Sufi Aesthetics

Studies in Comparative Religion
Frederick M. Denny, Series Editor

Sufi Aesthetics

Beauty, Love, and the Human Form in the Writings of Ibn 'Arabi and 'Iraqi

CYRUS ALI ZARGAR

The University of South Carolina Press

Published by the University of South Carolina Press
Columbia, South Carolina 29208

www.sc.edu/uscpress

Manufactured in the United States of America

20 19 18 17 16 15 14 13 12 11 10 9 8 7 6 5 4 3 2 1

Library of Congress Cataloging-in-Publication Data

Zargar, Cyrus Ali.
Sufi aesthetics : beauty, love, and the human form in the writings of Ibn 'Arabi and 'Iraqi / Cyrus Ali Zargar.
p. cm. — (Studies in comparative religion)
Includes bibliographical references and index.
ISBN 978-1-57003-999-7 (cloth : alk. paper)
1. Sufism—Doctrines. 2. Aesthetics. 3. Perception (Philosophy) 4. Ibn al-'Arabi, 1165-1240—Criticism and interpretation. 5. 'Iraqi, Fakhr al-Din Ibrahim, d. 1289?—Criticism and interprtation. I. Title.
BP189.3.Z36 2011
297.4'167—dc22

2011010278

This book was printed on Glatfelter Natures, a recycled paper with 30 percent postconsumer waste content.

Contents

Series Editor's Preface

This study addresses Sufi mystical poetry within the conceptual universe of the poets themselves, which is a world of aesthetic awareness rooted in love and connected to ontology and humans in relation to divine reality. The author addresses love and beauty as understood and celebrated by two great Sufi poets who created their art in a most productive era of such discourse. Of particular significance is the author's straightforward treatment of erotic verse, which is a major emphasis of Sufi poetry animated by profound adoration of the human form as a foundation of their aesthetics.

This book is grounded in a profound mastery and understanding of the Arabic and Persian texts of the Sufi poets studied, as well as the vernacular secondary sources within this discourse. Specialists will value this study as a major contribution to literary theory. It is also accessible for thoughtful readers to appreciate, whether in academic settings that encompass mysticism, Islamic studies, and literature courses or among the general reading public, which includes large numbers worldwide who love to learn about Sufi mysticism both for intellectual stimulation and personal enlightenment.

Frederick M. Denny

Preface

The following book considers closely the writings of two thirteenth-century Sufis, Muhyi al-Din ibn al-'Arabi and Fakhr al-Din 'Iraqi. Patience is the reader's only prerequisite, for a study of the "aesthetics" of vision and the human form in the complex thought of these mystics often requires extensive explanation until we can finally reach the interpretive heart of the matter toward the end of the book. If you, like me, have long marveled at the human experience of beauty, then I hope you enjoy, as much as I did, discovering a perspective that is so distant yet so insightful and relevant.

A Note about Readings

I have avoided a biography of either Ibn 'Arabi or 'Iraqi, mainly in hopes of relative brevity, but also in recognition of the efforts of others in this regard. In English, Julian Baldick, William C. Chittick, and Peter Lamborn Wilson have considered closely the life of 'Iraqi, and Claude Addas's carefully researched biography of Ibn 'Arabi has been translated from the French, among others who have concerned themselves with one or even both of these mystics.

For an astute overview of Ibn 'Arabi's ontological and cosmological insights, one can refer to the writings of William C. Chittick, since I have concentrated on one particular aspect of this worldview and, thanks to his efforts, can avoid reiterating what would have to be a long discussion. I also have been able to avoid a broader discussion of aesthetics as founded in classical Sufi thought, on account of the accomplishments of Seyyed Hossein Nasr, Titus Burckhardt, and others. There are other important and related topics, such as *sama'*, the Sufi practice of "audition," and wine imagery, that are intimately connected to the thematic and historical contexts of this book yet covered only briefly herein because of limitations. Again, I refer inquisitive readers to the bibliography for resources.

Text Editions

As for the most relevant primary texts, the edition of Ibn 'Arabi's *Fusus al-Hikam* I have used corresponds to the A. E. Affifi edition, printed in Beirut in 1946, here reprinted in Tehran in 1991, although all page numbers correspond. The edition of *al-Futuhat al-Makkiyah* used throughout this book is the one published in 1997 in

Beirut by Dar Ihya' al-Turath al-Islami. It is a reprinting of the Dar Sadir edition, based on the Bulaq edition published in Cairo in 1911, which is often cited in studies of Ibn 'Arabi. Unfortunately the Dar Sadir edition is no longer in print or in the market, so those introduced more recently to Ibn 'Arabi often do not have ready access to it. In order to make citations accessible to most, I have cited both versions but have placed the more available Dar Ihya' edition first in every instance and have included its line number. The *Tarjuman al-Ashwaq* cited throughout was also published by Dar Sadir in 1961, which I have favored mainly because of its conformity with the commentary and a dearth of more authoritative, carefully edited versions. The edition of Ibn 'Arabi's commentary on his *Tarjuman al-Ashwaq*, the *Dhakha'ir al-A'laq, Sharh Tarjuman al-Ashwaq*, is that of Muhammad 'Abd al-Rahman al-Kurdi (Cairo, 1968), an edition used by Michael Sells, Chittick, and others. Sometimes, however, the edition of *Tarjuman al-Ashwaq* published by Reynold A. Nicholson in 1911 seems to have been more discerningly edited than the Dar Sadir edition—such instances are indicated in the endnotes.

As for 'Iraqi, the main text used throughout for the author's complete works is a critical edition published as a second edition in 1382 *shamsi-hijri*/2003–4 by Nasrin Muhtasham. This is, as far as I know, the most recent edition of 'Iraqi's collected works, and the editor has carefully compared fifteen manuscripts, eight of which pertain to 'Iraqi's *diwan*. This edition is referred to as *Kulliyat*. Despite its strengths, because of difficulties inherent in editing 'Iraqi's collected works, this text has been complemented by two other editions. For the *Lama'at*, this study makes use of Muhammad Khwajawi's 1992 critical edition as a second reference. For all other instances, a reprinting of Sa'id Nafisi's revised edition of 'Iraqi's collected works has been employed; this edition is cited as *Diwan*. Important textual variances are indicated in the notes.

All translations are mine unless otherwise indicated.

Diacritical Markings

I hope that the lack of diacritical markings does not confuse anyone, but diacritics serve a somewhat strange purpose anyway, since those who understand them usually do not need them. In case there are some ambiguities, the index and bibliography both include diacritical markings. In such instances, the markings I use correspond to those of the *International Journal of Middle East Studies*, with a few minor adjustments; most notably, I add an *h* to words ending in *ta' marbutah* and prefer a long *i* and one *y* for the *-iyya* ending suggested by *IJMES*. Also, because many of the authors quoted here use Arabic terms and phrases in Persian contexts as part of an Arabic-Persian Sufi vocabulary, I have transliterated all Persian names and words using Arabic consonant and vowel transliteration equivalents, except, of course, when the consonants in question do not exist in the Arabic alphabet.

Acknowledgments

This book would not have been possible without the guidance and generosity of others. I thank Augustana College for its New Faculty Grant and continued support. I must mention and thank Hamid Algar, whose encouragement helped this project blossom and whose erudition continues to inspire me. It is to him that this book is dedicated. I owe appreciation to James T. Monroe for all his advice and kindness. Moreover, my sincere gratitude extends to Wali Ahmadi, William C. Chittick, Omid Safi, Sarah Skrainka, Dawud Salman, and everyone else who helped this work flourish within the context of other voices. I should acknowledge, furthermore, all those scholars of Sufism and Ibn 'Arabi, classic and contemporary, whose years and even decades of research, having built a framework of study, often go too easily unnoticed. Thanks are due to Mohammad-Javad Shabani and Ali Qasemi for their help in reconfiguring the two diagrams that appear in chapter 1; to my editors for their care and sensitivity with this text; to Munir Shaikh for painstakingly preparing the general index; and to my friends at the Augustana College Thomas Tredway Library, especially those at Interlibrary Loan, for their proficiency and indefatigability. I am grateful to every student I have had at Augustana College for teaching me how to (try to) explain the unusual. I thank my wife for her love, my mother for her encouragement, and my brother for his skepticism. I thank my children for their always-equipped comic relief and their unquestioning affection. I owe to my father a work ethic that will never come near his and an inclination to open-minded inquiry that I cherish even more now, sixteen years after his death. The flaws that you will inevitably encounter in this book are, of course, my own, *wa ma tawfiqi illa bi-llah.*

Introduction

Less bounded by logic and the expectations of reason, dreams seem to create their own rules. A friend might appear in the form of someone else—and yet the dreamer never hesitates to recognize her. A person might even change forms in the duration of a dream, or fly, or experience non sequitur shifts in health, or meet those who have died. Abstract concepts such as "strife" might appear in tangible forms such as animals or the wind. Yet while often strange and unpredictable, dreams do observe the boundaries of human experience. Forms, lights, symbols, sounds, and scenes in the dream world all have some basis in the world of wakefulness. In other words, dreaming does not propose an entirely new method of perception, nor does it introduce visions or thoughts completely unfamiliar to the human imagination. Rather, a person comes to the dream world with presuppositions, memories, and familiar faculties (especially sight and audition). What the soul encounters during the unconsciousness of slumber is not material like the world of the outer senses; that is certain. Equally certain, however, is the *seeming* materiality of the soul's experience: The soul sees in forms. This fascinating and yet everyday phenomenon of dreaming gives us a starting place for discussing visionary experience in the Sufi tradition.

This is not a book about dreams. Rather, this book considers those who encountered the world around them with the spiritual clarity we might only have in dreams: medieval Muslim mystics, who apperceived the divine in matter and in forms. However distant we may feel from the proclamations of the Sufis, in our most profound dreams we have all beheld the abstract in images and sounds. We have all "seen," via representational forms, that which cannot be seen: deceit, friendship, emotions, hopes, and meaningful abstractions. While this differs from mystic experience, we can at least begin to familiarize ourselves with mystical claims of encountering meaning in sensory fashion. I hope that by reflecting on the altered *perception* claimed by mystics, through this example as well as throughout the present book, the complex and contradictory *language* of mysticism will come to new life. Islamic mysticism particularly yearns for such new life. After all, a labyrinth of misunderstandings, surrounding Islamic mysticism and even Islam itself, has arisen from a failure to acknowledge the relevance of vision. By considering the sensory as a vehicle for that which the soul beholds, the imaginative literature of Islamic mysticism will seem far less imaginary. The erotic poetry produced by medieval Muslim mystics will seem far less allegorical. Moreover, the paradise found in the Qur'an, in the sayings of the Prophet Muhammad, and in centuries of Islamic literature, will seem far less simplistically profane.

Let there be no ambiguity about this. This study, while focused on a particular school of witnessing and love found in the world of Sufism, responds to questions raised by those who have mishandled the Islamic tradition. Some, coming from a perspective in which neat distinctions between sacred and profane or spiritual and corporeal must exist, have failed to understand Sufi expressions of eroticism in poetry. Others have taken the matter even further. Recent discussions of the Qur'anic paradise as an abode of meaningless sensual pleasure, as a meeting place for lascivious, self-righteous fanatics, have so misunderstood the spirituality and vision behind Qur'anic paradisal imagery that a new perspective is necessary, one informed by some of the most profound instances of contemplation on Islam's sacred sources. While it might take many chapters to work through the complexities of this vision and its workings, my hope is that, by the end of this book, one can understand that what is granted to mystics in this world can be granted to the believer in the next, namely, visions of God, his attributes, and his names, in a manner that corresponds to the propensities of the human experience and acknowledges the purposefulness of that human experience.

Thus it is that this book, much like the writings of the Sufis it discusses, largely concerns vision, especially the envisioning of the divine in forms. If the word "beauty" also arises, it is only because God, when seen, is the Absolutely Beautiful. Seeing God—as impossible as that may or may not be in this temporal world of ours—stands as the apex of spiritual felicity, not only in Islamic mysticism, but even in the Qur'an itself.

Vision in Islamic Mysticism

It is reported in the Qur'an that when Moses requested to see his Lord more directly, two things occurred. First, he was told of the hopelessness of such immediate vision. Second, he was told to gaze upon a mountain. When his Lord disclosed himself to that mountain and it crumbled, Moses fell in a swoon of bewilderment. It is significant that the term "self-disclosure" (*al-tajalli*), used by certain medieval Muslim mystics to describe God's all-pervasive manifestations throughout the cosmos, derives from this one Qur'anic passage. After all, in the context of this verse (7:143), God's awesome manifestation takes place wholly on account of the longing of one of his very elect friends for direct vision. Not only is this longing for vision one of the major preoccupations of mystics in the Islamic tradition, but vision's relationship to divine manifestations becomes an important theme in medieval Sufi texts. More generally speaking, one can also argue that mystical experience concerns and certainly affects perception above all else.

Yet among the less carefully considered dimensions of the Sufi tradition is the matter of mystical perception and the vision of beauty it entailed, a vision often proclaimed but, when approached from the outside, usually either misunderstood or described in far too general terms. The relevance of beauty to the tradition, especially in the seventh/thirteenth century, when contemplative writings concerning this matter flourished, appears in many emphatic pronouncements that perceptive encounters with divine beauty in human forms can occasion ecstatic love in a manner unlike and unrivaled by anything else. For this reason, what follows is a study of perception, beauty, and the applications of these two concepts according to the writings of medieval mystics in the Islamic tradition, especially two mystics who will concern us centrally. For this reason and for this reason alone, I have used the word "aesthetic" in this book's title. The intention here is not to summon the various complex connotations this word has acquired. Rather, Sufi theoretical literature explicitly proposes its own understanding of beauty—discussed here with an emphasis on one object of beauty, the human form. The word "aesthetic," then, aims solely to capture the observation that there existed among such mystics a distinctive mode of perception, one that resulted in an evaluation of beauty related both to the cosmos as well as to the individual human experience. I argue that many writers, readers, speakers, and listeners have applied this evaluative system to poetry, whether in composing such poetry or in interpreting it.

Two Visionaries in the Sufi Tradition

Both of the mystics to be discussed lived during the sixth/twelfth to seventh/thirteenth centuries (Hijri dates are followed by Common Era dates), and both can be called "Akbaris." The term "Akbari" derives, in fact, from a title of esteem given to one of the subjects of this study: Muhyi al-Din Muhammad ibn 'Ali ibn al-'Arabi (560/1165–638/1240), known as *al-shaykh al-akbar,* that is, the "Greatest Shaykh." This term is often applied to those who had direct association with Ibn 'Arabi or his students and yet can be expanded to include those who sympathized with and even adopted his cosmological and ontological vision. Our second Akbari mystic, Fakhr al-Din Ibrahim ibn Buzurjmihr ibn 'Abd al-Ghaffar 'Iraqi (ca. 610/1213–1214 to 688/1289), spent seventeen years of his adult life associated with the Indian Suhrawardis in Multan and was introduced to his teacher, Ibn 'Arabi's most eminent student, Sadr al-Din al-Qunawi (d. 673/1273–1274), relatively late in his saintly career. Other than when pertinent to the topic at hand, the biographical details of these two mystics will not concern us here, especially since they have been discussed ably elsewhere. Claude Addas has written a carefully researched biography of Ibn 'Arabi, and Julian Baldick has discussed the life of 'Iraqi, among others who have concerned themselves with one or even both of these mystics. Of some interest to this study is the merging of two Sufi traditions, Ibn 'Arabi's from the West and the Suhrawardi tradition from the East, to comment on one particular phenomenon in mystical perception: witnessing and experiencing love for the divine in forms. As indicated by the compatibility of these two traditions, the general principles of witnessing and beauty are not restricted at all to the Akbari tradition; for many of the Sufis mentioned, witnessing might be considered any accomplished mystic's definitive occupation. There is, however, a unique and insightful perspective given to matters of witnessing in the cosmology of Ibn 'Arabi.

The Cosmology of Witnessing

In the case of both mystics, witnessing and love together pervade the entire cosmos. This might be expected from 'Iraqi, who openly sympathizes with a Suhrawardi forefather, Ahmad Ghazali (d. 520/1126), whose treatise *Sawanih* alludes to a cosmology of love. The pervasiveness of love and witnessing has been less discussed, however, with regard to Ibn 'Arabi. For both of these authors, witnessing and love result from one omnipresent reality: existence itself. This oneness is real and all-inclusive, to such an extent that a complete distinction between God and creation amounts to a sort of idolatry, since it posits the independent existence of that which maintains a constant state of need vis-à-vis God. This notion of oneness manifests itself in an understanding that the cosmos consists of realms, realms that affect one another so that every stage or realm closer to absolute existence dominates and becomes manifest in the stage beneath it, that which is further from absolute existence. Lower realms, those further from pure existence, moreover, determine the mode of manifestation or "form" for those ontologically above them.

Because of this cosmological system, all things have spiritual significance and reflect the highest source from which even God's very own names have come. Ibn 'Arabi and 'Iraqi often describe this descent of pure existence as a settling of the unbounded in more bounded locales, or as a matter of meaning and form. Meaning is pure spirit, while form is that which allows the mystic to interact with meaning. This relationship is sometimes depicted in terms of a word: If one were to trace a written word back to its original source, one would be led to a very abstract thing, namely, an idea in the mind. This idea, unbounded by the sensory, takes on the shape of a mental word. This word can then become pronounced on the tongue and written onto paper, in both cases involving composite letters that make it up. The abstract has now become concrete, stage by stage, and meaning has now entered the boundaries of form; generosity, for example, has become a giving hand. For Ibn 'Arabi and 'Iraqi, this process occurs throughout creation, so that everywhere one looks, meaning has become manifest in form. Yet since meaning itself has derived from the Real (the name "the Real," *al-haqq*, refers to God as himself, not necessarily related to his creation), this process constitutes a divine self-disclosure. The specifics of this phenomenon are discussed in more detail, but this paradigm serves as the basis for perception and beauty according to Ibn 'Arabi and 'Iraqi.

No less significant than the cosmos in discussing perception and beauty is the soul. The soul receives all that surrounds it, from supersensory meaning to the physical world it senses. Ibn 'Arabi proposes a system of perception focused on the soul as receiver. While the soul does have an important creative hand in the process, its encounter with the beautiful (and thus with the divine) depends on its own inclinations and the physical constitution to which it corresponds. Existence is one reality, but as different souls receive it—according to the constitutions of those who possess such souls—existence can be perceived variously. It is because of this that, according to Ibn 'Arabi, beauty and ugliness are relative matters.

Beauty and Lovability

Beauty in the writings of both of these mystics corresponds to "lovability," that is, the extent to which a perceived object evokes love in its perceiver. This too is not distinct from receptivity. Every perceiving subject has a predisposed inclination to loving itself; it searches for that which corresponds most to itself. When it sees that which serves as its mirror, it delights, deems that object beautiful, and experiences love. On one hand, this explains human fascination with other human beings. Nothing in creation resembles one human more than another human. On the other hand, this explains why the truly beautiful is the divine; the divine is existence itself, an existence that each of us can recognize as our own mirror image, since a breath from the divine spirit corresponds to the very soul of every person. The gnostic (a word used in place of the Arabic *'arif*, which describes a mystic accomplished in esoteric knowledge of God) constantly senses that his or her perception corresponds to God's perception. Thus, for the gnostic, the beautiful is the Real. One important caveat must be mentioned: The gnostic cannot witness the Real outside of the boundaries of form. Put simply, it can be said that while *unveiling* occurs outside of form, the *witnessing* of that which is acquired through unveiling occurs within form and within some sort of matter (what is called "matter," however, need not be material in the physical sense).

Because of the formal human correspondence mentioned above, the form in which God's self-disclosures are most fully witnessed is the human form. The human form not only evokes great love but also, in the thought of Ibn 'Arabi, provides a comprehensive cosmological perspective.

Reading Sufi Literature as a Result of Sufi Aesthetics

Here it should be admitted that, to some extent, the impetus for this study has been the failure of many researchers to consider the mystical significance of ambiguous erotic verse. This is perhaps nowhere more apparent than in the case of a poet unrelated to this study and thus mentioned only briefly in it: Shams al-Din Hafiz of Shiraz (d. 792/1390). The concern that has existed in the study of Persian and Sufi literature over his historical person, whether he was a sincere mystic or a libertine, has aroused a more important question, one overlooked in discussions of the poet: Considering such ambiguity, why was the poetry of Hafiz so well received in the world of Sufism? In other words, the *reception* of ambiguous erotic lyric poetry must come from a set of values, a point implied by a later Akbari-influenced poet, 'Abd al-Rahman Jami (d. 898/1492), in his analysis of Hafiz. Jami comments that although it is not known whether or not Hafiz was a formally initiated Sufi, nevertheless "his utterances accord with the disposition of this [Sufi] group to such a degree, that the like cannot be said of anyone else."[1]

Many of those researchers who have concerned themselves with Hafiz, including Jan Rypka, Seyyed Hossein Nasr, and Ehsan Yarshater, have determined various degrees of veracity in the claim by Sufis that the poet was one of their own. From a purely historical perspective, their concern is justified. Most have discussed the matter in terms of symbol systems, allegories, and sacred-versus-profane imagery. None, however, has offered a systematic explanation presenting the mystical appreciation for such ambiguities and sometimes seemingly farfetched interpretations of his poetry as a matter of reception, perception, and the evaluation of beauty, that is, aesthetics. The same applies to any other poet in classical Persian and Arabic literature whose works were *received* as having mystical significance, when their original context was either clearly for a human beloved or ambiguous at best. This might even include a number of poems by 'Iraqi, whose collected poems undergo categorization in the sacred-profane dichotomy offered by Julian Baldick. It should be added here that real equivalents for the words "sacred" and "profane" did not exist in the vocabularies of the Sufis who are discussed. Medieval Sufism did have a concept of *'ishq-i majazi* (metaphorical love) and *'ishq-i haqiqi* (real love), but these are far different in signification. The metaphorical always indicates the real and relies on the real for its very existence, just as the real is known through the metaphorical; the two are inseparable. (Thus even the word "metaphorical" must veer from accepted English usage to convey accurately the meaning of *majazi.*) A far better manner of understanding love and images of love in the context of these Sufis is to consider carefully their own terms, theories, and assertions.

While one might point out here that the word "aesthetic" did not exist either, it should be borne in mind that, while "profane" and "sacred" demand sharp divisions, the word "aesthetic" points to a unity indicated in Islamic mystical writings—an evaluative experience of beauty. In this regard, it is a word that helps those of us outside the tradition to approach a mode of perception restrictedly esoteric. The word "aesthetic" also places a phenomenon in the world of Sufism in a framework that allows one to relate perception and evaluation to artistic expression. This relation, while left somewhat unsaid in the writings that concern us, undoubtedly existed.

The application of the comprehensive vision of these gnostics to poets possibly outside of their own tradition (such as Hafiz) or even clearly outside of their own tradition should not be seen as unnatural. While for some commentators this may have been a mere matter of words, for many, the mystical terms in their commentaries represented envisioned realities. It was not a matter of usurping beautiful poetry; rather, some commentators expressed cosmological reverberations that they actually beheld in such poetic imagery. Such is definitely the case for Ibn 'Arabi's commentary on his own collection of amorous verse, the *Tarjuman al-Ashwaq*. Nevertheless, it is not difficult to see why those exposed to Ibn 'Arabi's love poems had and still have their doubts, especially considering the saint's earnest and sometimes even raw expressions of human-to-human love:

Soft breeze of the wind, hark! Relay to the horned oryxes of Najd
that I uphold the promised pledge, the one of which you are aware.
Say to the tribe's girl: "Our rendezvous is the off-limits pasture,
in early-morning moments, Saturday, at the hills of Najd,
upon the red bluff, by the stones piled high along the way,
at the right side of the streams and the solitary marking."
If what you report is real, and if she truly suffers
for me the agonizing yearning that I suffer
for her, so, in the heat of a sweltering midday, we will meet
in her tent, secretly, abiding by the truest of promises;
then she and I will divulge all we have undergone of love-longing,
and of the extremities of affliction and the pains of ardor.
Are these meaningless dreams? Or auspicious sleep-omens?
Or talk of a time in which talking was my blessedness?
Maybe the one who put these wishes in me will make them appear
before me, so that their gardens give as gifts their gathered blossoms to me.[2]

Ibn 'Arabi's worldview and commentary suggest that all levels of artistic representation within such a poem thrive simultaneously: the tribal girl associated with Najd, the woman she represents, and the human-divine communications captured in every image. The echoes of spiritual significance a lover of God discerns in such poems, as clarified by the poet himself in his commentary, serve as the focus generally of this book and specifically of its final chapter.

Fascinatingly, as Ibn 'Arabi's teachings spread, so too did the propensity to write poetic commentaries, particularly on the erotic mystical poetry of 'Umar ibn al-Farid (d. 632/1235), as well as Sufi glossaries of often sensual imagery. Some, including scholars of Ibn al-Farid, have argued that such interpretive endeavors neglect the particular outlook of the poet. Clearly, however, the Akbari School advocated a way of seeing all things that had the potential to subdue other forms of interpretation, rereading literature outside of its own tradition and even outside of the Sufi tradition. Moreover, Akbari-inclined Sufis relentlessly related their observations on desire and beauty to existence itself, so in many ways it mattered little whether the writer was commenting on poetry or on the Qur'an; since their statements referred constantly to a larger ontological vision, the implication was that such interpreters commented on the reality of everything. When one considers the interpretation of poetry in this light, as an aesthetic matter, a matter that relates to vision, then anxieties concerning the application of Akbari terms to other traditions might disappear, be alleviated, or at least seem more sincere.

Method and Organization

This book considers perception and beauty from the point of view of Sufis who never explicitly convey an aesthetic theory as such. Hence one main function of this study has been to analyze relevant passages within the writings of these mystics to determine the nature and applications of this vision. In support of developing an understanding beyond simply the observations of one author, this study is comparative. There are certainly noteworthy differences between these mystics, other than the fact that 'Iraqi writes mainly in Persian and Ibn 'Arabi writes exclusively in Arabic. While 'Iraqi comes from a Persianate, Suhrawardi background, Ibn 'Arabi is associated with the Sufis of al-Andalus. While 'Iraqi's language is usually poetic and terse, Ibn 'Arabi often employs the language of the exoteric Islamic sciences, albeit in a manner peculiar to him. In his *Lama'at,* 'Iraqi to some extent represents the nexus of these two traditions. Yet more important than the differences are the similarities. In the values they share concerning love, beauty, and the human form, Ibn 'Arabi and 'Iraqi proclaim an unspoken aesthetic system. Moreover, while this system's details differ from Sufi to Sufi, the general principles are shared by a number of mystics, who even refer to the view they have in common as a *madhhab* or "school of thought." In other words, through comparative methods, this study outlines a general aesthetic view.

The focus throughout this book on source texts reflects the premise that the keys of interpretation for Sufi assertions, practices, and expressive undertakings lie in their own contemplative writings. This has been the case not in order to diminish other valid approaches to Sufism, Islamic studies, or literary studies, but because of the postulate that mystical experience resists external rational methods and can only be discussed, even if vaguely, through the language used by such mystics. The errors of seeking a comprehensive or even analogous understanding of the tradition's experiential dimensions should lead one to find solace, instead, in a more limited and textually based instance of insight.

The organization of this study should allow for a careful, step-by-step understanding of perception, beauty, and the application of these concepts in poetry, in that order. The first consideration is perception according to the writings of Ibn 'Arabi, with special focus on that which relates to witnessing, especially witnessing in forms. Following this, perception, form, and meaning in the prose and poetry of 'Iraqi are examined, and then beauty as found in the writings of Ibn 'Arabi, which leads to a discussion of beauty and the human form in the writings of 'Iraqi.

Ibn 'Arabi's emphasis on the beautiful human form, the perfection of witnessing in the female form, and the experience of love are linked to a network of loosely affiliated Sufi writers who saw themselves as members of the "School of Passionate Love." 'Iraqi can be placed in the context of this very school, focusing more specifically on a Persian tradition of love and witnessing, a tradition that clearly preceded Ibn 'Arabi. Also examined are the *shahid* or "visionary testimony" in this Sufi tradition, as well as a discussion of gazing at beardless young men, a practice shaped by gnostic aesthetic values. In other words, while the aesthetic system at hand resulted in and was bolstered by poetry, a recorded art, it had the same relationship with an unrecorded practice, that of gazing, a practice that seems to have sometimes been quite an intense experience, involving staring, the recitation of poetry, and weeping. The focus here, again, is on theoretical matters as relayed in the writings of a number of Sufis.

Applying all these principles leads, arguably, to the most significant artistic mode of expression in Sufism: poetry, here particularly erotic or amorous lyric poetry, because of its relationship with beauty and the human form. Of emphatic concern are misunderstandings of the poetry of these two mystics, as well as the commentary of Ibn 'Arabi on his own amorous poems. Ibn 'Arabi's lyrical poems clearly emanate from someone with a sincere and insightful love of the beautiful female form, just as their commentary results from a gnostic who is aware of the limitless and universal significance of sensual experience. What emerges is an often neglected perspective on Ibn 'Arabi—the mystic admirer of human beauty, the aesthete, and the poet. Mystical significance aside, 'Iraqi too is an earnest love poet, but effective love poetry is, under the aesthetic values proposed, essentially mystical.

While few comparisons are made here to mystics outside of the Islamic tradition, those acquainted with interpretations of the ardent Song of Songs, or with the poetry and commentaries of St. John of the Cross, will possibly sense that they have wandered into familiar spiritual gardens. Perhaps mysticism is in many ways a universal language, and the experiences shared by mystics in various traditions, times, and locales ring with a tone more similar than different, superseding the particularizing limitations of the world's religions. Even within a specific religious tradition, mystics often indicate the superiority of the universal to the particular. St. John notes, in emphasizing that which is at once shared and individual in mystical experience, that the explanations to his "Spiritual Canticle" have been written in the "broadest sense so that individuals may derive profit from them according to the mode and capacity of their own spirit."[3] In other words, while mystical love poetry is broad enough to speak to each individual who has shared in this encompassing love of God, commentaries specify and define, thus running the risk of excluding the variegated meanings potential in the poems they dissect and the hearts they address. Nevertheless, as attested to by St. John's undertaking, there is a time for commentaries. When ambiguity muddles meaning instead of inspiring it, when misunderstandings become commonplace, when the poet's audience fails to fathom the depths of his or her verses, then explication allows for necessary connections to be made. There will doubtless be a continuation in the effort to relate the discoveries of Islamic mystics to other esoteric traditions, yet I hope it is undertaken with a consideration of this community's unique particulars. To a large extent this book's purpose is to explore the *uniqueness* of the medieval Islamic mystical tradition, a tradition in which human beauty can be sacred, truly sacred, in a manner not at all metaphorical and justified by the most foundational religious sources. The reality of visionary experience is beyond us and, according to the Sufis in question, incomprehensibly universal. Yet such discoveries must begin with an inquisitive consideration of the particular, an exploration of the self.

CHAPTER 1

Perception according to Ibn 'Arabi

God in Forms

Before any discussion can take place regarding divine beauty and its expression in amorous poetry, it is necessary to establish the *experience* of divine beauty. Because the poetry of Ibn 'Arabi and 'Iraqi concerns itself with encounters and observations that they refer to as a vision, this segment asks an important preliminary question: What exactly is it that the person accomplished in esoteric knowledge of God, the gnostic (*'arif*), perceives? In the end, since this vision must be directly experienced, it escapes the boundaries of language. Not surprisingly, then, it seems that Ibn 'Arabi's efforts to articulate and analyze this unspeakable perceptive experience yielded diverse sets of terms.

Each set of terms presents this vision differently, from a certain perspective, and is often described in the language of the Qur'an or prophetic narrations (of course, Ibn 'Arabi's use of these terms is also a commentary on their original usage in the revealed sources). An interpreter of Ibn 'Arabi must acknowledge the varying nuances that these groups of words offer—because the abundance of concepts and terms in the writings of Ibn 'Arabi is an attempt to achieve some accuracy in articulating that which ultimately must be tasted.

What I offer here is not a complete presentation of perception in the thought of Ibn 'Arabi, which would be a useful undertaking, but one that would require a separate and lengthy study. After all, *shuhud*—a term referring to "witnessing" in a general sense, the most basic and definitive perceptive experience of the mystic and that most relevant to our discussion—involves the entire experience of the gnostic, including his or her knowledge of the divine attributes, the divine names, the entifications, and practically anything that the privileged insight of the gnostic can assert. Rather, presented here are certain key points, especially those that relate to the experiential visions related to beauty and love and thus often found in Sufi poetry.

The Importance of Witnessing to Ibn 'Arabi's Thought

Traditionally, Ibn 'Arabi has been classified as the great expositor of Islamic mysticism's most famous theory of existence—the Oneness of Being, or *wahdat al-wujud*.

A number of Ibn 'Arabi's statements point to a lack of any concrete distinction between the Creator and creation, such that everything seen is none other than the Real, and that created entities possess their own separate existence in only an illusory way:

There is no creation seen by the eye,
except that its essence/eye is the Real.
Yet he is hidden therein,
thus, its [creation's] forms are [his] receptacles.[1]

Yet William C. Chittick, among others, has rightly taken great pains to illustrate that not only did the phrase *wahdat al-wujud* (Oneness of Being) emerge and gain currency after Ibn 'Arabi's death but also the terms and technicalities of this theory are often not explicitly found in his writings.[2]

Ibn 'Arabi was not primarily concerned with forming an ontological philosophy or with arguments and proofs because the greatest proof for him was that which he acquired through direct witnessing. He was, however, concerned (and, one might say, primarily concerned) with vision, and that which he presents in his writings is—first and foremost—a way of *perceiving* things, witnessing the Real in both the mundane and the lofty, in the "spiritual" as well as the "worldly" and material. For Ibn 'Arabi, "everyone in *existence* is Real / and everyone in *witnessing* is a creation."[3] That is, in terms of existence, the created things lack self-sufficient being, so that all is God. In terms of witnessing, however, creation and creation alone—on account of having nothing, being in a sense ontologically poor—has the ability to receive *wujud*/existence and engage in *shuhud*/witnessing.

Creation is receptive and, like an uncluttered mirror, serves as the means for God to witness himself. Throughout this process, creation is both seer and seen, and yet the actual seer and seen are God. Moreover, this "seeing" or "witnessing" is for Ibn 'Arabi the primary purpose of creation. For Ibn 'Arabi, the Real created the cosmos in order to see himself.[4] In making such a statement, Ibn 'Arabi alludes to a well-known prophetic narration, one in which God speaks in the first person: *"I was a Treasure—I was Unknown, so I loved to be known. Hence I created the creatures, and made Myself known to them, so they knew Me."*[5] In other words, the very impetus for all of creation proceeds from the Real's love to be known, and his love to be known or "witnessed" justifies and maintains creation's ongoing existence. As Ibn 'Arabi states, "Were creation not witnessed through the Real, it/he would not be," and "were the Real not witnessed through creation, you would not be."[6] The phrase "Oneness of Witnessing," if interpreted according to this understanding, is almost as adequate a description of Ibn 'Arabi's system as the phrase "Oneness of Being," despite the fact that interpreters of Ibn 'Arabi have placed far less importance on *shuhud*/witnessing.[7]

Witnessing: To Know That Which Is Seen

With regard to Ibn 'Arabi, the numerous perceptive perspectives that will be described broadly fall under the umbrella term *shuhud* or *mushahadah,* both translated here as "witnessing." Judging from Ibn 'Arabi's description of *mushahadah* in chapter 209 of his central work *al-Futuhat al-Makkiyah* (The Meccan Openings), a chapter devoted to this topic, *mushahadah*/witnessing is foundational for the gnostic. In fact, witnessing serves as the first requirement or first sign of becoming a gnostic or *'arif.* Before achieving such witnessing, the wayfarer is merely a novice, since only after the wayfarer is "called to witness" do terms such as "place" (*makanah*) or "station" (*maqam*) apply to him or her:

When you are called to witness, you are confirmed, my lad!
Then place and station are in order for you.
So you witness him with your intellect in a veiling,
for the place of his witnessing is powerful, unwished for.
You witness him through himself in everything—
"behind" does not apply to him, he has no "in front,"
and you are tranquil in seeing him, so tranquil.
Through him there is ascertainment and peace.[8]

In this chapter, Ibn 'Arabi describes *mushahadah*/witnessing as that important visionary ability to see things as they really are, not as they merely appear to be. Even when reason or the senses dictate that a perceived object must correspond to one thing, the gnostic gifted with witnessing knows that indeed that object is something else.

Ibn 'Arabi gives two important examples from the scriptural sources of those who lack this ability, those who lack "knowledge of that which is witnessed," in order to teach through negative example. The Queen of Sheba, named "Bilqis," exclaims that the throne she sees in Solomon's court resembles her own throne (*"it is as if it is it!"* 27:42), unable to see that her very own throne has indeed been instantaneously transported into the court of Solomon. This is on account of the boggling distance that separates her court from Solomon's court, a distance the instantaneous circumventing of which reason must reject. Second, the companions of the Prophet see the young and handsome Dihyah al-Kalbi as Dihyah al-Kalbi even when the angel of revelation Gabriel takes on the form of the young man. In other words, in one example, a person lacking vision (the Queen of Sheba) cannot see an object of vision as itself, and in another example, a group (the companions of the Prophet) cannot see an object of vision representing something else.[9] That which most people see, in other words, corresponds to their sense of reason but does not correspond to reality. The various planes of existence are infused with meaning, communications from God, and symbolic significance—yet only those granted *mushahadah*/witnessing have awareness of the true states of things.

Making Sense of Terms

The use here of two different terms—*mushahadah* and *shuhud*—to describe one experience, "witnessing," should not be offsetting since the two terms can be interchanged in Ibn 'Arabi's writings. Sometimes, however, the two terms do maintain distinct definitions and are part of a set of terms that describe more broadly "witnessing," each with its own subtle difference in meaning. When the two are distinct, *mushahadah* can refer to a specific grade and type of esoteric knowledge, while *shuhud* usually refers to the general experience of witnessing as creation's receptive orientation toward existence and sometimes refers to "presence" or being manifest. A third term, *ru'yah* (vision), at times refers to a visionary experience more intense than *mushahadah,* one that is direct in that it makes no use of an intermediary. Distinguishing *mushahadah*/witnessing from *ru'yah*/vision, Ibn 'Arabi defines *mushahadah* as "the witnessing [*shuhud*] of the evidential locus [*shahid*] in the heart from the Real," which—unlike *ru'yah*—is "fettered by signs" or, one might say, "signifiers" (*quyyida bi-l-'alamah*).[10] That is, the mystic first encounters the divine in the realm of formless and absolute meaning, where interaction is direct and incomprehensible. This leaves a mark within the heart—a trace or "testimony" or "evidential locus." The witnessing of that testimony or *shahid* results in *mushahadah.*

This description of *mushahadah*/witnessing parallels the definition of *'ilm* (knowledge) by classic Islamic philosophers as the "presence of a thing's form in the intellect."[11] Just as (for the philosophers) things and the relationships between them leave traces of their forms in the intellect, so too, according to Ibn 'Arabi, does that which is witnessed leave a trace of its form in the soul.[12] It is thus interesting to note that Ibn 'Arabi seems to offer witnessing as an esoteric counterpart to the knowledge described by philosophers—a sort of knowing that occurs not in the intellect (*al-'aql*) but in the heart (*al-qalb*) or soul (*al-nafs*), since Ibn 'Arabi alternately recognizes both as the site where the form of the witnessed (*al-mashhud*) abides.[13] Much like the functioning of the intellect, which uses that which is known to understand the unknown,[14] the heart uses that which it knows and has witnessed to behold the hitherto unwitnessed, unknown, or unexperienced. Thus this witnessing occurs through preconceptions and is not wholly receptive.

A wholly receptive vision that involves no preconceptions applies only to *ru'yah*/vision, for "*ru'yah* is not preceded by knowledge of the seen, while *shuhud*/witnessing is in fact preceded by knowledge of the witnessed."[15] For this reason, vision (*ru'yah*) has immediacy and is an unattained goal for many even from among the highest ranks. According to Ibn 'Arabi, for example, Moses' expressed wish to "see" God (7:143), establishes that he longs for something beyond *mushahadah*/witnessing, since according to Ibn 'Arabi even those below the rank of prophet partake in *mushahadah*/witnessing. Hence *mushahadah*/witnessing is a type of *ru'yah*/vision bound by the knowledge of the viewer, and *mushahadah*/witnessing is more readily available, at least in preresurrection life, than true *ru'yah*/vision.

Also, Ibn 'Arabi tells us that *mushahadah*/witnessing involves an opening or divine display on a lower level than *mukashafah*/unveiling. Ibn 'Arabi defines and contrasts these two terms, *mushahadah* and *mukashafah*, in chapters 209 and 210 of *al-Futuhat al-Makkiyah*, in which he comments on the usage of these terms as part of the developed technical vocabulary of the Sufis.[16] While Ibn 'Arabi's overall discussion proves very original, his specific, threefold Sufi definitions of *mushahadah*/witnessing and *mukashafah*/unveiling closely parallel those from Abu Hamid Muhammad al-Ghazali's (d. 505/1111) section on Sufi terms in *Kitab al-Imla' fi Ishkalat al-Ihya'* (The Book Resolving Uncertainties in the Ihya'), a text written in response to criticisms of his masterpiece *Ihya' 'Ulum al-Din* (The Revival of the Religious Sciences).[17] In *Kitab al-Imla'*, al-Ghazali seems to have wanted to prove his ability to use Sufi terms in what had become part of a technical vocabulary, since he, like Ibn 'Arabi, does not usually confine himself to such usage in his major writings.

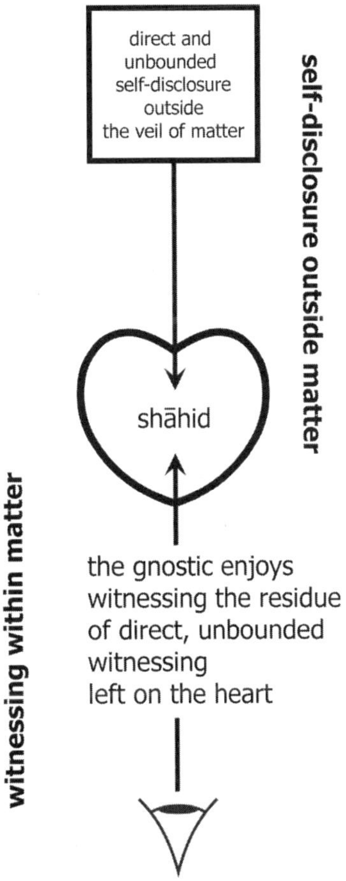

The definitions based on al-Ghazali's text will not concern us for now. It suffices to know that Ibn 'Arabi agrees with al-Ghazali that unveiling exceeds witnessing in excellence, despite the fact that some earlier masters held witnessing to be higher than unveiling.[18] While witnessing is a pathway to true knowledge, Ibn 'Arabi contends, unveiling is the full attainment of that pathway to knowledge. While witnessing relies on the *physical* senses, unveiling relies on the *spiritual* senses.[19] Ibn 'Arabi explains that while *mushahadah*/witnessing concerns perceiving the luminary forms of things with respect to their quiddities (*dhawat*), *mukashafah*/unveiling concerns perceiving abstractions or ideal meanings (*ma'ani*).[20] Moreover, while *mushahadah*/witnessing relates to that which is named, *mukashafah*/unveiling is governed by the Names (*al-asma'*). As Ibn 'Arabi says,

"Unveiling is for us more complete than witnessing" because "unveiling makes subtle that which is gross, while witnessing makes gross that which is subtle."[21] In other words, *mushahadah*/witnessing involves receiving unseen self-disclosures (*al-tajalliyat*) in forms. Form is "gross" (*kathif*) with respect to meaning, which due to its formlessness is subtle (*latif*).[22] Conversely, *mukashafah*—in its function as an unveiling—strips the self-disclosure of its forms and reverts to the meanings behind it. For Ibn 'Arabi, *mukashafah*/unveiling brings with it an understanding that cannot be attributed to *mushahadah*/witnessing, an understanding that results in "verification" (*tahqiq*). While *mushahadah*/witnessing involves perceiving through a recognition of unity or oneness, *mukashafah*/unveiling bestows upon the wayfarer something more than mere perception: an *understanding* of that which has been hitherto merely witnessed.

Lastly, Ibn 'Arabi on occasion distinguishes between two perceptive experiences of the mystic: beholding a divine self-disclosure in matter (*tajallin fi maddah*) and beholding a self-disclosure outside of matter (*tajallin fi ghayr maddah*).[23] Here "matter," not necessarily carrying all the classical philosophical connotations of the term, refers to that which allows for form, much in the way that letters (the "matter" of words) allow for an ordering of letters (the "form" of words) that express a meaning.[24] Self-disclosures outside of matter correspond to the mystic's experience of pure meaning, divorced from any form or restrictions (*al-ma'ani al-mujarradah*).[25] Here the mystic encounters the divine outside the parameters of anything known or knowable by the human faculties. Since this self-disclosure is completely unknowable, and since humans reckon that which they do not know as distant, a self-disclosure outside of matter is a self-disclosure of distance (*tajalli al-bu'd*). On the other hand, self-disclosures within matter are knowable, thus arousing in the mystic a sense of proximity and love; as one would expect, a self-disclosure in matter is termed a self-disclosure of proximity (*tajalli al-qurb*).[26] The distinction should sound familiar, for it parallels much of what has already been discussed concerning gnostic perception: Ibn 'Arabi relates self-disclosure outside of matter to direct vision (*ru'yah*) and self-disclosure within matter to witnessing (*shuhud*).[27] Most significantly, the differentiation between self-disclosures outside of matter and those within matter refers to a descent of gnostic experience, where the gnostic encounters the divine in unbounded, less-bounded, and, finally, bounded dimensions. Yet all that seen in the bounded dimension of form has its correspondence in the world of meaning, for as the gnostic descends levels of existence, "the Real descends with him."[28]

What the gnostic has experienced in the realm of unbounded meaning accompanies him forever—it leaves an impression (the *shahid* discussed above) that he reencounters in the realm of representation (or imagination) and sense. This means that the gnostic, having experienced pure spirit or pure meaning, later experiences meaning *through the medium* of matter, whether that matter be physical, imaginal, or luminary. This reexperiencing of meaning through the medium of matter and form is precisely the experience of *shuhud*/witnessing.[29] Thus matter, according to Ibn 'Arabi, since it allows for form, makes perception through the human faculties possible; each of the faculties (comprising imagination, reflection, memory, form-giving, fantasy, and reason) has a certain type of "matter" that corresponds to it.[30] Knowledge acquired outside of matter is profound, overwhelming and pure, but—lacking any reference point in the known world—it cannot be expressed.[31] On the other hand, knowledge acquired within matter corresponds to most of that which can be discussed and hence most of that which Ibn 'Arabi discusses in his writings; inspiration (*ilham*), for example, always occurs in matter, as does witnessing (*shuhud*).[32] Ibn 'Arabi's discussions of beauty and love chiefly concern self-disclosures within matter.

While subtleties in Ibn 'Arabi's terminology of witnessing do deserve attention, the aim of this discussion is to provide a general understanding of perception according to Ibn 'Arabi, one that allows us to interpret in a more genuine way certain recurring visionary themes, especially those that relate to Sufi lyric poetry. Since that which is acquired outside of *shuhud*/witnessing, in the realm of pure meanings, is raw and inexpressible, the focus here is on knowledge and experiences acquired through *shuhud*/witnessing—much as it is in the writings of Ibn 'Arabi. Moreover, because of the broad nature of the word *shuhud*, especially because of its including witnessing at every level of existence, I have chosen this word to describe the general beholding of divine beauty that occurs for the gnostic.[33]

Imagination and the Inlets of Perception

In seeking to share the vision that Ibn 'Arabi presents, there are certain experiences and faculties that allow one to peek into the One Reality he describes. The imagination serves as an able indicator for man to visualize the ease with which his Creator creates—as well as the somewhat illusory existence of other-than-God. By simply imagining an object, I as a human have the ability to bestow it with existence—mental existence, of course.[34] Clearly, the human capacity for attentiveness (and hence creation) cannot be compared with the divine attentiveness.[35] Still, similar to God's creation of the cosmos, the mental image I have created proceeds from my knowledge and is sustained through the attention I give to it; if I forget it even for an instant, it disappears. According to Ibn 'Arabi, all that which we know as existence is an "imagination within an imagination, and true existence [*al-wujud al-haqq*] is only God with respect to his essence, his absolute self, not his names."[36] This is because everything other than the essence of God, which is pure being, is surmised; it lies somewhere between pure being and nonbeing. Only the divine essence can be said to exist in a complete and unimagined way, and anything that is not completely "being" does not completely exist in any real sense. Everything else can be said to "exist" only because it rises from and is maintained by God's knowledge or, one might say, imagination.

In other words, there is a collective imagination, of which all creation is a part: This is what we know as "existence." There is also each individual existence, what one might call each individual "point of view," which constitutes another imagination: "You are an imagination, and all that you observe which you consider to be other-than-yourself is an imagination too."[37] One's point of view is in fact a phantom, because it has no reality; it exists only to allow one to know a part of existence as a whole. Hence it is a *personal* imagination within the *collective* imagination that is external existence (*al-wujud al-khariji*).[38]

As should be apparent from such descriptions, for Ibn 'Arabi the imagination (*khayal*) is something far more concrete than an abstract mental ability. The imagination, as Henry Corbin has famously discussed at great length, can be said to correspond to a "plane of being" or "plane of consciousness," in the words of Corbin, or "an isthmus" (*barzakh*), in the words of Ibn 'Arabi.[39] Imagination is an isthmus because it constitutes an intermediary realm in both the macrocosm (the cosmos) and the microcosm (the human being). From the perspective of macrocosm, there is the world of spirit and the sensory world. That which connects these two worlds, allowing form to envelop spirit and allowing meaning to be found in material or sensory things is the imaginal realm. Ibn 'Arabi often points out that, as cause is to effect, so too do the divine self-disclosures (the cause) emanate throughout the different levels of creation (the effect). Realities on the level of the identities (*al-a'yan*) become manifest in the world of spirits, which become manifest in the world of representational forms (*mithal*), which become manifest in the sensory world. Therefore the sensory world always corresponds to realities occurring in the hidden or spiritual world, even if most are unaware of this fact. When spirit takes on form in the exterior world around us, it does so in the *objective* imaginal realm (*al-khayal al-munfasil*).

As for the microcosm, the individual human being, the soul's imaginal realm serves much of the same purpose—except that it is particularized, suited for the individual knowledge of the soul. The soul interprets spiritual openings and occasions of witnessing according to the sensory experiences it has come to know. It is this faculty of *subjective* imagination (*al-khayal al-muttasil*) that allows the human viewer to see the spiritual significance of sensory forms. Viewed from this perspective, the imagination serves as an in-between point or *barzakh*/isthmus for spirit and sensory perception. Actions and entities in the world of pure spirit are formless when compared to the world of sense. Conversely actions and entities in the world of sense have dense forms—yet with respect to spirit, they lack meaning. The imagination is a mediator between these two antithetical realms. Imagination gives form to meanings, which originate in the world of spirit. It also infuses sensory forms with meaning.[40]

The human senses serve an important purpose in this process; the imagination cannot function without them, for they are initial and fundamental sources of knowledge. It is through the senses that man begins to learn and attain gnosis, gradually relating that which has been acquired through sensory perception to the spiritual world. The information gathered by the senses becomes the raw "matter" required by the imagination to create forms. The senses "lift" to the imagination that which they collect, where the intellect (*al-'aql*) can employ the "form-giving faculty" (*al-quwwah al-musawwirah*) to give such matter forms that facilitate the acquisition of knowledge. Since, however, much of that which the intellect seeks to know transcends matter or form, such as the divine attributes, the intellect must rely on "fantasy" (*al-wahm*) to create the forms needed to have some understanding. In this regard, fantasy outranks intellect in its powers of imagination. In a similar process, the faculty of fantasy (*al-wahm*) can use the form-giving faculty to generate forms not only in service to the intellect, but also for its own ends, although in a much more fleeting manner.[41] Since sensory knowledge is "levied" or collected and stored in the imagination and therein used by the soul to know things both sensory and supersensory, Ibn 'Arabi describes the imagination as a "treasury" (*khizanat al-khayal*) or a "treasury of taxed revenue" (*khizanat al-jibayat*).[42]

During dreams, the soul, like a king, acquires access to the treasury of imagination. Then, formless meanings—that is, what we might call "abstract concepts"—can take on forms. Knowledge, for example, appears as milk.[43] For many, the imaginal realm is only accessible during sleep. For the gnostic, however, this imaginal power allows him to see during wakefulness that which others see only during dreams, and it allows for the acquisition of knowledge through *shuhud*/witnessing.[44]

Yet even in the case of the gnostic, the forms of these visions correspond to that which is known by the senses, since, after all, the primary stage of knowledge acquisition for all humans is sensory. It is for this reason that the soul's rational and spiritual cognition often corresponds to sensory forms, to representations suitable to the human perspective. Spiritual realities, while in themselves unbounded, must assume certain representational or imagined forms in order for a human knower to perceive them. Two phrases in the writings of Ibn 'Arabi reflect this idea: *al-tamaththul* (assuming representational forms) and *al-takhayyul* (assuming imaginal forms).

The difference between these two parallel terms is not always clear, since both often appear side by side as one phrase in the writings of Ibn 'Arabi. The word *al-takhayyul* functions in a number of ways. It can be used to describe the faculty of imagination (*quwwat al-takhayyul*), the Imaginal Realm (*'alam* or *hadrat al-takhayyul*), or the process whereby meaning and spirit can take on sensory forms (*al-takhayyul*). Whenever used together, the terms *al-takhayyul* and *al-tamaththul* describe an important imaginal process: Presenting themselves to the gnostic, unbounded, or less-bounded entities take certain forms—forms that are perceived as having limits such as shapes, colors, bodies, or voices, even though the gnostic knows that such limits are merely representational or imaginal and not binding.

An example of *tamaththul* in the Qur'an would be the angel Gabriel's appearing to Mary in the form of a man (19:17). The verse describing this scene is helpful because of the terms used, specifically the verb *tamaththala: "We sent to her Our spirit* [*ruhuna*] *so he assumed for her the representational form* [*fa-tamaththala laha*] *of a shapely man."* Although Ibn 'Arabi tends to favor citing Gabriel's appearance to the Prophet Muhammad in the form of the handsome Dihyah al-Kalbi as an example of *al-tamaththul,* he does mention the encounter between Gabriel and Mary in numerous places, including his commentary on his own poetic collection, *Tarjuman al-Ashwaq* (The Interpreter of Desires).[45] In this instance, Gabriel, described as God's spirit, clearly neither occupies a real body as a sort of indwelling nor abandons his less-bounded spiritual qualities by appearing in such a form. Rather, it is Mary as a viewer who sees him as such, and the image that she sees is only a representative counterpart to that spirit, a counterpart or form necessary for Mary to have contact with him.

Even on the highest levels of human perception—that enjoyed by the prophets and saints—spiritual realities are dressed in sensory forms. This includes, for example, the Prophet Muhammad's interactions with the angel Gabriel.[46] Because of the visionary natures of these phenomena, *tamaththul* and *takhayyul* occupy a central position in the poetry of Ibn 'Arabi, since forms witnessed by the gnostic are projected from the Imaginal Realm, and the lover-poet yearns on account of these very forms.[47] The ability to see the imaginal, to perceive the supersensory in sensory forms, renders the human being more receptive than (and thus superior to) meanings or spirits.[48] This ability allows the human being to function as a comprehensive receiver, since the Imaginal Realm, which brings together the supersensory and the sensory, is the widest of all realms. Common folk experience this while asleep or after death, but, as has been said, the gnostics have access to the confluence of meaning and sensory form while awake in this world.

While sensory experience is an important part of *shuhud*/witnessing, nevertheless, the perceptive experiences of the gnostics cannot be compared to that which common perceivers see. The common perceiver sees the imaginal realm as unreal and the sensory realm as real. For the gnostics, the opposite is true—the supersensory realm is actual, while the material, physical world has an illusory quality to it.[49]

Ultimately, the most significant experience of the gnostic is witnessing the Real, but it is not enough to say that the gnostic sees only the Real and naught else. Rather, the gnostic's very senses testify to the Oneness of Being, such that the gnostic has almost no experiences of his own. Instead the gnostic is cognizant that the Real sees through his senses and that the Seer and the Seen are both the Real. Or, since no substantive distinction can be made between the gnostic and the Real, one might say that both Seer and Seen are the gnostic.[50] This is supported by one of the most important and frequently cited narrations in the writings of Ibn 'Arabi, a hadith which he uses perhaps more than any other to explain the perceptive experience of the gnostic. The hadith is a *hadith-qudsi,* meaning that the narration relates the words of God in the first person: *"My servant draws near to Me through nothing I love more than that which I have made obligatory for him. My servant never ceases drawing near to Me through supererogatory works until I love him. Then, when I love him, I am his hearing through which he hears, his sight through which he sees, his hand through which he seizes, and his foot through which he walks."*[51]

In the chapter of the *Fusus al-Hikam* (Ringstones of Manifold Wisdom) concerning the Prophet Hud, Ibn 'Arabi interprets this hadith in a surprisingly literal way, reminding his audience of the profound implications of this narration. (Very often, Ibn 'Arabi will uncover intimations of his vision in traditional sources by means of uncommonly literal interpretation.) Ibn 'Arabi explains that multiplicity always leads back to oneness, since, in the case of this narration, no distinction is made between the Essence of the Real (which is one), the various limbs (which are many), and the servant (who is one).[52]

Ibn 'Arabi uses the wording in the narration cited above to illustrate that different branches and instances of knowledge actually reflect one reality, much like, in his words, water varies in taste depending on its location. Alluding to the Qur'anic verse describing different waters as "pleasant and sweet-tasting" versus "salty and bitter-tasting,"[53] Ibn 'Arabi argues that the differences in water tastes are due to the differences in the places wherein water stands (*ikhtilaf al-biqa'*), yet water itself is one reality (*haqiqah wahidah*). The various limbs and sensory organs, too, possess knowledge specific to them, even though the reality they observe is one. Each organ of

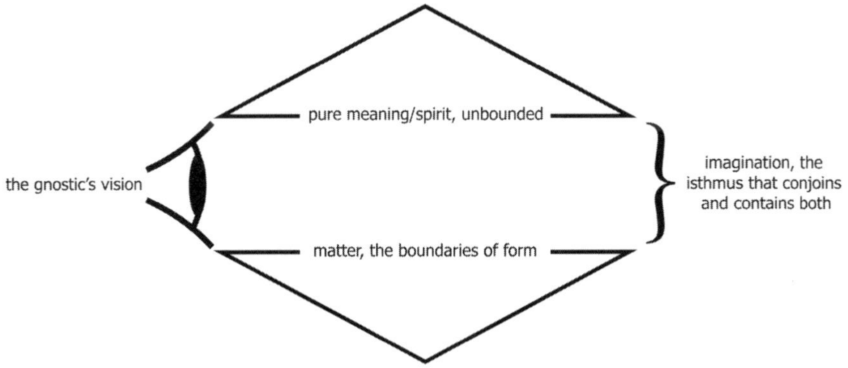

perception knows things according to its own capacity and preordained inclinations, that is, their "tastes" differ.[54] In truth, however, the different sorts of knowledge to which the organs have access are various perspectives of one reality, since the branches of knowledge unique to each organ ultimately lead to one unified source (*min 'ayn wahidah*). Moreover, not only is the Perceived in all actuality one, but the perceiver—that is, the human soul—combines the disparate reports of each organ into one perceived reality. After all, the soul as perceiver is one as well.

Practical Considerations in Monitoring Imagination

A detailed account of man's main organs of perception and action can be found in an early interpreter of Ibn 'Arabi, who was, like 'Iraqi, a disciple of Ibn 'Arabi's great disciple, Sadr al-Din Qunawi: Mu'ayyid al-Din Jandi (d. ca. 700/1300). A discussion of the organs of perception in Jandi will clarify, first, the practicalities behind Ibn 'Arabi's theoretical focus on the imagination; second, the extent to which Ibn 'Arabi's teachings affect the perception of the gnostic; and third, the connection between the physical senses and *shuhud*.

Jandi's discussions of the various organs are framed in his discussion of self-surveillance (*muraqabah*), that is, watching over that which one sees, hears, and does, because the wayfarer must begin to control that which enters his heart.[55] At the end of each day, having undertaken constant self-surveillance, the wayfarer then performs self-reckoning (*muhasabah*), that is, he takes into account all that which he has performed by means of his eight organs—the eye, ear, tongue, hand, stomach, private parts, feet, and heart. Taking into account the deeds and states of *eight* faculties, according to Jandi, is specifically the way of the Seal of the Saints, that is, Ibn 'Arabi.[56] Before the time of the "Great Shaykh," wayfarers only took into account the activities of the seven physical body parts mentioned above, without reckoning the "heart" or the soul separately, that is, without reckoning the various bestirrings (*khawatir*)—inspirations both negative and positive—that affect the heart: "In these eastern lands, those known as 'Sufis' and those who appear to be 'shaykhs' have no knowledge of this practice [of *muhasabah*]. In the west, however, the important Sufi shaykhs and verifiers have engaged in it. Yet they restricted their reckoning to the seven organs, nothing more. Once the period of the Seal of the Saints was realized and the Shaykh—may God be pleased with him—came along this way, he added another station to this reckoning of the self. By adding this station, he sealed the practice of self-reckoning. The Shaykh—may God be pleased with him—would take his soul into reckoning with respect to bestirrings [*khawatir*] as well."[57]

This is verified by Muhyi al-Din's own assertions in *al-Futuhat al-Makkiyah* regarding self-reckoning. Ibn 'Arabi remarks that, while his teachers recorded their words and actions in notebooks, reviewing these registers after the evening prayer (*salat al-'isha'*), "I surpassed them in this regard, since I recorded bestirrings."[58] By vigilantly watching over the bestirrings of the soul, Ibn 'Arabi was able to efface the superfluous activities of the soul and thus perfect his attentiveness to the meaningful: "I used to record that which my soul said to me and what it imagined, in addition to my words and actions. I would take my soul into account, like they did, during that time, and would bring out the notebook, taking the soul to task for all that which bestirred it, that which it said to itself, that which from such [bestirring and self-speaking] became manifest to the senses in terms of both words and actions, and that which it intended in every bestirring and instance of self-speech. Hence bestirrings and superfluous thoughts were lessened to only that which had meaning."[59] As can be seen from Jandi's analysis of this undertaking, Muhyi al-Din's contribution to the practice of self-reckoning involves something more profound than merely his introduction of a higher ethical station, namely, watching over the bestirrings of the heart. Rather, the end goal of this practice—perceiving the true Perceiver and the true essence of the soul, which is the Real—corresponds to one of Ibn 'Arabi's distinctive teachings.

According to Jandi, by correctly fulfilling the conditions for self-surveillance and self-reckoning, the wayfarer gains mastery over the bestirrings (*khawatir*) that enter his heart—whether divine (*ilahi*), angelic (*malaki*), from the lower soul (*nafsani*), or Satanic (*shaytani*)—until he ultimately becomes "illuminated by the secret of the self-disclosures of the divine essence, names, and attributes."[60] Although the matter is practical, the theoretical terminology of Ibn 'Arabi's school colors Jandi's account. This indicates that Ibn 'Arabi and his students discerned an important interdependence between *theories* about witnessing the One Reality and *practices* perfecting the wayfarer's ability to witness. Moreover, Jandi's description of the organs over which the wayfarer must be watchful, especially the eye and the ear, emphasize the extent to which realizing the Oneness of Being affects the gnostic's perception. According to Jandi, the right of the Real and the right of one's eye is to "see all that which appears to this organ from the Real as the Real, and not to see anything other than the Real at all, because, in fact, other than the Real there is no existent or witnessed except that which is [due to] imagination [*khayal*] and fantasy [*wahm*]."[61]

Bear in mind that Jandi describes a process of visual interpretation that begins with physical sensory perception and ends with witnessing the Oneness of Being. It is the *physical* eye with which he first concerns himself in this section; this is clear from his description of the eye as "the instrument of understanding seen things, that is, radiances, lights, surfaces, bodies, colors, figures, shapes, frames, forms, and nothing else."[62] Yet the functions of the physical eye give rise to the soul's ability to perceive unseen realities. The senses—here vision—are the soul's introduction to the phenomena that surround it, since, according to Jandi, "God—Glorified and Exalted—has bestowed on the human *spirit* understanding of seen things by means of this organ [the eye]." With respect to the "inner" senses, each organ has an unseen counterpart, and that counterpart has a further-unseen counterpart, each of which affects the other. According to Jandi, the eye has a form, a spirit, and a reality: "Its form is obvious [that is, the physical eye is its form]. The spirit of the eye is the 'heart's eye' which is also called 'insight' [*basirat*]. The heart's eye sees nothing other than the face of the Real, which is an abstracted [*ma'qul*], luminary form, eternal without beginning or end." The reality of the eye, which Jandi tells us is its "ultimate purpose," is to engage in the most sublime degree of witnessing possible for the gnostic: "Comprehending the manifestness of the Real in the identities of seen things [*a'yan-i mubsarat*]."[63] According to such an understanding, the physical sense of vision is a degraded instance of *shuhud*/witnessing.

Elsewhere Jandi explains the correlation between outer organs such as the eye or ear and inner faculties such as the heart by outlining successive grades of reality; every outer reality has an inner one, and the physical eye or ear is the outermost reality of the divine seeing or hearing: "The inner aspect of your body is the soul [*jan*]. The inner aspect of the soul is the heart [*dil*]. The inner aspect of the heart is the divine secret [*sirr-i ilahi*], in which the Real is veiled. The inner aspect of the secret is the Real."[64] This reverse emanation of the senses, from the physical eye to the heart's eye to the reality of the eye, reflects an understanding—based on the Oneness of Being—that levels of interconnected manifestation exist, where the physical body serves as an outer manifestation of the soul, and the reality of the soul is the Real itself. Jandi tells us, for example, that, because the sensory faculties are the outer form of the soul's knowledge, and the soul is the outer form of the Real and his attributes, "hearing derives from the realities of the name All-Knowing [*al-'alim*]."[65]

Jandi's account emphasizes vision, which should not be surprising since the sense of vision has a status above the other senses in the writings of Ibn 'Arabi and his school. The poetry and prose of the Akbaris often describes witnessing in terms of seeing with the eyes, because, in the words of Ibn 'Arabi, "even though man has been given many organs, he contemplates and sees exclusively through the use of his eyes; therefore the eyes occupy in him a position analogous to the one that lovers occupy in the cosmos."[66] That is, the eyes are the organs singularly most capable of knowing the outside world, just as the lovers are more adept than God's other creatures at serving as the divine mirror through which they know him and he knows himself.

Yet the wayfarer's sense of hearing also serves an important purpose, especially with regard to communicating the divine speech, and like vision, hearing undergoes a transformation as the veils of otherness are lifted. Hearing's primary function, according to Jandi, is acquiring knowledge—specifically knowledge of the two revealed sources, the speech of God and the narrations of the Prophet Muhammad.[67] At the most basic level, such hearing concerns merely listening to the outer form of the Qur'an and the words that make up the traditions of the Prophet.

Yet for every outer sense there is an inner reality, and the inner reality of hearing is to surpass the outermost meanings transmitted by these holy sources and delve into the secrets of gnosis. With the outer ear one listens to the outward form of God's speech, but with the inner ear, which is "the soul of the ear and the ear of the soul," one can listen directly to "the speech of the Real." The speech of the Real surrounds every listener, even when he or she is unaware of it. The voices and sounds of those around him are in fact the speech of the Real. Once one lifts the veils of "others" (*aghyar*), removing "the cotton of heedlessness from the ear of awareness," one gains access to the audition of the divine speech. At this exalted station, the gnostic can hear the divine voice telling him to "do this and avoid that" (*chunin kun ya makun*). Of course, just as with the eye, Jandi's advice applies to not only advanced mystics but also novice wayfarers. Jandi explains that even those who have not reached the level of the "Achieved Ones" (*kamilan*) can engage in "sweet, intimate prayers with the Real." In accordance with the power of attentiveness (*tawajjuh*) and concentration possessed by the mystic, the mystic converses with the Real. As this propensity for conversation intensifies, and becomes constant, the gnostic experiences perpetual conversation, hearing God in all things. Intimate conversation with the Real is the outcome of perfecting the inward sense of hearing, just as seeing the Real in all places and eventually witnessing him in the identities themselves is the outcome of perfecting the inward sense of sight.

The result of attaining gnostic hearing—constant conversation with the Real—should explain much of the dialogical lamentations and rejoicings of Sufi poetry. The gnostic, having undergone the perceptive transformation described, communicates longingly with the relentless Voice that occupies him. Ibn 'Arabi expresses the amorous potentials of tuning the physical senses to divine self-disclosures, and the difference between the senses of hearing and sight, in a poem from *al-Futuhat al-Makkiyah:*

The ear is in love and the eye is in love,
distinct because of the gap between [direct] source and [indirect] report.
Thus, the ear loves intensely that which my fantasy depicts,
and the eye loves intensely that which is sensed in forms.[68]

One can see here that the difference between hearing and seeing (or the ear and the eye) relates to prominence and grades of directness: The eye witnesses forms directly, while the ear receives reports of forms depicted for it by the faculty of fantasy (*wahm*). Thus the eye, being the most immediate of senses, is also the most prominent. Of course, both senses cause the gnostic's longing for the beloved to escalate. For one aware of the Reality behind the forms of the cosmos, every sense is enamored.

A general rule can be applied in fact to all the perceiving senses: Without gnosis, the created form or effect is perceived, while with gnosis, one only perceives the

Real. All that which is seen, heard, or known in any way corresponds to the Real. Of course, at an even higher station of insight, the gnostic does not merely perceive that all things are the Real; rather, the gnostic loses all self-identity, so that the Real is both perceiver and perceived.

Seeing with Both Eyes: *Tanzih* and *Tashbih*

While the gnostic at times perceives no distinction between creation and Creator, the intellect knows something else to be the case. God transcends all form, so that the gnostic's vision, in which the cosmos is the form of the Real, encroaches on the incomparability of God. In describing this paradoxical experience of the gnostic—seeing the cosmos as the Real while knowing that it is not he—Ibn 'Arabi often employs the terms *tashbih* (immanence or similitude) and *tanzih* (transcendence), terms that describe two far-reaching religious tendencies.

Although both terms, *tashbih*/similitude and *tanzih*/transcendence, have a special sense for the gnostic, they apply to religious language in its most basic form as well. In order to have any means of approach to God, humans necessarily compare his acts and attributes to that which they know: their own human acts and attributes. Not only names such as "the Seeing" and "the Hearing," but also names such as "the Merciful" and "the Forgiving" can be attributed to a human as fittingly as they can be attributed to God, with the exception that in relation to God these names are absolute. For Ibn 'Arabi, God has not only permitted such descriptions of himself, he has indeed encouraged them, for in the Qur'an and narrations he has described himself by certain names, attributes, and actions with qualities of *tashbih*. Of course, there are certain limits to considering God through descriptions of similitude; if one exceeds these limits, one falls into the most censurable of all practices, namely, *shirk*, associating others with God, declaring him to be like others or others to be like him. There must always be an acknowledgment that descriptions of God based on similitude fall short of him; otherwise, God becomes confused with his creation.

For uninitiated persons, it is the intellect that is susceptible to the dangerously erroneous conclusions of *tashbih*/similitude, since it employs similitude to comprehend the One who cannot be comprehended. If left unbalanced by an understanding of God's transcendence, the intellect will impose created attributes upon the Real, falsely supposing that God hears as humans hear, has fluctuating emotions, or somehow corresponds to human perfections. For the gnostics, however, the hazard of similitude stems not from the intellect but from vision; the gnostics risk considering absolutely true that which they see as one reality. In both cases, it is *tanzih* that establishes that God is exalted above anything known or witnessed of him.

From the mystic's perspective, the cosmos is the form of God, while from reason's limited view, the cosmos is merely a created entity. Both aspects of creation must be perceived in order for a gnostic to possess what Ibn 'Arabi considers a proper outlook, an outlook that he often describes as seeing with both eyes, alluding to the Qur'anic verse *"Have We not bestowed him* [that is, the human] *with two eyes?"* (90:8): "One eye is that through which he who changes states is perceived, while the other eye is that through which state-changing itself is perceived. . . . Each eye has a path. So know Whom you see and what you see. For this reason it is correct that, *You did not throw when you threw, but God threw* (8:17). The eye through which you perceive that the throwing belongs to God is different from the eye through which you perceive that the throwing belongs to Muhammad. So know that you have two eyes, if you possess knowledge. Then you will know for certain that the thrower is God in a corporeal Muhammadan form. Assuming representational forms [*al-tamaththul*] and assuming imaginal forms [*al-takhayyul*] are nothing but this."[69] As is the case here, the writings of Ibn 'Arabi consistently emphasize perceiving two realities at once: The cosmos and all in it is he, but it is also not he. God has appointed for each person two eyes, with which each person should be cognizant of God as cosmos, on the one hand, and cosmos as cosmos, on the other.

In the Qur'anic example mentioned above (8:17), God's self-attribution of Muhammad's throwing a handful of sand and pebbles at the battle of Badr, highlights this dichotomy of two concurrent realities. It was God who threw, in reality, even though one cannot deny that a human being with a physical form also threw. The Qur'an does not simply say it was God who threw (*Allah rama*). Rather, it denies human action while simultaneously affirming it: You did not throw (*ma ramayta*) when you did throw (*idh ramayta*), but God threw (*wa lakinna Allah rama*). Clearly there is a duality of action—you threw and God threw—although, since the ultimate source and granter of action is God, the overall sway of the verse according to Ibn 'Arabi favors God's actions over human ones (that is, the conclusive meaning of the verse favors "you did not throw"). Obviously there would be no throwing, in fact, no entities whatsoever, if not for God's causing these things and bestowing existence on them. Yet it would also be impossible for there to exist any throwing at all if there were not the corporeal form of Muhammad, the sand and pebbles, and all the other limits required for human action. Thus God's throwing requires certain limits in order to be actualized. The gnostic perceives these limits while also perceiving the reality behind them; he sees both the moved and the Mover, or, in the words of Ibn 'Arabi, he sees God as thrower and also the corporeal Muhammadan form as the locus of this divine action. (Muhammad, as the exemplar Perfect Man, represents the greatest locus for divine manifestation, which makes this example particularly fitting.)

The balance between similitude and transcendence is one between intimacy and awe, proximity and distance, the heart and the intellect. Ibn 'Arabi repeatedly associates transcendence with reason and observes that God has also verified reason's conclusion that he cannot be known.[70] The transcendent God of reason cannot be loved because he surpasses all comprehension or proximity. In fact, Ibn 'Arabi tells us that without superhuman knowledge, that is, revelation, humans would be left with the unlovable, transcendent God of reason: "If we were left only the intellectual proofs used by rationalists in knowing the divine essence—that it is *not* such-and-such and *not* such-and-such—no created thing would love him. But when the divine reports came, in the languages of religious law, telling us that he *is* such-and-such and *is* such-and-such, in matters the outer senses of which contradict rational proofs, we loved him for the sake of these positive attributes."[71] As Ibn 'Arabi explains, God's direct communication with man, that which transcends reason, tells us that God *is* certain things, allowing for *tashbih*/similitude, proximity, and hence love. It is for this reason that a spiritual temperament inclined toward love emphasizes *tashbih.*

Similitude or *Tashbih:* The Way of Lovers

The contraposition of transcendence and similitude is a central theme of Ibn 'Arabi's chapter "The Wisdom of Transcendence in the Nuhian/Noachian Word" in the *Fusus al-Hikam,* a chapter primarily concerned with the ways in which gnostics know the Real, the most evenhanded of whom are the heirs to the Prophet Muhammad. We have established that transcendence is negative knowledge, knowledge that God cannot be known, for he is "hidden from all understanding."[72] Yet that which transcendence soberly opposes—knowledge of God based on similitude—has an intoxicating allure that brings many lovers of God to shun transcendence. Ibn 'Arabi discusses this allure in his esoteric reading of chapter 71 of the Qur'an, which focuses on Nuh/Noah's unheeded efforts to guide and save the idol-worshipping people of his time. The polytheists, according to Ibn 'Arabi, represent the practitioners of immoderate similitude.[73] They reject Noah's message of a transcendent God because it demands that they abandon the immanent Reality that they have come to know and that arouses love in them.

These adherents to similitude are especially affected by one of its facets, associating the soul or "self" with their Lord and thus seeing the soul as the Real. In the words of that important narration mentioned above, in which God describes the effect of becoming the object of his love, God has become for each adherent of similitude the *hearing through which he hears, his sight through which he sees, his hand through which he seizes and his foot through which he walks,* but here in an excessive way. This confusion between self and Lord, a result of annihilation in God (*fana'*), causes these practitioners of similitude to see God in the cosmos.[74] Since the practitioners of similitude have merged self and Lord, and since he has become for them their inner and outer senses, the outside world perceived by those senses is nothing but God.[75] Thus they possess the "piercing" eyesight that results from *tashbih.*[76]

The vision of *tashbih*/similitude results in knowledge, a knowledge that brings with it love.[77] Yet such knowledge has a bewildering effect on the gnostic, one which

Ibn 'Arabi describes as *al-hayrah*, or "perplexity."[78] Perplexity in the language of Ibn 'Arabi is directly related to love, for while "reason ties down its possessor," love has the opposite effect: "Among the attributes of love [*al-hubb*] is waywardness [*al-dalal*] and perplexity [*al-hayrah*], although perplexity is incompatible with reason. Truly reason brings you together, while the better of the two [love] strews you apart!"[79] These idol worshippers / gnostics have uncovered a reality of the human soul that, when known, strews them apart. To ask them to relinquish this painful, inebriating, yet enrapturing knowledge in favor of transcendence, which is a negative knowledge, or what might be called a willed ignorance, is futile. It is because of their status as immoderate and uncompromising lovers that the idol-worshipping "knowers" deserve both blame and praise. On the one hand, they have abandoned transcendence completely, which is blameworthy, but on the other hand, these polytheists represent the gnostics themselves, for the gnostics are in a sense inclined to the way of similitude, that is, the way of love and vision.

Similitude (*tashbih*), beauty, and love cannot be separated from one another in the worldview of Ibn 'Arabi and his school. To some degree, this relates to the interconnectedness of love and witnessing in the thought of Ibn 'Arabi: "When the Real is one's beloved, [that person] experiences perpetual witnessing [*al-mushahadah*]. Witnessing the Beloved, like food for the body, causes [the lover] to grow and increase—as his witnessing increases, so too does his love."[80] As has been discussed, witnessing involves matter and form; it cannot be attributed to the World of Pure Meaning or, even less, the unknowable divine essence. It is a form of similitude. Since, as seen in the passage above, love is intimately connected to witnessing, one can conclude that lovers rely on visions of *tashbih*/similitude. Ibn 'Arabi alludes to the relationship between witnessing, love and *tashbih* in a concise phrase explaining that when God allows his servant to love him with the same sort of love that he has for his servant, then "he has granted witnessing [*shuhud*] and has blessed him with the capacity to contemplate God in the forms of things [*bi-shuhudihi fi suwar al-ashya'*]."[81] The phrase "forms of things" is of particular importance, for God in forms is the God of *tashbih*.

This witnessing only fuels the blaze of the gnostics' love first kindled by God, so much so that they risk becoming immoderate. It is for this reason that Ibn 'Arabi emphasizes the importance of seeing with two eyes: an eye of *tashbih*/similitude and an eye of *tanzih*/transcendence. Practicing a sort of justice, the gnostic gives each thing its *haqq*, its "due" or its "right," that is, the gnostic acknowledges the inimitable perfection God has given to each individual existent thing.[82] Such a person recognizes that the multiple existents were created wisely and must be recognized as individual existents, despite the veracity of the gnostic's vision that all things are the Real. He or she partakes in the pleasures of witnessing and love while also acknowledging the proper limits of his or her vision. By doing so, the gnostic can control the dangers of excess and remain within the boundaries of those who preserve proper etiquette with respect to God.[83] It is with such dangers of excess in mind that Ibn 'Arabi states, "God has given me an excessive share of love, but he has also given me the ability to control it."[84]

Having here established that the gnostic witnesses divine disclosures in forms and undergoes love in the vision of *tashbih*/similitude, we can bring this difficult chapter to an end. While many of the terms and specificities of this vision pertain to Ibn 'Arabi alone, the general experience of witnessing and many of its concomitants are shared by other Sufis, Akbari and non-Akbari alike. In fact, Fakhr al-Din 'Iraqi saw baffling correspondences between the Akbari worldview and the love language of Persian Sufism. In the case of both Ibn 'Arabi and Fakhr al-Din 'Iraqi, the vision of *tashbih* is of particular importance to matters of love and the human form, and thus poetic expression. Indeed, much of the language of love in Islamic mysticism emerges from an orientation toward witnessing and *tashbih*.

CHAPTER 2

Perception according to 'Iraqi

Witnessing and Divine Self-Love

In many important ways, the writings of Fakhr al-Din Ibrahim ibn Buzurjmihr 'Iraqi differ from those of Ibn 'Arabi. While Ibn 'Arabi's copious prosaic output in Arabic often sounds scientific, 'Iraqi, whether in verse or in that which remains of him in prose, writes in the language of love, mostly in Persian, and concisely so. It is for this reason that the congruity found in the writings of these two mystics deserves mention. Beyond that which resulted from 'Iraqi's association with Ibn 'Arabi's main visionary inheritor, Sadr al-Din al-Qunawi, Fakhr al-Din's entire corpus of written works confirms many of Ibn 'Arabi's descriptions of witnessing. Perhaps, in writing his "Flashes" or *Lama'at,* 'Iraqi sought to display the conformity of witnessing and love that exists between Ibn 'Arabi's teachings and those of his own Suhrawardi tradition. Whether or not that is the case, Fakhr al-Din chose to focus his attention on the significance of witnessing and love to Ibn 'Arabi's ontological vision. In fact, 'Iraqi can be considered to have specialized in these two subjects, namely, witnessing and love.

The Creational Basis of Witnessing

Repeatedly in the works of 'Iraqi, particularly but not exclusively the *Lama'at,* one encounters his view of creation and its relationship to *shuhud*/witnessing. The story of creation according to 'Iraqi is one where Love wanted to look upon itself. Having witnessed itself, it became infatuated and took on two identities that perpetually long for one another: lover and beloved. All of creation springs from the divine yearning for the Self, and all witnessing is in fact the divine act of self-admiration. Thus for 'Iraqi, the process of creation is one of self-love, then self-speaking,[1] and finally self-witnessing. The designation *'ishq* (passionate or desirous love), when attributed to the essence of the Real, indicates that the divine essence inherently yearns for itself. In this regard, it is its own impetus to self-speaking and self-witnessing. Moreover, much like the independent divine essence, the word "love" can stand conceptually on its own as an abstract concept, without any lover or beloved to cause it to be realized. Yet in order to be witnessed and known, "love" necessitates a lover (who puts this relationship into action) and a beloved (the object of this two-way relationship). That is, while "love" can be independent, it can only be *known* through lovers and objects of love. So too, 'Iraqi tells us, does the entirety of creation stem from the self-manifestation of "love," a self-manifestation without which love would never be known, heard, or witnessed: "The words 'Lover' and 'Beloved' are derived etymologically from 'Love,' but Love upon its mighty Throne is purified of all entification, in the sanctuary of its Reality too holy to be touched by inwardness or outwardness. Yet, that it might manifest its perfection (a perfection identical both with its own Essence and its own Attributes), it showed itself to itself in the looking-glass of 'lover' and 'beloved.' It displayed its own beauty to its own eyes. It thus became viewer and viewed, which caused the names 'lover' and 'beloved' and the attributes of 'seeker' and 'sought' to appear."[2] Especially significant here is that the attributes of lover, beloved, seeker, and sought (*'ashiqi, ma'shuqi, talibi, matlubi*) all result from Love's self-witnessing (from the attributes of *naziri* and *manzuri*). The Real's admiration for his own beauty brings about the entirety of creation, an object of love derived from himself in which he admires himself.

Self-Admiration as Witnessing

The centrality of God's love for himself, a love that pervades all things and becomes actualized as the divine self-witnessing and the divine self-speech, can be seen in a succinct, threefold saying in the *Lama'at:* None loves God other than God; none sees God other than God; and none mentions God other than God.[3] This is a key point for 'Iraqi: Self-love, self-witnessing, and self-speech, which in reality are divine actions, pervade the entire cosmos. Every lover reenacts the divine self-admiration and sees in his object of love none other than himself. Yet the human reality is a breath from the divine essence, so that the human self is indeed the divine Self. Hence the achieved lover sees not only himself but also God in his object of love. When the human lover sees God's beauty in an object of vision, he shares in the divine self-witnessing: "All that exists is a mirror for his beauty—thus everything is beautiful. Undoubtedly he loves all things. Or to be precise, he loves himself. Every lover you see loves none other than himself, for in the mirror of the beloved's face, that lover sees none other than himself. Hence he takes no one other than himself as a beloved. [As it says in the prophetic hadith,] *'The securer* [of faith] *is a mirror for the Securer,'* and God is 'the Securer.' This [hadith] clarifies everything."[4]

All things, as 'Iraqi repeatedly mentions, are mirrors for the beauty of God. One can deduce from this that admiration of all beauty or any object of beauty is in fact admiration of the Source and Giver of that beauty. Glancing at the beautiful face of a human being, for example, would resemble this divine act of self-admiration. Such a view of created beauty—enacting divine self-admiration by staring at ravishing human faces—is not only a possible interpretation of the creation story related by 'Iraqi and other like-minded Sufis but also, in fact, explicitly stated, sanctioned, and probably put into practice by 'Iraqi. The love that human lovers experience for human beloveds, like the love a gnostic experiences for the divine beloved, derives from *shuhud* (witnessing). One can see why, then, *shuhud* would serve as the primary motivation for Sufi amorous poetic expression, and it should not come as a surprise that *shuhud* is arguably the central theme in almost all of 'Iraqi's poems. In fact, it is difficult to find a poem in 'Iraqi's *diwan* that cannot somehow be related to the theme of *shuhud*.

It is a simple matter to say that the gnostic sees God in all things, but the details of such witnessing are far less discernible. While the prose writings of Ibn 'Arabi are more direct, it sometimes involves a great degree of interpretation to determine in the writings of 'Iraqi the particulars of *shuhud*/witnessing. 'Iraqi's descriptions are succinctly stated in the language of love and through the medium of amorous poetry (or, in the case of the *Lama'at*, amorous prose), as opposed to the sometimes deceivingly scholarly prose of Ibn 'Arabi.[5] Often one line in the poetry of 'Iraqi corresponds to an entire chapter of Ibn 'Arabi's *al-Futuhat al-Makkiyah*.[6] A proclivity for terse, poetic language holds true even in 'Iraqi's prose work, *Lama'at*, where each of the observations made in our discussion of Ibn 'Arabi concerning *shuhud* can be found in condensed form. Perhaps resulting from the theoretical nature of *al-Futuhat al-Makkiyah*, as opposed to the amorous nature of the *Lama'at*, the very terms used to describe *shuhud* also differ in the writings of these two saints. While Ibn 'Arabi's prose descriptions of *shuhud* make use of terms from *ahadith* and the Qur'an, 'Iraqi phrases his descriptions of *shuhud* in terms and symbols common to classical Persian poetry—wine, boys, and infatuated lovers. Yet despite these differences, the visions of Ibn 'Arabi and Fakhr al-Din 'Iraqi for the most part do correspond and maintain a certain parallelism.[7]

State-changing

Clearly Fakhr al-Din's writings verify Ibn 'Arabi's descriptions of the gnostic's witnessing the cosmos constantly "transmutate" or change forms to reflect the infinity of God's manifestations, a phenomenon known as *tahawwul*, or "state-changing."[8] In fact one *lam'ah* of the twenty-eight *lama'at* of 'Iraqi (that is one of the twenty-eight "flashes of light," each of which can be considered a chapter), the fifth flash, concerns *tahawwul*/state-changing. One can find a remarkable degree of consistency in content between Fakhr al-Din's metaphorical description of state-changing and excerpts from Ibn 'Arabi's writings: "Every instant, the Beloved shows a different face in a mirror, and at every instant appears in a different form. This is because form—in accordance with the altering of mirrors—varies at every instant. And at every breath, the mirror—because of the altering of states—also varies."[9] The phrase "every instant" or "every breath" (*har dam*), repeated twice in this segment, like the parallel phrase "every breath" (*har nafas*) seen once, tells us that we are dealing with the same "indivisible moment" (*an*) that Ibn 'Arabi often describes, that smallest unit of time within which God constantly re-creates the cosmos in a different form.[10] In fact, Fakhr al-Din refers directly to the indivisible moment toward the end of this chapter, in his citation of verse 55:29, *"Every day* [or instant] *he* [God] *is upon a new affair."*

Like Ibn 'Arabi and probably inspired by Ibn 'Arabi's interpretation of this verse, 'Iraqi sees here an allusion to the constant re-creation of the cosmos. Every instant God regenerates every created thing, but in a different manner. Thus all things are inconstant and changing—while God remains constant and unchanging. 'Iraqi's predecessor Ibn 'Arabi tells us that, from a different perspective, the continuous changing of the cosmos can be seen as God's own perpetually changing states.[11] As the receptacles of God's manifestation vary at every moment, one might say that the Real, the Object of reflection in the mirrors of creation, takes on new appearances. While this might seem blasphemous to any competent theologian, for God is perfect and thus unchanging, Ibn 'Arabi and 'Iraqi suggest that such variation is undeniably true, that even if the divine essence remains the same, God's acts and traces unceasingly vary.[12]

Significant to *shuhud,* both Ibn 'Arabi and 'Iraqi see the constant changing of the cosmos as reflective of the fluctuations of the heart, so that variations witnessed externally seem to imitate or mirror variations occurring internally. Fakhr al-Din makes clear that the perpetual alteration of the cosmos, the varying of God's "states" or "affairs" and the fluctuations of the heart, are all in fact one reality. It is the realization of this reality that renders one a gnostic:

> It has been reported [in a prophetic hadith] that *"the heart is like a feather in the wide, barren desert, which the winds keep turning inside and out."* The source of these winds could very well be that wind about which Mustafa [the Prophet] said: *"Do not revile the wind, for truly it is from the breath of the All-Merciful."* If you want that a waft from the fragrances of this breath reach your sense of smell, gaze into the workshop of *Every instant he is upon a new affair* [*sha'n/shu'un,* 55:29] until you see it apparent that the variety of your states comes from the variety of his affairs and acts. Then you will come to know that "the color of the water is the color of its container," which has the same sense as saying the color of the lover is the color of the beloved.[13]

As the Real assumes his infinitely and instantaneously altering forms, the gnostic's heart, which follows its Beloved invariably, also changes forms. In this sense, both 'Iraqi and Ibn 'Arabi compare the gnostic lover's heart to a "goblet of love," since it contains the wine of love, which Ibn 'Arabi equates with divine self-disclosure.[14] According to Ibn 'Arabi, it is only the heart of the human lover, "and not his intellect nor his senses," that possesses the ability to conform to its self-permuting divine beloved: "The heart alternates from state to state, just as God—who is the beloved—is *every instant upon a new affair* (55:29). Thus because of his love's attachment, the lover varies along with the variations of the beloved in his actions, like a pure, uncolored, glass cup varies on account of the variations of the liquid located inside it. The color of the love[r] is the color of his beloved, which is a quality that only belongs to the heart."[15]

In other passages, Ibn 'Arabi clarifies that the gnostic heart, on account of the superiority of human knowledge and the comprehensiveness of human existence, is transformed to reflect the divine self-disclosures in a manner more accurate than the cosmos. This reflective perfection is often supported through a hadith in the divine first person: "My earth and My heavens do not contain Me, but the heart of My (believing) servant contains Me."[16] The heart's ability to "contain" the Real corresponds to its malleability and receptivity, which causes it to alter as instantaneously as that which it reflects: the states or "forms" of the Real.

Of course, there is a certain ambiguity between the heart as a container and the divine manifestations it contains; it is unclear at times exactly which affects the other, or if the changing of the heart and the self-disclosures of the Real are one indivisible reality. The effect on the gnostic, however, could not be clearer: The heart that turns wittingly with the State-changer becomes keenly sensitive to beauty and its infiniteness. This sentient, ever-changing heart relates very directly to the way 'Iraqi and Ibn 'Arabi understand the gnostic's love for God and for his manifestations in creation, and as such it plays an important role in their lyric poetry. It has been referred to famously in the poetry of Ibn 'Arabi as the heart "receptive to every form" (*qabilan kull surah*).[17]

Here the observations of a certain Ightishashi-Kubrawi commentator on Fakhr al-Din's *Lama'at* are of great use. Shaykh Shihab al-Din Amir 'Abdallah al-Barzishabadi al-Mashhadi (d. 872/1467), when commenting on this chapter, concerns himself centrally with the varying capabilities pertaining to loci of manifestation (*qabiliyat-i mazahir*). As Shaykh Shihab al-Din tells us, the various mirrors of manifestation exist merely because of the multitude of capabilities.[18] Yet Barzishabadi also discusses the topic of the heart's expansion (*bast*) and contraction (*qabd*), describing these two alternating states of the heart as "the property of the attributes of Fortifying-ness (*mu'izzi*) and Inhibiting-ness (*mani'i*) of the Real." Clearly, with respect to the heart of his servant, as *al-mu'izz* (the Fortifier), God draws his servant close, but as *al-mani'* (the Inhibitor), God also pushes the servant away.

Yet Barzishabadi's statement implies more than the prevalent idea, supported by a canonical hadith, that God maneuvers the heart of his servant in whatever way he wishes.[19] Rather, Barzishabadi maintains that the heart in fluctuating between these two states merely exhibits the attributes of its creator, God, who possesses attributes that are in seeming diametric opposition.[20] Here Barzishabadi asserts that the heart, just like its Creator, is both *al-mu'izz*/fortifying and *al-mani'*/inhibiting and fluctuates between these two states. Hence the expansion and contraction of the heart is more than simply a divine act of pulling close or pushing away; it is a perfection found in God's own attributes.

Such knowledge means that the true gnostic, who has known his Lord, accepts equally the varying states, recognizing the perfection in each, such that "constriction is just like expansion, and being melted is just like being tenderly caressed."[21] The gnostic no longer concerns himself with the fluctuations of his heart, instead seeing such fluctuations as the heart's duty, for the heart must conform to the self-disclosures of God, who is the Changer of Hearts (*muqallib al-qulub*).[22] In order to serve as the supreme locus of manifestation for God, who is *every instant upon a new affair*, the heart must constantly change. Barzishabadi's observations are important because they highlight the more practical ramifications of 'Iraqi's and indeed Ibn 'Arabi's descriptions of *tahawwul*/state-changing. For 'Iraqi, state-changing and, more generally, witnessing pertain not only to what the mystic witnesses outside of himself, but also—and more important—to that which he witnesses inside himself, in his heart. The heart varies in its states, and in doing so it follows the precedent of the cosmos and of its Creator.

The Cross-eyed Fool

Ibn 'Arabi's injunction that mystics see with "two" or with "both" eyes is also reflected in 'Iraqi's writings, although far less noticeably so. This is because gnostics such as 'Iraqi, especially when expressing their experiences in poetry, celebrate love, immanence, and beauty, in other words, all that which Ibn 'Arabi tells us pertains to the eye of *tashbih*/similitude, while only sometimes acknowledging (at least in the case of 'Iraqi) the validity of the eye of *tanzih*/transcendence. For the most part, 'Iraqi describes a condition where he no longer sees a barrier between creation and the Real, so that in effect he no longer sees anything but God. Countless passages in the works of Fakhr al-Din state this directly. Often, the mystic makes clear that his *belief* that nothing exists but God is based upon his *vision* wherein he sees nothing but him. This is the main theme of a *tarji'band* (a series of stanzas held together by a repeated refrain), the very refrain of which, in italics below, revolves around the ephemeral and unreal quality of everything but God:

Since other than you, there is no one I see,
I will articulate nothing other than this:
That in this universe there's no one other than you;
other than you, no one is the eternal existent.[23]

The gnostic as beholder is a mirror upon which the divine self-witnessing takes place. Such a gnostic plays a receptive part in the divine self-witnessing and as a result plays a receptive part in the divine self-speech. After all, this unity of witnessing results in a unity of speech, wherein all of creation springs from and is maintained by the Real's speaking to himself, as can be seen in a different stanza of the *tarjiʿband* mentioned above:

To see other than you is to make a mistake
—such is the view of the right-speaking folk.
Since he sees none else other than Self,
thus he speaks to no other, only himself.
For in this universe there's no one other than you;
other than you, no one is the eternal existent.[24]

Yet we see in this very poem, the *tarjiʿband* quoted above, that the gnostic's vision possesses a multilayered quality as well, even if it is only mentioned concisely, in one double line, or *bayt:* "Sometimes one, sometimes you become many— / can the intellect ever accept what I just said?"[25] The poet here alludes to visions of unity and multiplicity. Important here, the rhetorical question he poses asserts that the intellect (*ʿaql*) has no access to this contradictory vision.

ʿIraqi's emphasis on the vision of *tashbih*/similitude leads him to mock those who see exclusively through the eye of *tanzih*/transcendence, those blinded by their intellects who cannot see that Creator and creation are one. A term he uses to describe such perceptionally inept souls is *ahwal,* or "cross-eyed," since a cross-eyed person perceives a second figure where there is merely one object. This blurred vision renders the onlooker ignorant that "all things are but imagined" and that only "he exists," as ʿIraqi states in a short *ghazal* concerned with the Oneness of Being:

First, in that world-depicting cup,
the entire cosmos' image was portrayed.
The Sun of Being glowed upon the cosmos—
all those images took [external] shape.
One Face and yet more than 1,000 mirrors!
One Whole and all these particularizations.
Leave aside these fetters troublesome,
so that your problem is completely solved.
All these images and forms are nothing but
the second image seen by the cross-eyed one.[26]

The term *ahwal* allows ʿIraqi to convey not only the falsity of acknowledging the existence of created things but also the foolishness of such an assertion, since the word *ahwal* carries with it a derisive connotation.

The Wine, the Cup, and the Saqi

It should also be mentioned that ʿIraqi inherits many descriptions of *shuhud* from the Persian poetic tradition, especially through images borrowed from the poetry of infatuation and intoxication. Often these images can be seen as corresponding to descriptions of witnessing found in the school of Ibn 'Arabi. It is probably more useful, however, to see these terms and images as common to the phraseology of Sufi amorous poetry that prevailed during 'Iraqi's age (and which he played a part in solidifying).

One set of terms important to witnessing concerns the drinking of wine: *sharab,* "wine"; *jam,* "goblet"; and *saqi,* "cupbearer" or "wine-server." In *Istilahat-i Sufiyah* (Technical Terms of the Sufis), a short glossary on the definition of poetic terms attributed to 'Iraqi, *sharab* refers to "the prevalences of desirous love [*ghalabat-i 'ishq*] along with deeds that incur blame," *jam* refers to "states" (*ahwal*), and *saqi* refers to "a cupbearer" (*sharabdar*).[27] Although it would seem logical to favor 'Iraqi's own definitions of such terms, I agree with Najib Mayil Hirawi and Chittick that the glossary attributed to 'Iraqi might not be his at all and might derive from a more coherent and identifiable text by Sharaf al-Din Husayn ibn Ahmad Ulfati Tabrizi (fl. 761/1360) titled *Rashf al-Alhaz fi Kashf al-Alfaz* (The Sipping of Glances in the Unveiling of Terms).[28] The two texts share a very specific, threefold structure, and most terms and definitions correspond closely, often word for word.[29]

Indeed, the incompleteness of the version attributed to 'Iraqi becomes clear when contrasting the very definition of *saqi*/wine-giver mentioned above with that in Tabrizi's *Rashf al-Alhaz.* Whereas 'Iraqi's supposed definition, "a cupbearer," seems incongruous and strangely unhelpful, providing a mere Persian translation for this Arabic word, Tabrizi's *Rashf al-Alhaz* defines the term as "the self-disclosures of love that bring drunkenness," a more consistently insightful definition.[30] Moreover and more pertinent, 'Iraqi's presentation of these terms in his actual poetry deviates from that described in these definitions. While this might tempt us to affirm confidently that the *Istilahat* is not 'Iraqi's at all, we must bear in mind that the glossary's author does not attempt to provide a consistent, one-to-one key to symbols for *anyone's* poetry, neither a cipher nor a literary commentary. Tabrizi, in fact, explicitly describes his intention to awaken a sense of spiritual profundity hidden in the vocabulary of the great Sufi poets, those who intended "*countless* meanings and realities in these short words."[31]

Regardless of their intent, these definitions do not aid in understanding the poetry of 'Iraqi. In the case of the wine, goblet, and cupbearer, instead of referring to the states and acts of the lover, these drinking terms can be found in the *ghazal*s of 'Iraqi to correspond to the paradox of witnessing that occurs for the gnostic, in which he witnesses both meaning and form (or Being and locus of manifestation) at once. One example of such usage occurs in a poem rejoicing at the persona's incorrigible lifestyle:

One cannot hold the scoundrel of the tavern in a monastery—
how can one contain the Phoenix in a corner of a nest?

With one flirtatious glance, Saqi, break repentances a thousand!
Seize *me* from *me* again, with that bewitching eye of yours.
So I can be freed from existing and from worshipping the self,
and in a drunken fervor, wreck the good and bad of fortune.
Since asceticism and devoutness are naught but showing off,
just us, the wine, and the *shahid*—in the corner of the tavern.
How merry is the drunkard! He's fallen in the tavern,
inebriated like the friend's eye, from the nighttime's revelry.
Is this really my lot? To see in drunk unconsciousness
him in the corner and me, vanished altogether?
Having seen within the wine's cup the reflection of the Saqi's comeliness
and having heard his voice from the plectrum of the *chaghanah*?[32]
This, this is life. All the rest is merely stories—
this is true fruition—all else is fairy tales.
The wine-house is the Saqi's beauty, the wine-drinker is his drunk eye,
the goblet is his lip, and all the rest is simply pretexts.
In 'Iraqi's vision the cup and wine and Saqi—
all three are one, though the cross-eyed fool sees one as two.[33]

Perhaps the most significant double lines in this poem, at least as concerns the topic of *shuhud*/witnessing, are the last two. Here 'Iraqi redefines terms having to do with consuming wine as representations of the Saqi/Wine-server's beauty, thereby obliging his reader or listener to reinterpret the poem as such.

The wine house (*maykhanah*) in which intoxication occurs is, in fact, the Saqi's beauty (*husn-i saqi*), presumably because the Saqi's beauty is the source of the loss of self-control and rapture the viewer experiences, just as the wine house is a place or source of intoxicating drinks. A more difficult equation to decipher: The wine drinker (*maykhwarah*) is the Saqi's own inebriated eye (*chashm-i mastash*). That is, the Saqi's eye, while drunk, also instills drunkenness in others. The wine drinker is the actor in the process of intoxication; it is his act of drinking that causes himself to become drunk. Similarly, in the act of witnessing, it is the Saqi's eye that causes all action, inebriating others through desire far more than through the wine he dispenses. The cyclical element in this image aims most likely at capturing the image of the Real admiring himself through the mirror of creation, captivated by his own beauty. 'Iraqi also tells us that the goblet (*paymanah*) is the Saqi's lip (*lab*) because it is only nearness to the Saqi—in the form of a kiss—that can allow the admirer to become intoxicated.

As if these formulas were not complicated enough, 'Iraqi ends the poem with one last mystical analogy: The cup (*jam*), wine (*sharab*) and Saqi are in actuality all one, according to "'Iraqi's vision" (*dar didah-i 'Iraqi*). 'Iraqi's use of the term *didah*, which can mean "eye" or "sight," tells us that these matters pertain to *shuhud*/

witnessing, which can relate to any of the senses but is often described in terms of seeing. The final hemistich clarifies that 'Iraqi's central concern in conflating cup, wine, and wine-giver is the affirmation of the oneness of Being through witnessing. The chastising of the *ahwal* (the "cross-eyed fool") who mistakenly sees "one as two" (*binad yaki du-ganah*) in this line serves as a key indicator. As was seen in the poem quoted above, 'Iraqi reproves the *ahwal* for assuming a separation between God and creation, imagining two separate entities when in reality the cosmos is only a phantom or shadow of the Real. Here, however, 'Iraqi speaks not of two but of three separate entities that are in actuality one. Most likely this final hemistich alludes to the issue of meaning and form. The cup, as a container, corresponds to form. The wine, as the reality captured in that container, corresponds to meaning. The Saqi, as the true actor, and as both lover and beloved, corresponds to the most ideal beloved, the Real. The poetic persona, who witnesses with the eye of unity, sees three things as one: form, meaning and the Agent who manipulates the two.

What I have dubbed "meaning" often also corresponds to "existence" in the poetry of 'Iraqi (as it probably does here), since the meaning or reality that all things make manifest through their forms is in fact existence. Such is explicitly stated by 'Iraqi in his *Lama'at,* where he again makes use of the wine-and-cup metaphor: "In one instant, the Saqi poured so much of the wine of existence into the cup of nonexistence that"

From the purity of the wine and translucence of the cup,
the colors of the cup and wine have mixed together!
All is the cup, and it seems there's no wine—
or all is the wine, and it seems there's no cup![34]

The gnostic, according to 'Iraqi, faces a contradiction in vision: He either sees only wine or only the cup that holds it. Verifying Ibn 'Arabi's statement that the gnostic "will never see both creation and the Real," 'Iraqi maintains that the gnostic sees either wine or cup, never both at once.[35] The gnostic sees in one instant the wine, which is existence, in its fullest sense corresponding to the Real. In another instant, the gnostic sees the cup, which is nonexistence, that is, the cosmos, since the cosmos is but a perceived reflection of the Real. It should also be noted that, in accordance with *tahawwul*/state-changing, this vision alternates back and forth between cup and wine, that is, cosmos and the Real—or, from another perspective, multiplicity and unity. That the gnostic witnesses a variation every instant can be seen in the sudden shift of the two final hemistichs quoted above: "All is the cup, and it seems there's no wine / or all is the wine, and it seems there's no cup." The juxtaposition of these two contradicting images is meant to convey the gnostic's instantaneously altering vision.

One can see that Fakhr al-Din's use of wine-and-cup imagery allows him to express the paradoxical vision of the gnostic as one of formlessness versus form. The liquid or seemingly formless "wine" is held and shaped by the form of a concrete "cup." For 'Iraqi, form lacks any real existence and is only conceived by the viewer; existence ultimately corresponds to formlessness. Yet without form, nothing in creation would be known, including the truth that all things are in actuality One formless thing. While the wine-and-cup metaphor ably captures this dilemma, 'Iraqi also expresses this in another metaphor he uses often, namely, the sea: "All is one thing: the wave, the pearl, and the sea, yet / the form [*surat*] of each has introduced distinction [*khilafi*]."[36]

Clearly the wave (*mawj*) is merely a movement or action of the sea (*darya*). So too the pearl (*gawhar*) comes from the sea's motion, since traditionally the movement of the sea's waves was believed to form the pearl. From the perspective of form, there are differences between these things. From the perspective of formlessness, however, they all constitute the sea and its movements. Working within the Persian poetic tradition, Fakhr al-Din uses a multitude of metaphors to convey contradictions in the gnostic's vision, especially fluctuations between form and formlessness. These manifold images and metaphors seem to be, in 'Iraqi's estimation, the least defective way of sharing gnostic experience.

Witnessing Form and Meaning

The contradiction between witnessing form and witnessing meaning (or form and "formlessness," a word that might better capture 'Iraqi's presentation of *ma'na*) receives much attention in the *Lama'at*. One vision brings with it a sense of love, proximity, or in 'Iraqi's words "pleasure" (*lidhdhat*), while the other vision results in a sense of bewilderment. The vision of form allows the viewer to witness the Beloved, in a multitude of loci, which brings pleasure to the viewer. The vision of formlessness, on the other hand, provokes a loss of identity, so that the viewer loses his identity and takes no pleasure in witnessing. In a third vision, one beyond both form and formlessness, the divine essence (*dhat*) reveals its imperviousness, which results in an experience beyond words. While 'Iraqi describes this last experience in terms of self-annihilation, clearly it is a more lasting and consuming experience than the vision of formlessness:

> The Beloved shows his face either in the mirror of form [*surat*], or in the mirror of meaning [*ma'na*], or beyond either form or meaning. If beauty [*jamal*] shows itself to the lover's vision in the robe of form, then the lover can derive pleasure from witnessing and gain strength from observation. . . . If [on the other hand] his splendor [*jalal*] makes an assault in the World of Spirits from behind the curtain of meaning, it seizes the lover from himself in such a way, that there remains of him neither trace nor name. . . . And [lastly] if the Beloved uncovers the veil of form and meaning from beauty and

> splendor, the awesomeness of the divine essence says thus to the lover: "Tell me who should remain in this town—either you or me / because the affair of governance [*wilayah*] is ruined by two."[37]

The two contrasting visions of form and formlessness correspond to the antipodal attributes of *jamal* (beauty) and *jalal* (splendor). The vision of form, which allows the gnostic to witness the beloved, induces pleasure.

Why does a vision of form bring pleasure, and why associate form with beauty? According to two commentators on 'Iraqi's *Lama'at*, Shaykh Barzishabadi and the famous Khwajagani/Naqshbandi poet 'Abd al-Rahman Jami (d. 898/1492), the vision of form allows for understanding on behalf of the viewer.[38] The viewer perceives a divine manifestation through some medium—the divine attributes or acts—so the viewer does not experience complete bewilderment or a loss of self. This medium allows the beloved to be witnessed, since, after all, nothing can be witnessed without the limitations of form. The proximity the gnostic experiences in witnessing the beloved brings him pleasure. Such is not the case with the manifestation of splendor, that is, the vision of meaning, which overwhelms the viewer. Here no form is involved, and hence the witnessed is completely unfamiliar. Because of the lack of form, the beholder must succumb to this unknown vision, distancing himself from all he knows and permitting no sense of proximity to the beloved. Therefore, since the gnostic experiences bewilderment instead of knowledge and distance instead of proximity, the vision of meaning does not bring pleasure.

Lastly, 'Iraqi describes a third, superseding vision. Here there is neither form nor meaning, and thus the experience demands an utter annihilation of the self, one more obliterating than the vision of meaning. It is a vision beyond words, and it is for this reason that 'Iraqi does not define this vision, offering instead merely one hemistich that highlights its lack of duality.

Further Exploration of the Triple Vision

A threefold, fluctuating vision such as that encountered above emerges as an important matter of perception not only for 'Iraqi but also for many Sufi writers in general. 'Iraqi, like others, proclaims that that which is seen constantly oscillates between unity and multiplicity and is superseded by a perplexing third vision:

In the vast ocean of Your being, the cosmos is but a wave,
which the wind of Your determining caused to roll toward every coast
One-hundred thousand gems of meaning and form at every breath
are made apparent and unseen by the billows of this ocean.
Yet again the sea of Your majesty, having suddenly struck a wave,
threw them all into the abyss of the ocean without shores.[39]

One cannot help but admire the manner in which the technicalities of witnessing, delineated at length by others, such as Ibn 'Arabi, appear in simple, fluid, and metaphorical form in the poetry of 'Iraqi.

As described here, in the eyes of the gnostic, the cosmos constantly fluctuates, continuously changes, as it oscillates between a state of being apparent (*payda*) and unseen (*nihan*), like waves that ebb and flow, uncovering and then covering. Yet in a third description, both visions fall away, and suddenly everything is drowned in an infinite and incomprehensible surge. In other words, the viewer witnesses the cosmos in its multiplicity shift from seen to unseen, where the forms of all things disappear behind a vision of unity and reappear as multiple entities. Then the gnostic encounters something more direct.

This threefold structure resembles a discussion in Ibn 'Arabi's writings alluded to earlier, one in which Ibn 'Arabi discusses Sufi usage of *mushahadah*/witnessing, relying heavily on Abu Hamid al-Ghazali's definitions. According to Ibn 'Arabi, for the Sufis *mushahadah*/witnessing designates three things: (1) witnessing creation in the Real, which is "the vision of things through the proofs of recognizing oneness"; (2) witnessing the Real in creation, which is "the vision of the Real in things"; and (3) witnessing the Real without creation, which is "the reality of certainty without doubt."[40] In the first, the gnostic sees a *multiplicity* of things, and the uniqueness of each of those infinite things points to the uniqueness of the Real that manages and maintains them. Since God is uniquely infinite, the cosmos tries to reflect God's infinite vastness through its infinite dissimilarities, that is, its innumerable, unique entities. Created things are limited, and yet they attempt to reflect the Limitless. Thus the created things have multifarious essences and continuously changing states, to serve—however deficiently—as a divine mirror. 'Iraqi refers to this in the lines above as the appearance of "one-hundred thousand gems" exposed by a receding wave. In the second sort of witnessing, the gnostic envisions *one reality* within all things, so much so that a vision of unity overpowers and engulfs multiplicity. 'Iraqi refers to this as the wave's return, covering everything else. The third is the most complete form of witnessing, where one undeniably recognizes the God one has worshipped all one's life. This corresponds to 'Iraqi's "abyss."

These three visions are often found in the classifications of witnessing by later Akbari-influenced Sufis, such as Jami, for example, and are not unlike distinctions made in other Sufi texts among *tafriqah* (dispersion), *jam'* (collection), and *jam' al-jam'* (collection of collection).[41] 'Abd al-Razzaq al-Qashani (d. 736/1335), a commentator on Ibn 'Arabi, offers a similar apportionment for *shuhud*, which he also divides into three types.[42] Here Qashani describes two visions, one of multiplicity and one of unity: (1) witnessing the differentiated (*mufassal*) in the undifferentiated (*mujmal*), which is "a vision of multiplicity in the unitary Essence," and (2) witnessing the undifferentiated in the differentiated, which is "a vision of unity in multiplicity."[43] These paradoxes express the gnostic's seeing the lifting of veils between the Real and creation—once the veils are lifted, multiplicity becomes a means to witness unity, and unity shows its multiple self-disclosures. In Qashani's vocabulary, the third, superseding vision corresponds to *shuhud* itself, which he describes as "a vision of the Real through the Real." These commentators agree that the gnostic does not have one constant manner of witnessing the Real, but rather engages in witnessing in three major ways, two of which are diametrically opposed and the last of which supersedes the other two.

Elsewhere, in the *Lama'at*, 'Iraqi describes this third, more direct vision as one that occurs when "the beloved uncovers the veil of form and meaning from beauty and splendor," so that "the awesomeness of the Divine Essence" overpowers the lover.[44] Here the mystic sees neither creation in the Real nor the Real in creation but, as Ibn 'Arabi describes it, "the Real without creation." The overpowering and awesome nature of this third vision can be seen in 'Iraqi's description of this all-enveloping wave as one originating in the sea of God's splendor or majesty (*darya-yi jalalat*).

An Admonition: Witnessing Oneness versus Unification and Incarnation

Perhaps because of his temperament, or perhaps because of the genres within which he writes, 'Iraqi seldom concerns himself with polemics. Yet in witnessing the divine in forms, especially the human form, Fakhr al-Din faces an issue so misunderstood that it requires an admonition, an admonition to the wayfarer and perhaps to the critic.[45] The two terms 'Iraqi confronts, *ittihad* (unification) and *hulul* (incarnation), were often applied to Sufis accused of, in the first case, claiming to become one with the Creator, and in the second, claiming that God indwells created beings, which many associated with Christian beliefs concerning Jesus. While this was a common accusation against many Sufis, 'Iraqi deems the matter resolved by a response that is simple and concise. Both of these misconceptions demand a multiplicity of essence (*dhat*). In other words, unification requires that two entities, with separate essences, become one. Incarnation assumes that one entity takes another entity as its exclusive dwelling place. 'Iraqi, however, asserts that the divine essence is unique and completely unaffected by the multiplicity of properties (*ahkam*). Just as one source of light can appear as multiple colors when refracted through glass, 'Iraqi illustrates, so too does the one unique essence allow for perceived multiplicity in the realm of properties. The gnostic is able to recognize the oneness of essence behind the exterior or veil of multiplicity. His claim to witnessing the divine in forms results from this vision of oneness. In this regard, the gnostic, far from being inclined to unification or incarnation, is a far truer monotheist than his less enlightened counterparts.

CHAPTER 3

Beauty according to Ibn 'Arabi and 'Iraqi

That Which Causes Love

One of the pivotal concerns of this discussion is beauty and its relationship to the human form. To explore the concept of beauty in Ibn 'Arabi demands that the reader be disengaged from equating one particular Arabic word, often *jamal,* with the English word "beauty." Ibn 'Arabi's discussion of this power of attraction, this alluring quality or this beacon to perfection, spans a series of words, including *jamal, husn,* and *tibah,* all of which are translated variously but which indicate one overarching conception of beauty in Ibn 'Arabi's vision. Ultimately Ibn 'Arabi's disparate accounts of beauty can be summarized by the definition "that which causes love."

The predominance of specifically human beauty in the language of Ibn 'Arabi (and Islamic mysticism) clearly results from the ability of the human form to arouse an intense and profound variety of love. Often misunderstood, the value given to human beauty by gnostics such as Ibn 'Arabi and 'Iraqi assumes an understanding that, just as the visible world is a divine mirror, the human form represents a comprehensive world, so that human beauty reflects divine beauty more completely than any locus of manifestation. By and large, the extolment of the human form by these two mystics—seen especially in their amorous poetry—betrays a reluctance to make a distinction between human and divine beauty.

Beauty and Its Relationship to Love

Ibn 'Arabi's conception of beauty can be summarized in a single sentence taken from *al-Futuhat al-Makkiyah* in which Ibn 'Arabi modifies a widely known hadith with a terse but suggestive phrase: "*God is beautiful and loves beauty,*[1] so he loves himself."[2] An exoteric understanding of this narration might simply state that, since God is beautiful, he loves beauty in things that are, like himself, beautiful. Ibn 'Arabi's interpretation of this hadith, however, underlines the reality that God is the truly beautiful to the exclusion of all others. Hence, he loves himself exclusively. Fittingly the citation of this hadith occurs in Ibn 'Arabi's chapter concerning the station of love (*al-mahabbah*), since in his writings love and beauty are inseparable. "Love is caused by beauty [*al-jamal*]," Ibn 'Arabi states, and "beauty is beloved by its very essence."[3]

Love and beauty are so interdependent in Ibn 'Arabi's thought that we might define "beauty" as "that which causes love."

Love is also caused by *al-ihsan,* a term that might be translated as "excellent action." At first in his chapter on the station of love, Ibn 'Arabi uses the term *al-ihsan* to introduce a series of ethical and practical means for acquiring God's love as delineated in Qur'anic verses, such that *al-ihsan* might appear as a sober counterpart to intoxicated attraction, an ethical pursuit of the proper path to attain love of and for God. Yet divine beauty inheres in any application of *al-ihsan,* so that we could easily translate *al-ihsan* as "beauty in action" or beauty realized in conduct (especially since, according to Ibn 'Arabi, *al-ihsan* derives etymologically from *al-husn,* or "comeliness").[4] To begin with, every action undertaken by the spiritual wayfarer reflects a *beautiful* divine name, so that, for example, God loves the penitent (2:222) because they have assumed his own oft-turning quality (9:118). Here Ibn 'Arabi reacts to a lexical feature of the Qur'anic virtue of repentance: The language uses the same name for a truly or unceasingly "penitent" servant (*al-tawwab*) and his or her "oft-forgiving" Lord (*al-tawwab*).[5] More explicitly, Ibn 'Arabi relates excellent action to witnessing divine beauty in his interpretation of the famous narration in which the Prophet Muhammad defines *al-ihsan* as *"worshipping God as if you see him, for if you do not see him, truly he sees you."*[6]

For Ibn 'Arabi, the first part of this narration, which advises one to worship God as if one sees him, means "worshipping him through witnessing [*al-mushahadah*]."[7] Witnessing divine attributes assumes witnessing beauty, since all of God's names and attributes are beautiful, referred to as the Most Beautiful Names (*al-asma' al-husna*).[8] In fact, while Sufi texts usually deem the divine majesty or splendor (*al-jalal*) antithetical to the divine beauty (*al-jamal*), for Ibn 'Arabi, even the gnostic's encounter with divine splendor springs from divine beauty.[9] The highest virtue, the peak of ethical perfection that is *al-ihsan,* demands tearing through many of the veils of otherness that separate every human from God and instead worshipping constantly and directly through vision. When one's knowledge corresponds perfectly to one's vision, as is the case with the Real, only then is one truly and perpetually *al-muhsin,* one who acts excellently or a practitioner of *al-ihsan.*[10] This interpretation of *al-ihsan* emphasizes the unity of the witnessed and the witness, such that the gnostic is directly connected to his object of vision. Thus the gnostic beholds beauty not in mere form or attribute but rather in his or her own knowledge and, one might say, in his or her very own existence.

While in chapter 178 of *al-Futuhat al-Makkiyah,* Ibn 'Arabi offers a number of causes for love, on occasion elsewhere he refers more directly to beauty as the panoptic and actual impetus of love and as a unifying force pervading the cosmos. After a prolonged discussion of love, its varieties, its creative power, and its infinite source, Ibn 'Arabi replies to a short inquiry posed centuries before by al-Hakim al-Tirmidhi: "From where?"[11] In other words, from where does this love that comprehends all existence come? Ibn 'Arabi's answer points to the primacy of divine beauty in responding to this question: "From the self-disclosure of his name 'the Beautiful.' The Prophet has said, '*God is beautiful and loves beauty*,' and this is a well-established narration. He [God] has described himself as loving beauty, and he loves the cosmos [which implies that the cosmos is beautiful]. Thus there is nothing more beautiful than the cosmos. God is the Beautiful, and beauty is loved by its very essence, so that the entire cosmos is a lover in love with God. Beauty is his fashioning spread throughout creation, and the cosmos is the loci of manifestation for him. Therefore the love of one part of the cosmos for another part has been granted by the love of God for himself."[12] Because this beauty covers all things—in other words, because all existents have a unique portion of divine beauty—"every thing is created with a disposition [*majbul*] to the love of itself."[13]

The Real has given existents his quality of self-love, so that when these existents see their attributes shared by other existents (such that they see their own beauty in others), this causes love. As Ibn 'Arabi mentions, this occurs on every level of existence: "Every presence has an eye from his name the Light with which it gazes upon his name the Majestic; that Light covers [the presence in question] with the robe of being. Thus every lover loves none other than himself. It is for this reason that the Real describes himself as loving the loci of manifestation, although those loci are essentially nonexistent. Love applies to those loci because of what becomes manifest [in them,] and he is the one who becomes manifest in them [*al-zahir fiha*]. The relationship between the one becoming manifest and the loci of manifestation is love."[14]

Here, instead of discussing the self-disclosure of God's name "the Beautiful," Ibn 'Arabi attributes the alluring characteristic that provokes self-love to God's name "the Light," because he describes the matter of existence. You will notice, however, the precedence of gazing or witnessing—and serving as a locus for the divine witnessing of Self—as the cause of love. Although Ibn 'Arabi avoids defining love, he describes love as the relationship wherein the lover becomes manifest in the nonexistent beloved. His statement seems somewhat general, pertaining not only to God viewing himself in the mirror of the cosmos but also to every lover viewing himself in the mirror of a beloved. Implicitly the beauty of every beloved lies in its nonexistence, in its function as something empty or receptive—in other words, as a place of self-display for its lover.

The Good in All Things

Ibn 'Arabi's view of beauty is no less encompassing than his view of existence, because, for him, beauty is an attribute of existence. Since all things derive their existence from one Being, all things share in his attributes to different degrees. The created things are therefore essentially and inherently beautiful. Ibn 'Arabi makes this clear in a chapter concerning speech, but his discussion of "speech" should not be taken too literally; in the vocabulary of Ibn 'Arabi all created things are divine words, since the phenomenon of being is in fact the ongoing speech of God. With this in mind, Ibn 'Arabi's statement that "speech [*al-qawl*] is all comely [*hasan*] or more comely" points to the comeliness and goodness of all things.[15]

Of course, from the human perspective not everything is beautiful; if such were the case, words like "vile" (*su'*) and "comely" (*husn*) would be meaningless. Ibn 'Arabi explains that the distinction we make between "vile" and "comely" is in reality a distinction we should be making between "comely" and "more comely." He explains that "every speech is comely, but the words that conform to personal desire [*waqif al-gharad*] are more comely." Ibn 'Arabi recognizes that personal taste—determined by a person's constitution (*mizaj*) or the balance of elements within him or her—causes that person to consider some things pleasant or beautiful and other things unpleasant or vile.[16] In considering comely versus vile, Ibn 'Arabi's discussion relates more to *acts* than to *things;* the term used to describe certain words as "vile," *su'*, really has more to do with determining certain actions to be unseemly actions, not with determining certain things to be ugly.[17] This is an important distinction, because it explains why Ibn 'Arabi emphasizes so decidedly that in determining actions as vile, "none should say this but God." God's determination of vile acts constitutes the *shari'ah,* Islam's legal code. His is the exclusive right to decide that which is vile, for his determinations are in accordance with the all-knowing divine wisdom, not based on subjective inclination or disinclination. Thus actions are only ugly or vile in two ways: according to the *shari'ah* or according to one's personal determination.

Moreover, the vile is vile only because of a decree, not because of something inherently evil or unseemly in it. After all, since everything is inherently comely, inherent evil or unseemliness does not exist. Yet just as God has established a system of hierarchical perfection, where some entities and actions receive more praise than others, so too does each person rank entities and actions in terms of perfection, considering some comely and others vile, or, if she possesses insight, considering some comely and others more comely. Such a notion of comeliness and vileness is stated explicitly by Muhyi al-Din: "In reality, there is nothing but the comely through relation and the vile through relation, for everything from God is comely, whether that thing be vile or bring about happiness. The affair is relative." One can conclude from this that comeliness or beauty exists in two modes: the gradated beauty known to all perceivers, and the omnipresent, inherent beauty known exclusively to the gnostics.

Relative Beauty and Taste

The matter of inclination and disinclination occurs elsewhere in the writings of Ibn 'Arabi, offering more insight into the matter of relative beauty and what might be termed taste. Muhyi al-Din's explanation of the phenomenon of taste—an inclination or disinclination to certain entities or actions—is significant because without such an explanation his view of all things as ultimately and inherently beautiful or good leaves little room for judgment. In the final chapter of *Fusus al-Hikam,* the chapter concerning the Prophet Muhammad, Ibn 'Arabi explains that receptivity is central to inclination. In other words, liking or disliking something, considering it pleasant or unpleasant, has little to do with the thing itself. The perceiving agent's predisposition determines such instances of judgment.

In this final chapter of *Fusus al-Hikam,* the terms Ibn 'Arabi uses for beauty and vileness, or good and bad, have to do with the senses of smell and taste: *al-tayyib* (goodly) and *al-khabith* (foul), terms that primarily describe pleasant and unpleasant odors and foods, but secondarily describe pleasant and unpleasant (or moral and immoral, lawful and unlawful) persons, acts, or objects.[18] The terms Ibn 'Arabi uses to describe attractive and repelling qualities have so far been determined by the revealed sources upon which he comments; the term *jamal* was found in the tradition quoted above describing God as beautiful (*jamil*) and One who loves beauty (*jamal*), while the terms *husn*/comely and *su'*/vile originate in verses of the Qur'an describing instances of speech.[19] This set of contrasting terms—*tayyib*/goodly and *khabith*/foul—is no exception. Often in the Qur'an these words are encountered referring to lawful or unlawful wealth or food.[20] Yet Ibn 'Arabi quotes a verse in which these terms refer to human beings (24:26): *"Foul words* [*al-khabithat*] *befit foul people* [*al-khabithin*], *and foul people befit foul words. Goodly words* [*al-tayyibat*] *befit goodly people* [*al-tayyibin*], *and goodly people befit goodly words. Those are they who are innocent of what they* [*others*] *say and for whom are forgiveness and a noble sustenance."*[21]

While translating the term *tayyib* as "goodly" instead of the more usual "good" might seem strange here, it coincides with Ibn 'Arabi's distinctive interpretation of the verse. For Ibn 'Arabi such descriptions point to the truthfulness of speech possessed by such women and men. After all, this verse is the conclusion of a series of verses revealed to absolve one of the Prophet's wives, clarifying that she speaks the truth about a calumny others spread concerning her. Conversely these verses chastise those who mischievously conveyed this rumor, declaring them to be liars.[22] Since speech is uttered through the breath, Ibn 'Arabi interprets this verse literally, describing those who are honest as possessing pleasant or fragrant breath (*tayyib*) while describing those who lie as possessing foul breath (*khabith*).[23] In other words, the breath of such women and men bears a smell that reflects the moral goodness or vileness of their speech.

Yet Ibn 'Arabi is quick to remind us, despite the moral implications of this verse, that "lawful," "moral," and "pleasant" are all relative judgments, determined by a discriminating entity, whether divine or not. Since all speech is a borrowed attribute from a divine source, all breath "is goodly, so the breath in question is goodly, but from the perspective of that which is praised and blamed, it is reckoned goodly or foul."[24] Only through the act of discriminating and comparing can something be determined comely or vile, goodly or foul. Moreover, since all things are inherently good, one can only deem the effects of an entity foul, not the entity itself.

According to Ibn 'Arabi, judging secondary effects is a method of discrimination put into practice by the Prophet Muhammad when he said, concerning garlic, that *"it is a plant the odor of which I abhor."*[25] It is relevant to Ibn 'Arabi that the Prophet did not find fault with the entity itself—which is, after all, created and thus good—but rather "that which is made manifest from it," namely, its odor. This illustrates the Prophet's awareness that judgment must be confined to that which has no independent reality: that which proceeds from created beings, not that which proceeds from God.

By mentioning the Prophet Muhammad's aversion to garlic's odor, Ibn 'Arabi invites a question regarding his own statements about judgment: Considering the Prophet's status as the finest example of the Perfect Man, can his judgments concerning the pleasant and the unpleasant be considered completely subjective, lacking a connection to that which is meaningful? Clearly, the answer must be no. First of all, this discussion of taste occurs in a chapter concerning three things made beloved to the Prophet: women, perfume, and prayer. Ibn 'Arabi's detailed analysis of the ontological and cosmological implications of this hadith should be enough to tell us that the Prophet's attraction or favor for certain things cannot be haphazard. Second, Ibn 'Arabi himself states that "once the affair was apportioned between foul and goodly, as we have established, then the goodly was made beloved to him [the Prophet] and not the foul."[26] In other words, Ibn 'Arabi asserts that the Prophet's inclinations are always toward that which should be praised and away from that which should be blamed.

But how can a personal preference epitomize some sort of olfactory perfection? In terms of the factors that cause one to dislike something, Ibn 'Arabi lists custom (*'urf*), a lack of suitability with one's nature (*mula'amat al-tab'*), personal aims (*gharad*), holy law (*shar'*), and lacking a perfection that one seeks (*naqs 'an kamal matlub*).[27] As 'Abd al-Razzaq al-Qashani points out, commenting on this passage, all these factors relate merely to the perceiving, "receiving" agent, not to the thing itself.[28] If the Prophet has perfect taste—that is, an inclination to all praiseworthy things and a disinclination to all blameworthy things—it is merely on account of the receptive perfection within himself. The Prophet's likes and dislikes reflect perfectly God's approval and disapproval of things. Thus there must be something blameworthy about the smell of garlic—from the divine decree—that causes the Prophet to dislike it, although Ibn 'Arabi does not elucidate precisely what this is. One possibility is that the Prophet's distaste for the smell of garlic reflects the legal pronouncement dissuading the eating of garlic before attending the mosque, since the pungent odor left on the breath of one who eats garlic is a potential nuisance to others.[29] This is not to say that the Prophet dislikes the odor of garlic in a conscious effort to submit to the divine decree but that the Prophet's very *constitution* corresponds to the divine will in the most precise way possible for a human being.

In fact, this is the most important point Ibn 'Arabi seeks to express concerning taste: All perceiving agents judge in accordance with their constitutions and find pleasure in that which corresponds to their own constitutions. According to Ibn 'Arabi, it is because of this that angels, who are purely spiritual beings, dislike the smell of human beings.[30] Spirit, lacking any of the imperfections of materiality, is not subject to change or decay. The human body, on the other hand, was made from a dry, black, putrid-smelling mud, according to the Qur'an (15:26, 28:33). Ibn 'Arabi comments that the word *masnun,* used to describe the putrid smell of the mud from which man came, indicates changeability of odor. Since angels are unchanging, they "detest it [man's odor] in accordance with their essence [*bi-l-dhat*]."

Contrarily, the scent of roses, one of the most pleasant fragrances from the human perspective, is repulsive to the dung beetle (*al-ju'al*) on account of its natural constitution (*mizaj*). Since the dung beetle possesses a foul odor, this insect enjoys encountering foul odors in the world outside itself. In other words, every discriminating entity has a predisposition—according to its constitution—to like that which suits it and dislike that which does not. Yet while inclination or taste is merely a relational effect, one should not mistakenly assume that attraction and aversion are devoid of profound spiritual implications. After all, everything in the physical world is a representation of unseen realities. It is clear, for example, that the dung beetle physically represents a spiritual phenomenon, for the dung beetle's aversion to that which higher beings (especially humans) deem pleasant represents the disinclination of morally corrupt people to the truth. The dung beetle, according to Ibn 'Arabi, represents those who confuse good and bad, or goodly and foul, determinations that have been made in creation according to the wisdom of God: "Whoever has such a constitution [like the dung beetle's] in terms of meaning and form [as opposed to mere physical constitution] is repulsed by Truth when he hears it and delights in falsehood. . . . Indeed, one who cannot distinguish between goodly and foul has no perception [*idrak*] whatsoever."[31] In other words, just as the dung beetle delights in foul odors and dislikes goodly fragrances, there are those who in spiritual matters are inclined toward falsehood and disinclined toward the truth.

On the other hand, in order best to recognize the divine reality of creation, one must resemble the Prophet in delighting in the praiseworthy and disliking the blameworthy, while at the same time acknowledging the limits of one's own constitution and seeing the good in all things. It is impossible, Ibn 'Arabi tells us, to merely see the good or goodly in all things, without judging some entities, effects, or actions foul. After all, the Source of all creation has deemed certain things to be "hated" and "loved," making judgments discriminating between goodly and foul that constitute the *shari'ah.* Such discrimination relates to God as Creator or God as Judge, while God as God loves the essences of all entities, which point back to him. Thus the most perceptive individuals are those who understand that their constitutions delight in particular experiences and things to the exclusion of others, while also recognizing the essential loveliness of existence and hence all things. This highest level of discrimination occurs when "the perception of the [essential] loveliness in a phenomenon distracts such a person from sensing its [relative] foulness."[32] This is the perception of a gnostic affected by realizing the Oneness of Being.

The natural constitution corresponds to a mode of reception for Ibn 'Arabi; in other words, that which descends from spirit into matter takes on the forms determined by matter. The physical human form, composed of humors or elements, determines the manner in which even the gnostic receives meaning, responds to it, and judges it as beautiful or otherwise. The powerful *physical* correspondence and attraction that exists between human beings allows for the most profound contemplation of meaning.[33]

Love and Beauty according to 'Iraqi

In an extremely concise and unguarded manner, 'Iraqi's seventh chapter of the *Lama'at* captures the most important principles concerning love and beauty made in Ibn 'Arabi's writing. Fakhr al-Din attests to Ibn 'Arabi's observation that love has primarily two causes: "It is not fitting for other-than-[God] to be loved; rather, it is impossible. Other than Essential Love, the cause of which is unknown, anything loved is loved either for comeliness [*husn*] or for excellent action [*ihsan*]. And these two belong to none but him."[34]

'Iraqi's mention of *husn* and *ihsan* as the primary causes of love coincides so evidently with Ibn 'Arabi's teachings that we can probably assume that Sadr al-Din al-Qunawi instructed 'Iraqi in the Akbari perspective on love's relationship to beauty and excellent action, an instruction probably based on chapter 178 of *al-Futuhat al-Makkiyah.* After all, Ibn 'Arabi's discussion of *jamal* and *ihsan* as causes of love appears in *al-Futuhat al-Makkiyah* and not in *Fusus al-Hikam,* the text often considered to be the impetus for 'Iraqi's *Lama'at.* Unlike Ibn 'Arabi, 'Iraqi does not articulate the visionary connection between excellent action (*ihsan*) and beauty (*jamal*). Yet he has implicitly conjoined beauty and excellent action by his replacement of the word *jamal* used by Ibn 'Arabi with the word *husn,* since *husn* and *ihsan* share a common lexical root.

'Iraqi describes a unity of love and a oneness of the beloved also seen in Ibn 'Arabi's writings, alluding to the distinction between those aware of their True Beloved and those who are oblivious: "In loving anyone, you love him. Wherever you turn your face, you turn it toward him, even if you do not know this."[35] 'Iraqi makes clear that all lovers are drawn to one exclusive source of beauty, some knowingly, others unknowingly. For example, while the legendary lover Majnun might "gaze upon Layli's beauty," nevertheless, the Source of that beauty is the Real and "Layli is nothing more than a mirror."[36] In his attraction to Layli, the lover Majnun—like all lovers—seeks a perfect and whole beauty, a beauty "other than which everything is ugly." This is true "even if Majnun is unaware."

Having asserted this, 'Iraqi cites the first half of the very hadith that serves as the crux of Ibn 'Arabi's discussion of beauty and love: *"God is beautiful."*[37] In his interpretation, 'Iraqi reads the hadith so emphatically that it is almost restrictive, or as 'Iraqi himself states, "It does not suit anyone other than him to be beautiful." On the one hand, only God is beautiful by essence—all other things have beauty because of his glancing upon them. On the other hand, every perfection, including and perhaps especially beauty, belongs to God. As 'Iraqi explains in a double line placed directly after this discussion, the absoluteness of God's beauty relates directly to the exclusivity of his existence: "The one who has no existence of his own, / how can he possibly be said to have beauty?" Here 'Iraqi turns his attention to the second half of the hadith concerning God's beauty: *"[He] loves beauty."* To which Fakhr al-Din immediately adds, "Beauty is beloved by its very essence." The influence of Ibn 'Arabi, who defines beauty in the context of this hadith in precisely the same terms (of course, in Arabic), is conspicuous here.[38]

The essential lovability of beauty has profound implications, suggesting a cosmology of love and beauty. The phrase that both 'Iraqi and Ibn 'Arabi use to explicate the hadith above, that "beauty is beloved by its very essence," hints at another hadith mentioned earlier, arguably the most foundational hadith in any version of a love cosmology: *"I was a Treasure—I was Unknown, so I loved to be known. Hence I created the creatures, and made Myself known to them, so they knew Me."*[39] The verb "loved" (*ahbabtu*) signals to mystics such as 'Iraqi and Ibn 'Arabi that divine essential self-love has effected creation, since, after all, God created all things out of the love to be admired. Beauty too must be loved. Thus the Real or Beauty (both are one and the same) is loved by its own essence, a love that seeks admiration. Through carrying out this admiration, even by gazing at human beauty, the achieved human, for whom God has become both sight and hearing, serves as a means for the true Admirer to witness that which is actually Admired. As is so often the case, 'Iraqi is forthright and brief in describing human admiration of human beauty as a means for God to admire himself: When Majnun, the legendary poet-lover, gazes upon his beloved Layli's beauty, writes 'Iraqi, the Real "beholds his own beauty through the eye of Majnun."

True Self-Love

One of the results of the cosmos being created according to the image of its Creator is the universality of essential self-love. ʻIraqi agrees with and virtually quotes Ibn ʻArabi in asserting that "everything has been created predisposed [*majbul*] to love of self."[40] This love of self causes all things, including the gnostics, to love "mirrors" in which the self can be seen; that is, seeing the self-in-other yields love. Of course, love of self can be either love of the True Self, that is the Real who has breathed into man his spirit and who is the reality behind all things, or, love of the false self, the veil of selfhood that allows one to perceive an individualized existence. ʻIraqi's emphasis is obviously on the former; if one loves the True Self, then one loves God in all things, and the lover sees everything either as reflections of the Real or as reflections of himself (for his true existence is none other than the Real): "The ultimate of this [reciprocal love of Self] is that the lover sees the beloved as his own mirror and himself as the mirror of the beloved. . . . Sometimes, this one is that one's witness, and that one is this one's witnessed. At other times, this one is that one's viewed, and that one is his viewer. Sometimes this one appears in the color of that one, and, at other times, that one obtains this one's fragrance."[41] Lover and beloved experience here commingled or even indivisible identities. It is significant that ʻIraqi usually describes the two participants in the phenomenon of love as "lover" (*ʻashiq)* and "beloved" (*maʻshuq*), avoiding any specification as to the nature of the lover and beloved. In other words, his descriptions of lovers and beloveds are general enough to include not only human/divine love, but also human-to-human love and in fact any entity that has experienced love for any other entity.

In the case of love, in its most general sense, the lover loves himself and sees that self in the beloved. A realization of the shared identity between lover and beloved is, according to ʻIraqi, the pinnacle of love accessible to humans:

Love displayed a face from beyond the veil;
when I looked at it, the face was my own.
I relegated myself, withdrawn to the side,
once it opened up its embrace to me [*kinar bigushud*].
Before my own countenance I prostrated,
at the instant when it exhibited beauty.[42]

Here the lover realizes that he worships and adores none other than himself—once the false self has been put aside. As ʻIraqi proclaims elsewhere in this penetrating *tarjiʻband,* the relationship of lover and beloved begins as one of dual individualities: "We were one, we appeared as two." But it is also subject to an awakening to true oneness, such that "through being, that apparition [of duplicity] became nonexistent."[43] In the context of divine love, it is at this point that the True Self and the Real become indistinguishable. This *tarjiʻband* also clarifies that *only* the human heart can serve as a perfect mirror, contain the divine self-disclosures, and thus allow the most comprehensive reciprocity possible between divine self and created locus:

Love traveled from the top of its street
passing the various levels altogether
It searched the Desert of Existence; immediately
every concealing place of nonexistence [that] it pursued shielded itself.
It sought a sign of its own form.
Once it looked at our narrow heart,
it discovered [that sign]. There, its trusted deposit [*amanat*]
it hid. And it brought out its own clothes,
dressed the soul [with them] and unburdened itself
of the encumbrance of these clothes.[44]

'Iraqi's use of enjambment here, aside from being somewhat unusual in classical Persian poetry, adds to the mysterious drive of these lines; the heart's relationship with Love is, after all, both mysterious and impassioned. With the correspondence between the heart and the divine essence (or Love) before him, the gnostic sees his heart's True Self as appearing in outer forms. This witnessing further provokes his love for the divine both within and without.

As opposed to the gnostic, who loves the True Self, the one unaware of the divine True Self, that is, the unknowing lover, loves his false individual self, which is actually but a veil. On account of the principle of self-love, this unknowing lover seeks what he imagines to be his "self," thus loving the individual human beloved merely in form. 'Iraqi rarely concerns himself with this false variety of self-love, and, when he does, it is often merely for the sake of admonition: "When your form has become the veil of your way, / obliterate [it]! So that your path becomes beautiful."[45]

Expressing one of the very common Sufi themes of his age, 'Iraqi clarifies elsewhere that this "form" hindering the "beautiful" (*ziba*) path to realization of meaning is the self, the *nafs* or *khud:*

Deliver me [oh, Saqi] from the selfness of my self
for from my self is the wound, and there is no balm;
Since my being is a veil for my self,
if it were not to exist, all the better: there is no grief.[46]

The one who discerns only externalities fails to realize that behind the false "form" (*surat*) of self, is the reality of God's omnipresence, the unadulterated beauty within all things. Similar to the observation made by Ibn 'Arabi that those who love merely outer form and merely to fulfill sexual pleasures love a form without spirit,[47] 'Iraqi chides those who sully love with mere sexual desire:

If, because of your heart's striving against you,
the transgressor and ascetic should seem similar to you,
arise from the lust that you hold within
so that one-thousand *shahid*s sit with you.[48]

Here 'Iraqi makes use of the double meaning of the term *shahid*, which can refer to an evidential locus or trace left from unveiling but also to a beautiful human being, especially in Persian Sufism to a beardless young man. While Ibn 'Arabi makes mention of this spiritless love in some detail, 'Iraqi usually merely alludes to it, as he has above. Interestingly the most famous and pertinent instance of benighted or purely natural love in the *diwan* of 'Iraqi is the biography that has traditionally accompanied it.

Limitless Beauty in the Limits of Form: The *Shahid*

One should not mistakenly assume that the metaphorical representation of form is merely for the spiritually uninitiated. Because of the process and limits of human perception, the gnostic, or any viewer for that matter, has no access to beauty outside the world of form: beauty, like excellent action (*ihsan*), is "veiled behind the curtain of intermediate causes and the faces of beloveds."[49] 'Iraqi candidly denies that love of pure meaning, a love untainted by the medium of form, might be possible for a human being, although clearly some have made claim to such: "Do not listen to professions of absolute love from the progeny of Adam, for where love's [fortified] city is, what business does the human have?" Since for 'Iraqi absolute love corresponds to the impenetrable divine essence, humans have no access to it and are thus forced to make use of intermediaries. 'Iraqi makes clear, much like Ibn 'Arabi, that creation's outer forms, indeed even material forms, act as these intermediaries, allowing for witnessing and the experience of love.

In fact, 'Iraqi describes love as the actor in the affair of making use of outer form to allow for witnessing. According to 'Iraqi, love acts as a bride-dresser, ornamenting reality by means of the metaphorical (that is, form) so that it becomes a means by which the viewer beholds and loves reality: "Love is a bride-dresser, skilled in the colors of makeup, / who bedecks reality in the color of metaphor."[51] In most of the poetry of 'Iraqi, the central focus of *shuhud*/witnessing corresponds to perceiving meaning in the form of the *shahid*. The *shahid*, a term that cannot be translated using one English word, is a testimony to the beauty of God, a locus of manifestation for the divine names to the fullest extent, and yet also, as has been mentioned, a human being in physical form.

It is in the very nature of human perception to expose the inner senses to meaning through the outer senses' experience of form. In fact, this is one of the central principles and justifications of the Sufi practice of gazing upon beautiful humans (*shahidbazi*), since such gazing awakens the heart to the beauty of the Real. A poem attributed to 'Iraqi uses a tone of avowal to relate this phenomenon in a seeming defense of *shahidbazi:* "I confess that the evidential locus [*shahid*] of the heart is meaning, / but what am I do? For the eye is form-seeing!"[52] In other words, the heart experiences witnessing and love, but only as a result of the human form, which is a means of display for divine beauty. Here clearly one discerns parallels to Ibn 'Arabi's assertion that divine beauty is completely unknowable in itself and relies on the medium of externalities, especially the human form, to be known.[53]

The witnessing of God's self-disclosures, which are strictly unbounded "meaning," leaves an imprint on the heart, namely, the *shahid*. The gnostic then perceives this *shahid* in the outer world, especially in the context of human beauty. The face of the human beloved therefore is a mere instance of what already exists in the gnostic's heart, a stamp of limitless beauty. Such a concept of the *shahid* can be found intimated in a *ghazal* about a beautiful Turk:

Bravo! Your beauty, the envy of Yaghma'i idols,[54]
union with you the longing of lovers who are zealous.
The bride of your comeliness no one discovers
in the bridal chamber, except for the eyes of the one watching,[55]
[All this is] through the attribute that you are in love with your own beauty,
not with anyone else's, but all that which conforms to the face you display.
The veil of your face is with your face in every state:
you are hidden from the whole universe, because you are so apparent.
I see your visage in anyone I observe;
all these beautiful idols appear to my eyes as you.
The entire cosmos I see through you, which isn't strange
because you are, within both eyes, vision itself.
Out of jealousy, so that no one recognizes you,
you adorn your beauty at every instant in varied garb.
How can you be ever found? Who ever reaches you?
Since at every breath you are at a different halting-place and location!
'Iraqi goes door-to-door, searching after you,
all the while, you are apparent, a resident inside his heart.[56]

A number of images used here pertain directly to the gnostic's envisioning of divine beauty in a human locale. First of all, the twice-repeated mention of idols (*butan*) refers, of course, not to statues of polytheistic devotion but to beautiful human beings, probably, considering 'Iraqi's other poetic descriptions and reports about his practices, young men or boys. This frames 'Iraqi's entire discussion of divine beauty within the context of human forms, for although Fakhr al-Din acknowledges the omnipresence of divine beauty by proclaiming that "all these beautiful idols appear to my eyes as you," he nevertheless makes clear that he witnesses this beauty in that which surrounds him externally, especially "idols." On the one hand, 'Iraqi clearly establishes his beholding of a unity of beauty, envisioning a self-admiring divine in all beautiful things.

Yet on the other hand, 'Iraqi also acknowledges the importance of human forms as a means to witnessing the sought-after divine beauty. This is seen especially in the final double line of the poem: "'Iraqi goes door-to-door, searching after you, / all the while, you are apparent, a resident inside his heart." This should not be taken as a stale proclamation that "God must be found within." After all, 'Iraqi has known from the outset that the divine is everywhere (including within his heart), and, having recognized this, there would be no need for him to search for the Beloved. Rather, these lines intimate that the persona has within him a "resident": the divine self-disclosure undifferentiated. This divine self-disclosure—which, as has been mentioned, can only be contained by the human heart—impels the gnostic possessing that heart to search in the outward world for loci of manifestation in which to view this beauty. That is, that which is contained inwardly is far too comprehensive and unfathomable to be witnessed; rather, its impression unfolds itself in the witnessing that occurs in the outer world. This is what causes the poet to go "door-to-door" despite his realization that the Real resides manifestly in his heart. Thus not only the beloved but also the lover is in love with "all that which conforms to the face" of the beloved, namely, external instances of the *shahid* imbedded in the heart. The gnostic saturated in the divine presence sees the contents of his heart in the natural world around him, as Fakhr al-Din proclaims elsewhere: "Once 'Iraqi was drowned, a life of remainingness he found; / The secrets of the Unseen in the World of Seen he sees."[57] 'Iraqi's description corresponds to other descriptions and definitions of the *shahid,* both in Ibn 'Arabi's terminology as well as that of an earlier Sufi, Abu al-Qasim Qushayri (d. 465/1072).[58]

Physical Spirituality and Spiritual Physicality: The Human-Godly *Shahid*

The *shahid* has in 'Iraqi's poetic descriptions a dual role. It is both the trace of a spiritual experience and the beautiful human form that testifies to the gnostic's witnessing. This duality is an essential element in 'Iraqi's poetry, in his description of a beloved that is at once human and Godly. The ambiguity in 'Iraqi's writings between physicality and spirituality is no accident or mere poetic device; rather, it is a result of his understanding of beauty itself. For 'Iraqi, the beautiful human form is subtle and spiritual, verging on immaterial. An earlier, philosophically inclined Sufi, Abu al-Hasan 'Ali ibn Muhammad al-Daylami (fl. 363/974), defines beauty as immateriality or subtlety, although to my knowledge an express statement to this effect cannot be found in 'Iraqi's works.[59] Rather, 'Iraqi makes this point through the poetic presentation of a human-godly beloved whose physicality is spiritual. Moreover, such a beloved captures the reality of beauty described here: purely spiritual meaning made manifest in the world of forms. Instead of a lengthy survey of 'Iraqi's poetry, a brief analysis of two poems illustrates this visionary paradox. The first describes a beloved whose dominance over the material world derives from the immateriality of his beauty:

A Christian boy, impudent, playful, a sugarcane-field [of deliciousness],
in every twist of his hair-lock is the deviation of a Muslim.
From the comeliness of his beauty every intellect is struck bewildered,
and from his dalliance and flirtation every soul has been enamored.
From his sugar-spilling ruby lips every heart is agitated,
and from his heart-adhering tresses hang red-coral jewelry.
His lively drunken eye scrutinizes every religious commitment,
the curled ends of his hair are infidel-belts, confined by each instance of faith.
On the dinner spread of the world his lip has added candy,
and the miracle of Moses has made his hair-lock a giant serpent.
The materiality [*nasut*] of his existence, through fineness and purity, each instance
displays a face of spiritual sublimity [*lahut*] in human form.
This beautiful Christian boy, in his animating speech,
has imitated the inimitability of Muhammad through an act of elucidation.
His ruby-lips with their sugared laughing have blown life into the dead;
his eye, in its mischievousness, has stolen the heart of a world.
Jesus-like in breath, from his lip, he gives to the dead one-hundred spirits,
so why every moment does he abduct hearts with his singing?
So that the one looking at his face would not be forced to travel,
he's appointed—through flirtatious glances—from each direction, an
overlooking guard.
From the eye he has shot out at every heart of those who long
an arrow with every glance and a spear with every eyelash!
He came out of the monastery, drunk on the comeliness of himself,
whosoever saw him became enthralled and perplexed.
The deacon saw his face: it became heliolatry;
if the ascetic were to see it, he would quickly become a monk.
Were the Sufi to see his face through this eye of mine,
he would worship the sun in a monastery, as devotedly as a monk.
The remembrance of his lip and teeth passed through my thoughts—
my eye began to scatter jewels, and my disposition became a sugarcane field.
I wanted to disseminate my soul before his face. The heart said:

"What place does a thorn have before a rose-garden?"
Were I to become the dirt upon his path, still he wouldn't place his foot on me;
God forbid that a Solomon should place his foot upon an ant!
No wrongdoing will be done to a human by the jinn race
because Solomon became the commander of all jinn.
As you see, 'Iraqi is so busy in both verse and prose
describing his beauty, that he has filled a whole *diwan*.[60]

While quite often the definitions in *Istilahat-i Sufiyah* attributed to 'Iraqi do not apply easily to particular poems, certainly the definition of *tarsa* (Christian), a phrase used to describe the boy beloved above, underlines the major theme of this poem. According to this glossary, the term *tarsa* refers to "meanings and realities . . . when they are fine [*daqiq*]."[61] The relationship between "Christian" and subtlety or spirit might derive from the traditional association of Jesus with spirit and immateriality in Islamic texts.[62] This association appears in 'Iraqi's description of the beloved's possession of a Jesus-like breath (*'Isa-nafasi*), one that bestows multiple spirits on the dead. Here too one sees the relationship between the beloved's beautiful material form and his powerful spiritual abilities; the description of the beloved's breath is meant to emphasize, of course, its sweet fragrance, a physical quality, one considered an important trait for a beautiful beloved to possess.

It is the spirituality of his physical form that endows the beloved with not only desirability, but also power. The beloved challenges the miracle of Moses through the attractiveness of his hair-lock (*zulf*). More surprisingly, the beloved's ability to speak beautifully, another important trait for an attractive person to have in the medieval Persian world, is spirit-enhancing (*ruh-afza*) and imitates the Prophet Muhammad's inimitable miracle: the Qur'an. The beloved is compared to Solomon, who, as 'Iraqi mentions, controlled the unseen jinn as well as other forces of nature. The idea here is that the beloved's worldly and otherworldly influence derives from his beauty alone. 'Iraqi's comparison of the beloved's comeliness to the miracles of prophets is not for mere hyperbolic effect. Rather, it reflects his intended aim of describing the beloved's physical beauty in spiritual terms. This becomes most explicit in a line that makes use of important mystical cosmological language: "The materiality of his existence, through fineness and purity, each instance displays a face of spiritual sublimity in human form."

In other words, to the beloved belongs a materiality (*nasut*) that is so fine, subtle, and pure (*lutf u safa*) that it makes evident the face of "spiritual sublimity" or absolute meaning (*rukh-i lahut*). The human form here is a luminous physical testimony to pure spirit. Only the human beloved can conjoin the highest and lowest realms of existence, *lahut* and *nasut* respectively, in one beautiful form. It is for this reason that the beloved leads men to infidelity; no one can maintain the religiously necessary division between God and creation when gazing upon the young man's nearly divine beauty. Therefore, on account of this sunlike beauty, no one, not even the deacon (*shammas*) or the ascetic (*zahid*), can refrain from worshipping him.

In a poem that praises the beauty of a wine-server (*saqi*), a task usually assumed by young men, 'Iraqi makes clear that the human beloved's beauty derives from his spiritual-material form, a marriage of high and low that is indeed far more beautiful than spirit or matter alone:

From grace [*lutf*] you, through-and-through, are spirit, wine-server [*saqiya*]!
What's lovelier [*khushtar*] than spirit [*jan*]? You're that, oh wine-server!
All the hearts inclining toward your countenance:
Go! For you're a charming heart-thief, wine server!
You so appear to me in every moment as if
from purity [*safa*], you're water streaming, wine-server!
While on the wine of love you may be drunk do not
haughtily ignore [your] drinking-colleagues, wine-server!
Make a pledge of wine, however false it is,
so you're not constantly compelled to make excuses, wine-server!
Allow yourself upon the lips to be kissed and see
the flavor of the water of vitality, wine-server!
I became the dirt before your door, so that from your cup
a sip you might pour out for me, oh wine-server!
From fineness [*latafat*] you cannot be grasped by anyone,
which is no wonder, for you are spirit, wine-server!
The ears of all the spirits are full of gems, since you
in utterance[s] pour out pearls, oh wine-server!
Your grace [*lutf*] and comeliness [*husn*] convinced my heart and eye:
you're apparent and you're [also] hidden, wine-server!
In this [whole] world for 'Iraqi there's not a gasp
of satisfaction upon your lips, oh wine-server![63]

The beloved as described in this poem possesses two celebrated traits: comeliness (*husn*) and fineness or subtlety (*latafat*). It seems that the "grace" (*lutf*) to which 'Iraqi twice refers also points to the beloved's intangible and almost angelic nature. The beautiful wine-server is indeed so subtle that he "cannot be grasped by anyone" (*nayabad kas*).

Yet this poem is not a praise of spirit or a purely spiritual being; 'Iraqi adores the wine-server because he is *more* appealing or lovelier than spirit itself (*khushtar az jan*). The wine-server is both material and immaterial, tangible and intangible, or, in the words of 'Iraqi, apparent and hidden (*ashkara u nahani*). The conjoining of these two contradictory qualities in one beloved yields his inescapable attractiveness. The wine-server metes out, of course, wine for his admirers, wine often representing passionate love in the poetry of 'Iraqi. This tells us that the wine-server serves as a medium by which the persona hopes to experience self-annihilating love. From the poetry and biographical details of 'Iraqi and his contemporaries, we know that this medium for experiencing witnessing and love was often a beardless young man. According to those partial to the practice of gazing at beautiful human beings, the intoxicating wine sought from such *shahid*s could not be found in equal measure elsewhere.

CHAPTER 4

Ibn 'Arabi and Human Beauty

The School of Passionate Love

One of the most distinctive, fascinating, and certainly poetically prolific movements in classical Sufism is that known in Persian as the "School of Passionate Love" (*madhhab-i 'ishq*). The word *madhhab* (school or way), often indicating a jurisprudential or theological allegiance within the various Islamic denominations, reveals the development of this identity for certain Sufis, an identity by which they considered themselves distinct from those outside of their tradition. In some cases, it might also imply a disdain for the overemphasis placed on a jurisprudential *madhhab* and a claim to have transcended the differences that separate them from each other. While love is arguably a common experience for the majority of practitioners of Islamic mysticism, the loose designation *madhhab-i 'ishq* comprised those enamored by divine beauty, often in the sensory world. Moreover, a clear predilection for witnessing God in forms, as well as allusions to the supremacy of the human form, often surround references to the School of Passionate Love. This is so much the case that witnessing absolute beauty in the sensory and admiring the human form (whether *poetically* through imagery or *practically* through gazing) seem to serve as unofficial principles of this unofficial school, at least for some. Any such uniformity found in reference to this *madhhab* reflects a commonality different from chains of initiation through the distinctive Sufi cloak (*khirqah*), inculcation of divine names (*talqin-i dhikr*), or instructive fellowship (*suhbah*). Rather, such references convey a unity of sensibility, emphasis, and outlook among those who did not necessarily have any formally binding affiliation.[1]

Attesting to the relationship between reference to this "school" and the practice of contemplating visions of beauty, 'Ayn al-Qudat al-Hamadhani's (d. 526/1131) description of the School of Passionate Love concerns gnostics enamored with God through direct witnessing.[2] Also, this often undefined but implied relationship between the School of Love and witnessing in forms appears in the poetry of 'Umar ibn 'Ali ibn al-Farid (d. 632/1235). Ibn al-Farid seems to allude to the School of Love early on in his "Poem of the Way," a poem that in many places, especially lines 239–64, could serve as a manifesto for witnessing the Real in forms and the poetic supremacy of the human form.[3] The Egyptian poet exclaims that "I was never confounded, until I chose your love as a *madhhab*," a pronouncement that intimates witnessing in form insofar as the divine beloved has here—at least in terms of poetic language and imagery—assumed the form of a beautiful female.[4] Similarly, Ibn al-Farid declares that "from my *madhhab* of love there is no egress for me / and if I incline one day away from it, I have forsaken my religion completely."[5] Although *madhhab* is not an uncommon word in Arabic love poetry, the reference here to the School of Passionate Love was clear to the poem's most famous commentator, Sa'id al-Din al-Farghani (d. 699/1300), a student of Ibn 'Arabi's preeminent student Qunawi. As is usually the case, Farghani translates the Arabic *hubb* (love) into Persian as *'ishq* (passionate love), a translation that, in this instance, for the commentator's audience, mitigates the lexical discrepancy between Ibn al-Farid and Persian adherents to the School of Passionate Love.[6] In another instance, Farghani's commentary associates "the Denomination of Passionate Lovers" (*firqah-i 'ashiqan*) directly and unambiguously with "the Passionate Lovers of the *Shahid*" (*'ushshaq-i shahid*).[7] Arguments for the validity and superiority of this way of love can be found in Ruzbihan Baqli's treatise *'Abhar al-'Ashiqin*, where, again, the author refers to "the School of the People of Passionate Love [*madhhab-i ahl-i 'ishq*]."[8] One sees a similar phrase used by Awhad al-Din al-Kirmani, when he asserts that "until a man has lost his head to the sword of passionate love / he has not become purified in the School of the Passionate Lover [*madhhab-i 'ashiqi*]."[9] Many of the adherents of this school whom I will discuss correspond to that group which Jami describes in his *Nafahat al-Uns*: "A congregation among the chief figures such as Shaykh Ahmad Ghazali and Awhad al-Din Kirmani occupied themselves in contemplating the beauty of sensory loci in forms, and in those forms witnessed absolute beauty of the Real—may he be exalted—though they were not attached to sensory form."[10]

Yet the phrase had fluidity; it was used sometimes by Sufi saints who disagreed upon the manner in which the knower fueled passionate love.[11] Indeed, although Mawlana Jalal al-Din Balkhi/Rumi (d. 672/1273) makes many references to the School of Passionate Love in his *Mathnawi-i Ma'nawi* as well as his *Diwan-i Shams*, one cannot group Rumi so easily with figures such as Kirmani, because of Rumi's expressed disapproval of the *practice* (though definitely not the *imagery*) of gazing at beardless youths.[12] As with any *madhhab*, the School of Passionate Love saw not only variances of interpretation but also criticism; the School of Passionate Love, as described by Kirmani, Baqli and others, even faced criticism from other Sufis. For example, Abu al-Hasan 'Ali ibn 'Uthman Hujwiri (d. 465–69/1072–77) comments that gazing at beardless youths has become a *madhhab*, one which he considers to be a remnant of the Incarnationist movement (*al-Hululiyah*).[13] Lastly, it seems that the infamy of abuses of this *madhhab* reached beyond the boundaries of Sufi discourse. In a satirical shadow play written in Cairo proximate to 'Iraqi's own stay there, the poet Shams al-Din Ibn Daniyal (d. 710/1311) comically refers to pederasty as its own *madhhab.* Considering the satiric inversion of Sufi terms in this play, it is highly likely that this phrase is an ironic response to abuses of a sort of *madhhab-i 'ishq* practiced in the poet's age.[14]

What was Ibn 'Arabi's relationship to this "school"? Moreover, how sympathetically would Ibn 'Arabi have responded to those adherents who proclaimed the supremacy of the human form for the goal of witnessing? Surely he was aware of these seminal figures and their provocative statements about witnessing divine beauty in the forms of human beloveds. Such can be seen in his mention of Ruzbihan Baqli's infatuation with a singing girl:

> The story is told of Shaykh Ruzbihan that he was afflicted with the love of a woman singer; he fell ecstatically in love with her, and he cried much in his state of ecstasy before God, confounding the pilgrims at the Ka'bah during the time he resided there. . . . When he was afflicted by the love of this singer, no one knew of it, but whatever he had with God was transferred to her. He realized that the people would imagine that his ecstasy was for God in its source. So he went to the Sufis and took off his cloak, throwing it before them. He told his story to the people, saying, "I do not want to lie about my spiritual state." He then became like a servant to the singer. The woman was told of his state and his ecstasy over her, and she learned that he was one of the great ones of the People of God. The woman became ashamed, and repented before God for the profession she had followed, by the blessing of his sincerity. She became like a servant to him. God removed that attachment to her from his heart, and he returned to the Sufis and put on his cloak.[15]

Most significant, this account highlights the complications that occur for the mystic in maintaining a distinction between the human beloved as a *medium* of love and the human beloved as an *object* of love. This is a major theme in Ibn 'Arabi's writings on love, one that parallels statements made by advocates of the School of Passionate Love, particularly advocates of gazing at human beauty. Also important to note here is Ibn 'Arabi's reference to an ecstasy that others mistakenly imagine is for God "in its source" (*'ala aslihi*). The "source" is what differentiates gnostic love from uninformed love, which is another major theme in Ibn 'Arabi's reflections on love. In other words love for human beings, its signs and symptoms, does not differ in any apparent sense from love for God. Rather, the gnostic must monitor himself, remain wary of the true motivating force behind his love for beautiful forms, and desist from loving women (or young boys) for their own sake.

It is not simply that Ibn 'Arabi was *aware* of this movement. Rather, his statements, poetry, and cosmological view suggest that he sympathized with the sentiment and contemplative methods of those whose allegiance was to the School of

Passionate Love and who advocated witnessing the divine in the forms of human beloveds. In a poem in his *Tarjuman al-Ashwaq,* Ibn 'Arabi famously describes a "Religion of Love" (*din al-hubb*) as a way particular to those possessing a heart receptive to every form of the divine; the heart, in other words, fluctuates to suit its Lord's state-changing quality ("My heart has become receptive to every form. . . . I profess the Religion of Love; to whatever direction turn its riding mounts, there love is my religion and belief").[16] This religion, as Ibn 'Arabi describes it, is epitomized by the legendary lovers of Arabic erotic poetry. It is important to note that both words used here, *din* (religion) and *hubb* (love), differ in definition and connotation from the words *madhhab* (school) and *'ishq* (passionate love). There is also, however, a parallel that cannot be ignored. The close relationship that Ibn 'Arabi discerns between love and the divine in forms, coupled with his focus on the great lovers of Arabic poetry and his emphasis on contemplating the divine in women, indicates that Ibn 'Arabi saw himself as a member of a religion of love, a tradition that experienced love for the ever-changing and self-manifesting divine, especially in the forms of beautiful human beings.

The Epitome of Beauty: The Human Form

Repeatedly the writings of Ibn 'Arabi affirm that no object of beauty more ably arouses human pleasure and evokes love than the human form. Considering Ibn 'Arabi's emphasis that attraction coincides with constitution, such an assertion seems like a simple statement about natural human inclinations, but the spiritual ramifications of human-to-human attraction fit into more extensive assertions about the nature of beauty and love. The potency of human-to-human attraction is indeed so overwhelming that Ibn 'Arabi often compares it with the love between gnostics and God, ranking these as the two most powerful loves: "Know that love only enraptures the lover in his entirety when the beloved is the Real, may he be exalted, or someone from among the lover's own genus [i.e., a human being], whether girl [*jariyah*] or boy [*ghulam*]."[17] Or as described elsewhere, a human being becomes annihilated in his or her totality either in the love of his or her Lord or in another human being who "is a place of self-disclosure for his Lord."[18] From this second quotation, it is clear that a human loves another human because he or she is a locus of divine beauty, although not all lovers know this. The process of contemplating God in humans finds further cosmological legitimacy in that the "Treasure"—that is, the Real in himself—has been collected and hidden in the form of the Perfect Man, or, translated more consistently with Ibn 'Arabi's thought, the Complete Human (*al-insan al-kamil*).[19]

Muhyi al-Din's observations about human beauty usually focus on the male viewpoint, especially the attraction of men for women (though he also comments on the attraction experienced by women for men and men for beardless youths). Indeed, as

Ibn 'Arabi explains in his final chapter of *Fusus al-Hikam,* the alluring quality of women for the male gnostic results from the heights of witnessing (*shuhud*) achievable in beholding and enjoying the female form, a witnessing unattainable through any other medium.[20] Ibn 'Arabi declares that humans cannot witness the Real divorced from matter (*la yushahad al-haqq mujarradan 'an al-mawadd abadan*).[21] Witnessing does not interact with pure spirit or meaning but occurs through the medium of matter, which permits the envisioning of the divine in forms. The medium of witnessing is not necessarily of physical matter (there are other types of matter in Ibn 'Arabi's thought), so it is remarkable that Ibn 'Arabi emphasizes the *physical* form of woman as the greatest medium for witnessing. He informs his audience that the witnessing of the Real in women is the greatest (*a'zam*), most perfect (*akmal*), and most complete (*atamm*) instance of witnessing.[22]

Inherent Love of Women

Ibn 'Arabi's discussion of contemplating the divine in woman, considered in detail by Sachiko Murata, originates in the Prophet Muhammad's declaration that women were one of three things made beloved to him.[23] As the hadith states, "*Three things have been made beloved of me from this world of yours: women, perfume, and the delight of my eye has been placed in the prescribed prayer.*"[24] These three things have also been made beloved of the heirs of the Prophet Muhammad, that is, those saints who have benefited fully from his infallible example and esoteric knowledge. Ibn 'Arabi is careful to mention that such heirs do not love these three things of their own accord; rather, like the Prophet, these three things have been *made beloved* to them.[25] The lack of agency in loving these three things means that women, perfume, and prayer exhibit inherent perfections that those possessing spiritual insight cannot help but love.

The love that the Prophet Muhammad and the achieved gnostics have for women reflects, in fact, a number of cosmological rules of beauty and attraction, the most fundamental of which can be described as "self-knowledge through the medium of otherness." Self-knowledge, arguably the very purpose of existence, has grades of ontological significance. On the most absolute level, the Real seeks to know himself through the process of creation, according to the famous hadith of the Hidden Treasure ("*I was a Treasure . . . Unknown, so I loved to be known*"). On the level of the individual human soul, another hadith, "*Whoever knows himself knows his Lord,*" beckons each seeker of the divine to pursue the true depths of the self or soul.[26] In both cases, the seeker needs an "other," a mirror that is similar but somehow detached.

Witnessing of the self in such mirrors results in a fervent longing for the self-in-other. Using a hadith in which God addresses the Prophet David, Ibn 'Arabi underscores God's longing for creation, a longing that outweighs the longing that creation has for God.[27] Since, in the case of the human, God breathed his own spirit into his creation, God's longing for the human is merely a longing for himself, that is, for the derivative of himself that he deposited in man. Because God created man from his spirit, he also endowed man with his form—that is, the form of the cosmos, since the cosmos is the form and mirror of God.[28] This means that man is the most complete of mirrors for the Real, in essence and form, such that the Real views himself most fully and longs for himself most urgently in man. Similarly man longs for himself through woman, who is an *other* receptive with respect to him in the same way that the cosmos is receptive with respect to God, and woman longs for herself through her active counterpart, man.

In accordance with the paradigm discussed above, Ibn 'Arabi refers to the attraction that women have for men as "the longing of the whole for its part."[29] Just as the human spirit has its source in God, Eve was created from a rib of Adam, a notion Ibn 'Arabi has doubtless received from canonical Sunni narrations.[30] As Muhyi al-Din explains in chapter 7 of *al-Futuhat al-Makkiyah,* Adam was first created without the faculty of desire (*shahwah*).[31] Once Eve was created, however, a mutual attraction arose because of the physical propensities effected by Eve's creation. Eve, having been created from a rib, acquired the traits of "curvature" (*al-inhina'*) and "inclination" (*al-in'itaf*), words that signify the shape of the rib, but also signify attachment and kind disposition. Because of these qualities, a woman is attached and sympathetic (*tahnu*) toward her children and husband. Moreover, and more important, since the rib from which Eve was made came from Adam, Eve's love for Adam is "a love of native place" (*hubb al-mawtin*).[32] Or as Ibn 'Arabi states in the *Fusus al-Hikam,* the longing of women for men is the longing of "a thing for its homeland" (*watanih*).[33] Eve longs for the place from which she came, namely, the body of Adam, and, since Adam and Eve are prototypes for the consequent human race, the love of all women for men is one of a derivative for its source. This of course parallels the love of humans for God, who in accordance with Ibn 'Arabi's understanding of the Qur'anic verses 15:29 and 38:72 (*"I breathed in him* [Adam] *of My spirit"*) is the Source of the human spirit.

Adam's longing for Eve also arises from this creative process, although the results are reversed and, in a sense, complementary. Just as, according to the hadith cited so often by Ibn 'Arabi, *"God created Adam according to his form,"* that is, God's form, so too has God created Eve according to Adam's form.[34] God witnesses himself in the form of man, one derived from himself; similarly, man witnesses himself in the form of woman, derived from himself. When the rib was taken from Adam, a void came about that had to be filled, for "there will not remain any emptiness in existence."[35] Thus in place of this void in Adam's side, God placed desire for Eve, a desire so forceful that at the time of union it "spreads throughout all the parts of his body."[36] Since the rib has come from Adam, the love of Adam for Eve is "a love of himself," for she is "a part from him."[37] Here the love of Adam for Eve resembles the love of God for creation, which is also a love of the Divine Self. Hence one can see that Adam sees in Eve that which God sees in his creatures, and Eve sees in Adam that which the creatures see in God.

The Beauty of Creative Powers

Expanding on the causes of human attraction, Ibn 'Arabi explains in chapter 380 of *al-Futuhat al-Makkiyah* that women allow men to actualize an inherent ambition: the act of creation. The desire to procreate comes from the very physical form of man, an action that requires an accommodating locale. Enlightened men, always more cognizant than other men, actually see in women a place of creation (*mahall al-takwin*).[38] Man, moreover, seeks perfection and, like his Creator, desires to produce nothing less than perfection (*al-kamal*). In terms of creation, there is nothing more perfect or complete (*akmal*) than human existence; thus no undertaking can outdo the creation of a human. Such cannot occur, of course, except in women. Hence, the love men have for women is a creative love. Ibn 'Arabi notes that this is an astounding situation, since woman has come from man (as his rib), is the source of man (as his mother), and yet also allows him to bring into being something identical to himself (a human child). Of course, for Ibn 'Arabi the significance of this creative attraction and the act of creation is its resemblance to the situation between God and the cosmos: God creates from himself the cosmos, which reflects his attributes (and is thus, in a sense, identical to him), and yet from this creation he comes to be the God-in-creation, acquiring manifestation from that which he created.

The potential to create leads the spiritual elect to love perfume as well. As Ibn 'Arabi tells us in the final chapter of *Fusus al-Hikam*, using an Arabic proverb, the "loveliest of perfumes is the embrace of the beloved."[39] The most compelling perfume is the natural fragrance of women—a scent that for Ibn 'Arabi indicates fertility and reproduction, one that, as he puts it, comes from the "odors of creation" (*rawa'ih al-takwin*).[40] In Ibn 'Arabi's vision, attraction or love arises from the complementary relationships that have been established in the first instances of creation. Since man comes from a creative entity, God, and has produced a creative entity, woman (who creates by bearing children), the love of creative feminine powers is inherent in him.

Cosmological Implications

The Prophet Muhammad's very wording in his narration of the three beloved things carries great meaning according to Ibn 'Arabi, reflecting not only man's inherent love of the creative powers of the feminine but also his stance in the cosmos and the order of creation. Ibn 'Arabi tells us that the three beloved things—women (*al-nisa'*), perfume (*al-tib*), and prayer (*al-salah*), in that order—are feminine, masculine, and feminine, in terms of Arabic lexical gender. Moreover, the first word in this series, *al-nisa'*, refers to *actual* female entities in terms of sex, namely, women. For Ibn 'Arabi this indicates the order of things in creation. First, the divine essence (*al-dhat*) is lexically feminine; from it proceeds all creation. Since the divine essence's powers of creation are absolute, it is represented by a *real* feminine word, the word for "women." Then comes a masculine word (*al-tib*), paralleling the masculinity of Adam, the first man and thus the first human soul. Although Adam is a man, his being represented by perfume means that he still retains within himself a scent of the divine creative powers, since, as Ibn 'Arabi has established, the truest of perfumes emits the fragrances of creation. Last in the series is a feminine word (*al-salah*), which reflects the feminine entity—Eve—who came from Adam's rib and from whom proceeds all of mankind. Since Eve creates only in a physical (and thus relatively unreal) sense, she is represented by a word that is feminine only lexically, not in actuality.[41] Thus the creative ability of women is merely a manifestation of the inherent propensity of the divine essence to create, bestowing on women a physical femininity that reflects the actual femininity of the divine essence. Just as Adam stands between two femininities—that of the divine essence and that of the woman who proceeded from him—the word "perfume" stands between the words "women" and "prayer," such that the very words of the Prophet Muhammad reproduce the ontological situation of the cosmos. By contemplating himself in woman, woman as his effect, and himself as the effect of God, all in one relationship, man has the ability to see himself as receptive vis-à-vis God, creative vis-à-vis woman, a Source for woman, an effect of God, and a medium through which God witnesses the affair in its entirety. This is the realization of triplicity that Ibn 'Arabi stresses so emphatically in the final chapter of the *Fusus al-Hikam*.

The threefold structure encountered—God, man, and woman—embodies a pattern of ongoing genesis throughout the cosmos. As Ibn 'Arabi repeatedly affirms, the creation of the cosmos involves triplicity (*al-tathlith*), a threefold process involving activity, receptivity, and bestowed activity. In Muhyi al-Din's manifold descriptions of the cosmos' genesis, a general pattern emerges in which three participants interact: (1) a divine source; (2) a medial participant, receptive toward the divine essence and active toward that which proceeds from it; and (3) a third participant, receptive toward the medial participant, active toward the rest of creation.[42] In some descriptions, the cosmos is described as having resulted from a process whereby the divine essence (*al-dhat*) engenders the Primary Intellect (*al-'aql al-awwal*), which consequently employs the Universal Soul (*al-nafs al-kulliyah*) to bring creation into being.[43] Or using a different set of terms, the essential light (*al-nur al-dhati*) becomes manifest in a process of speaking; here the medial participant is the Breath of the All-Merciful (*al-nafas al-rahmani*) and the third participant is called the Cloud (*al-'ama'*).[44] Often, the medial and third participants mentioned above are described as male and female respectively, or as Adam and Eve, and the interchange between them that allows creation is dubbed by Ibn 'Arabi as conjugal union (*al-nikah*).[45] This is perhaps most evident in Ibn 'Arabi's description of the Pen and the Preserved Tablet, which unite in an active-receptive or male-female relationship to write out the letters and words that correspond to all created things.[46]

Also, it is clear from Ibn 'Arabi's descriptions of these various sets of terms that the medial and third participants are in fact one reality; in that reality's functioning as a locus of reception it is called a "tablet," for example, since words are imposed upon it, while in its functioning as a generative medium, it is called a "pen." When seen as one indiscernible reality, this receptive-active entity is often described as the "Muhammadan Reality" (*al-haqiqah al-Muhammadiyah*), where Ibn 'Arabi attributes both the medial participant and the third participant of the cosmos' genesis to the essence of the Prophet Muhammad.[47] Here it must be understood that the "Muhammad" who lived for a duration of time in the Arabian Peninsula is merely a manifestation on the physical plane of the created entity most proximate to the divine essence. This proximity is such that the Muhammadan Reality precedes any other existent and occupies an axial position in the generation of all things.[48]

Comprehensive Witnessing

In understanding the significance of the male-female relationship, one must bear in mind that, in Ibn 'Arabi's vision, the greatest witnessing of existence is that which is most comprehensive. Ibn 'Arabi establishes this early on in the *Fusus al-Hikam* in his discussion of Adam, where he asserts the superiority of Adam to the angels and indeed any other created thing. Adam serves as the supreme mirror in which God witnesses himself—that is, witnesses himself through the witnessing of Adam—because Adam as the first Perfect Man possesses an unparalleled comprehensiveness. Adam as the prototype of the Perfect Man enjoys a comprehensiveness that causes him to be both the "very polishing" (*al-jala'*) that elicits the cosmos' reflectivity in its function as the divine mirror, as well as the "spirit" vis-à-vis the cosmos, which serves as the "form" of this mirror.[49] In other words, Adam is the essence or inner reality of the cosmos on account of his comprehensiveness.[50] The human reality that Adam represents also comprehends two polar attributes—receptivity and activity, or femininity and masculinity, for "humanness [*al-insaniyah*] is a coming together of male and female."[51]

In order for a human to possess the comprehensiveness that allows for complete witnessing, that human must possess qualities of femininity as well as masculinity, servitude as well as mastery. Of course, no witness possesses these traits in a manner as balanced or as complete as Muhammad, the most complete of Complete Humans (or Perfect Men), and it is for this reason that his witnessing is ideal.[52] Muhammad as an ontological phenomenon, not merely as a historical figure, possesses perfect receptivity as well as borrowed activity. This means that Muhammad sees himself as a completely receptive servant vis-à-vis God, an empty container that can serve as a locus of manifestation for all the divine names. On the other hand, he also sees the cosmos actively or creatively, as his effect, all in all yielding a witnessing unsurpassed in any other existent. Ibn 'Arabi notes the relationship between receptivity, bestowed activity, and witnessing in describing the purely passive and receptive origins of the Muhammadan Reality: "When he [Muhammad] was created quintessentially a slave, he never once sought mastery, rather remaining in a state of prostration, steadfast in his being purely receptive [*munfa'ilan*], with the effect that God created through him that which he created, thus conferring upon him the rank of activity [*fa'iliyah*] in the World of the Breaths."[53] Muhammad hence embodies the paradox of creation. Through his absolute servitude, his being the most subservient or receptive of existents, Muhammad acquires a sort of mastery: a comprehensive creative ability, such that in relation to creation he is both a Source and a Cause, witnessing creation from a Creative point of view and manifesting God's dominance and vigilance over his creatures.

As a pair, Adam, who is active, and Eve, who is receptive—and in fact all men and women—embody Muhammad's cosmological synthesis (femininity and masculinity, receptivity and activity, servitude and lordship) on the physical plane of existence.[54] Male-female attraction and union allows the gnostic to witness the Real in a comprehensive, Muhammadan manner, as both active and receptive. It is for this reason that man's witnessing the Real in woman supersedes all other manners of witnessing and that those gnostics who emulate the Muhammadan ideal love women so profoundly.

Those Oblivious to the True Beauty of Women

Of course, the love of women is a witnessing and love of God only for those aware of that which Ibn 'Arabi describes, those who—like the Prophet Muhammad—love women because of the "completeness of witnessing in them."[55] One who enjoys women without such knowledge and insight merely seeks pleasure and indulges in that pleasure in a manner similar to beasts. The form of comprehensive union is present in such attraction, but it lacks the "spirit" that exists only for one who understands and sees that man's enjoyment of woman actually corresponds to the Real's enjoyment of himself.[56] After all, true agency always belongs to the Real, even though he achieves his will through intermediaries; that is, in reality the object and subject of witnessing is the Real, but through the medium of man.

Nevertheless, Ibn 'Arabi admits that he too once lacked proper knowledge of women and love for them. For eighteen years of his life, after he entered upon the path of spiritual perfection, he detested women and union with them because he lacked understanding of the true status of male-female attraction and union.[57] After acquiring knowledge that, for the reasons outlined above, God has made women beloved to Muhammad and those who imitate his spiritual faultlessness, Ibn 'Arabi proudly states, "I am the most tender of people toward them [women] and the most observant of their due, because of the insight that I possess in this matter, an insight that comes from [their] being made beloved, not from a natural love; only one given knowledge and understanding from God knows the value of women."[58]

One who possesses such knowledge realizes that through male-female attraction and union, human lovers recreate the genesis of the cosmos, the first and truest instance of love and fulfillment; all participants, divine, medial, and third, are included in their love. Their love comprehends both poles of existence: cosmos and Real, created and Creator, passive and Active, feminine and masculine. It is for these reasons that love for women—if undertaken with proper gnosis—is a "divine love" (*hubb ilahi*).[59] Despite the fact that the form of male-to-female attraction and union is physical, the witnessing, longing, and love that occur therein has a spirit or inner reality that Ibn 'Arabi deems "divine."

Gazing at Beardless Youths

Considering the cosmological significance of the female gender to Ibn 'Arabi's account of love and beauty, one might assume that he would not approve of male admiration for the beauty of young men, a beauty so often celebrated in the Persian Sufi texts of this age. After all, simple biology dictates that beardless male youths, while depicted as somewhat androgynous in Persian poetry, still cannot represent the same creative feminine faculty that Ibn 'Arabi emphasizes. It is perhaps with this in mind—along with the observation that Ibn 'Arabi's erotic poetry, like that of his Egyptian counterpart Ibn al-Farid, revolves around the godly female form—that some scholars have asserted Ibn 'Arabi's opposition to gazing at beardless young men.[60]

Yet while man's enjoyment of woman has the exclusive potential for a certain meditation on the created order, gazing at beardless youths grants the accomplished gnostic (and only the accomplished gnostic) a different contemplative perspective. In outlining this perspective, Ibn 'Arabi's double definition of "recent ones" (*al-ahdath*) exemplifies his unexpected and shifting use of words:

> [We turn our attention] to companionship with "recent ones" [*al-ahdath*], that is, both beardless youths [*al-murdan*], and the People of Innovations who create praiseworthy imitated customs [*al-tasnin al-mahmud*] in the religion, a practice that the Lawgiver has conceded to us. The gnostic gazes [*yanzur*] at the beardless youth because he is smooth [*amlas*]. That is, there is no growth on his cheeks, like a sleek rock. The sort of earth that is called *marda'* [the feminine singular of the word for "beardless" mentioned above] is that which has no vegetation upon it. Thus the beardless youth reminds the

> gnostic of the Station of Detachment [*maqam al-tajrid*], and [the gnostic gazes because the youth] has more recently been with his Lord than an older person. The Law [*shar'*] has taken this into consideration in the matter of rain.[61] The closer something is to its original creation, the nearer it is in signification, the more exalted in sanctity, and the more plenteous in drawing mercy to itself, than the one who is older and distant from this station. As for why [these beardless youths] are "recent ones" [*al-ahdath*], it means that they are fresh from their Lord. In their companionship is a recollection of their newness by which one discerns his eternalness—may he be exalted. This is an instance of proper reflection [*i'tibar*] and a connecting path. If [the "recent one" in question] should be of the recent ones in declaring new imitated customs [*ahdath al-tasnin*], then he is supported by [God's] saying, may he be exalted, whenever a recent reminder [*dhikr muhdath*] comes to them from their Lord [21:2], or whenever a recent reminder comes to them from the All-Merciful (26:5). The one who blames has not accepted [the divine message] heartily. This is how the gnostics consider the matter. As for novice wayfarers [*al-muridun*] and Sufis [*al-sufiyah*], the companionship of recent ones is forbidden to them, because of the predominance of animal desire in them. This is because of the intellect, which God has placed in opposition to it. Were it not for the intellect, natural desire would be praiseworthy.[62]

Ibn 'Arabi has here combined ingeniously two aspects of the practice of gazing at beardless youths: first, the cosmological reason for choosing young men as objects of aesthetic contemplation and, second, the answer to objections raised that this practice falls outside of the Prophet's established way, the *Sunnah.* While only one term equivalent to "gazing" arises in this passage, Ibn 'Arabi's concentration on the physical features of beardless youths, particularly their smooth, hairless cheeks, clarifies that such is his intent. The beauty of a beardless young man lies in his youthful countenance, a reminder to the man of awakened perception that the object of contemplation in question has arrived more recently from the realm of potentiality into the realm of external existence.[63]

The notion that ontological freshness is a sort of beauty can be found intimated in an earlier treatise on beauty and love by the Sufi philosopher Abu al-Hasan al-Daylami, who categorizes proximity with relation to Universal Beauty as one factor causing an entity to be beautiful. Noteworthy here is al-Daylami's reference to a hadith alluded to in the passage by Ibn 'Arabi above, narrated by Anas ibn Malik: "We were with God's Messenger (God's blessings and peace be upon him) when rain fell upon us. . . . God's Messenger (God's blessings and peace be upon him) laid aside part of his attire, so that the rain would hit him [uncovered]. We asked, 'Why did you do this?' He replied, *'Because it is recent from its Lord* [*hadith 'ahd bi-rabbihi*], *may he be exalted.'"*[64] Supporting his assertion that any entity recently with its Lord has sway over one more distantly created by him, Ibn 'Arabi refers more directly to this hadith in the *Fusus al-Hikam* and highlights the ability of a simple substance (rain) recently with its Lord to have a subduing effect (*sakhkhara*) on even a divine messenger who receives revelation but is, in terms of creational chronology, more distant from his Lord.[65]

In the case of beardless youths, companionship with them yields another realization indicated by Ibn 'Arabi: God's eternalness. That the observer has aged while creation continually pours forth young human beings should remind the observer that the Source of creation is eternal and continually new.

One last indication that in a passage about *suhbah* (companionship) Ibn 'Arabi refers to gazing—although his abstruse language and reluctance to mention gazing directly seem to point to atypical timidity—is his insistence that anyone other than achieved gnostics (*al-'arifun*) should not enjoy the company of the beardless. This includes novice wayfarers (*al-muridun*) who have recently taken the path and "Sufis," a term that, when contrasted with the term *'arif*/gnostic, has the connotation of a simple albeit pious person observing the path of traditional spiritual and ethical training, not just in the works of Ibn 'Arabi but also in Rumi's statements.[66]

Lastly, lest one dismiss the practice of gazing at beardless youths as an innovation and blame those who associate with such innovators, Ibn 'Arabi defends keeping the companionship of those who undertake *tasnin*, that is, the creation of imitated customs. As he points out, God has conceded this matter to men of spiritual ability. Here, in using the unusual word *tasnin*, Ibn 'Arabi refers to a hadith that *"whoever leaves an exemplary established way in Islam* [*man sanna fi-al-islam sunnah hasanah*] *will have its reward and the reward of all those who practice it after him, without any reduction in their reward."*[67] Of course, to consider the practice of gazing at beardless youths an exemplary established way might be considered somewhat presumptuous, and, in fact, many (including Rumi) would regard the latter portion of this narration more applicable to the practice of gazing: *"Whoever leaves an evil established way in Islam* [*man sanna fi-al-islam sunnah sayi'ah*] *will bear its burden and the burden of all those who practice it after him, without any reduction in their burden."*

Nevertheless the liberty of the saints in creating new practices by this point had become somewhat of a truism in certain Sufi circles, as can be seen in the reminder Ibn 'Arabi's preeminent disciple Sadr al-Din al-Qunawi (d. 673/1273–74) gives to the Parwanah of Konya in response to his consideration of banning *sama'*: "Indeed, the innovation [*bid'at*] of the Friends of God is like customary practice [*sunnat*] of the noble prophets, and the Friends know what the wisdom behind it is. Whatever issues from them is not without the prompting of the Almighty."[68] Ibn 'Arabi's reference to two almost identical verses in support of such new practices is somewhat strange, if only because—while the portion quoted of each of the two verses is neutral—that which follows is strikingly condemnatory. Of course, the portion quoted supports Ibn 'Arabi's statement, and, moreover, to the man of insight, each meaning derived from the verse is a revealed meaning, which is Ibn 'Arabi's point; revelation is an ongoing affair. The gnostics, sensitive to the true universal significance of the physical world around them, should be permitted to introduce practices verified by their insight and constant communication with the Real.

It is such insight that allows Ibn 'Arabi to make his final statement somewhat boldly: Natural desire (*al-shahwah al-tabi'iyah*) itself would be praiseworthy if not for the intellect (*al-'aql*). While it is not unusual for medieval Islamic writers, including Abu Hamid al-Ghazali, to consider the functional benefits of the faculty of sexual desire,[69] Ibn 'Arabi takes the matter one intuitive step further. Since all of creation is essentially good and permissible, desire itself cannot be blamed, especially since it joins together separated entities, enkindling within them natural love, which is a means to something that approximates divine love. In the divine-human dialogue that is law, only reason—not natural or animal desire—has the ability to hear. Reason draws boundaries and makes judgments, and while they are a great service to moral human beings, restraining them from desire's tendency to neglect divine commands, such determinations are distant from the pervasive goodness of all things.[70] Of course, while here intimating the praiseworthiness of desire, Ibn 'Arabi limits concupiscent contemplation of human beauty to male-female relationships, for reasons grounded in both his cosmology and divine law. Ibn 'Arabi seems to be aware of the risks of experiencing sexual longing for young males, as can be seen in his repeated mentioning that the most intense experience of love occurs for a beloved that is either a "girl" (*jariyah*) or a "boy" (*ghulam*).[71] (It should also be mentioned that, in discussions of love, Ibn 'Arabi often assumes that the lover in question is a mature male.) Moreover, a contemplation of human beauty that arises purely from sexually motivated companionship, without contemplation of the divine, is "defective" (*ma'lulah*), according to Ibn 'Arabi.[72] This is because, as we have seen, appreciation for the beautiful human form must always be accompanied by an informed recognition of the divine presence.

Three Levels of Love, Three Levels of Beauty

While Ibn 'Arabi's vision eludes definition and classification, it can be described as emanational in that the realms of existence come from a Source, share the same binding reality, affect one another, but also differ in the precision with which they reflect the divine names and thus the clarity with which they allow one to perceive. This is especially significant when it comes to beauty and love because, to Muhyi al-Din, beauty or the power to evoke love has different meanings in accordance with the level of existence on which the admiring lover perceives. According to Ibn 'Arabi, the levels of love are three: the divine (*al-hubb al-ilahi*), the spiritual (*al-hubb al-ruhani*), and the natural (*al-hubb al-tabi'i*). While the parameters and signs of these three loves differ, lovers on the lower levels of spirit and nature imitate the pattern set by the divine love of Self. The Real's love for himself effects the creation of a mirror; this mirror has no actual existence, especially with respect to the Real. The mirror is merely a passive locus in which the Real unburdens his love, releasing the existence-bestowing breath that Ibn 'Arabi calls the "Breath of the All-Merciful." The more nonexistent and thus receptive that mirror is, the better it reflects and thus the more beloved it is. In similar fashion, all lovers "create" their beloveds and all beloveds are in fact nonexistent. Whether the gnostic experiences divine, spiritual, or natural love, in any case, the beloved lacks both existence and necessity, for it is a fashioning of the lover.

In order to understand this, we first return to Ibn 'Arabi's chapter on love in *al-Futuhat al-Makkiyah,* chapter 178. Referring to the hadith that serves as the nucleus of his account of gnostic perception, the hadith that describes God's becoming the very faculties of his servant, Ibn 'Arabi turns his attention to the narration's introductory words.[73] Recall that in this first part of the hadith, God proclaims that his servant draws near to him, in the first instance, by fulfilling obligatory duties. This drawing near continues and intensifies through recommended or supererogatory deeds (*al-nawafil*), and it is on account of these supererogatory deeds that eventually God loves his servant. Once God loves his servant, God becomes the servant's *hearing through which he hears, his sight through which he sees, his hand through which he seizes, and his foot through which he walks.* That "extra" or supererogatory deeds result in God's love is a central point for Ibn 'Arabi. For him, an important cosmological lesson underlies God's love of non-obligatory additions or augmentations of worship. Just as a lack of necessity or an extraneous addition of worship arouses God's love, so too can all excess (*ziyadah*) be understood as a cause of love. This is because all lovers, in their act of loving, reproduce the creational love of God, who saw in creation nothingness (as opposed to his existence) and a lack of necessity (as opposed to his necessity, in that he is the Necessary Existent or *wajib al-wujud*): "A cause of love is supererogatory things, which are augmentations; the world is an augmentation in being, such that he loved the world because it was supererogatory, so that it became his hearing and his sight—until he loved none other than himself."[74] Considering that augmentation (*ziyadah*) is a cause of love, and beauty is "that which causes love," it might be fair to describe augmentation (*ziyadah*) as a sort of beauty. Regardless, since creation imitates the pattern of love set by God, augmentation arouses love in the created things just as it does in the Creator. That which causes God to love things, a lack of being and a lack of necessity, also causes each lover to love his beloved—every beloved is both nonexistent and unnecessary.

Of course, a number of misgivings might arise when such an assertion is made, the most immediate of which concerns God's function as a beloved. After all, God is not only a subject of love, a lover, but often also an object of devotion, a beloved. How can it be said that God as a beloved is nonexistent or unnecessary? One has to remember here that the lover does not love God directly, for it is impossible to have any direct knowledge of God without intermediaries; even on the most exalted level, the divine names act as intermediaries. In the case of *shuhud,* the God that is witnessed and thus loved by the gnostic has taken on forms through the gnostic's imaginal powers. The gnostic has encountered some reality but has come to witness and love that reality only through "creating" a beloved within the imagination. Thus the beloved in forms neither has absolute existence or necessity: "The beloved, who is nonexistent, although he does happen to be nonexistent, takes on representational forms in the imagination, thus possessing one of the many types of existence that is perceived by the imaginal vision in the imaginal realm by means of the eye that suits it."[75] Even if the lover adores something in the sensible realm, still, the lover does not encounter that beloved object directly; it is filtered through the lover's senses and formed anew in the imagination before it becomes an object of love. In other words, every lover creates his own beloved.

Similar to the divine love of self that results in the universe, the lover first loves himself or loves the True Self, then projects that love outward, creating a beloved. Ibn 'Arabi refers to this phenomenon in terms used to describe conjugal states, usually of women: "It is incumbent to thank God since / she is a virgin for me, and I have been previously wed."[76] As Ibn 'Arabi explains, the term "virgin" (*bikr*) signifies that the beloved is untouched by existence.[77] The term that refers to a person formerly wed (*thayyib*), however, signifies that the lover's love has caused and thus in a figurative sense preexisted the beloved. According to Ibn 'Arabi, "I have loved before that, so that I am a person previously wed"; like one once married, the source/lover has experienced love, returning to that experience upon the creation of the beloved. The beloved's virginity, mirroring the purity of nonexistence, results from her later entry into the narrative of love and her being an unwitting object of the lover's desire to see and know. This beloved has an autonomous will and yet emanates from the lover's experimental knowledge. In other words, there is a parallel between individual acts of love and the love that brought the cosmos into creation, the love that God attributes to himself when asserting in the famous narration that *"I loved to be known, so I created creation."*[78] Just as God created the universe so that we might know him, "*we* only create for *him,* so that we might know him."[79] We, the created things, attempt to share in divine love by creating our own beloved, thus experiencing the divine quality that caused creation and acquiring some knowledge of our Lord. This is why Ibn 'Arabi tells us that the beloved does not exist: it is the lover's limited enjoyment of an infinite longing.

The nonexistent beloved results from the lover's stopping short in aiming at the object of love, choosing a particular beloved, when in fact the *real* object of love for any lover is infinite and divine Love itself: "I am a beloved of Love, if only you knew, / and Love is our beloved, if you only understood!"[80] The failure of human lovers to know the true object of love can be seen in Ibn 'Arabi's lamentations "if only you knew" and "if you only understood." Of course, this failure varies according to the different levels or grades of love that exist. One on the spiritual level of love is more aware of his actual love object than a lover engaged in natural love, yet both have chosen objects of love rather than love itself. These lovers share in the portion of divine love that God has caused to "diffuse throughout every possible entity attributed with existence, and [to which he has] coupled a pleasure beyond which there is no higher pleasure."[81] It is a bounded form of that infinite love on account of which God makes himself manifest throughout the cosmos: "One part of the cosmos loves another with a limited love derived from absolute love."[82]

These differences in the levels or grades of love result, to some degree, from the proximity possible between lover and beloved on that stage of existence. Can two physical bodies become one? In the material realm, the closest union possible—as Ibn 'Arabi mentions—is sexual union, but even then there is an evident separation, and each party maintains an individual identity. On this level of nature, the lover maintains his distinct will and uses the beloved to achieve his amatory objective, gratifying the desire that flows through his constitution like "water in wool."[83] If this sounds selfish, it is precisely Ibn 'Arabi's point. The "lover" on the level of natural love loves little more than the self that is constructed by physical desires. His love is not aimed at "the beloved herself."[84] According to Ibn 'Arabi, natural love is "the love of the common masses, the aim of which is union through the animal spirit, such that the spirit of each lover is [actualized as] a spirit for its possessor only through sensual pleasure and the provocation of desire; its ultimate fulfillment is the sexual act."[85] Such a lover acknowledges the boundaries set by the natural realm and experiences love exclusively within those boundaries, thus unable to perceive beyond them.

On the level of spirit, the merge is far more complete and the interchange more exact; this is so much the case that the wills or the desires of the two parties merge into one, such that the lover wills whatever his beloved wills and vice versa.[86] As Ibn 'Arabi explains, giving and receiving on the level of spirit avoids the limits of bodies, with the effect that the merging of spirits is harmonious and perfectly reciprocal:

> Spiritual love is removed from the definition [of natural love] and distant from measure and figure, because the spiritual faculties have an inclination that is relational. Thus, when relationships in the inclinations of lover and beloved become more comprehensive than gazing, hearing, or knowing, that

> is [spiritual] love. Yet if there is a deficiency, and the relationships come up short, then it is not [such] love. The meaning of "relationships" is that the spirits whose business it is to give and bestow are turned toward the spirits whose business it is to take and lay hold; those spirits suffer when there is a lack of reception and these spirits suffer when there is a lack of effusion. . . . Each of these two spirits exerts its full capability in the love of the other.[87]

Clearly, boundaries in the spiritual realm are far more attenuated than boundaries in the natural realm. Here the lover and beloved merge in a manner more abstract and conceptual than natural love, since, after all, their wills or desires become one, so much so that the lover resembles the beloved.[88] Ibn 'Arabi explains in fact that in the case of spiritual love, the chosen beloved must be capable of having a will (*iradah*), otherwise the lover has no will to imitate and make his own. Still, on the level of spirit, the "self" remains and the union is imperfect.

It is only on the level of divine love that no distinction can be made, for the divine essence is not a "self" that serves as a barrier. Moreover, creation (the object of his love) is his mirror, so one cannot speak of God and creation as two disjoined entities. In other words, lover and beloved are one: "His love knows no beginning or end. . . . The essence of his love for his servants is precisely the beginning of their creation, from the first created entities to the last ones ad infinitum. The relationship of God's love to them is the relationship of his creational-ontological disposition [*kaynunatihi*]: it is with them however they might be, in their state of non-existence or existence."[89] While Ibn 'Arabi intermittently attributes divine love to human beings, he pronounces that divine love in its plenary sense cannot be achieved by humans. Yet the human love that most resembles divine love (which Ibn 'Arabi often simply calls "divine love") demands an almost complete loss of self.

While the barrier between a human lover and his beloved cannot be completely removed, the distinction between "self" and "other" can be reduced to almost nothing. On this level of love, the gnostic lover realizes the Oneness of Being. Things are inseparable, including the lover and the Beloved, such that everything is beautiful and everything is beloved. If it were fair to posit a "divine perspective," the human version of divine love would most correspond to such a perspective, since the Real sees only himself in all created things, thus admiring the beauty of all things and loving them. One who loves with the human version of divine love adores all created things, for "the sign of divine love is a love for all created things on every realm [of existence], supersensory, sensory, imaginal, or subjective-imaginal."[90] In a *qasidah* that begins his chapter on love, Ibn 'Arabi refers to this uniquely human brand of divine love, one that involves a union of *both* spirit and body:

The ultimate fulfillment of love for a human is his union
spirit to spirit and body to body;

the ultimate of union with the All-Merciful is heresy,
for without doubt his *ihsan* [excellent action] is a part of my *ihsan*.
If I cannot depict him in a form, then I know not whom I adore;
my soul and his depiction in forms reject any rational arguments.[91]

The lover has committed heresy (*zandaqah*) because, using the eye of *tashbih*/similitude, he has associated himself or his soul with his Lord and has denied any boundary between them. Thus the excellent actions (*ihsan*) of the Real and the actions of the lover are inseparable. Another act of heresy is the depicting of the Real in forms, for God is beyond forms and limitations. Yet the lover must see the Real in forms (as mentioned, *shuhud* demands such) in order to know the beloved and experience love. While these statements are beyond the intellectual boundaries of any rational argument (*burhan*), they are proven by the reality of the soul (which is inseparable from its Lord), its experiences, and the witnessing of the Real in forms (*taswirihi*), an envisioning beheld firsthand by the gnostic lover.

In ranking these three loves, one might assume that Ibn 'Arabi places divine love as most exalted, spiritual love directly below, and natural love as the lowest form of love, but as is often the case in Ibn 'Arabi's writings, matters are not that simple. First, as has been mentioned, divine love cannot be perfectly achieved by a human lover. The human reality (*al-haqiqah al-insaniyah*) as it develops within the limits of the human frame is limited by its constitution, and on account of this constitution, preference is inevitable and a pure divine love of all things impossible. For this reason, man's love is limited to the spiritual and the natural: "The relationship of love to us is not the same as the way love is related to him. The love pertaining to us, because of that which our [human] reality can accommodate, is divided into [merely] two parts: that which is called 'spiritual love' and 'natural love.' Our love for God, the Exalted, takes place with both loves simultaneously, although this is a matter difficult to imagine."[92] Again, contrary to what one would expect, Ibn 'Arabi does not emphasize here the superiority of spiritual love. This is because natural love and spiritual love must coexist for complete human love; they have a complementary relationship intrinsic to human perfection.

Man loves with "both loves simultaneously," because he is a balance of both the spiritual and the natural worlds, spirit and body, and it is this combination that yields his comprehensiveness. On the one hand, man can experience the natural world, which allows him to produce forms in the imagination, which bestows on him proximity and love, and which gives him a taste of the level of being closest to nonexistence. On the other hand, the spiritual reality of man—his spirit—is an inhabitant of the highest supersensory realm, a direct result of God's command, a breath from the divine Breaths; the spiritual love man experiences puts him in contact with a much more sublime sort of intimacy. As Ibn 'Arabi explains, while loving

God simply for himself (which is spiritual love) does outweigh loving God selfishly, or simply for oneself (natural love), the combination of spiritual love and natural love surpasses even the selfless spiritual love he has described: "Some of us love him for himself. Others from among us love him for the combination [*al-majmu'*] [himself and ourselves, that is, himself and his manifestations in creation], which is more complete in terms of love, since it is more complete in terms of gnosis of God and witnessing. This is because some of us have gnosis of him through witnessing [*shuhud*], and thus love him for the combination. This [loving him through the combination of himself and creation] is because witnessing is not possible unless in a form, and form is composite [*murakkabah*], such that the Beloved possesses a composite form."[93]

Since the natural world allows witnessing the Real in forms, it is a necessary part of the complete gnostic love that Ibn 'Arabi describes: loving God in his sensory as well as supersensory manifestations. Although this might not be equivalent to true divine love, it is the closest human beings can come to divine love; it is, after all, an effectively comprehensive love of both the high and the low. As was made clear in our discussions of perception, the "low" or the natural realm provides the observer with the material needed to interact consciously with the supersensory realm. The lover uses his presence in the natural realm to interpret his interactions in the spiritual realm, all the while recognizing the relative illusoriness of the natural realm. In this way, the lover acknowledges the "self" (the self or soul that is a product of his natural or physical existence) while also negating it.

Conclusion: Loving Humans with Divine Love

The key, then, to complete love or "divine love" is merging spiritual and natural love, while acknowledging the true object of love: the Real. If such occurs, the gnostic is then able to love another human being with divine love. After all, the gnostic sees the Real in that human beloved, such that the beauty of the human beloved is divine. In such a case, the representational beloved can vary or even be multiple in number, for the true Beloved is invariably the Real.

According to Ibn 'Arabi, such an acknowledgment of the True Beloved in various loci is ably captured in a poem by the 'Abbasid caliph Harun al-Rashid (r. 170/786–193/809), whose statement so impresses Muhyi al-Din that he quotes and explicates it twice in *al-Futuhat al-Makkiyah.* In fact, the instances of this quotation occur in the two sections of *al-Futuhat al-Makkiyah* where Ibn 'Arabi discusses natural, spiritual, and divine love, namely, chapter 178, on love, and the segment of chapter 73 where in questions 116 through 119 Ibn 'Arabi engages with inquiries concerning love posed earlier by al-Hakim al-Tirmidhi. Notwithstanding Ibn 'Arabi's epiphanic commentary, the poem was clearly written without any esoteric or spiritual significance. According to the contemporary historian Baqir Sharif al-Qurashi, al-Rashid's impetus for these lines was his infatuation with three singers from among his slave girls, Ghadir, Maridah, and Haylanah:[94]

Three delightful maidens possess my bridle
and have alighted in every place of my heart.
Why, when all of creation coils in fright of me,
do I obey them—although they constantly disobey me!
This is nothing other than the dominion of passion
with which they prevail more mightily than my dominion.[95]

Ibn 'Arabi tells us that there is a "concealed secret" behind Harun al-Rashid's use of the phrase "my bridle" (*'inani*), speaking of the bridle as one instead of attributing a separate bridle to each of the three beloveds who has sovereignty over him.[96] Such language reveals a unified desideratum: The enthralled caliph "loves exclusively One Meaning actualized for him by these three girls." In other words, the girls are mere representations of one Beloved Source, and for this reason they are described as alighting *together* in each place of the lover's heart.[97]

Yet the power of these beloveds should not be attributed to themselves. In a separate discussion of these same lines, Ibn 'Arabi clarifies that it is *not* the beloved who humbles or has power over the lover.[98] In fact, the beloved is "owned" (*mamluk*) and overpowered (*maqhur*) by the lover, because the beloved is created by the lover; the preceding lines from al-Rashid illustrate this in a particularly pertinent manner, since he does in fact own his beloveds, who are literally his slaves. Yet clearly, despite the power that he has over them, the lover still suffers abasement vis-à-vis his beloveds; the caliph has become humbled and even degraded before his slave girls. As Ibn 'Arabi argues, it is love itself that dominates and abases the lover, exemplified in the caliph's attribution of dominion (*sultan*) not to the girls but rather to love or passion itself (*al-hawa*). Ibn 'Arabi here intimates that an indivisible and powerful entity—love—results in the lover-beloved relationship, remains the source of that relationship, and maintains its dominance over the two complementary parties it has created from itself. Like the candid observations of 'Iraqi's *Lama'at*, Ibn 'Arabi's more guarded comments point to a belief that Love corresponds to the divine essence. After all, according to the hadith of the "Treasure . . . Unknown," the divine essence "loved" to be known even before creation or the manifestation of the divine names, and created all things as mirrors for himself because of this essential love of himself. Consequently love permeates the cosmos, drawing all things toward one another. This attraction is Beauty, the common alluring Source that pulls every lover toward every beloved, seen in Ibn 'Arabi's observation that these three singing girls represent a unified Meaning. There is an implication here and in many other observations that the quality that draws the Real to himself is also Beauty and that perfect Beauty corresponds to the Real, as attested to by Ibn 'Arabi's understanding of the hadith "*God is beautiful and loves beauty,* so he loves himself."[99] While the form of the beloved may vary, Beauty (or, if one prefers, "belovedness") pertains exclusively to the Real.

Despite the ontological precision that he discerns in al-Rashid's language, it is important to note that Muhyi al-Din does not necessarily mean to assert that the caliph is aware of the divine reality of this love. Lovers have a tendency to be precise when it comes to describing the symptoms of the sway of their beloved(s), which explains the validity of all love poetry, even when the beloved is exclusively human. The accuracy of lovers in describing love is due to their attention to its effects and concomitants, for these are phenomena common to all lovers, those aware of their true Beloved as well as the oblivious. As we begin to apply Ibn 'Arabi's concepts of beauty and love to his lyric poems, it becomes increasingly clear that love and beauty are each One Reality, communicated through universal terms and images but subject to degrees of perception.

'Iraqi and the Tradition of Love, Witnessing, and *Shahidbazi*

Sufi writers in the time of 'Iraqi more or less concurred that the human form is the apex of media that allow witnessing, even if they did not always state such explicitly. While the term *shahid* at times did refer to the remnants of an encounter with the divine names in the heart, and only metaphorically to the human form, a movement within Sufism increasingly began to associate the *shahid* with the human form, especially that of a beardless young man, and resulted in not only one of the most important poetic images in Sufi literature but also one of the most controversial practices of certain Sufis, namely, gazing at beautiful faces.[1] The name given to this practice in Persian was *shahidbazi,* a term that might be translated as "entertaining oneself with the *shahid,*" a term negative in connotation, sometimes implying pederasty. It must be made clear, however, that for the Sufis in question *shahidbazi* was in no way a sexual practice. Rather, it might be described as a platonic (what I would argue is an aesthetic) appreciation of divine beauty in human forms, one affected by a preexisting cultural appreciation for the beauty of beardless young men in some parts of the medieval and classical world, an appreciation that, outside of the context of Sufism, often was sexual.

Another word connected to this practice, in both its Sufi and non-Sufi applications, especially when it involved mere glances, was *nazar,* or "gazing," a word that has a somewhat jurisprudential connotation because of debates within the Muslim world regarding this practice, debates discussed by Joseph Norment Bell.[2] The writers below seem to prefer the term *shahidbazi,* which, more than the noun *nazar,* appears in their own works, despite or perhaps because of the sense of frivolity and licentiousness it carried.[3] Many of those Sufis to be mentioned seem to disregard or even fear the reputation of an upright Muslim, because of the dangerous sins of arrogance or ostentation that accompany public acknowledgments of probity. (Ironically these same Sufis sometimes flaunt their status as saints as well.)

Those Sufis mentioned previously who proclaimed a binding affinity for the School of Passionate Love (*madhhab-i 'ishq*) will now be considered in their function as contributors to a tradition of *shahidbazi.* Such a connection between the *madhhab-i 'ishq* and contemplative *shahidbazi* is telling, perhaps indicating that, in certain contexts, the former designated the latter.

The end goal of gazing at the human form was, of course, *'ishq,* passionate love (here for the divine), another term of great controversy in this time. Many Sufis maintained that God could be loved passionately, while others Sufi and non-Sufi alike held that passionate love anthropomorphizes God. One should not mistakenly assume here that all those opposed to applying the term *'ishq* to God were simply punctilious literalists who doubted the centrality of love (*mahabbah*) to the Qur'an or the Sunnah. That God is the Loving (*al-wadud*) and man has the capability to love him and be loved by him is clearly established in the text of the Qur'an.[4] Rather, the subtleties of Arabic's rich vocabulary yield a plurality of words translatable as "love" but varied in connotation.[5] While words such as *hubb, mahabbah,* and *wadd* express healthy, nurturing forms of love, the word *'ishq* signifies a love that is excessive and—in its original usage—desirous.[6] While excessive love for God—if possible—might even be applauded, *desire* for God, especially one that in its original lexical context is of an erotic nature, encroaches dangerously on God's transcendence.[7] Of course, certain gnostics would declare that even ardent longing for God is possible when he is witnessed in forms, particularly the beautiful and hence loveable form of human beings.

Why beardless youths were the beautiful human beings of choice is a matter outside the boundaries of this discussion, which focuses on the theories and legends that drove *shahidbazi.* Khaled El-Rouayheb has studied closely the homoerotic culture of the Arab-Islamic world during the Ottoman period, including love and admiration for beardless youths, its function as a disposition for certain "aesthetes," and the matter of gazing among Arabic-speaking mystics.[8] Sirus Shamisa has written much about pederasty in the medieval Persian-speaking world and its literary expressions, devoting part of his attention to placing Sufi *shahidbazi* within that larger context.[9] In his study of the influential Persian poet Farid al-Din Muhammad ibn Ibrahim 'Attar (d. ca. 617/1220), Hellmut Ritter (d. 1971) devotes a chapter to this phenomenon of love for the divine in human form within the Sufi tradition, a chapter that in its service as a respectable catalogue merely begins the discussion concerning the theoretical ramifications of *shahidbazi* and its place in the development of Sufi thought.[10] Since Ritter's book treats the legacy of 'Attar in great detail, including themes shared by 'Attar and his literary descendant 'Iraqi, very little mention has been made of 'Attar in the already detailed discussion below, despite this figure's archetypical position vis-à-vis Sufi *shahidbazi.*[11]

Of course, the tradition of love and witnessing focused on the human *shahid* and inherited by Fakhr al-Din was so prevalent in the centuries preceding 'Iraqi, that it is too abounding to consider in full here. What follows instead is an analysis of certain key figures who contributed to the culture of *shahidbazi* that Fakhr al-Din 'Iraqi so admired, allowing us to consider his understanding of beauty and the human form as a natural continuation of this tradition. This is an important undertaking, because, as attested by the sheer number of hagiographies documenting the practice of *shahidbazi* by saints, the notion of a saintly precedent seems to have been the central means by which this practice was legitimized, a practice that Ibn 'Arabi himself lauds as an innovation (*bid'ah*), a divergence from the *Sunnah*. Earlier authors, here unmentioned, such as Abu al-Hasan al-Daylami and Abu al-Qasim al-Qushayri, while acknowledging the distinct status of human beauty, often illustrated the importance of the *shahid* in its more abstract sense to classical Sufi thought. Later thinkers in the Persian Sufi tradition, including and especially the influential Ahmad Ghazali, began to emphasize more candidly the human form as the supreme evidential locus or *shahid*. While 'Iraqi may or may not have been directly exposed to all that will be mentioned, the writings and behavior of these mystics represent a general progression in Sufi thought that certainly did affect 'Iraqi.

Ahmad Ghazali: *Shahidbazi* as Saintly Behavior Beyond Reproach

Iraqi's continuing emphasis on love and its derivation for the gnostic from witnessing the divine in forms, especially human form, was certainly given dimensions of theoretical significance from his association with al-Qunawi. Nevertheless, his views on the cosmological and spiritual predominance of love and its application in the appreciation of beautiful human forms are most indebted to an existing trend in Sufism, one emphasized most it seems in Persian-speaking circles. Perhaps most interesting, part of 'Iraqi's affinity for the teachings of Ibn 'Arabi and al-Qunawi might have resulted from the concordance these mystics experienced with regard to love and witnessing. It is not unlikely also, considering some of the parallels that will be obvious to the reader, that Ibn 'Arabi himself knew and appreciated the teachings of 'Iraqi's central Persian predecessor, Ahmad Ghazali (d. 520/1126).[12]

Clearly the most significant model for 'Iraqi's presentation of *shahidbazi* can be found in the writings and biography of Ahmad Ghazali, a seminal figure in the Suhrawardi Order to which 'Iraqi belonged.[13] The influence of Ghazali is apparent not only in many of the statements 'Iraqi makes in his writings, especially in the *Lama'at,* but also in his introduction to the *Lama'at,* where he explicitly mentions Ghazali's *Sawanih* as the paradigm for his work: "A few words will be dictated through the spiritual moment's tongue in exposition of the stages of passionate love (*'ishq*), according to the established ways of the *Sawanih,* so that it might serve as a mirror for every lover's beloved."[14]

Fakhr al-Din's statement of intent presents a contrast between the immediate moment (*zaban-i waqt*), those flashes of inspiration that occurred sometime during his association with al-Qunawi, and what he has acquired from the past, his acquaintance with Ahmad Ghazali's teachings and the established ways (*sunan*) put forward in the *Sawanih.* In other words, his treatise is a product of the new and inspired immediate present as well as a tradition that, as a shaykh in his mid- to late fifties, he has mastered.[15] The impetus for 'Iraqi's composition of the *Lama'at* was to share the discoveries and unveilings that had occurred to him through his acquaintance with al-Qunawi and the teachings of Ibn 'Arabi, but it is significant that 'Iraqi chose to do so in imitation of a standard work the text of which (or the author of which) was recognized enough to be designated as having "established ways" (*sunan*). The love-cosmology of Ghazali's treatise, where the divine essence is equated with Love, provided 'Iraqi with the opportunity to express Akbari teachings concerning existence in the language of love and witnessing.[16] Indeed, the "cosmology" of the *Lama'at* seems to be an attempt by 'Iraqi to use Akbari teachings to make explicit what he deems implicit in the work of Ghazali.[17]

Considering the *Lama'at* as a product of the generation of Sufis introduced to Ibn 'Arabi's teachings through al-Qunawi, many of whom commented on and reassessed the poetry of Ibn al-Farid, the sayings of Hallaj and Rabi'ah, or other Sufi maxims and *ahadith,* one can place the *Lama'at* among the body of Akbari works that find more conspicuous cosmological significance in traditional sources valued by Sufis. Still, in terms of imagery and style, the *Lama'at* resembles Ghazali's work far more than it resembles anything written by Ibn 'Arabi or his students. 'Iraqi's ability to create and maintain a style focused on love and in the language of more traditional Persian Sufi treatises, while still containing the core principles of the Akbari school, seems to be the reason for its celebration among Akbari-inclined Sufis who read and commented on it.[18] Yet it is not simply the style and tone of the *Sawanih* that one finds in 'Iraqi's *Lama'at.* Indeed, Ghazali's view of witnessing and love, a view that found execution in Ghazali's practice of *shahidbazi,* is a direct precedent for 'Iraqi's thought, in a manner comparable to the influence Ibn 'Arabi's teachings must have had on 'Iraqi.

Of course, the very thesis of the *Sawanih* is perhaps the singular most important premise of *shahidbazi* as 'Iraqi understands it: namely, that the divine essence is Love, and mirroring this primordial reality, the relationship of lover/beloved in which the Real admires and seeks himself results in and permeates the entire cosmos.[19] This unbounded love celebrated throughout the *Lama'at,* becomes realized in the gaze of the lover upon the *shahid,* and this theme, too, can be found in Ghazali's *Sawanih.* Ghazali emphasizes that love begins with the faculty of vision, and it is only through the act of gazing that the wine of love can intoxicate the heart: "The secrets of love are hidden in the letters of the word *'ishq* [passionate love]. *'Ayn* and *shin* are love [*'ishq*] and *qaf* symbolizes the heart [*qalb*]. When the heart is not in love, it is suspended. When it falls in love, then it finds acquaintance. Love begins with the eye and seeing. This is intimated by the letter *'ayn* at the beginning of the word *'ishq.* Then the lover begins to drink the wine [*sharab*] saturated with longing [*shawq*]. This is intimated by [the letter] *shin*. Then he dies to his self and is born through [the beloved]; [the letter] *qaf* suggests [his] subsistence [*qiyam*] through [the beloved]."[20] Again, one notices that without vision, love cannot be. While clearly this vision does refer to witnessing (*shuhud/mushahadah*) in a spiritual sense, one should remember that witnessing cannot be completely separated from vision experienced within the material realm. In fact, Ghazali's writings indicate that it is from the *physical* eye that love first springs; this, along with the eye's ability to shed tears, cause the physical eye to be the primary inlet and outlet of the heart's experience of love.[21]

Is the object of this vision, the *shahid* that arouses love, necessarily a young man? While mention of Sultan Mahmud and his young male beloved Ayaz does appear twice in the *Sawanih,* there is little in the text to suggest that this is more than a motif that had become standard in Persian love literature.[22] Of course, biographical accounts confirm Ahmad Ghazali's admiration for the beauty of young men. Nevertheless, the very outlook presented in the *Sawanih* also seems to have brought inspiration to Sufis such as 'Iraqi who spoke and wrote about divine love, witnessing, and the human form, an outlook in which Love is the axis of all creation and witnessing or gazing at beauty allows one entry into the presence of Love. There are a number of instances where Ghazali presents themes of love, witnessing, and beauty: "I said: Oh idol, I thought you were my beloved. / Now, as I keep looking, I see that you are none but my soul."[23] When quoted and interpreted by Ghazali, these lines establish a few important points. First, it is significant that the poet seeks his beloved—which in this instance might be the Real—within a beautiful being, the word "idol" (here *sanam*) often serving as a metaphor for a beautiful person in Persian poetry. Second, there is the phrase "keep looking" (*nigah hami kunam*) which suggests prolonged gazing as a natural act in the phenomenon of love. Third and last, there is the confusion between the beautiful beloved and the poet's own soul, a point emphasized later by Ghazali. This alludes to the true unity of lover and beloved, and intimates that the soul exists only to witness and love. Still, the most powerful argument he makes is one that will resonate in the writings of Sufis generations after him, one that we have seen in *al-Futuhat al-Makkiyah* of Ibn 'Arabi and the *Lama'at* of 'Iraqi. It is that God himself is Beautiful and loves his own beauty, and, significantly, it is an argument supported by the prophetic narrations: "Now, know that '*God is beautiful and loves beauty.*' One must either be in love with that beauty or with the lover of that beauty. This is a great secret."[24] Of course, here in the *Sawanih,* as indicated in Ghazali's description of a "secret," the full implications of this hadith are left to the reader. Nevertheless, many of the foundational doctrines of a cosmology of love, an emphasis on witnessing, and an inclination to *shahidbazi* can be found in his treatise.

As is the case with most major figures in Sufism, Ahmad Ghazali's biography serves as a factor of influence comparable to his famous composition. The plenitude of hagiographies within the Sufi tradition indicates that the remembered example of any saint was of no less significance than his written legacy. When discussing Ghazali's influence on Fakhr al-Din, the actual historical time line of Ghazali's life carries less weight than the manner in which Ghazali's life was recorded by Sufis for Sufis. Judging from such hagiographical texts, if Ahmad Ghazali's practice of *shahidbazi* can be seen as a predecessor to 'Iraqi's, it is mainly in two ways.

First, like 'Iraqi, Ghazali displays an almost deliberate obliviousness to the chastisement of others; in fact, often Ghazali's quests for beautiful faces seem to have been calculated attempts to bring reproach upon himself.[25] Second, like 'Iraqi and many medieval Sufis seeking love and witnessing in the human form, Ahmad Ghazali focused his attention on preadolescent males. Ghazali's interest in young men is well documented in Sufi literature, as Nasrollah Pourjavady indicates in a recent study on the subject.[26] Stories of Ghazali requesting a beautiful boy's presence from the pulpit—and in one instance kissing him publicly—can be found in numerous sources, including Shams-i Tabrizi's (d. 645/1247) *Maqalat* as well as the *Talbis Iblis,* a treatise in which 'Abd al-Rahman ibn al-Jawzi (d. 597/1200) criticizes what he deems heterodox in Islam's various denominations and expressions, including Ghazali's companionship with young men.[27]

Unlike Ibn Jawzi's polemical work, Pourjavady's study of Ghazali's encounters with young men tells us much about *shahidbazi* as part of Sufi disagreement and exchange in the seventh/thirteenth century, especially since its focus is on Shams-i Tabrizi's account of Ghazali.[28] Shams, fittingly, presents Ghazali's *shahidbazi* practices as another instance of erratic behavior by a saint whose actions should not be questioned. While Shams does seem to have some hesitations speaking about *shahidbazi,* at other times he eagerly expresses sympathy with Ghazali's admiration of human beauty and seems to admire many of Ghazali's shocking outings with young men as an effective testing of allegiances.[29] Since Shams was known to have tested allegiances himself, it is not unlikely that he sees in Ahmad Ghazali a kindred saint.

One story in Shams al-Din Ahmad-i Aflaki's (fl. 754/1354) *Manaqib al-'Arifin* has Rumi's son Sultan Walad describe Shams-i Tabrizi as being "greatly provocative" and "testing" Mawlana Rumi by requesting a *shahid.* When Rumi brings his own wife, Kira Khatun, Shams clarifies that he seeks "the graces of a delicate beautiful boy [*shahid pisari*] who will serve me."[30] After Rumi presents Shams with his own son, Sultan Walad, Shams also requests wine to be brought. Aflaki, who maintains that Rumi, Shams, and other Mevlevis were opposed to the practice of gazing at young men, comments that this was nothing more than a test of Rumi's patience.[31] Still, it is noteworthy that not only wine—clearly forbidden by Islamic sacred law—but also the company of a young man was considered a request abominable enough to be a worthy assessment of Rumi's confidence. This, along with Shams's need to defend Ghazali, indicates that many saw *shahidbazi* as unacceptable behavior for the pious.

A recurrent theme in Shams's accounts, after all, is the doubt that Ghazali's association with young men arouses in his followers. On one hand, the apprehension they have that his intentions might be ill tells us that the temptations of pederasty were well known and perhaps common. On the other hand, the disgust that his followers display tells us that pederasty was considered Islamically unacceptable. In this regard, associating with beautiful young men is often juxtaposed with other doubtful or even illegitimate activities, such as gambling, chess playing, or loitering in the *hamams*, both in Shams's account of Ghazali and in Aflaki's account of Shams.[32] Concerning such practices, the Sufi writer Fadlallah ibn Muhammad al-Majawi, in a treatise concerning jurisprudential ordinances from the perspective of the Indian Suhrawardi order to which 'Iraqi belonged, mentions "him who plays with backgammon, chess, and beardless boys" as belonging to those who cannot lead the daily prayers.[33] The frequent company of beardless youths was clearly a practice associated with society's scoundrels.

Thus, aside from witnessing divine beauty in a human face, Ghazali's association with boys might have also allowed him the opportunity to battle with the narcissistic human ego within every person, the *nafs* that seeks the praise of others. In other words, his suspicious interactions with young men might have been an act in the spirit of *Qalandari* Sufism; often major figures in Sufism used censurable words or conduct to draw the reproach of others upon themselves for the sake of extirpating arrogance. Of course, one problem with such an interpretation is that Ghazali, in most of the stories Shams narrates, salvages his reputation as a saint through paranormal deeds, in one instance reading his disciple's mind after the Prophet Muhammad has vindicated the saint in a dream, and, in another instance, placing his foot in live embers while he enjoys the company of a young man.[34]

Lastly, and perhaps most interesting of all, one also learns through these accounts of Shams and Ghazali that *shahidbazi* was—for the ranks of the saints—often ultimately tolerated. I have already mentioned Rumi's acquiescence to Shams's request for a young man. Similarly Shams reports that when Ghazali requests from the pulpit for a certain comely young man to be placed before him, otherwise refusing to continue speaking, his wish is promptly fulfilled at the command of the Atabeg (*ra'is*).[35] The sway of sainthood and its ability to normalize otherwise unacceptable behavior must be considered here. It was perhaps this very sway that led to the reception of *shahidbazi* among medieval Sufi figures.

'Ayn al-Qudat al-Hamadhani: Medial Love

While much less is available concerning the practice of gazing at human beauty in the biographies of Ahmad Ghazali's student 'Ayn al-Qudat al-Hamadhani (d. 526/1131), his writings indicate a strong inclination toward love, witnessing, and *shahidbazi*. Aside from these statements in his writings, 'Ayn al-Qudat's close association with his master Ahmad Ghazali signals his sympathies toward the general outlook of the *Sawanih*.[36] The devotion of al-Hamadhani to his master and the consequent influence of Ghazali on al-Hamadhani should not be underestimated. In his *Zubdat al-Haqa'iq* (The Quintessence of Realities), 'Ayn al-Qudat emphasizes the transformative and immediate effect of Ghazali upon him, such that after less than twenty days of serving as Ghazali's disciple a great unveiling occurred for him, freeing him from the hindrance he had faced in his spiritual life.[37] The "master" to whom he refers to in his discussion of *shahidbazi* below is also probably Ghazali, which tells us that *shahidbazi*, like most other practices in the Sufi tradition, is possibly transmitted from teacher to student.

A passage in 'Ayn al-Qudat's *Tamhidat* (Preliminaries) summarizes one of *shahidbazi*'s most basic aims, to allow a taste of real love for the divine (*'ishq-i haqiqi*) through metaphorical love for that which is created (*'ishq-i majazi*): "In the metaphorical *shahid*, which is a beautiful face [*ruy-i niku*], a portion of the *shahidbazi* of reality has been inscribed upon hearts. That reality can become represented [*tamaththul*] in this beautiful form. May my soul be sacrificed for the one who is a worshipper [*parastandah*] of the metaphorical *shahid*, for being a worshipper of one's real *shahid* is rare. Yet do not suppose that I speak of love for the self, which is base desire, rather, I speak of the love of the heart—and this love of the heart is rare. Wait until you reach that station wherein 70,000 forms are presented to you, and you see each one as your own form."[38] While al-Hamadhani's passionate and suggestive style eludes any absolutely explicit mention of the human form, the major themes of *shahidbazi* are apparent. The sentiment that human-to-human love facilitates and allows love for God and enjoyment of God's beauty is implied here as well as elsewhere in al-Hamadhani's writings. Moreover, this passage affirms the possibility of witnessing oneself in the beauty of foreign forms.

Most striking, as seen in another passage in the *Tamhidat*, is the similarity of al-Hamadhani's account of love and witnessing to Ibn 'Arabi's three levels of love outlined previously: "My dear! I do not know if I should speak of the love of the Creator or the love of the created. The varieties of love are three, although each sort of love has its own various grades: minor love [*'ishqi saghir*], major love [*'ishqi kabir*], and medial love [*'ishqi miyanah*]. Minor love is our love for God the Exalted. Major love is God's love for his servants. Medial love—alas! I dare not say it, because of how meager in understanding we have become. Yet, God-willing, a little of it will be said through allusions [*bi-ramz*]."[39]

Although 'Ayn al-Qudat refrains from mentioning this third type of love directly, context and the continuation of his discussion tells us that it is the love of humans for humans; bear in mind that he begins this passage expressing similarity between love "of the Real" and love "of the created," almost conflating the two. Human-to-human love is medial (*miyanah*) not only because it is a lesser realization of God's love for us but also because it—when undertaken with proper gnosis—is superior to minor love, that is, human love for a transcendent God. Medial love supersedes minor love for the very same reason that Ibn 'Arabi emphasizes the combination of natural love and spiritual love over spiritual love alone. By making use of the world of form, the lover can elevate the experience of love beyond that which is purely spiritual (and thus unknowable) and that which is purely material or natural (and thus lacking gnosis) to that which is comprehensive.

There is another implication in these three levels of love that risks perhaps greater condemnation, namely, that medial love is a means for the human realization of minor or even major love. Similar to Ibn 'Arabi's discussion of the lover imitating God's relationship toward his creation, 'Ayn al-Qudat's undisclosed statement might allude to the capacity of human-to-human love to allow love from the lordly perspective, if such a phrase may be used. Thus, just as the Real uses creation as a mirror, a human looks upon another human, seeing in that human either his divine cause or perhaps even, as Ibn 'Arabi claims, his creative effect. The use of natural form to witness the supersensory is a key concept behind the practice of gazing at human beauty, and it is perhaps because of the ignominy surrounding this practice (and surrounding celebrations of love by Sufis more generally) that 'Ayn al-Qudat restrains his pen. One must bear in mind that doctrines and practices of Sufis who emphasized love and witnessing were under suspicion in a climate unsuitable for controversy, as can be seen in 'Ayn al-Qudat's own execution, which, although undertaken probably for political ends, was justified by charges of heresy.[40]

Prudence can perhaps also explain why 'Ayn al-Qudat alludes to the Sufi practice of *nazar* or gazing at beautiful human faces through the citation of prophetic narrations: "Friend! Listen to this report that awakens the elite of the Muslim nation. He has said, '*Beware of gazing at beardless youths, for truly theirs is a color like the color of God.*'[41] And elsewhere he has said, '*I saw my Lord on the Night of Mi'raj in the form of a beardless adolescent with short, curly hair.*'[42] Seek [the explanation of] this too in the World of Representation [*'alam-i tamaththul*]."[43]

These narrations are part of al-Hamadhani's consideration of *tamaththul,* the assumption by spirit of representational forms, which includes as an example the Angel Gabriel's appearance in the representational form of a comely man both for Mary and for the Prophet Muhammad and his companions. The author's mentioning of Gabriel's formal actualization as a comely man, in two separate instances, means that these narrations take place within the context of human and specifically male beauty. By including the first hadith in a discussion of *tamaththul,* al-Hamadhani reads the phrase "color of God" quite literally, even perhaps justifying the practice of gazing at beardless youths for those accomplished enough to be exempt from the Prophet's warning. After all, according to al-Hamadhani, this narration awakens the "elite" (*khawass*) of the Muslim nation (*ummah*). While for the uninitiated it is a warning, for others it is a testimonial of vision and love; the first hadith establishes the Godly quality of young male beauty, and the second hadith would be sufficient evidence for some to consider glancing at a comely youth as part of the prophetic *Sunnah,* although such a reading of the hadith borders on interpretive manipulation. While 'Ayn al-Qudat does not directly advocate gazing at beardless youths, he does rely on an authoritative source to allude to this practice. Of course, the word "authoritative" is not exactly appropriate here, since *ahadith* such as this are conspicuously absent from any of the canonical hadith collections. Rather, these narrations provide an aura of authority and, perhaps more important, indirect statement.

Having established what might loosely be called a "prophetic precedent," al-Hamadhani engages his listener more directly, highlighting the spiritual rank that can be achieved through *shahidbazi:* "Alas! What do you know of what this station can do to someone?! I am a disbeliever if all that has been given to me has not come from this very station. Wait until an atom from this station is shown to you in a representation from the world of form. Then you will understand what this hopeless person is going through! Do you know what this station is? It is *shahidbazi.* What do you hear? Alas, have you never had a *shahid,* and have you never then had your liver torn to shreds because of the love and jealousy for that *shahid?*"[44] While these lines might seem direct, 'Ayn al-Qudat maintains the ambiguity of the term *shahid,* which can refer (simultaneously) to the "evidential locus" within the gnostic's heart or the human form witnessed in the natural world. Such ambiguity is maintained by the lines that follow, lines that concern the oneness of the witness (*shahid*) and the witnessed (*mashhud*) and the realization that "witness" and "witnessed" are roles that are variously assumed by the Real and the gnostic.[45]

Yet his exposition of *tamaththul* becomes even more complicated when al-Hamadhani quotes and expands upon two double lines from "our shaykh," which probably refers to Ahmad Ghazali:

On account of that idol *shahid,* the soul lost its life;
the heart, in seeking union with him, became irremediable.
He, unprovoked, hid himself from us,
Disbelief and Islam became, to us, alike.

> Alas! *"I saw my Lord on the Night of Mi'raj in the most beautiful of forms."*[46] This "most beautiful of forms" is *tamaththul.* If not, then what is it? *"Truly God created Adam and his children upon the form of the All-Merciful"* is another type of *tamaththul.*[47] Oh! The [sway] of his names! One of those names is *musawwir,* which means Form-giving. But I say that he is *musawwar,* that is, Form-displaying. Do you know in which bazaar these forms are displayed and sold? In the bazaar of the elite. Hear it from [the Prophet] Mustafa, blessings be

upon him, when he said, *"In Paradise there is a bazaar in which forms are sold."*[48] This is what is meant by *in the most beautiful of forms.*[49]

It is the juxtaposition of the discussion of the *shahid* and of the divine in human form that indicates al-Hamadhani's true objective. His concern is the divine as *musawwar,* the divine in forms, and although he leaves his audience to make the necessary connections, his emphasis is on the "most beautiful of forms," that which was given to "Adam and his children," namely, the human form. While the phrases above quoted in italics refer to *ahadith,* one should not assume that the proof of witnessing the divine in human form rests on traditions; rather it is that which has been acquired from "the bazaar of the elite," from mystical experience and insight.

'Ayn al-Qudat's use of the term *tamaththul* to describe all varieties of actualization in form means that his discussion is far less detailed than what we saw in Ibn 'Arabi. What al-Hamadhani offers, however, is an intimate view of the bewildering effect of seeing the divine in forms, especially the human form. In this regard, lest one reduce *shahidbazi* simply to gazing at young men, one final passage from al-Hamadhani's *Tamhidat* accentuates the gnostic visual experience behind *shahidbazi,* one tightly intertwined with the eternal and otherworldly beauty of the Prophet Muhammad. After explaining that, according to narrations, the first created thing was the light of Muhammad and that the Real makes himself manifest in forms suitable to the viewer, 'Ayn al-Qudat discloses an important and personal spiritual event: "At this station, I, 'Ayn al-Qudat, saw a light emerge from him. I also saw a light emanate from me. These two lights projected and conjoined, becoming a beautiful form, such that I remained bewildered in this state for some time. This is *In Paradise there is a bazaar in which forms are sold.* The [narration of] *I saw my Lord in the most beautiful of forms* here shows itself. Oh! Listen to these words: the terminus [*intiha*] and convergence [*ittisal*] of all wayfarers is with the light of Mustafa. Do I not know with whom is the terminus and convergence of Mustafa? *He who has seen me has seen the Real* sufficiently illustrates these words."[50]

Here al-Hamadhani alludes to his own spiritual status, having achieved union with the light of the Prophet Muhammad, known as "Mustafa." Moreover, as he intimates, union with the light of the Prophet yields the most direct vision of the Real possible for the wayfarer. One must bear in mind, however, that the author mentions these achievements in the context of representational forms and *shahidbazi,* citing his experience as the ultimate realization of seeing the divine in the "most beautiful of forms" of the prophetic hadith, which, as we know from a differing version, is the form of a young adolescent. The practice of *shahidbazi* and the sublime visual experience 'Ayn al-Qudat outlines are related; the latter is the visionary pinnacle of the first. Obviously *shahidbazi* as al-Hamadhani describes it is neither in any way carnal nor is it distant from the human form.

Ruzbihan al-Baqli: A Defense of *Shahidbazi*

The famous gnostic lover from Shiraz, Ruzbihan ibn Abi Nasr al-Baqli (d. 606/1209), must be mentioned in almost any discussion of *shahidbazi* in the medieval Persian-speaking world, in part because of the explicit reference made in his writings to God's appearance in the human form. In his *Kashf al-Asrar* (The Unveiling of Secrets), an autobiographical account of mystical experiences, Ruzbihan expressly describes seeing God "in the form of Adam" or, on at least two different and perhaps more relevant occasions, seeing God "in the appearance of the Turks" or "in an appearance of beauty like the Turks, with a lute of papyrus wood in his hand, which he seemed to play, provoking me to an increase in desirous love and yearning."[51] In the medieval Persian world, young male Turks were considered paragons of homoerotic beauty; in the latter example, this power to attract is only intensified by the seductive potential of music. While Ruzbihan does not necessarily here describe witnessing the divine through the physical form of a human in the natural world, instead possibly alluding to an imaginal form, the images in his spiritual diary—particularly the last one—affront all oppositions to descriptions of the divine-in-human or to the language of *'ishq*.

It is perhaps because of unguarded statements such as these that Baqli's love for the human form became legendary in Sufi narratives. Indeed, one such narrative mentions alternatively Ahmad Ghazali and Ruzbihan as lovers of the faces of beautiful boys:[52] the *'Ushshaqnamah*, a *ghazal*-embedded *mathnawi* poem about lovers in the *shahidbazi* tradition once attributed to 'Iraqi but recently, through the efforts of Julian Baldick, deemed spurious.[53] Herein the poet assigns to Ruzbihan the very story Shams-i Tabrizi tells of Ghazali; the account describes Ruzbihan as having his foot rubbed by a beardless youth (*amrad*), and, when the suspicious Atabeg witnesses this scene for himself, Ruzbihan places his foot in burning embers replying, "While my eye might be enamored [*hayran*], / my foot is indifferent [*yaksan*] toward the two [*shahid* and fire]."[54] This double attribution might suggest that major Sufi figures known for their allegiance to *shahidbazi* were easily confused with each other, seen as united and almost indistinguishable in their expressions of love for the divine-in-human.[55]

Legend aside, there is much historical evidence that Ruzbihan did indeed enjoy the company of beautiful faces and possibly considered such company an important element in achieving ecstatic witnessing. From among those faces, certainly the beautiful *qawwali* singers that Ruzbihan praises would be male, but unlike Ghazali and 'Iraqi, Ruzbihan's admiration for the human form was not restricted to young men.[56] In at least two accounts, Ruzbihan can be found admiring the beauty of females. Jami narrates the first in his *Nafahat al-Uns*. When a mother advises her daughter to keep her beauty concealed, Ruzbihan interjects that "beauty is never content to be alone, and it desires nothing other than to be close to desirous love;

for truly beauty and love vowed to one another in pre-eternity never to separate."[57] That this statement excited great ecstasy (*wajd*) in Baqli's companions (so much so, Jami comments, that some died) reminds us of the centrality of mystical experience in anecdotes such as this. Such accounts must be considered as products of the powerful relationship of love and beauty between the divine and the gnostic, reified in the realm of human beauty. Another instance of Ruzbihan's captivation with female beauty is perhaps less visual than auditory: Ibn 'Arabi's aforementioned account of Ruzbihan's infatuation with a singing girl.

Most powerful of all, however, are Ruzbihan's own statements concerning the subject of *shahidbazi:* "He made the Adamic race the lamp-niche of his splendor's light, the resplendence of his attributes, and the settling place of the manifestation for the projection of his self-disclosure. Moreover, he bound the hearts of some with others, on account of the dominance of the light of his power and the witnessing of his attributes."[58] In this passage from the introduction to his treatise on beauty, love, and man's relationship with God, *'Abhar al-'Ashiqin* (Jasmine of the Lovers), Ruzbihan clarifies that it is man whom God has chosen above all others as the vehicle for his beauty. Moreover, he describes the love between humans as resulting from witnessing the divine attributes (*mushahadat sifatih*); such a relational link is the fundamental basis for *shahidbazi.* As Ruzbihan continues, the indispensability of *shahidbazi* to the spiritual path becomes increasingly evident. Relying heavily on the work of the Sufi and philosopher Abu al-Hasan al-Daylami, Ruzbihan presents his treatise as a response to a request posed by a female beloved, somewhat similar to Ibn 'Arabi's interlocutions to Nizam in the *Tarjuman al-Ashwaq.*[59] The question she asks—"What does this love [between us] have to do with that love [for God]?"—eventually takes the shape of a request that Ruzbihan should "explain human desirous love [*al-'ishq al-insani*] as part of Godly desirous love [*al-'ishq al-rabbani*], in the Persian language, in a concise book."[60] The female beloved's question points to a contention held by certain theologians and specialists in jurisprudence that the term *'ishq* cannot be applied to man's relationship with God.[61] Unfortunately the defense of *'ishq* for the divine, undertaken by a number of Sufis, including Ruzbihan in his *'Abhar al-'Ashiqin,* is beyond the boundaries of this study.[62] Ruzbihan's closely related defense of *shahidbazi,* however, does deserve mention.

According to Ruzbihan, this witnessing of the divine in human form is both a result and a cause of love for the divine. In other words, an accomplished lover enjoys witnessing divine beauty in human loci, yet one can also become an accomplished lover of God by first witnessing beauty in the human form and experiencing love for such beauty. In fact, to become a lover of God without initially making use of the medium of the *shahid* is a rarity: "The beginning of all lovers proceeds from the path of *shahid*s [*shawahid*], except some of the elite from among the People of Recognizing Oneness, for whom witnessing of the universal occurs in the heart without the witnessing of transient beings. This is among the very rare occurrences from the unseen."[63] The elementary function of the *shahid* in this treatise does separate it somewhat from the tradition of *shahidbazi* as seen elsewhere in the writings of Ahmad Ghazali or 'Iraqi. In the *'Abhar al-'Ashiqin,* Ruzbihan speaks mainly of witnessing the human form and human-to-human love as a precursor to real love for God, not necessarily as an ongoing visionary practice.[64]

Still, mention of appreciation for human beauty by the most accomplished of souls, the Prophet Muhammad, does indicate that this elementary practice need not ever be abrogated by the mystic. One passage, for example, juxtaposes two traditions from the Prophet with two sayings from the great early saint Abu al-Fayd Thawban ibn Ibrahim al-Misri (d. 246/861), known as Dhu al-Nun. This citation of a Sufi forefather might indicate that Ruzbihan aims to convince not only exoteric scholars of the legitimacy of gazing at human beauty but also some from within the Sufi tradition:

> [Another testimony for the legitimacy of chaste love is] his saying, peace be upon him, "*Whosoever has loved desirously, maintained chastity, hidden that love, and died, has died a martyr.*"[65] Also, he has said, peace be upon him, "*Whosoever has within himself love* [*hubbah*] *and predominating longing* [*ghalabah*] *by* [the grace of] *God, for God, and in* [pursuit of the pleasure of] *God loves the face of a beautiful person* [*wajh al-hasan*]."[66] And Dhu al-Nun has said, may God's mercy be upon him, "He who becomes intimate with God [*man ista'nasa billah*], becomes intimate with every beautiful thing and every pretty face." And he has also said, "The one who becomes intimate with God, becomes intimate with every beautiful thing and every goodly form. In such things, there exist secrets for the People of Gnosis [*ahl al-ma'rifah*] the uncovering of which is not befitting except for those suited to it. Hence, whoever divulges [these secrets] to those unsuited has earned thereby punishment and the [divine] tribulations that set an example."[67]

In defending the admiration of beautiful faces, Ruzbihan also relies on the Qur'anic account of the story of Joseph, although his interpretation of key events from chapter 12 of the Qur'an seems to be based almost entirely on intuition. Ruzbihan describes Jacob's love for his son as an *'ishq* resulting from the beauty of "that witness [*shahid*] to the Real," Joseph.[68]

Two potential objections might arise here. First, there is no immediate Qur'anic proof that Jacob's love for his son has anything to do with his beauty. Second, to use the language of *nazar* and *shahidbazi,* describing the love of this father for his son as *'ishq,* while referring to the prophetic figure of Joseph as a *shahid,* might strike more conservative readers as blatantly irreverent. An earlier and subtler version of this defense might be found in Ruzbihan's main model for this treatise, al-Daylami, who also cites Joseph as the most eminent example of beauty, whose beauty "was one of

God's miracles," so much so, in fact, that whenever a woman saw him, "she would cover her face for fear of becoming infatuated with him."[69] The allusion by al-Daylami to chastity here is significant, especially since when Ruzbihan al-Baqli writes on the topic of Joseph's beauty some two centuries later, he considers Zulaykha's infatuation with Joseph to be one of two factors for which God qualifies this story as "the greatest of all stories," the second factor being Jacob's regard for his beautiful son.[70] In other words, the restraint that one encounters in al-Daylami's discussion of human beauty, as opposed to the candor of a later Sufi such as Ruzbihan, might indicate that gnostic lovers in al-Daylami's age were generally more conservative with respect to the issue of divine beauty in the human form.

Unfortunately, the parameters of this study preclude a lengthier consideration of Ruzbihan's treatise on love and human beauty, which is quite simply one of the most complete presentations on this topic among the writings of classical Sufism. More than merely defending *nazar* or *shahidbazi,* Ruzbihan, following the example of al-Daylami, presents an aesthetic system with love and the human form as its foundation. Matters pertaining to ugliness, the beauty of nonhuman objects, and grades of beauty can be found in his *'Abhar al-'Ashiqin.* Such concern with definitions, exceptions, and categories means that the basis of a theory of beauty is present in this work. For example, Ruzbihan provides an extremely detailed analysis of the process of perceiving and coming to love the beautiful.[71] Ruzbihan's expansive consideration of beauty and the human form verifies that mystical experience affects not only the gnostic's perception but also his sensibility—his awareness of the manner in which the Beautiful becomes manifest.

Awhad al-Din al-Kirmani: The *Shahid* of Form and the *Shahid* of Meaning

The name of Awhad al-Din al-Kirmani (d. 635/1238) is one of perhaps three or four that must be mentioned in any discussion of Sufi *shahidbazi* in the medieval Islamic world. Kirmani was well known to have championed this practice. Aside from this, Awhad al-Din, like 'Iraqi, traced his lineage to Ahmad Ghazali through the Suhrawardi line. In his interaction with Akbari mystics, Kirmani also resembled 'Iraqi. Indeed, Kirmani was held in great esteem by Ibn 'Arabi and in perhaps even greater esteem by Sadr al-Din al-Qunawi, both of whom were his contemporaries. Ibn 'Arabi recounts an incident told to him by Kirmani concerning the latter's loyalty to a sick *shaykh* with paranormal abilities in the eighth chapter of *al-Futuhat al-Makkiyah.*[72] As for al-Qunawi, his reverence can be seen in a request from his will that "they should shroud me in the clothes of the Shaykh [Ibn 'Arabi], as well as in the [customary] white winding cloth, and spread out in my grave the prayer-rug of Shaykh Awhad al-Din al-Kirmani."[73]

Not everyone expressed such affection for Kirmani. In fact, disdain for his cavalier practice of *shahidbazi,* which included "tearing the shirts off beardless youths and taking them chest-to-chest" when *sama'* sessions became especially intense, moved some to serious criticism.[74] Shihab al-Din Suhrawardi (d. 632/1234), nephew of Abu al-Najib al-Suhrawardi (d. 563/1168), the eponym of the Suhrawardi Order, accused Kirmani of being an innovator (*mubtadi'*), that is, one who adds illegitimate practices to that which should be limited to the Sunnah.[75] Clarifying that Suhrawardi's objections were to *shahidbazi,* Jami comments that what Shaykh Suhrawardi probably meant by referring to Kirmani as an innovator is "that it is said that in witnessing reality he had recourse to forms as loci of manifestation and witnessed unlimited beauty [*jamal-i mutlaq*] in the forms of bound things [*muqayyadat*]."[76] Yet like 'Iraqi, who sometimes stands outside the boundaries of the more conservative Sufi circle while still maintaining his reverence for it, Awhad al-Din is reported to have replied to Suhrawardi's comment that "it is an honor enough for me that my name was uttered on the shaykh's tongue."[77] Then there is of course the oft-cited meeting between Kirmani and Shams-i Tabrizi: "As has been mentioned, Shams al-Din Tabrizi, may his secret be sanctified, asked him, 'What are you doing?' He said, 'I am gazing at the moon in a basin [of water].' Shams al-Din said, 'If you do not have an abscess on the back of your neck, why don't you simply look at the moon in its sky?'"[78] While this encounter has often been cited as evidence of Shams's opposition to witnessing the divine in human forms, such a conclusion is not supported by the story alone.[79] It does, however, indicate that Kirmani's hallmark in Sufi hagiographies is his practice of witnessing in forms. This infamy surrounding Kirmani's practice of *shahidbazi* can also be seen in the comments of Mawlana Rumi's disciples that Kirmani "is one who plays with *shahid*s [*shahidbaz*] but he is also one who plays fairly [*pakbaz*]."[80] Perhaps Kirmani's composition of a number of *ruba'iyat* defending *shahidbazi* was motivated by their author's notoriety; on the other hand, it is possible that Kirmani's staunch defense of the practice helped publicize his reputation as a *shahidbaz.*

While the collection of Kirmani's poetry is not great—here limited to selections from his *ruba'iyat*—relatively speaking he has much to say about the *shahid.* The *shahid* is an expression of limitless beauty in the confines of form and, in its human manifestation, love for the beauty of the human *shahid* accords with human nature. Love of beauty, argues Kirmani, is undeniably human:

Even if one's lower nature does not become restive because of form,
he whose *heart* does not become disturbed, is not [true to] himself.
I have seen kings and paupers, good and bad.
There is no one who does not delight in beautiful forms.[81]

It is because of the inevitability of loving human beauty that Kirmani confesses to it; it is better to be honest and sincere than a cowardly hypocrite. In a somewhat defiant tone, Awhad al-Din often divulges his love for gazing at *shahid*s:

I am one who enjoys *shahid*s [*shahidbaz*]. Anyone who denies it,
once you look into the matter, does this very act night and day.
Those whom you see, they all enjoy *shahid*s [*hamah shahidbaz and*].
They simply have no gall—that's why they deny.[82]

Those who enjoy gazing at the *shahid* should not be condemned. Only those who do so with sexually desirous intent behave in a blameworthy manner. Kirmani expresses this point in a *ruba'i* that parallels a *ruba'i* of 'Iraqi we have seen:[83]

Whenever a glance occurs because of your passion,
your actions too will doubtless be out of place.
If you restrain yourself from that lust you have,
a *shahid* will fall at your feet, wherever he might be.[84]

It is not clear, in this case, who influenced whom, but the parallel between the *ruba'i* of Kirmani and that of 'Iraqi again illustrates that the topic of *shahidbazi* was debated and defended within Sufi circles—where ideas were shared and borrowed.

Yet the practice of *shahidbazi* is not simply a matter to be defended; it is an important spiritual practice as well. Indeed, gazing at human beauty is the highest form of witnessing and thus the most direct manner in which to advance in terms of love for God:

The soul is a pure child and a *shahid* is its wet-nurse;
shahidbazi is continuously its means for growth.
This beautiful [external] form that you see
is not that *shahid*, but is rather a shadow of it.[85]

If Kirmani's stance seems obstinate, it is, he claims, because nothing else opens the eyes like the *shahid*. The self-disclosures witnessed through the *shahid* inspire unwavering resolve in the *shahidbaz*, the one who enjoys the *shahid*:

My heart will not retreat even a speck from the *shahid*.
My eye is not opened by anything but the *shahid*.
Busy yourself with yourself! What do you want with us?
I am—even if you are not—an enjoyer of the *shahid* [*shahidbaz*].[86]

Moreover, *shahidbazi* itself is a matter that demands of the practitioner purity of heart and sincerity; the lover shuns the estimation of others and devotes himself fully to the cause of love and witnessing. Conversely, in a manner similar to 'Iraqi, Kirmani depicts asceticism as subject to hypocrisy:

If you have an aspiration for that which you love passionately,
throw your head at the feet of those with green fuzz on their face [*sabz khattan*].

Nothing will be gained from hypocrisy and the monastery—
[oh] people of purity, the call of *shahidbazi*![87]

Yet the most significant distinction Kirmani makes in his poetry is between the *shahid* of form (the object of beauty at which one gazes) and the *shahid* of meaning (the beautiful divine self-disclosure that takes form as its medium). The form of the *shahid* is necessary because "meaning cannot be seen except in form."[88] The *shahid* of form allows for the *shahid* of meaning; the latter is the objective, while the first is but a means to it:

I am a slave, and the *shahid* is what's worshipped by my heart,
thus seeing the *shahid* is what's praised by my heart.
I do not give my heart to the *shahid* of form because
that primary *shahid* is what's sought by my heart.[89]

Kirmani warns the *shahidbaz* that "it is not good, if you do not see the *shahid* in the *shahid*," that is, the *shahid* of meaning in the *shahid* of form.[90] In fact, the *shahid* of form can be troublesome for the lover. Perhaps the trouble to which Kirmani alludes is the struggle to refrain from loving the medium itself—or perhaps the image of a coy and tormenting *shahid* is a poetic necessity, inseparable from the tradition of love poetry Kirmani has inherited:

That comely boy, even if he is a *shahid* and a flirt,
is a *shahid* only of form, while meaning is something else.
Seek meaning, if you know anything about the *shahid*,
for this *shahid* of form is nothing but a headache.[91]

Because the gnostic must use his human faculties to experience spiritual realities, he is compelled to pursue beauty in the *shahid* of form; otherwise, the *shahid* of form is not at all the true *shahid* sought by the mystic. In fact, the *shahid* of form is only called a *shahid* "because of the moment's [ecstatic] tongue [*zaban-i hal*]," a result of the confusion between form and meaning experienced by the mystic.[92] Two levels of perception take place simultaneously: the eye, according to Kirmani, sees form, but the heart sees meaning.[93] The complexity of this experience, while described candidly in the *ruba'iyat* of Kirmani, becomes the impetus for the more ambiguous image of a human-godly beloved found in 'Iraqi's *ghazals*. Of course, the genre of the erotic *ghazal* lyric demands far more subtlety than the epigrammatic *ruba'i,* a genre which Kirmani has favored. It is important to note, however, that a perceptive experience common to mystics who practiced *shahidbazi* found varied expression in their writings according to genre—whether theoretical prose, esoteric erotic poetry, or the witty and brief *ruba'i.* The individual spiritual inclination (*mashrab*) of each mystic apparently prompted the genre most often chosen to relay this shared experience.

Sadr al-Din al-Qunawi and the Poetry of Ibn al-Farid al-Misri

Here mention should also be made of Kirmani's famous associate, Sadr al-Din al-Qunawi, who while well known for his devotion to and admiration of Ibn 'Arabi, in fact recognized a pronounced albeit secondary admiration of Kirmani. While it might seem strange to mention Sadr al-Din al-Qunawi, known for his philosophically orientated writings, in a discussion of *shahidbazi,* such should not be the case. His devotion to Kirmani, his approval of 'Iraqi's *Lama'at,* and writings attributed to him indicate that, at the very least, Qunawi considered the witnessing of divine manifestation in forms to be legitimate and of spiritual benefit.[94] Whether Qunawi was a practitioner of *shahidbazi* cannot be said, but he certainly sympathized with its principles.

Such an emphasis on love and witnessing can be seen in a work attributed to Qunawi, *Tabsirat al-Mubtadi wa Tadhkirat al-Muntahi* (The Novice's Enlightenment and the Expert's Reminder). The treatise's author quotes at least one *ruba'i* by Kirmani and another that resembles closely a *ruba'i* by Kirmani and, more significantly, encapsulates Kirmani's thought:

When my head's eye looked into that meaning,
I saw form, but the soul saw meaning.
I gaze at form with the eye of my head because
Meaning cannot be seen except in form.[95]

The poem emphasizes gazing at form, doing so with the physical "head's eye" (*chishm-i sar*), and seeing meaning *only* through form; these are the foundational premises of *shahidbazi.*[96] As Chittick has mentioned, this treatise probably does not belong to Qunawi, written perhaps instead by a student—or even rival—of his, Nasir al-Din Juwayni (or Khu'i).[97] Nevertheless, the fact that 'Aziz al-Din Nasafi (d. before 700/1300), a disciple of a friend of Qunawi, *believed* Qunawi to be the author suggests that Qunawi's reputation included an emphasis on passionate love and witnessing in forms, a point further verified by Qunawi's known proximity to Kirmani.[98]

Also illustrating Qunawi's inclination toward the school of love and witnessing is his fascination with the poetry of 'Umar ibn 'Ali ibn al-Farid, the master of the Arabic Sufi erotic lyric. Intense interest in Ibn al-Farid's poetry seems to have begun with al-Qunawi, crystallized with his students, and spread to later generations of Akbaris.[99] In fact, grouping al-Qunawi and Ibn al-Farid together in the subtitle above can be justified in that it is not unlikely that 'Iraqi's exposure to Ibn al-Farid was the outcome of his association with al-Qunawi. As the commentaries written by his students indicate, al-Qunawi encouraged the careful reading of Ibn al-Farid's poetry in a manner similar to his emphasis on teaching Ibn 'Arabi's *Tarjuman al-Ashwaq.*

Motivated by the request of his teacher al-Qunawi, Sa'id al-Din al-Farghani (d. 699/1300) wrote two commentaries, first in Persian then in Arabic, on the famous poem (*qasidah*) of 'Umar ibn al-Farid known as both *Nazm al-Suluk* (The Order of the Way) and *al-Ta'iyah al-Kubra* (The Greater Poem Rhyming in "T"). In fact, al-Farghani acknowledges that it was Qunawi who "lifted the enigmatic lock from the fortified citadel that is this poem" and enlightened the author on the meaning of each particular hemistich, which signals a series of regular lessons.[100] In his introduction affixed to Farghani's commentary on Ibn al-Farid's poem, al-Qunawi himself seems unable to contain his admiration for Ibn al-Farid, "one of the great men of the People of the Real," who "collected and versified the comprehensive sciences and lordly realities . . . in such a splendid, forceful, eloquent and articulate manner as was not feasible for anyone before him," which apparently includes Ibn 'Arabi.[101]

As al-Qunawi mentions in this short passage, he regrets that in his visit to Egypt in the year 630 Hijri, he was not able to meet with the then-living Ibn al-Farid. Qunawi explains that later, in the year 643 Hijri, after returning to Egypt from Syria, he began to meet with a group composed of "men of learned excellence, great ones from the People of Tasting, and reputable persons," to analyze the poem and comb through its difficulties, a gathering that shifted locations from Egypt (Cairo), to Syria (Damascus), and to Anatolia (Konya). Only one figure from this gathering, al-Farghani, was able to penetrate the poem after a long while "with an enlightened understanding and a purified mind," later bringing the commentary to Qunawi for his approval.[102] The enthusiasm Qunawi expresses for Ibn al-Farid's poem and his student's accomplished commentary on it seem to have spread. Like al-Farghani, Qunawi's student 'Afif al-Din al-Tilimsani (d. 690/1291) wrote a commentary on Ibn al-Farid's *Nazm al-Suluk*. 'Abd al-Razzaq al-Qashani (d. 736/1335), a pupil of Qunawi's pupil Mu'ayyid al-Din Jandi (d. ca. 700/1300), also wrote a commentary on this poem, as did Qashani's pupil Sharaf al-Din Dawud al-Qaysari (d. 751/1350).

Most relevant to this discussion, the manner in which Farghani interprets Ibn al-Farid's poem in the commentator's *Mashariq al-Darari* (Rising Places of the Luminous Bodies) affirms the principles of *shahidbazi*. Thus Farghani's discussion hints at gazing upon the human form when he translates Ibn Farid's "do not profess absolute beauty to be bound" as a warning that absolute, real beauty, which is the Presence of the Beloved, merits the lover's attention, so "do not focus your attention on external love-play and external *shahidbazi*."[103] *Shahidbazi* here might not refer to human forms (and certainly is not limited to them), since all that which is seen in the natural and imaginal worlds, aside from human beings, corresponds to form and can serve as a testimony or *shahid* to beauty. Still, Farghani's emphasis on the possibility of becoming attached to "*shahid*s of form" (*shahidan-i surati*) and external *shahidbazi*, when seen in light of similar pronouncements by Kirmani and 'Iraqi, might allude to a communal context that sometimes verged on such dangers.

Indeed, elsewhere, Farghani explicitly translates al-Farid's pronouncement that the beloved appears to her lovers in every "place of manifestation" (*fi kull mazhar*) as "in every *human* form and place of manifestation."[104]

Like other associates and disciples of al-Qunawi, 'Iraqi shows a fondness for the poetry of Ibn al-Farid, quoting him in the *Lama'at,* the most pertinent occasion of which is a reference in the *Nazm al-Suluk* to human beauty as a stratum of infinite divine beauty. Here Ibn al-Farid gives absolute beauty, undoubtedly divine, a feminine dimension: "Every comely man's beauty from Her pulchritude is / borrowed, in fact, the beauty of every comely woman too."[105] While this is all that 'Iraqi quotes, he almost definitely intended to capture some of the force of Ibn al-Farid's continuing lines:

By means of [Her pulchritude], Qays became frantic for Lubna. Yes, each lover
['*ashiq*] does,
such as Majnun for Layla, or Kuthayyir for 'Azzah.
Each of them longed ardently for the characteristic of Her wearing
the form of a sort of beauty, appearing brightly in the beauty of a form.

Reference to witnessing the divine in beautiful forms and the divine quality of human-to-human love can be found throughout this *qasidah,* one that excels in maintaining a sense of ambiguity in its description of a female human-godly beloved. The similarities between this poem of Ibn al-Farid and Ibn 'Arabi's teachings concerning human beauty are striking: the human beloved loved only for its human beauty as a case of mistaken identity,[106] envisioning the divine in forms through the faculty of imagination (*takhayyul*),[107] and Gabriel's appearance in the guise of Dihyah as an instance of spirit in human form.[108] The similarities here point not to transmitted teachings but to a shared affinity for witnessing the divine in human form and experiencing profound love through that perceptive experience.

The Shaykh of San'an and the 'Iraqi Biography

Considering the glossary and *mathnawi* poem improbably attributed to 'Iraqi, both of which concern the three central themes of this book (beauty, love, and the human form), and considering depictions of the saint such as that in the *Majalis al-'Ushshaq* of Kamal al-Din Husayn ibn Isma'il Gazurgahi (fl. ninth/fifteenth century), clearly Fakhr al-Din 'Iraqi stood out in the collective memory of Sufis and their admirers as a sagacious man of God, a poet, and a lover of the *shahid*—what we might call a Sufi aesthete. Indeed this term, "aesthete," to a certain extent suits the remembered personalities of other Sufi saints near 'Iraqi's time, those scornful of the hypocrisy of others, absorbed in the divine qualities they encounter in the physical world around them, and able to enjoy life's pleasures—beautiful faces, sounds, and words—with complete indifference to them. I have already discussed the theoretical dimensions of the *shahid* and appreciation for the *shahid* in 'Iraqi's writings. Equally important to the tradition of love and witnessing, however, is the Qalandar-aesthete portrayal of 'Iraqi's life in Sufi writings, a portrayal that has become inseparable from his poetry. Hence, let us explore 'Iraqi's own contributions to the *shahidbazi* tradition not so much as an entirely historical figure but as the embodiment of an ongoing hagiographical legacy.

While the hagiographical sources available do not provide a reliable biography of Fakhr al-Din 'Iraqi, at least in terms of detail, they do illustrate the significance of the *legend* of 'Iraqi in the medieval Sufi world. The anonymous biography affixed to 'Iraqi's *diwan* was composed less than a century after the poet's own death, most likely by someone who considered himself the spiritual descendent of Shaykh Fakhr al-Din, considering the biographer's mention of chains of oral narration (*tawatur*) and his description of 'Iraqi as the Shaykh of Shaykhs of this Order (*shaykh al-shuyukh al-tariqah* [*sic*]).[110] This account becomes the basis for other hagiographical narratives, for example, that of Jami in his *Nafahat al-Uns,* or—one that places 'Iraqi's biography emphatically in the *shahidbazi* tradition—the *Majalis al-'Ushshaq* of Gazurgahi.[111] The significance of 'Iraqi's biography lies in a narrative pattern found in it, one that embodies the transition of metaphorical love (for a human being) to real love (for the divine), a pattern seen repeatedly in the literature of this age. Remember that the creed of *shahidbazi* rests on a privileged esoteric appreciation of natural human beauty, the result of a saintly return to the love of humans known externally by all. In other words, the pattern found in 'Iraqi's biography supports a central *shahidbazi* principle: "Metaphor is the bridge of reality [*al-majaz qantarat al-haqiqah*]."[112]

By observing the pseudo-hagiographical narrative of the Shaykh of San'an as related by 'Attar in his *Mantiq al-Tayr* (Language of the Birds), one can discern a pattern similar to the biography of 'Iraqi.[113] Put simply, the Shaykh of San'an is a man of unsurpassed piety, with a following of four hundred disciples. He has a dream that takes him to Byzantium. Upon seeing a beautiful Christian girl there, the Shaykh falls deeply in love, so much so, that he renounces his life of piety and camps out in the alleyway before her abode. After he beseeches her to respond positively to his love, she sets four conditions before him: In order for her to become his, the Shaykh must burn the Qur'an, drink wine, declare his infidelity to Islam, and prostrate himself before an idol. While somewhat reluctant at first, eventually the Shaykh acquiesces to each of these demands. When the Christian girls sets one more condition, that he tend her pigs for one year, the Shaykh of San'an consents to that as well. It is here in his abased and wretched state that the Shaykh's disciples find him once again. While at first they decide that he cannot be helped, the promptings of one particularly devoted friend eventually bring them to join together in a forty-day-and-night vigil for the Shaykh's recovery. Through their efforts, especially those of the devoted friend, a dream of the Prophet Muhammad gives news of his intervention and the Shaykh's consequent return to piety. The Shaykh is reunited with his students. His Christian beloved repents, becomes Muslim at the Shaykh's hands, and dies. While one might be tempted to call the Shaykh's repentance a "reversion," 'Attar makes it clear throughout that the Shaykh's fall was a means for the purification of his soul. His obsession with the Christian girl was an opportunity to relinquish everything—even Islam—for the sake of love, and a divinely decreed apparatus allowing the acquisition of sincerity and the absolute repudiation of ostentation, hypocrisy, and arrogance.

'Attar tells the story of the Shaykh of San'an as if he and his audience are to consider it historically true, beginning it in the hagiographical style: "The Shaykh of San'an was the spiritual authority (*pir*) of his age."[114] As noted by Hellmut Ritter, a number of biographical tales assume this motif.[115] In the *Mustatraf fi Kull Fann Mustazraf* of Baha' al-Din Muhammad ibn Ahmad al-Ibshihi (d. ca. 850/1446), the fallen shaykh is named Abu 'Abdallah al-Andalusi and the devoted disciple who saves him is al-Shibli. Ritter recounts six stories in all that "attest to this abandoning of the faith for the sake of love."[116] Interest in stories resembling that of San'an suggests that many Sufi practitioners were on the lookout for living hagiographical examples of the conversion of metaphorical love (*'ishq-i majazi*) to real love (*'ishq-i haqiqi*). Traces of this story are apparent in Ibn 'Arabi's account of Ruzbihan Baqli's love for a singing girl, a love that brings Baqli to throw off his cloak and become her servant, as described previously. Most significant, the biography of 'Iraqi also follows this pattern and, as such, becomes an all-inclusive commentary on his *diwan*.

The pattern here described can be summarized as three stages: readiness, immolation through natural or "profane" love, and achieving gnosis through repentance. In order for a moral misjudgment to be considered a fall, a figure must begin from a place of considerable personal piety. In other words, just as a depraved person does not *succumb* to profane love, when a devout person does, it is a story worth telling. Moreover, there must be a preexistent stimulus that occasions the event. The dream that the Shaykh of San'an sees in which he worships an idol (*buti*) in Byzantium becomes his impetus for leaving.[117] Since, as an accomplished shaykh, he would be able to discern a true dream from a Satanic insinuation, one must interpret the dream as a divine prompting that will allow the shaykh to abandon all for the sake of love, thus purifying himself of attachment to reputation and rank. Just as the Shaykh of San'an is a man of religious practice and knowledge (*ham 'amal ham 'ilm*), the biography of 'Iraqi emphasizes Fakhr al-Din's learning and devoutness before gazing at the beautiful Qalandar boy.[118] The narrator tells us, for example, that 'Iraqi came from a family of scholars and learned men, an observation verified by 'Iraqi's letters to his brother; that 'Ali ibn Abi Talib, the second patriarch of the Sufi tradition, foretells his impending greatness; and that at the age of five he memorized the entire Qur'an in nine months and acquired all religious sciences by the age of seventeen.[119] Such devotion to Islam and the religious sciences adds the element of irony to 'Iraqi's moral capitulation.

'Iraqi's readiness to succumb to profane love can also be seen in his inclination to matters of beauty even as a child, which includes his ability to recite the Qur'an in a manner so stirring that "anyone who heard the modulations of his voice became restless," a voice that caused his amazed neighbors to sit up all night waiting for him to begin his assigned Qur'anic recitation practices and caused non-Muslims to embrace Islam.[120] A more significant inclination to beauty and love can be seen in 'Iraqi's boundless affection for his fellow schoolmates, from whom "he could not spend one moment away"—young boys being, of course, standards of human beauty in the medieval Persian world. The anonymous biographer's description of Fakhr al-Din as a sort of aesthete explains 'Iraqi's susceptibility to the beauty of the Qalandar boy, one that is inaugurated by his hearing the intoxicating musical poetry recital of a traveling group of Qalandars.

In the second stage of the story, again like the Shaykh of San'an, 'Iraqi abandons learning and piety for the sake of a beloved, here a young Qalandar boy. While the Shaykh of San'an is somewhat compelled to convert to Christianity for his beloved, 'Iraqi undertakes his conversion to this antinomian sect wholeheartedly, perhaps because in this case the disbelief in question is less egregious, or—more likely—because the mission of the Qalandars coincides so readily with 'Iraqi's newly acquired inclination to heedlessness. Nonetheless, the theme of "disavowal of reputation" is maintained here by giving allegiance to a group whose identifying communal trait is the disavowal of reputation. In the passage describing 'Iraqi's surrender, beauty leads to love, which, in turn, leads to abandoning oneself:

> He glanced at the Qalandars, seeing in their midst a boy whose beauty was without peer, a boy most charming to the hearts of lovers. The beauty of this boy was such that, were a Chinese figure-painter to see a tress of his hair, he would be confounded. For a second time, the falcon glanced, and the bird that was his heart fell into the snare of passionate love. The fire of passion incinerated the harvest of his intellect. He slipped his arm under his frock and removed it from his body. He took the turban off his head and gave it to those Qalandars. He then began to recite this *ghazal:* "How good it would be for you to be my heart-possessor, / my drinking-companion, my intimate, and my beloved! / The whole world could not contain me in such cheerfulness, / if, for one instant, you'd be the solace for my every sadness!"
>
> After some time, the Qalandars left from Hamadan for Isfahan. Once they had gone, yearning overpowered him. The Shaykh's state changed drastically. He cast aside his books. . . . The tongue of traditional learning [*zaban-i qal*] became the tongue of the present moment [*lisan-i hal*]. One who once

possessed intellectual arts went mad [*majnun*]. . . . Having travelled for two miles, he caught up to them, and recited this *ghazal:* "Boy! Play in the Qalandar style [*rah-i qalandar bizan*] if you are our match, / because the street of devoutness appears long and distant to me!"

Once they saw him, the Qalandars celebrated much. Immediately they sat him down and shaved off his eyebrows, making him of the same "color" as [*hamrang*] themselves. In the companionship of these vagabond Qalandars, Shaykh Fakhr al-Din treaded *'Iraq-i 'Ajam* [Western Iran].[121]

The passage above highlights an important change: transcending traditional learning for the sake of direct experience. This is not an uncommon theme in medieval Sufi texts; knowledge acquired through books, especially in its capacity to instill arrogance in its possessor, becomes a barrier, hindering a person from direct experience. Only falling in love can obliterate this barrier, because it demands of those it afflicts the abandonment of everything, including one's faith and one's reputation. The lover's loss of self results in another important theme: his taking on the same "color" as the beloved, whether such should demand becoming Christian, a Qalandar, or—in one account from the *Mantiq al-Tayr*—a dog keeper.[122] In all these instances, as well as in the love cosmologies of Ghazali and 'Iraqi, in order to take on the beloved's color, the lover must first lose his own. In terms of gnostic love, the lover's loss of his own color or his own will, such that, in the words of 'Iraqi, "he loves whatever the friend loves," leads to the identity confusion that allows for the Real to become the lover's hearing and sight.[123] Lastly, this immolation of the self in love turns the lover into a poet, a theme found in the oft-cited story of Layla and Majnun and one also intimated by the narrator of 'Iraqi's biography. The passage quoted above is the first passage in which the narrator ascribes the recitation of poetry to 'Iraqi, so that, once 'Iraqi becomes a lover, he also becomes a poet. Of course, one cannot rely on the attribution of 'Iraqi's poetry to specific instances in his life by the narrator, but the connection of love to poetry in the narrator's rendition is striking.

Quite often the last stage of the story, that of repentance, involves the intercession of others. In the case of Ruzbihan's infatuation with the singing girl, a story that only imperfectly follows this pattern, his friends inform the singing girl that Baqli—who has become her enamored servant—is in fact "one of the great ones of the People of God," which prompts her to repent from her occupation as a singer. Yet Ibn 'Arabi attributes to God the actual removal of attachment to her from Ruzbihan's heart. In the case of the Shaykh of San'an and 'Iraqi, a spiritual authority brings the lover to proceed beyond metaphorical love for love of the Real. As mentioned, the Prophet Muhammad intervenes on behalf of the Shaykh of San'an, removing the black "dust from his path."[124]

The powerful spiritual figure in 'Iraqi's case is the Suhrawardi master Baha' al-Din Zakariya (d. 661/1262). When 'Iraqi and his Qalandar cohorts visit him at his *khanaqah* in Multan, Zakariya notices that 'Iraqi differs from the Qalandars in his possessing "complete readiness" (*isti'dad-i tamm*) for the path of self-perfection.[125] 'Iraqi too notices an overpowering attraction to the shaykh, so much so that he warns his companions that, if they do not leave together, the shaykh will ensnare him "like a magnet attracts iron."[126] In his attempt to flee, however, 'Iraqi is foiled by an auspicious windstorm. He repents, returns to the shaykh, and undergoes the discipline of the path, particularly the period of isolation or *khalwat*. It is here that 'Iraqi's capabilities as a selfless lover cause him to excel. 'Iraqi reaches a state of *wajd* (ecstasy) in only ten days and recites a poem on the eleventh day about wine and beauty. The narrator mentions that Zakariya normally discouraged the recitation of poetry, in keeping with Shaykh Shihab al-Din Suhrawardi's customary way of reciting only Qur'an or prophetic traditions in isolation. Yet the poetry 'Iraqi recites while in this retreat again shows his particular spiritual aptitude as a gnostic lover, which is verified by Shaykh Baha' al-Din Zakariya who comments to 'Iraqi's jealous peers that the recitation of poetry "is forbidden for you, but not for him."[127] 'Iraqi's sincerity and capability for inner excellence, which to some extent seem to result from the purification he has undergone as a lover, bring the shaykh to arrange for his own daughter to marry 'Iraqi and for 'Iraqi to become his main successor or *khalifah* (a point rightly contended by Baldick).[128] The conspiracies of 'Iraqi's jealous peers eventually bring him to flee, and the next stage of 'Iraqi's life begins.[129]

While the above account is unreliable and explicitly wrong in certain aspects of 'Iraqi's life, the general outline is supported by a letter 'Iraqi writes to his elder brother Qadi Ahmad, complaining of their separation:

> This stranger, once he left Baghdad, after encountering great adversity, committed himself to the service of that esteemed uncle Sharaf al-Din 'Abd al-Salam, may God designate him with peace. Having discovered that he [Sharaf al-Din] was busy with his post and rank, absorbed in learning and teaching—while the heart of this broken man had tasted a little of the flavor of the water of freedom [*hurriyat*] and had discovered the delight of leisure [*faraghat*]—he did not want [to cause] a disturbance. He stayed there for no more than around 20 days. He decided to go to Sham. From there, he came toward 'Iraq [Western Iran], concerning which: "In the curve of the polo-stick, like a ball, / I was being struck, wandering hither and thither."
>
> Neither did he have a firm footing in religion, nor did his pen cross out this world. He had neither knowledge conjoined to good deeds, nor a good deed kneaded by sincerity. I had remained irresolute for one or two years, at the apex of insensibility and misfortune, in the desert of inability, failure and disappointment, until the Pre-eternal Succor took the hand of this fallen person and showed this lost one the path to his Governing Excellency, the Lordly Shaykh, the Splendor of the Real and the Religion [*Baha' al-haqq wa-l-din*]

> Zakariya, may God sanctify his powerful spirit. I spent 17 years attending him: "What happened is among the things I will not mention; / So assume the best and don't ask for information."[130]

'Iraqi then continues, revealing that he had planned to visit his father until he learned of his death. This passage alludes to a period of moral obliviousness, followed by the intervention of Shaykh Baha' al-Din Zakariya. While the narrator is certainly mistaken concerning 'Iraqi's 25 years of discipleship (it is 17), 'Iraqi's love for a young man and his wanderings with the Qalandars are neither negated nor affirmed. Certainly the Qalandar spirit of uninhibited wandering and freedom is present.

Two important points must be made here. First, although 'Iraqi's legendary love for a young man serves as an instrument for his recruitment to the path of self-perfection, 'Iraqi continues to observe the practice of gazing at beardless youths seemingly throughout his life. In other words, *shahidbazi* is reported to have begun as a profane practice emerging from metaphorical love but persists as a spiritual practice emerging from love of the Real. The evidence for 'Iraqi's postrepentance *shahidbazi* inclination found in various hagiographical sources coincides with that found in his poetry. There is, for example, the accusation made by 'Iraqi's colleagues in the Indian Suhrawardi Order that 'Iraqi's "time is absorbed in poetry, and his isolation is with beardless youths," an accusation never contested by the narrator.[131] There is also his playing with young boys in Tokat and his request to the Parwanah, Amir Mu'in al-Din Sulayman (r. 654/1256–676/1277), who fails to impress 'Iraqi with gold, to bring him instead a certain *qawwali* singer named Hasan, whose "beauty was peerless" and who had a following of nearly ten thousand men in love with him.[132] In addition, there is his payment of a salary of eight dirhams a day to a shoemaker so that the shoemaker's son is not compelled to put leather to his beautiful lips, as was required for fashioning shoes. Instead, 'Iraqi and his companions visit the boy every day, gaze at him, recite poetry, and weep.[133] In the continuing appreciation of young male beauty even after he has repented and converted to the spiritual path, 'Iraqi to some extent represents the Sufi *shahidbazi* tradition itself. 'Iraqi's love for a young boy becomes a gnostic love for the beautiful reality within the human form. Similarly the School of Passionate Love had found in pederasty—a sexual and illicit practice—a licit practice devoid of sexual longing, namely, *shahidbazi.* Moreover, it seems that 'Iraqi inherited from the *shahidbazi* tradition precisely the most pivotal thing that he bequeathed to it: a saintly precedent.

A second observation that can be made about 'Iraqi's biography concerns the soul. The process of having unique potential, succumbing to sin, and repenting from that sin to achieve great spiritual heights epitomizes the story of the soul so celebrated in the Sufi tradition. The pattern of descent and ascent (*nuzul wa su'ud*) describes the journey whereby the soul, whose origin is divine, descends to the earthly sphere, undergoes tests and hardships, and emerges with a knowledge of itself and its Lord far greater than it had in its original, innocent state.[134] Just as metaphorical love allows the lover to become enamored with the Real, so too is the entire worldly plane metaphorical, an instrument by which the soul comes to know reality. Of course, this theme of the soul's necessary abasement and edifying rise transcends the story of the fallen lover. It is of the utmost importance to the Islamic spiritual path in general and leaves its trace in numerous manuals of wayfaring and Sufi biographies, including that of Ibn 'Arabi.[135] This theme can even be discerned in the Qur'an itself, according to some interpretations.[136]

The Qalandar as Sincere Lover

It is interesting to note that when contemporary scholar Muhammad Akhtar Chimah describes those Sufis who deem passionate love as being the best means to self-purification, his emphasis is on love's ability to obliterate "self-worship" (*khud-parasti*) because love "sets aflame the very foundations" of self-worship, and the love of forms—a bridge to the love of the Real—absorbs the lover to the point that he forgets himself.[137] Another method to do away with love of self is, of course, to do away with the self's most evident proof of its own excellence: the approbation of others. This is the call of the Qalandar in medieval Sufi literature, a call which rendered the Qalandar an essential metaphorical figure in the School of Passionate Love. The Qalandariyah, a marginal and antinomian manifestation of Sufism which had at one time been more of an undefined movement based on the Malamatiyah, would also became a literary image found in the poetry of Hakim Majdud ibn Adam Sana'i (d. 525/1131), 'Attar, and many who followed them.[138] The Malamatiyah, a movement within the world of Islamic mysticism that began probably in the third/ninth century in the region of Khurasan, advocated abstemious resistance to the sin of ostentation (*riya'*).[139] The Qalandar takes the disavowal of public approval found in the Malamatiyah movement a step further, by challenging social norms and sometimes even Islamic law, actively bringing blame upon himself, whether through shaving all the hair on the head and face, wandering in a vagabond manner dressed in animal skins or sometimes virtually nude, engaging in song and dance, ignoring the daily prayers, and in extreme instances, making use of intoxicants, gambling, and practicing pederasty, among other examples.[140] Thus while Shaykh Shihab al-Din Suhrawardi says of the Malamati that he "strives to conceal acts of worship," he remarks that Qalandars "devastate customs."[141] Moreover, the Qalandar as a poetic theme in medieval Persian literature captures, perhaps more than any other, the religious sentiment of the time. In a setting where piety resulted in not just the respect but also the devotion of others, the temptations of insincerity and ostentation were considered powerful. Sincerity, which is supposedly the Qalandar's primary religious concern, was thus highly valued, especially so among those who advocated that a true lover should sacrifice his identity for the beloved and be heedless of the approval of others. How fitting that the beloved of *shahidbazi* assumed the legally unsanctioned and socially mistrusted form of a beardless youth, thus further verifying the sincerity of such lovers.

As J. T. P. De Bruijn has pointed out, Sufi saints such as Ahmad Ghazali and Ruzbihan Baqli employed images of the Qalandar and places of ill repute associated with the Qalandar (specifically the "ruins," or *kharabat*) in a positive manner, to portray the abject lover.[142] Thus a key contribution 'Iraqi's legacy makes to the *shahidbazi* tradition is the bolstering of this very relationship between love for the Real and the Qalandari spirit of spurning reputation. This occurs first and foremost in 'Iraqi's poetry, which often presents as its persona a dissolute lover, using images associated with the Qalandars, such as wine and gambling.[143] 'Iraqi's arguably most famous *ghazal* describes this persona as a lover so wretched that he belongs not in the sanctuary of the Ka'bah but in the convent (*dayr*), a place medieval Sufi poets often associated not just with disbelief but also with imbibing wine:

Boy! Give me Magian wine, if you are our match,
for ours no longer is the desire for asceticism and devoutness.
I deemed the *khanaqah* paltry, and I have no love for the reformer.
Fill up the wine-goblet, bring it to me. How long will you just stand there?!
Neither gold, nor silver have I. Not a heart, or a religion, or pious obedience—
Just me and my beloved in the corner, and the tune of helplessness.[144]
I am not the type for asceticism or wariness of God, bring me the cup of wine!
For—in truth—I have repented of ostentatious worship.
If the wine is not pure, then bring me dingy dregs,
because the heart and eyes find in dingy dregs illumination.
I went to the house of gambling and saw everyone playing fairly.[145]
Once I went to the monastery, I found everyone deceitful.
Now that I've broken my repentance, don't you ever break your promise;
ask me, this broken man, "How and where do you happen to be?"
Surrender wine to me, because I have repented from asceticism,
for in being an ascetic I saw naught but self-displaying boastfulness.
Free me from the sorrow of time with wine for an instant:
one cannot find relief from the world's sorrows except in wine.
Once I became drunk on wine, church and Ka'bah were the same;
union, separation—both the same, once I abdicated the self.
I went to circumambulate the Ka'bah—they didn't let me in the sanctuary,
saying, "Go! Who are you to come into the Ka'bah?"
In the night I pounded the convent's door, hearing a call from within:
saying, "Come on in 'Iraqi, for you're our drinking pal as well!"[146]

The Qalandari element is quite apparent in this poem, seen especially in the contrast between ostentatious asceticism and drunken indifference, which might explain editor Sa'id Nafisi's inclusion of a double line explicitly using the term "Qalandar" at the beginning of this poem.[147] The true lover shuns the externalities of religious piety, in Qalandar fashion—so much so that he embraces his status as a heretic and sees no difference between the Christian church and the Muslim sanctuary (a theme also found in the poetry of Ibn 'Arabi and the story of the Shaykh of San'an). Moreover, and more important, he values sincerity above all else, finding such sincerity in the gambling house and the tavern, both places where flagrant sin, the diametric opposite of pious ostentation, can be found. The gambler is not a businessman, coldly calculating investment and return; rather, like the lover, he risks everything to acquire what his heart seeks. The Qalandari variety of sincerity, presented here so forcefully, expresses poetically the same ideal found among Sufis such as Ahmad Ghazali and Awhad al-Din Kirmani, who tested their pupils' allegiances, flouted their own reputations, and thus converted publically acknowledged wrongs into saintly rights.

The power of this particular *ghazal* is in the immediacy and repetition of the persona's command to be brought wine, an immediacy that allows his disavowal of piety to seem like a self-revealing aside. Such honesty adds to the sense of sincerity surrounding the 'Iraqi persona, one that becomes the poet's hallmark and an important contribution not only to Sufis inclined to the School of Passionate Love but also to classical Persian poetry in general. Candid sincerity becomes, for example, a key trait in the poetry of the Shirazi poet Shams al-Din Muhammad Hafiz (d. 792/1390).[148] In the case of 'Iraqi, since examples of the Qalandari theme can be found throughout his *diwan,* other poems need not be cited. The legendary biography of 'Iraqi also seems to have further established the relationship between 'Iraqi-the-*shahidbaz* i-practitioner and 'Iraqi-the-Qalandar, especially since it interprets 'Iraqi's poetic references to the spirit of the Qalandariyah as occurring from his inclusion in their circle.

Since all the sources available on 'Iraqi indicate such, without evidence to the contrary, there is no reason to doubt that 'Iraqi was indeed himself at one point a Qalandar or, synonymously, a *jawaliqi.* The term *jawaliqi* (sometimes *jawlaq* or *jawlaqi*) signifies the weighty sacklike woolen cloth (*jawaliq*) that identified the Qalandars, worn perhaps in imitation of Jamal al-Din Sawaji (d. ca. 630/1232–1233).[149] In support of 'Iraqi's affiliation with the *jawaliqi*s, Baldick cites the historian Hamdallah ibn Abi Bakr Mustawfi (d. after 740/1339–1340), who applies the term *jawaliqi* to 'Iraqi in his *Tarikh-i Guzidah,* written in 730/1330, only about forty-two years after Fakhr al-Din's death.[150] As Baldick notes, Mustawfi, a writer from Qazwin (a city relatively close to 'Iraqi's city of Hamadan), exhibits surprising familiarity with the person of 'Iraqi. Perhaps more important than that fact, the depiction of 'Iraqi in Sufi texts written after his death, aside from his legendary biography, unfailingly includes his transformative association with the Qalandars, seen, for example, in an account of 'Iraqi's conversion in the *'Ishq-namah,* a *mathnawi* by Sayyid Nizam al-Din Mahmud al-Da'i ila Allah, known as Shah Da'i Shirazi (d. 870/1465).[151] As Baldick mentions, Da'i's reference to 'Iraqi's preconversion allegiance to the "Qalandars-of-form" (*qalandar-suratan*), which implies thereby that in his repentance he will become a Qalandar-in-meaning, reveals much about sympathy for the Qalandari spirit among more conservative Sufis, such as Da'i.[152] Da'i's account of 'Iraqi's transfer of metaphorical to real love (phrases used in his narration) is an excellent example of the assertion that, while Qalandars follow the path of innovation (*rah-i bid'at*), the true Qalandar spirit belongs to initiated Sufis.[153]

Over and above 'Iraqi's formal affiliation with the Qalandars, a number of observations from his biography depict him as embodying the Qalandari spirit well after his discipleship and training under Baha' al-Din Zakariya. In a manner something like the poet-lover Majnun, it is reported that while in Tokat 'Iraqi disappeared for three days, only to be found in the mountains "naked from head to foot with only one shirt," spinning in the snow, sweating, and reciting poetry.[154] 'Iraqi's image as one reluctant to be tied down is supported by his letter to Qunawi, which describes a painful self-imposed exile that takes him from Rum to Damascus, Jerusalem, and finally Medina, where he awaits commands from the unseen (perhaps the Prophet or the deceased Ibn 'Arabi).[155] It is also supported by 'Iraqi's leaving Multan supposedly because of his disinterest in the rules of the order, leaving 'Uman because of wanderlust (*ranj-i rah*), leaving again from Tokat to Cairo and then from Cairo to Damascus.[156] More significant, 'Iraqi's Qalandari-spirited desire to bring blame upon himself and thereby weaken his ego might have compelled him (and others) to enjoy the company of young boys so often and so conspicuously, a phenomenon seen in the story of Ghazali told by Shams-i Tabrizi. Intentionally seeking the disapproval of others would not be unusual for 'Iraqi, especially considering that upon being paraded honorifically through Cairo, he is reported to have removed his turban (*dastar*) and laudatory cloak (*taylasan*), thrown them to the ground, and thus aroused the ridicule of others, for this very purpose.[157] While the extent and particulars of his Qalandari practices are unknown, nevertheless, the worldview of the Qalandar is clearly discerned in his poetry. This is significant because the tone and themes of hagiographic accounts tell us that the complementary ideals of sincerity and adventure, rooted in the image of the Qalandar, helped render the censurable vice of enjoying the company of beautiful young men into an antinomian virtue.

Shahidbazi: Medieval Sufism's Great Interpretive Error?

The Qalandari call to sincerity and to love God with such focus that one fears not the *"blame of any blamer"* (Qur'an 5:54) did indeed resonate with the ethical aspirations of many in the medieval Muslim community. Nevertheless, regardless of the spirit behind it, *shahidbazi* serves as a striking example of certain practices that, while justified internally, consistent with the values of certain Sufi circles, do not do as well externally when judged by the standards shared between those Sufis and the greater Muslim community. Such incongruity seems to have left a suspicious mark on the Sufi tradition (even if such suspicions are largely unjustified).

While the boundaries of academic discourse might necessitate forbearance from applying a certain moral system or code of ethics to a separate time, place, religion, or culture, one can demand that any tradition abide by its own standards. Especially in the context of medieval Islamic texts, the doctrines of Sufis, who often considered themselves more rigorous practitioners of the moral-ethical code of the Qur'an and the Sunnah, can be expected to display compliance with these twin sources of guidance. Both sources are clear concerning the virtue of sexual modesty and avoiding illicit attraction. One example is the Qur'anic verse, *"Tell the male believers to lower their gaze and protect their private parts,* [for] *that is purer for them."*[158] Another example is a warning against even approaching forbidden sexual conduct, *"Do not come near to fornication,"* which demands precaution in matters that might lead to unsanctioned sexual desire.[159] These verses are emphasized by numerous traditions encouraging wariness in looking at those of the opposite sex who are not legally sanctioned sexual partners. Thus the Prophet's response to Jarir ibn 'Abdallah's question about the inadvertent gaze (*nazar al-fuja'ah*), that he must turn away his eyes, warns against even seemingly harmless glances, which verge too closely upon the temptation of impassioned looks.[160] Perhaps more emphatic is a warning by Imam Ja'far al-Sadiq (d. 148/765), a revered authority for Sufis, Shi'is and traditionalists who considered his statements to represent knowledge acquired from a chain of his forefathers leading back to the Prophet Muhammad (a statement cited also by Abu Hamid al-Ghazali): "Gazing [*al-nazar*] is a poisoned arrow from among the arrows of Iblis. How many a [momentary] glance has brought extended grief!"[161] It would seem a matter of common sense to extend these injunctions against gazing at women to those who, by the time of 'Iraqi, had become considered women's equals or sometimes even their superiors in terms of attraction—beardless youths. While differences of opinion existed (as El-Rouayheb has displayed in detail), and while advocates of the practice, such as 'Abd al-Ghani al-Nabulusi (d. 1143/1731), often presented evidence of the scriptural and even prophetic soundness of gazing admiringly at young men, they must have noticed that the weight of reliable revealed sources favored precaution and that their arguments almost always rested on obscure traditions or farfetched interpretations brought in ex post facto to support something that ultimately rested on saintly intuition.[162]

Yet since any discussion of the Islamic legitimacy of actions must also be considered by jurisprudential standards, the topic is far too involved to be discussed here.

Suffice it to say that many Sufi theoreticians found fault with the practice of gazing at beardless youths, especially those who emphasized that the Qur'an, Sunnah, and the various interpretations of these sources within legal schools were scales by which judgments against scripturally unfounded or even perverse practices could be made. It is with such in mind that Abu Hamid al-Ghazali, not to be confused with his brother Ahmad mentioned earlier, declares that "gazing [*al-nazar*] at a boy's face with sexual desire is legally forbidden." Of course, since the case was often made that gazing can be devoid of such desire, al-Ghazali is compelled to add that "rather, gazing is not permitted for anyone whose heart is affected by the appearance of a beardless youth, in such a way that he perceives any difference between him and a bearded person."[163] In other words, any man who would consider a beardless youth "beautiful" in the same manner that he would consider a woman beautiful is forbidden from gazing at him, even without the presence of sexual desire, including the accomplished gnostics mentioned hitherto. Abu Hamid considers gazing at beardless youths a tremendous affliction (*afah 'azimah*); quoting an unnamed source, al-Ghazali comments that the companionship of beardless youths is more dangerous for a young pious man than a deadly predatory beast.[164] The danger in gazing at beardless youths is magnified even beyond the danger of gazing at women because, while a man enamored with a woman can find permissible expression of his love in marriage, there exists no Islamically legal means for the satisfaction of love for a bearded youth, as al-Ghazali notes.[165]

The concern expressed by Abu Hamid seems to result from a problem facing the men of his time, even and perhaps especially those who undertook the spiritual path, those who often, as al-Ghazali remarks, avoided marriage with the intent of devoting themselves entirely to self-betterment (al-Ghazali does not necessarily discourage avoiding marriage for the wayfarer). With such arguments in mind, considering that each of the Sufis discussed expressly sets the Qur'an and the Sunnah as moral standards for himself and his readers, one should not be hasty to declare a jurist who fiercely condemns *shahidbazi*, such as 'Abd al-Rahman ibn al-Jawzi, a mere literalist lacking appreciation for Islamic spirituality. It emerges clearly from his writings that Ibn al-Jawzi was also deeply concerned with an Islamic society that he saw as decaying in terms of not only corrupt beliefs but also corrupt practices—especially pederasty. For example, after a discussion of egregious actions undertaken by Sufis in their companionship of beardless youths, Ibn al-Jawzi mentions that Ahmad Ghazali responded to a letter accusing him of loving his Turkic male slave by kissing the young man between the eyes.[166] Here al-Jawzi expresses his indignation: "I am not surprised by the actions of this man and by his casting off the covering of modesty from his own face. I am only surprised by the quadrupeds present there, how they remained silent, failing to disavow him!"[167] Perhaps Ghazali's actions do not surprise Ibn al-Jawzi because, in his estimation, *most* self-proclaimed Sufis (*akthar al-sufiyah al-mutasawwifah*) engage in replacing the natural inclination for women with gazing at beardless youths.[168]

Ibn al-Jawzi's statement concerning the Sufis brings me to my second point. It seems that in the process of disdaining their individual public reputations, Sufis who practiced *shahidbazi* failed to consider adequately the reputation of Sufism as a whole within the medieval Islamic world, despite the real effects that it had. Comments by practicing Sufis opposed to *shahidbazi* as well as those outside of the tradition indicate that Sufism's reputation within the Islamic world suffered greatly because of the practice of *shahidbazi,* one of several practices that a multitude of *shari'ah*-minded Muslims deemed blatantly antinomian. Mawlana Rumi, who was at the very least an acquaintance of 'Iraqi, laments that among his contemporaries "a Sufi has become in the estimation of these base people / needlework, sodomy, and nothing else," referring not only to relationships with beardless youths but also the practice of ripping (and hence sewing) clothes in moments of ecstasy during *sama'*.[169] Clearly, Mawlana was among those who saw the practice of *shahidbazi* as dangerous because of its normalization and the adoption of this practice as a tradition of the saints; thus he comments that the famous practitioner of *shahidbazi* Awhad al-Din Kirmani "left a bad legacy for the world," a legacy reprehensible enough that the saint will be accountable not only for his own action but also *"the burden of all those who practice it* [*wizr man 'amila biha*]."[170] Here Rumi quotes the prophetic tradition concerning *tasnin,* creating a precedent in practice to be followed by others, the very tradition that Ibn 'Arabi alludes to in order to *defend* the companionship of beardless youths.[171]

Sirus Shamisa comments that, in the time of Rumi, abuses of *shahidbazi* were common enough in *khanaqahs* that it became known as the "sickness of the shaykhs" (*'illat al-mashayikh*); such a term might actually indicate that the perception of a serious problem persisted, even if pederasty was not as widespread as rumor would have it.[172] As another example, the Mamluk biographer of the Prophet and poet Abu al-Fath Muhammad ibn Sayyid al-Nas (d. 734/1334) attributes to Sufis six traits: "copulating with pretty boys, drinking wine, eating hashish, dancing, singing and pimping."[173] The Shirazi poet Hafiz, in bewailing the unfairness of his reputation, points to the popular conception that Sufis ogled young men: "The Sufis are all drinking pals and gazers profligate [*nazarbaz*], though / in the midst of all of this, it befell that broken-hearted Hafiz was infamous."[174]

Hafiz seems to mean here that Sufis take part in that which the rest of debauched society enjoys, as can be inferred by comparing this double line to another from his *diwan:* "I am a drinker, a vexed soul, a scoundrel, and a profligate gazer [*nazarbaz*] / and who in this whole city is not the same as I?"[175] Widespread depravity is an important theme in Hafiz' *diwan,* as seen here, but the first double line quoted tells us that Hafiz and his contemporaries expected more from those devoted to the spiritual path. The sinister, clandestine, and even hypocritical nature of Sufi *shahidbazi* is captured in a double line by another Shirazi poet, Abu 'Abdallah Musharraf al-Din Sa'di (691/1292): "The moral enforcer covertly watches the scoundrels, / unaware of the Sufis practicing *shahidbazi*."[176] In other words, the Sufis are even more cunning than the morals police (*muhtasib*) when it comes to undertaking the nefarious act of pederasty. Again, it might not require a large percentage of hypocritical self-professed saints and ascetics to disillusion those inclined to accept their piety. While the true extent of *shahidbazi* and its abuses in the medieval world perhaps cannot be known, certainly some amount of damage had been done, even if by the few.

A final point must here be emphasized. Abuses of *shahidbazi* did certainly occur, and it was a practice both without precedent in the prophetic Sunnah and dangerously close to a breach of conduct. Nevertheless, there is nothing to suggest that the gnostics discussed were insincere in their claims that it was for them a practice devoid of licentiousness. In fact, never do the texts discussed thus far refer to *shahidbazi* as pederasty. Rather, in the experience of the mystics in question, *shahidbazi* was a profound instance of witnessing, as has been seen. Ironically enough, an anecdote from the *Talbis Iblis* of Ibn al-Jawzi provides an excellent final illustration of this fact. Ibn al-Jawzi relates that Ahmad Ghazali, gazing at a rose in his hand and turning his attention to a young man's face, back and forth repeatedly, ignores a group of men around him.[177] When one member of the group hints at the saint's discourtesy and asks if they are disturbing him with their presence, Ghazali replies, "Yes, by God [*ay wa-llah*]." Here the narrator states that this reply aroused from the group the clamor of ecstasy (*al-tawajud*). Both the intensity of emotion and the use of a sexually neutral flower indicate that the desired aim in gazing here is indeed nothing other than witnessing, in the lofty sense of the term. Ahmad Ghazali's reply has the qualities of a gnostic absorbed in love and meditative vision. His desire for sheer beauty can be seen in the switching back and forth between a human face and a flower; neither alone can fully capture that which Ghazali seeks. While the practice was considered bizarre by those outside the tradition, and is still considered bizarre by many of us who research it today, it must be understood within the context of witnessing meaning within form, which is, after all, an experiential affair. Notwithstanding this, it is difficult to deem inculpable such gnostics not only for their lack of foresight, but also for the indifference and even disdain they held and expressed toward the perceptions of other intelligent Muslims.

The Amorous Lyric as Mystical Language

Union of the Sacred and Profane

With discussions of vision and beauty now behind us, we proceed to study the pertinence of these phenomena to the amorous lyric, an artistic form favored by Ibn 'Arabi, 'Iraqi, and other Muslim mystics. The phrase "amorous lyric" aims to be an equivalent for certain versified genres used by both saints, lyrical forms concerned with love. Very often, mystics did not create new genres to convey their experiences, working instead within established genres. Such is the case, for example, in Sufi exegetical undertakings, where esoteric commentators employed an existing genre—the *tafsir*—as a medium for their insights.[1] So too did the amorous poem, whether from the Arabic *nasib* or from the Persian *ghazal*, find itself a new medium for the expression of love enhanced by gnostic awareness. In this process, lyric poetry acquired new *meaning*, even if *form* did not always reflect this change.

Needless to say, the poems of Ibn 'Arabi as well as 'Iraqi are shaped by the long poetic traditions that precede them. References to many of the images and motifs of the pre-Islamic *nasib* as well as the 'Udhri tradition of amatory verse can be found in Ibn 'Arabi's *Tarjuman al-Ashwaq*. The influences of the *nasib* on Sufi poetry, handled quite ably in Jaroslav Stetkevych's analysis of Ibn al-Farid as well as in the writings of Emil Homerin and (especially in the case of Ibn 'Arabi) Michael Sells, need not be discussed here.[2] Similar to Ibn 'Arabi, following the path laid down by other Persian-speaking Sufi poets before him, 'Iraqi makes use of themes and tropes from the courtly *ghazal* and *qasidah*, from which the poet has ultimately inherited his oft-used image of wine, for example. The concern here, however, is to view these poems not diachronically, as the culmination of various poetic traditions, but rather functionally, as an expression of the vision of love in Sufism. In that regard, juxtaposing the poetry of Ibn 'Arabi, which derives from the Arabic literary tradition, with the poetry of 'Iraqi, which derives mainly from the Persian literary tradition, allows us to push these formative factors temporarily into the background, focusing for now on one feature shared between them: poetry about human beauty with far-reaching spiritual significance. Hence the concern here is almost exclusively for matters of theme and imagery, not poetic form. It is hoped that through this method an important question can then be addressed: Why would amorous verse, often blatantly sensual in its depictions, become the main artistic medium for the vision that has been hitherto described? That poetry has historically dominated the Islamic arts does not suffice to explain "mystic" affinity for amorous poetry. Rather, there is a homogeneity in aim and experience that renders love poetry such an able medium for the gnostic.

The Methodology of Ibn 'Arabi's Commentary: Hermetic or Aesthetic?

The method of this study has been to consider, up until now, the vision of the mystics at hand and the function of the human form in this vision and, currently, to apply this vision to the poetry shaped by their perceptive experience. Such has been the case because to do otherwise, to engage in mistaken analogies about amorous Sufi poetry, might cause one to misconstrue the poetry of these mystics as somehow distinct from their vision and their claims to gnostic meaning as somehow disingenuous.[3] Such misinterpretations indeed occurred in Muhyi al-Din's own lifetime, serving as the impetus for his commentary on his *Tarjuman al-Ashwaq*. When two of his disciples requested that Ibn 'Arabi write his commentary, they did so because, in the words of Ibn 'Arabi, "they had heard one of the jurists of Aleppo deny that this [collection of poems] resulted from divine secrets and that the Shaykh [Ibn 'Arabi] dissimulates so that [the poetic collection] is ascribed to propriety and religion."[4]

Of course, the familiarity of these pupils with Ibn 'Arabi's work and their offense at these suggestions itself signifies that the original collection of poems without commentary served as an elucidator of spiritual realities. The title of the work, moreover, which literally means "the interpreter of desires," is perhaps enough of an indication of the collection's aim. Yet more than simply a defense, the commentary on the *Tarjuman al-Ashwaq* also underscores the visionary dimensions of amorous poetry in general and mystical amorous poetry in particular.

It is understandable that one who approaches the *Tarjuman al-Ashwaq* and its commentary separately, without considering Ibn 'Arabi's other discussions of beauty and the human form, would see the commentary as an artificial dressing cloaking the poems. This is the case with Jaroslav Stetkevych's critique of Ibn 'Arabi's commentary, undertaken in his seminal and otherwise excellent *The Zephyrs of Najd:*

> A very elaborate example of a symbolic commentary comes from the great mystic and hermetic symbolist Ibn 'Arabi, who (supposedly under stress but undoubtedly also as his own afterthought and further search for meaning) provided his otherwise poetically undistinguished lyrical collection, appropriately entitled *The Interpreter of Desires,* with a fastidiously detailed quid pro quo "interpretation." But his commentary appears trapped in its own hermeneutic logic, detached and esoteric. His poetic text would hardly have been served by anything else, however, if the modest amount of mystical substance contained in it was to be salvaged and the general symbolic pretense

> maintained. In brief, the result is that the commentary develops largely its own sphere of content, treating the poetry merely as a "point of departure," and the poetry, going its own traditional ways, never quite manages to warrant the flights of the symbolic imagination of the commentary.[5]

Here Stetkevych presents Ibn 'Arabi's commentary as an instance of medieval, mystical hermeneutics, "dense in symbolic texture but restricted in experiential scope," one that relies on etymology and the formalistically "motivated association of concepts to the exclusion of sensory perceptions."[6] Underlying these observations is an assumed distinction between honest sensory perception and abstract and hypothetical mystical terminology. Of course, the refutation of such assumptions lies in the observations and claims of these very mystics, who swore affirmably that their mystical terminology resulted from something witnessed, often through the medium of the physical senses. The outcome was superlatively far from being "restricted in experiential scope." The phrases that Stetkevych uses to describe Ibn 'Arabi's commentary, such as "quid pro quo," "keys," "codes," and, above all, "hermetic," reveals his presumption that Ibn 'Arabi's method revolves around words, words that do not necessarily expand upon the experiential significations of the poem's words. In the coming pages, I will respectfully disagree with Professor Stetkevych's position.

A key difference between Stetkevych's interpretation of Ibn 'Arabi's method and what has been presented throughout this book can be found in his analysis of the victory of the sacred over the profane in Islamic thought. In many ways, Stetkevych's conception of the miracle of the Qur'an belies his conception of Sufi commentaries on poems derived from the *nasib*.[7] Stetkevych is certainly correct that the miracles of Muhammad and Moses subverted and rendered incapable the valued marvels of their own ages, poetry and magic respectively. What Stetkevych fails to mention, or at least consider fully in declaring that with such miracles "the stronger magic wins," is the incomparability of prophetic miracles to their profane counterparts.[8] A miracle is a divine suspension of the probable that often makes use of the external medium of its opponents and bears many of the traits used by them, and yet renders them impotent to respond or recreate it. Similarly the love language of gnostics bears the traits and externalities of profane love but has within it a level of vision and gnosis that would render the profane lover impotent to understand. This is what Ibn 'Arabi intends in commenting on his own poetry. Ibn 'Arabi did not mean for his commentary to be an exclusive and overbearing interpretation of his amorous lyrics, but rather evidence of echoes of meaning in both language and vision. Proof of that lies in the fact that he did not deem a commentary necessary in his first version of the *Tarjuman al-Ashwaq*. Proof can also be seen in the observation made by Stetkevych himself that one image is often interpreted in multiple ways in various instances. Certainly some commentators did abuse the language of Sufi interpretation and employed the device in a line-by-line and word-by-word genre that often forced them to make mystical observations when there might not have been much to say other than repetition. Ibn 'Arabi, however, hopes not to provide keys or codes for his lines of verse but to capture and express their profoundness and even ambiguity.[9]

There is no dearth of poems in the *Tarjuman al-Ashwaq* that illustrate the aesthetic perspective offered by Ibn 'Arabi's commentary. Still, considering the focus of the present study on the human form, it would be most useful to observe a poem with particularly erotic imagery, such as poem number 46 cited below. Here Ibn 'Arabi's nostalgic yearning for the beloved shifts from a potential problem, the longing caused by separation, to an offered solution, the persistence of the beloved in the lover's consciousness:

Between innards and beautiful wide eyes a desire is at war,
and the heart, from that war, is in a state of perdition.
A sweet-lipped girl, dark-lipped, honeyed where she is kissed—
the testimony of the bee is what appears in its white, thick honey.
Plump are her ankles, darkness over a white moon,
On her cheek the redness of sunset, a bough on dunes of sand,
Beautiful, well-adorned, she is not married,
She laughs showing teeth like brilliant hailstones, white, clean, and sharp.
When it comes to ignoring, she is serious, but she plays at love frivolously,
and death is what lies between such seriousness and such play.
Never does the night blacken except that comes upon its trail
the breathing-back-to-life of morning, a fact known since olden times.[10]
And never do the easterly winds pass a lush grassland
that contains girls with large breasts, virginally bashful, playfully passionate,
except that, in their light blowing, the breezes cause to bend and to disclose
the flowers and freshly-cut herbs that are carried by the girls.
I asked the east wind about them, so that it might inform me,
it said, "What purpose is there for you to acquire such information?
In al-Abraqayn and near the Pool of al-Ghimad and near
the Pool of al-Ghamim, I left the tribe so recently;
No plot of earth has possessed them." So I said to the wind,
Where is the escape, when the steeds of yearning are in pursuit?[11]
Far be it! They have no residence except in my consciousness,
so wherever I am, there is the full moon—expect this!
Doesn't she rise sun-like only in my fantasy, and set only in
my heart? Gone is the inauspiciousness of the moringa tree and willow!

There is no cawing for the crow in our alighting places,
nor can he inflict a wound in the order of togetherness.[12]

This is an expressly sensual poem, one that includes the name of Nizam subtly in the concluding line mentioning the "order of togetherness" (*nizam al-shaml*).[13] Ibn 'Arabi's allusion to a specific female beloved should thwart any false assumptions that the poem or its commentary stem from a system of representations, where the beloved is a transcendent God and the expression of love mere allegory. While one must not deny the sincerity of its author in claiming that these poems result from "divine inrushes and spiritual down-sendings," still his other claim that "with every name I mention in this section [of my collected poems] I allude to her [Nizam], and in every abode over which I weep I intend hers," should remind the reader that the physicality of this poem is as real as it seems.[14] Over and above Ibn 'Arabi's observations about his own poetry, the images within the poem emphasize colors, parts of the human body, and the effect of human beauty on the persona.

Contrary to Stetkevych's suggestion that Ibn 'Arabi's interpretation belongs to "the philological, dichotomy-based tradition of commentary which aims at a construction of meaning through extrapoetic equivalences," Ibn 'Arabi's commentary on this poem illustrates that such observations (from the gnostic perspective) do not stray from the poem itself, nor is it less "poetic" or even "erotic" to make connections between the human beloved and God.[15] Indeed, the commentary by its very nature deifies the human form far more than the poem alone. One excellent example of this occurs in Ibn 'Arabi's explanation of the phrase "plump of ankle" (*rayya al-mukhalkhal*), which the poet glosses as "stout of shank" (*mumtali'at al-saq*), allowing him to make reference to a Qur'anic phrase. The part of the Qur'anic verse in question, "the day when the shank is exposed [*yawm yukshaf 'an saq*],"[16] refers idiomatically to the terribleness of Judgment Day, which results from God's overwhelming attributes of might. Here Ibn 'Arabi intends to draw a parallel between the awesome and vanquishing beauty of the beloved and the awesomeness of God. Elsewhere Ibn 'Arabi has clarified that beauty itself can possess might and dominance, which in the context of God's attributes Ibn 'Arabi calls the "majesty of beauty" (*jalal al-jamal*).[17] By applying this to the human beloved, the poet comments on the spiritual implications of human beauty, a beauty comprehensive enough that it relays even the overpowering attributes of God. What Ibn 'Arabi conveys to his readers is an accurate description of the effects of human beauty, one with which any sensitive lover would sympathize. The plump ankle of the beloved is not here a code or metaphorical allusion to God's awesomeness. Rather, its sway on the lover results from God's awesomeness made manifest in the natural world.

One sees Ibn 'Arabi's ability to conjure up the unity of the sensual and supersensory in his commentary on the poem's personification of the wind. The wind describes its passing over the travelers as having occurred "from proximity" (*'an kathab*), which may be taken to mean "recently." According to Ibn 'Arabi this phrase illustrates the Prophet Muhammad's fondness for rain because it is *"recent from its Lord"* (*hadith 'ahd bi-rabbihi*), in the hadith quoted earlier.[18] More than simply commenting on his poem, Ibn 'Arabi here makes an observation concerning the hadith itself and thus interprets the Prophet's actions (allowing the rain to fall upon him) as resulting from being stirred by a certain kind of beauty. Rain, young faces, and a fresh vernal breeze all carry the aura of recent creation, and their beauty derives from a beaming sense of new life. The smells and sights of creation play an important role in the aesthetic values of Ibn 'Arabi and serve to conjoin his admiration for the female (and young male) human form to the divine source of all things. It also comments powerfully on the reason behind the wind's effect on lovers.

Yet perhaps the finest illustration of the intentional ambiguity between human and divine beloved in this poem occurs in its final lines. The poem indicates in its two penultimate double lines that the beloved can no longer be separated from the lover because she persists in his consciousness or mind (*khaladi*); this accords with the definition of *shahid* that has been seen, a continuing trace that remains in the gnostic's heart and that he enjoys witnessing in the world exterior. The connection between a persistently imagined beloved and the remnants of witnessing within the heart appear in Ibn 'Arabi's commentary on the image of the crow, which no longer "has the influence to bring disunion to togetherness, since the realities show us that there is no veil after self-disclosure and no erasure after inscription upon the heart."[19] The projection of the heart's *shahid* onto the world of forms is a point evident in the poem itself, not wanting elucidation for those aware of Ibn 'Arabi's vision, but still emphasized in the commentary. Indeed, one version of the poem more directly refers to the *shahid,* on account of a variant reading of the phrase "they have no residence except in my consciousness" (*maghnan siwa khaladi*), which in the alternate version reads "they have no *meaning* except in my consciousness" (*ma'nan siwa khaladi*). Either word points to the true location of the beloved *shahid,* namely, the gnostic heart, an observation that Ibn 'Arabi clarifies: "In saying, *Far be it! They have no meaning . . . ,* the poet intends the Prophet's saying (blessings and peace be upon him), which he narrates from his Lord: *'My earth and My heaven do not contain Me, but the heart of My believing servant contains Me.'* Therefore, it [the heart] is a location for God's gnosis and a place for the divine self-disclosure."[20] Indeed, the heart might be considered the setting of this poem, a setting the expansiveness of which appears most vividly in the poet's commentary.

The perceptive centrality of the heart can be seen in Ibn 'Arabi's discerning various levels of divine manifestation in the poem's reference to sunrise and sunset. Sunrise alludes to forms in the imaginal realm (*'alam al-tamaththul*). Sunset alludes to a comprehensive or all-containing realm (*al-sa'ah allati dhakarnaha*): the human heart, which achieves the gnosis of God. This is a significant distinction. While this sensual poem on the surface seems to acknowledge one realm of existence, that of the natural world and the physical beauty within it, Ibn 'Arabi's commentary considers the spiritual, imaginal, and natural realms and adds to it the realm of the human heart, which contains all else. Earlier in his analysis of this poem, Ibn 'Arabi comments that "the only veil for the hearts of the gnostics impeding their perception of the Highest Panoramas [*al-manazir al-'ula*] is the natural realm [*al-'alam al-tabi'i*]." The term "Highest Panoramas" is, to my knowledge, specific to Ibn 'Arabi's commentary on the *Tarjuman al-Ashwaq*, not found or at least not commonly used in either his *al-Futuhat al-Makkiyah* or his *Fusus al-Hikam*. The Highest Panoramas seem to correspond to God's attributes neither in their function as sources for the names of God nor in their function as universals, but in their function as loci of witnessing for the heart. In other words, whereas the universals (*al-umur al-kulliyah*) represent God's attributes insofar as they are applied to all things (for example, strength in its multiple manifestations of all that which we would deem "strong"), the Highest Panoramas indicate the attributes when seen through a vision of reversion, a looking back from loci of manifestation to their sources.[21] While veiled for the mystic, the purely supersensory Highest Panoramas still act as a source of vision for these gnostics and of existence for all things (since things exist only through gazing upon the Panoramas, even if behind a veil). Because of the veiling quality of the natural world there is no perceived discrepancy or conflict for the gnostic between the contradictions and adulterations of the natural realm (literally, the "realm of mixed components and permeation," *'alam al-akhlat wa-l-tadakhul*) and the Highest Panoramas. In other words, the gnostic's vision perceives harmony. The heart, however, senses a discrepancy and agonizes because of it.

Hence the heart is, as the poem's opening lines indicate, in a state of war because of its own ontological poverty contrasted with the intimations of perfection it senses. Clearly the natural world serves as a *necessary* veil, one that not only allows the gnostic to experience a vision of unity but also actually increases his longing. The separation between beloved and lover, perceived by the heart, excites the sense of yearning, passion, and aspiration to union. The veil allows for the longing to *un*veil. This is true of the veil that exists between the Highest Panoramas and the heart that discerns the limits of the natural world. It is also true, however, for the distance that separates the poet from his beloved, allowing him to see her and desire her. Her eyes provoke a feeling of urgency and pain inside him, in his "innards" (*al-hasha*). Just as each realm of manifestation and existence necessarily affects that which it subsumes, so too does the beloved's exterior (her eyes) affect the poet's interior (his entrails). One sees then that there is nothing artificial about Ibn 'Arabi's reading. Quite to the contrary, the interpretation he offers highlights gnostic realizations about human-to-human love.

Lastly, aside from furthering the awareness of profundity in the amorous lyric and in the Sufi amorous lyric, and in addition to warding off misunderstanding, Ibn 'Arabi's commentary also represents the significance of amorous poetry for the spiritual path and the ability of amorous poetry to exteriorize the sense of love in mystical experience. It is likely that one reason for the emphasis on teaching and commenting on such poetry in the Akbari school was this very effect. In justifying his commentary, Ibn 'Arabi states, "I allude in these [pages of commentary and poetry] to lordly gnostic learning, divine lights, spiritual secrets, noetic sciences, and admonitions based on the Islamic tradition; I rendered the expression of all this in the language of the amorous lyric [*ghazal*] and playfully erotic poetic depictions [*al-tashbib*], because souls fall passionately in love with such expressions."[22] Here Ibn 'Arabi is not reducing his poetry to allegory or a representative system but is justifying the need for amorous poetry among Sufis. Why do souls fall passionately in love with expressions of human-to-human love? Because such is a vehicle for recognizing human-divine love, in much the same way that human beauty is a vehicle for witnessing divine beauty. In this regard, the *Tarjuman*'s commentary serves as an important inducer of *tashbih*/similitude for the gnostics. It localizes or humanizes lofty spiritual concepts, so that one can actually begin to *love* something as supersensory as the Highest Panoramas or further one's love of the sublime. The language of the commentary, therefore, in drawing connections between the language of contemplative Sufism and amorous poetry, brings into the realm of vision and love that which might still be abstract for the novice wayfarer. For the more advanced spiritual wayfarer, the sense of sympathetic acknowledgment aroused in hearing these connections is central to perceiving the beauty of the poem and the masterfulness of the commentary.

Far from being a quid pro quo or hermetic analysis, Ibn 'Arabi's manner of interpretation assumes that the poem itself is a manifestation of the experience of beauty, subject to the very grades and realms of existence possessed by the human form. Conjoining the human beloved and the divine in forms is the gnostic's experience of beauty. In other words, the gnostic sees the human form and therein the divine self-disclosures—his experience brings the two together, or at the very least, recognizes their unity. His expression of that experience in words is what remains of the meeting place or *barzakh* between two levels of existence: form and meaning, matter and spirit, or human beauty and the divine presence. The gnostic's words do more than simply capture the human beloved or her effects; they do so through the medium of his enlightened experience. Thus the words of the poem become the form that captures meaning. This artistic form, unlike the human form, is shaped solely by the lover-perceiver. Meaning has now taken two forms, the human beloved and the recorded experience of that beloved; the first is determined by existence, the second is determined by the gnostic's experience of existence. The delight in poetry derives from its ability to recreate this meaningful form of recorded experience in the hearts of those exposed to it. Ibn 'Arabi's commentary, while never directly propounding such significance to poetry, inherently elevates the recorded poetic experience of love to a level of signification far beyond mere emotion or mere words. Only that which captures meaning deserves the sort of analysis that Ibn 'Arabi offers.

Sacred-Profane Ambiguity: An Aesthetic Value

In his doctoral dissertation, "The Poems of Fakhr al-Din 'Iraqi," Julian Baldick undertakes to divide the poems from 'Iraqi's *diwan* into a number of categories, including those that are "Sufi," those that have "no overt Sufi content" and thus "could be either sacred or profane," those which "show the influence of Ibn 'Arabi," and those "in which there is inconclusive evidence for the influence of Ibn 'Arabi," among others. While I would not normally subject an unpublished dissertation to critical scrutiny, Baldick's is an important undertaking, both in its capacity as an accomplished historical study and as one of the few existing English resources on 'Iraqi.

Considering Baldick's interest in placing 'Iraqi's poems in a historical context, the attempt to categorize them in such a manner would make sense, if, that is, 'Iraqi's poems were less ambiguous. Baldick himself seems to recognize the shortcomings in this approach in commenting that "given the nature of the material, such rules may evoke some derision."[23] While in some instances Baldick's approach does successfully place the poetry in a historical context useful for understanding the poet's frame of reference, there remain two major flaws in Baldick's very premise, a premise that anticipates distinctions between sacred and profane, and Akbari and non-Akbari Sufi poetry: "Thus we insist that if a poem has no overtly Sufi element in it then it may well be considered profane: given the long-standing tradition of the *ghazal* before 'Iraqi, the poet is to be seen as making contributions to an established genre rather than having a clearly defined addressee, human or divine. If the overtly Sufi content of a poem exceeds two lines (by line we mean a *bayt* not a *misra'*, which we call a half-line), then it is to be classified as Sufi; if the amount is two lines only, then it can be said to have 'some' Sufi content; if it is less, it can be said to have a little. Further subdivisions are made according to theme: these categories are naturally arbitrary, and poems could easily be moved from one to another."[24] As seen in Baldick's last sentence, the ambiguities in 'Iraqi's poetry have brought the literary historian to hesitate in ratifying the categories he has created. Perhaps more problematic than the exceptions to the rules Baldick establishes is the quantifying of Sufi content. Even one hemistich indicating gnostic insight comments on the entirety of the poem. Moreover, as seen in Ibn 'Arabi's case, even poems that lack any explicitly mystic dimensions are often viewed as a homogeneous output of mystical experience.

A second problem with Baldick's divisions is the assumption that Ibn 'Arabi's teachings will necessarily show themselves as somehow different from the declarations of previous Sufis. With regard to the Akbari element in 'Iraqi's poems, Baldick remarks that such influence is "clearly evident in some poems, and possibly in others," advising his readers to consult a source on Ibn 'Arabi's thought.[25] Of course, here the main complication is that poetry and prose inspired by the teachings of Ibn 'Arabi does not necessarily need to be inundated with Akbari terms or concepts. On the surface, the *Tarjuman al-Ashwaq*—its commentary aside—lacks signature Akbari vocabulary. Moreover, even the *Lama'at,* which is perhaps 'Iraqi's most conspicuously Akbari work, manages to make reference to Akbari teachings in a manner at times so subtle that Hamid ibn Fadlallah Jamali (d. 942/1536) considered the text to be inspired by the Suhrawardi Sadr al-Din 'Arif (d. 684/1286), the son and successor of Baha' al-Din Zakariya (d. 661/1262), and not the Akbari Sadr al-Din al-Qunawi.[26] Lastly, even non-Akbari Sufi poets, such as Ibn al-Farid, or poets that were not Sufi at all or even spiritually inclined, such as Harun al-Rashid, were considered to have composed suitable material for Akbari commentary. This reminds us that, in the arena of poetry and love, Ibn 'Arabi did not present observations that demanded the awareness of poets, but rather a commentary on what every lover knows about love, whether consciously or unconsciously.

Let us reconsider, however, Baldick's mention of poems that have merely one double line of explicit Sufi reference. Baldick notes that it is common in the poetry of 'Iraqi for the poet to use the *takhallus* (the concluding double line of the poem in which the poet's pen name is often mentioned) to "introduce, at the end of a poem, which up to now could have been sacred or profane, a Sufi theme."[27] This accurate observation tells us much about the place of erotic imagery in the gnostic vision of 'Iraqi. A sudden introduction of mystical language or mystical concerns does not indicate that the poet has contorted or forced a sacred interpretation of what is in actually profane poetry. Nor does it imply that the mystical double line included differs in any meaningful way from the purely profane verse surrounding it. To the contrary, the lack of candidly sacred language can betray an assumption on the poet's part that there is no real difference between profane and sacred themes; therefore there is no need to be explicitly "Sufi." (If, moreover, these lines were additions made to a collection of profane poems after the poet's conversion to the Sufi path, then his discretion in adding so little and leaving so many poems unchanged would illustrate the suitability of profane poetry to mystical meaning.) Thus one should be aware that the mystical significance of the images in the entirety of an erotic poem can be indicated by a mere double line or hemistich, or need not be indicated directly at all.

One can see the manner in which 'Iraqi *suggests* sacred meaning, as opposed to directly stating it, in a poem that mainly concerns the beloved's enchantingly beautiful hair:

From behind the veil came the wine-server, with a goblet in hand;
he not only rent our veil—he also smashed our repentance.
He displayed a beautiful face; we all went into a frenzy.
Once nothing remained of us, he came, sitting on our laps.
His tress loosened its knot, the fetter was lifted from our hearts,
My soul detached its heart from the world and tied it to his hair-tip.
In the snare that is his hair-tip we all remained bewildered,
and from the cup of wine that is his ruby lips, we all became besotted.
The heart lost its self-control, once it clasped one of his ringlets—
He causes all that he can reach to drown in stupefaction.
Once his chain-like ringlets fettered the bewildered heart,
it became freed from the world and rescued itself from existence.
The heart was lost to his hair-tip; I sought [it] back from the ringlet;
his lip said: "Be happy that it has now adhered to us!"
The heart sat gleefully with the friend, since it had forsaken soul:
it conjoined soul with beloved and cosmos, having cut off both the worlds.
From his teasing glance and his face, sometimes I'm drunk and sometimes sober,
and from his ringlet and his lip, sometimes I don't exist, and sometimes I do.
There used to be a time when, wishing to utter something of the secrets,
I would become afraid of others and would speak allusively.[28]

In some respects, the references in this poem to the beloved's being (*hasti-i 'u*), to an attraction that affects the entire cosmos, to cutting off from both worlds, and to an unnamed plurality of lovers seems to ensure that the beloved here is divine. Yet while one might consider this poem (and numerous others like it in 'Iraqi's *diwan*) manifestly mystical in its description of a godly beloved, nevertheless, deified images of the beloved can also serve as effective hyperbole, so that ambiguity is maintained. This poem seems even more ambiguous when juxtaposed with 'Iraqi's other poems, many of which use these same images to describe a beloved seemingly disengaged from any divine predications. 'Iraqi is also careful to avoid hints of transcendence in these descriptions. In other words, the intended in this poem might be a deified human beloved, or perhaps the divine subjected to the language of *tashbih*/similitude, or—most likely of all—the beloved in its most comprehensive sense, which is at once the human *shahid* and the Source of all beauty.

In accordance with Baldick's observation, the final double line seems to clarify that its poet is indeed a gnostic, or at least someone privileged with esoteric knowledge of the beloved. The persona no longer represses secrets, because his lack of concern for reputation means that he no longer fears the scrutiny of outsiders. To some extent this secret seems to be that the beloved *is* divine—which is only a perilous statement if the poem signifies a human (or at least excessively humanlike) beloved.

The power of these poems lies in the realization that, once one labels it a celebration of the sacred, the high degree of similitude or immanence in it seems almost blasphemous. On the other hand, once one labels it a celebration of the profane, the deified and clearly mystical images in it render such love for the human form almost blasphemous.

Another important theme in the poem above is that the heart has a will of its own, not subject to the practical considerations of the persona. The beloved does with the heart what he wills, and the persona must succumb. Very often in the poems of Fakhr al-Din, concern for the heart and its states pervades. This focus on the beloved's effects on the heart allows the poet to maintain an indeterminate tone, one that seems to humanize the divine and deify the human simultaneously:

Today my heart can hold nothing but the friend.
It is constricted for that reason: no others can be held within.
In my flooded eyes but for the friend no one appears,
and no one but the friend is in this enduring heart of mine.
Nevertheless, I am gleeful, that in this my narrow heart
grief can find no cure—rehabilitation is not an option.
If ever this soul in my body should be without the friend,
it is afflicted to the utmost. It cannot bear this burden.
Where is the cup of wine of love for him, so that I can get drunk? Because
in the feast of union with him, no one sober can be found.
Where are his entrapping hair-tips to snag away this heart?
For no one remains with-heart within the tangles of his hair-locks.
Once love-for-him invades, the soul vacates its cell,
Once such love makes its home there, dwellers cannot be found.
This drop of blood, after being colored by his ruby lips,
from glee—like the pomegranate—within the skin can't be contained.
I'm not bothered by the hostile words of enemies because
there are no troubles in this heart for me, when I'm with him.
I took gifts for the heart: soul, body, religion, reason.
The heart said, "Be gone! For here is empty of all four.
If you really want to enter, put *'Iraqi* aside
for in the sanctuary of souls, the infidel's belt cannot exist."[29]

Baldick includes this poem in the category of "Sufi *ghazal*s, love poems," probably on the basis of the last two double lines.[30] Of course, if one ignores these concluding lines, the poem becomes completely ambiguous. Even with the final lines in consideration, it would not be farfetched to require that a true lover in the profane sense should abandon "soul, body, religion, reason" for the sake of his beloved. The lover, in both sacred and profane contexts, must abandon all. It is noteworthy, however, that the persona must negotiate not with the beloved but with his own heart. Again 'Iraqi depicts the heart absorbed with the beloved, while the persona watches helplessly from a distance. Among the things that the persona must abandon is the soul. In this poem and elsewhere, 'Iraqi describes the soul (*jan*) as if it were an encumbrance, not only in the poem's closing lines but also in describing the soul's escape once love invades. In an alternate version of this poem, this theme is emphasized in the penultimate double line: "My soul struck the heart's door, it [the heart said], 'Leave, for this instant, / with the friend, in this secluded cell, there's no room for [other] convent-dwellers.'"[31] Thus, considering the undesirable quality of *jan*, it might be better to look upon the word as "life," or even "existence." The poet must abandon his own existence for the sake of the beloved. Is this mystical experience? Yes, but not strictly so. It is an experience common to all lovers who lose themselves in an intensity of desire and must negotiate with their own recalcitrant hearts. Thus much of what renders this a successful poem is the careful use of the language of lovers, as opposed to the language of Sufi experience. Even if mystical or religious themes are stated explicitly, a sense of subtlety and obscurity still surrounds them. If the sacred vocabulary of Sufism were presented in too forthright a manner, then the descriptions of the beloved and his effects would seem a mere poetic device or allegorical trope. Rather, by maintaining ambiguity, 'Iraqi captures the genuineness of this experience for all lovers.

A Glance at Persian Sufi Glossaries

Of course, an important treatise attributed to 'Iraqi might seem to counteract the desired ambiguity discussed hitherto. In the *Istilahat-i Sufiyah*, an author identified as 'Iraqi offers neat equivalents for many of the terms common to sensually amorous poetry. Here, however, along with the matter of dubious authorship, the matter of genre must be carefully considered. The *ghazal* is a mode of ambiguity. The commentary or the glossary can be a mode of disambiguation, but it is one not intended to supersede or nullify the ambiguity that exists in poetry. Rather, it simply exists to verify the spiritual or sacred dimension of these images.

Moreover, while Sharaf al-Din Tabrizi's glossary, *Rashf al-Alhaz fi Kashf al-Alfaz*, probably served as the source for the less cohesive collection attributed to 'Iraqi, a very brief consideration of these glossaries will further illustrate the integral relationship that Sufis discerned between the externality of words and the resonating strata of beauty within them. Tabrizi's response to the use of erotic and vinous terms in the Persian poetic tradition is extremely sensitive to the relationship between meaning and form, sensitive enough that one definitely could imagine 'Iraqi as the text's author, even if some definitions do not correspond to usage in the poetry of 'Iraqi.[32] In fact, Tabrizi shows an almost tangible allegiance to the worldview presented throughout this book, seen in his observation that "the World of Meanings cannot be perceived except in the clothing of form."[33] The supersensory nature of meaning demands that it assumes the forms of either actions or words that can be grasped in sensory or rational fashion.[34] Yet such words, especially those describing the human body, are not merely tools for understanding, since, as Tabrizi notes, a prophetic hadith verifies that *God created Adam according to his form:*[35] "Once the intoxicated nightingales and peacocks of *A-last* beheld this [human] form, and once they began chirping melodiously, they brought original poetic order to the words 'lock of hair' [*zulf*] and 'mole' [*khal*], made each a locus of manifestation for profound meaning, and caused realities and subtleties to appear in such a manner."[36]

Were one to trace these words back to their ontological origins, in other words, one would find that words indicating human beauty have their origins in a cosmic appreciation of the divine-human resemblance. Thus the essential meaning of such words has a profundity that transcends the external meaning observed by most. Tabrizi's theory that the etymological origins of words describing human beauty stems from the admiration of angels (whom he describes poetically as nightingales and peacocks) for the divinely mirroring human form closely parallels a statement made more candidly by Mahmud Shabistari (d. ca. 740/1339–40) in his *Gulshan-i Raz* (Flower-garden of Secrets): "According to me, these terms [*alfaz*] that undergo esoteric interpretation / were established with those meanings from the very outset. / Applying them specifically to sensory things is the custom of the common. / How would a commoner comprehend what that [original] meaning is?"[37] Shabistari posits that sensual terms became applied exclusively to human features through a process of materialization, implying that the lexical origins of words such as "lip" and "mole" are immaterial. His interest in poetic terms yet again indicates that the supersensory significance of words relating to the human form and wine drinking became an important matter in the Akbari tradition, as did the extraction of sublime meaning from those words through commentaries and Sufi glossaries.

While one might assume that such cosmological etymologies strip words of any nonsacred significance, the brilliance of the glossary (both that attributed to 'Iraqi as well as the parallel glossary written by Tabrizi) lies in accurately portraying the language of beloveds, lovers, and love in its most sublime human context, namely, the gnostic-divine relationship, without abrogating the profane. To give one example, the glossaries define "comeliness" (*husn*) and "beauty" (*jamal*) in a manner that differentiates between essential beauty (*husn*) and beauty realized as instances of belovedness (*jamal*). Comeliness is "what they call the collection of all perfections in one essence, and this belongs only to the Real."[38] Such perfections belong to the Real, but are borrowed by others; in its fullest and original sense comeliness applies only to the divine essence. Beauty is "what they call the making manifest of the beloved's perfections through the extreme longing and seeking of the lover."[39] In other words, while comeliness is an absolute and abstract trait, beauty results from the *application* of comeliness to a relationship between lover and beloved. Beauty is comeliness observed and admired. Also, one might notice that in defining *husn,* which is an essential trait, the author specifies the Real. In contrast, when defining *jamal,* which can be applied to existents, the author defines it as pertaining to the "lover" and "beloved," more general terms applicable to any two entities, include humans loving other humans. Such precision validates all grades of beauty while still asserting the ongoing divine generation of that beauty.

Love Poetry as a Model for Gnosis

When Ibn 'Arabi refers to famous sets of lovers from Arabic poetry, he often does so with great respect and even admiration, going so far as to label the peak of gnosis—the culmination of witnessing and ecstasy—as the "Religion of Love," whose heroes are Bishr, Hind, Qays, Layla, Kuthayyir, 'Azzah, and all those who loved or were loved with all their being.[40] In celebrating these figures, Muhyi al-Din not only wishes to describe the desire and longing aroused for the mystic in witnessing but also aims to show the universality of love and its successive degrees. Those whose love is aimed at a human beloved undergo an experience parallel to gnostic love, an experience in which the lover derives pleasure and proximity from witnessing. Moreover, the uninitiated lover has actually come to know affection for one particular divine self-disclosure and one particular divine name, whether that name belong to the mistress "Layla" or to the idol "al-'Uzza."[41] The central difference is that, while the lovers in Arabic poetry love a particular instance of beauty, the gnostics love the Source of beauty. Lovers of human beloveds witness beauty in one particular form, while the gnostic witnesses the perfection behind all forms, the one who takes the entire cosmos as his form and yet still cannot be captured by form. Ibn 'Arabi clarifies this point when commenting on a couplet in one of his most famous poems from the *Tarjuman al-Ashwaq:*

> "Ours is a model in Hind's lover Bishr and in their counterparts / and in Qays and Layla, and in Mayya and Ghaylan."
>
> The poet mentions lovers of the created world—those enraptured by desirous love for girls secluded in forms—from among those Arabs enslaved by love. By "their counterparts" (*ukhtiha*), he means Jamil ibn Ma'mar and Buthaynah, Bayad and Riyad, [Qays] ibn al-Dharih and Lubna, and others like them. He uses the word "love" (*al-hubb*) because that which is love for us and for them is one reality, except that they have desirous love for the beloved in the created world while we have desirous love for the Source. Otherwise, the conditions, concomitant traits, and mediate causes are one. We can take these lovers as a model, for God the Exalted captivated them and afflicted them with love for humans like themselves only in order to make them

> proofs over anyone who claims to have love for him and yet fails to love with the same passionate intensity that these lovers had. For love had taken away their sense of reason and annihilated them from themselves on account of their witnessing *shahid*s of their beloveds in their imagination. Thus, more fitting [than a human beloved] for the one who makes claims to love is the One who is his hearing and his sight, He who outdoes his [i.e., the human lover's] drawing near by drawing near to him double-fold.[42]

The lovers of Arabic amorous poetry are superb models (*uswah*) on account of the intensity of their devotion and the self-annihilation which they undergo. Strictly in terms of sentiment, the experience of all-consuming natural love and gnostic love have enough in common to be considered one reality. Their symptoms do not merely parallel the effect of love for God on the gnostic, but rather, the utter self-resignation of these lovers stands as a paradigm for anyone who claims to love God.

Of course, while the *manner* of love practiced by these lovers is commendable, the *object* of their love is not fully and correctly perceived. Since gnostics know that the Real is the Source of beauty and hence the conclusive object of love, their rank as lovers outstrips all others. This is no minor point. Ibn 'Arabi emphasizes that while every lover ultimately loves the Real, only the gnostics are aware of this fact. While at times he might seem to praise all lovers, he also expresses a disparaging view of those who love created things. In his chapter on love in *al-Futuhat,* Ibn 'Arabi mentions that while the lover "does not love anyone except for his Creator," lovers of created objects are "veiled from him the Exalted through the love of Zaynab, Su'ad, Hind, Layla, this lower world, the dirham, status, and every beloved in this world."[43] Note that here Ibn 'Arabi includes objects of love that in classical Sufi texts are objects of contempt against which one must guard oneself: status (*al-jah*), wealth (*al-dirham*), and the most blameworthy of all, the lower world itself (*al-dunya*). Poets have wasted their words on created existents while unaware, but the gnostics "do not hear a poem, or a riddle, or a panegyric, or an amorous *ghazal,* except that in it is he who is behind the veil of forms."[44] Thus the importance difference between gnostic and profane lovers is awareness and the intensity that results from awareness:

> To [comprehend] what we mention, is it not fitting to consider Qays the Mad in his love for Layla, how it annihilated him from himself? Likewise we consider the people of bewildering love [*walah*] and the lovers to be greater in terms of pleasure and mightier in terms of their love for God than those who love members of their own [human] species. The divine form in the servant is more complete in terms of resemblance than the resemblance within species, [and love occurs between entities sharing a resemblance of form]. It is not in the capability of someone from your species to be your hearing and sight. Rather, his [or her] ultimate limit is to be your *heard* and

> your *perceived*—in the passive sense. When the servant perceives through a truth that is more complete, then his pleasure is greater, his desire mightier. This is befitting to be the desire of the People of God.[45]

Such observations concerning the universality and degrees of love have important repercussions in gnostic applications of poetry. First, sincerity and proficiency in declaring the experience of love becomes a standard by which poetic expression is considered successful. A successful poem is one that is able to recreate best the experience known and shared by all gnostic lovers, indeed by all lovers, since the experience of love is in fact one. It matters little if this lover is a gnostic or not, in fact, because of the unity of all love. The poet must merely be a true lover, able to capture the lovability (i.e., beauty) of his beloved and its effect on himself; this representational form (the poem), if effective, will then induce a parallel experience in its audience. Those with gnostic insight will recognize the spiritual significance of the recorded experience at hand and the corresponding beloved. It is because of this unity of love that both Ibn 'Arabi and 'Iraqi praise with such esteem lovers from the profane poetic tradition. Numerous examples of admiration for lovers from the profane poetic tradition, mentioned in the writings of Ibn 'Arabi, have been cited. While not often, 'Iraqi too refers to lovers from the profane tradition; some occasions in the *Lama'at* where 'Iraqi mentions Layla and Majnun have been cited. Similarly, in a *tarji'band* attributed to 'Iraqi, the names of famous lovers underscore the severity of the poet-persona's love:

The bird that is my soul has broken inside—
in the air of love for you it takes to flight:
Farhad's passionate love and the face of Shirin,
Mahmud's head and the dirt of the feet of Ayaz.[46]

The universal language of love allows mystics in the Akbari tradition (and in other traditions sympathetic to this notion of love) to apply their method of interpretation to any earnest love poem. One example mentioned earlier is Harun al-Rashid's lines written for his singing slave girls, interpreted with gnostic dimensions by Ibn 'Arabi. In the *Lama'at,* 'Iraqi applies two double lines from the Saljuq panegyrist Awhad al-Din Muhammad Anwari (d. ca. 582/1186) to gnostic experience:

Those who gaze deeply at your beautiful face,
when they view it acutely from various angles,
see in your face the faces of themselves:
The differences in depictions arise from this.[47]

Clearly—for 'Iraqi—the court poet Anwari's perceptivity and insight into the effects of a beautiful beloved, even in the profane sense, have given his lines mystical veracity. Indeed, in this case, the resemblance of such verse to that of the mystics is striking but easily explained. As is evident from the *ghazal* as a whole, Anwari, in exaggerating the effects of his human beloved, has deified his object of admiration. By elevating his beloved to an ambiguously human-divine status, he has rendered his profane poem suitable for gnostic contemplation. This ontologically justified universality of love so expands the domain of poetic commentary that, in a paper presented to an English-speaking audience on beauty, love, and poetic expression in Persian Sufi poetry, for example, one contemporary Iranian critic refers as easily to the sonnets of William Shakespeare as to the poetry of Jami, Rumi, or Hafiz.[48]

Language Unbounded by Reason: Poetry as a Contradictive Medium

In considering poetry, especially amorous poetry, as a medium of expression for the vision of the gnostic, it is now necessary to return to some declarations made by Ibn 'Arabi in chapter 178 of *al-Futuhat al-Makkiyah,* particularly those concerning the illogical and irrational nature of love: "If I cannot put him in a form, then I know not whom my soul loves / and his being placed in forms cannot be proven logically."[49] Regarding the matter of love and witnessing, Ibn 'Arabi recognizes the inevitability of perplexity for the gnostic, who sees and adores that which is contrary to reason: God in forms. To some extent, Ibn 'Arabi and those gnostics who referred to this experience and its effects seemed to be aware of the contrast between their descriptions and that which had been asserted in traditional Islamic theology and philosophy. According to Islamic logicians, contradictories cannot both be true, so that a syllogistic argument is easily refuted if a "combination of contradictories" (*ijtima' al-naqidayn*) occurs in it. Ibn 'Arabi alludes to the supralogical and contradictory experience of the gnostic lover, in fact of the lover more generally, in his chapter on love, among other instances:[50] "Love's necessary concomitants dress me in its ipseity / with the dress of contradictories [*naqidayn*], like one present and mentally absent."[51] While contradictories are not at all the same as opposites, for Ibn 'Arabi, the meeting of opposites characterizes the lover's contradictory experience, one that results from his unique position in the cosmos:

> Among the properties of love [*al-mahabbah*] is that the lover, in his loving, combines opposites, in order to resolve his having been created in a form, on the one hand, with that which he possesses of free will, on the other. This difference [of form versus will] is that which lies between natural love and spiritual love, which the human being alone combines. Quadrupeds love but, unlike the human, do not combine opposites. The human combines opposites in his act of loving only because he has been created according to his [that is, God's] form, who described himself through opposites in saying, *He is the First and the Last, the Outer and the Inner.*[52] Love combines opposites in this manner: Among the necessary attributes of love is union with the beloved. Also, however, among the necessary attributes of love is that the

> lover loves that which the beloved loves, and the beloved loves separation. If the lover loves separation, then he has acted against the dictates of love, for indeed love seeks union. Yet, if the lover loves union, he has also acted against the dictates of love, for indeed the lover loves that which the beloved loves and does not act [on his own]. Hence the lover is thwarted [*mahjuj*] in every case. The ultimate of combining these two opposites is to love the beloved's love of separation, not separation itself, and also to love union.[53]

The lover is in a baffling situation in terms of what he wills. Like all creatures of form, especially in the natural realm, he is subject to desires. Conversely his spiritual qualities bestow him with a cognizant will of his own, so that he can choose to obey his desires or the will of his beloved. No longer is will something that pertains only to himself: He must now choose to sacrifice his will for the will of the beloved, even when the beloved has willed that which is contrary to love itself, that is, separation. The lover is faced with a contradiction.

Of course, the major contradiction the lover faces is one that has been discussed: the vision of God in forms, which contradicts reason itself. Elsewhere the relationship between love and *tashbih* was mentioned; it will be recalled, for example, that while rational proofs serve the central purpose of establishing the divine transcendence, "when the divine reports came, in the languages of religious law, telling us that he *is* such-and-such and *is* such-and-such, in matters the outer senses of which contradict rational proofs, we loved him for the sake of these positive attributes."[54] In other words, the language of *tashbih* arouses love in spite of the limits of reason, which opposes it. Thus, considering the contradictions and combination of opposites faced by the lover, the most accurate word that describes his situation is perplexity (*al-hayrah*). Herein lies the importance of poetry, especially amorous poetry that can portray perplexity and a crisis in self-will, without the burdens of logic and continuity found in discursive prose. This is one reason that imaginative and emotive poetry stands as the language of all lovers, whether gnostic or otherwise.

The poems in Ibn 'Arabi's *Tarjuman al-Ashwaq* not only often describe the separation and consequent longing so common to the Arabic *nasib* but also, more generally, convey a sense of perplexity central to the experience of love:

If only I knew whether they were cognizant
of the heart that remains within their possession.
And my heart—if it could somehow just apprehend
the mountain-pass which they traversed.
Do you suppose they made it safely?
Or do you suppose that they have perished?
The lords of love-longing [*al-hawa*] are perplexed
in love-longing and are near inescapably entangled.[55]

On its own, without considering the commentary, this poem depicts a caravan departed, having taken with it the heart of an enamored lover. In futility he wonders about the journey of his beloved's caravan, the perils that they have faced, and their arrival. It ends with a statement on the hopeless condition of the lover, who must tolerate separation and nescience. Applying to it Ibn 'Arabi's commentary adds to this poem not only a gnostic dimension but also a dimension of spiritual-romantic narrative. According to Ibn 'Arabi, while he circumambulated the Ka'bah reciting these lines, he felt upon his back the strike of a hand with a "palm softer than silk."[56] His attention turned suddenly to a girl "from among the girls of Rum," more comely of face, sweeter of speech, more able in interpretation, and more endowed with gnosis and beauty than all the people of her time. She demands that he read the poem back to her, and she takes him to task for complications of spiritual significance that she has already discerned in each line. As she commands him to read every next line, she disputes each time the poet's observations and chides him. Interestingly Ibn 'Arabi does not reject her critique, at least not directly, offering instead only praise for her perfect insight and thereupon offering his own commentary. This narrative is here mentioned because it too becomes a part of the poem's connotative situation. It is significant that a female beloved described in very sensual terms has interrupted Ibn 'Arabi's moment of communication with the divine, seizing his attention. Considering that in Ibn 'Arabi's vision God interacts with the cosmos through all media in a complexity of interrelations, this dialogue, like all dialogues, occurs between the gnostic and the Real on a certain level. Moreover, the central theme of the poem, perplexity, is realized in the unexpected and brazen challenge of a beautiful woman. The profane and sacred elements of Ibn 'Arabi's account and poem cannot be distinguished; one enhances the other.

The commentary too offers its own perspective on the poem's themes of separation and perplexity. Ibn 'Arabi's discussion of the line questioning the beloved's safe arrival ("Do you suppose they made it safely?") brings to light the necessity of separation for existence, both the existence of an idealized beloved in the mind of the lover and the existence of all things in the will of God. Reflecting on this hemistich, Muhyi al-Din comments that "the Highest Panaromas, with respect to their being panoramas, have no existence except insofar as they have one to view them."[57] His statement points to the centrality of witnessing to existence. The Real looks upon potentialities among the Immutable Identities in order for those identities to be granted existence; if he were to cease his gaze, they would cease to exist. On the receptive side, the extent to which all of creation witnesses the Real determines its receptivity and thus its existence. By drawing a comparison between this cosmological phenomenon and the lover's apprehension about his beloved and her caravan, Ibn 'Arabi comments on the role of imagination in existence. One moment, the lover visualizes his beloved's safe arrival, so she exists. The next moment, he visualizes her perdition; thus she ceases to exist. Her well-being, in fact, her very being, has become a function of his imagination. This parallels the Real's maintenance of creation merely through his gazing or active knowledge. Again, the created order becomes imitated and realized in the relationship between human lovers and human beloveds. One also sees from this observation that the separated beloved is a *more* intrinsic part of the lover than the present beloved. Separation itself has become an important factor in her continued idealized existence—she can now exist perfectly and eternally in his heart, a theme already seen.

According to the commentary, this poem also represents the relationship between the Muhammadan Heart, receptive to all forms, and the Highest Panoramas, the end point of all witnessing. Such a heart can reach such heights of selfless absorption in gazing that it almost ceases to exist. Yet without the gazer, that which is "seen" also becomes nonexistent. Thus, like an intense light that causes temporary blindness, the seer and the seen flash in and out of existence in flickers of intensity. (This corresponds to the poem's description of the caravan, safe one instant, annihilated another instant.) The Muhammadan Heart functions so because of its ethereal nature, standing close to nothingness, unblemished by "being bound by stations," a perfect mirror of selflessness and reflexivity that assumes all forms.[58] No stations separate that heart from the Highest Panoramas, so its view is the most proximate possible; hence the fervor described.

Ibn 'Arabi's commentary on the final double line reaffirms the passage quoted above from *al-Futuhat al-Makkiyah,* asserting that the demands and desires brought by love cause the lover to face contradictories (*al-naqidayn*). Again, the lover's desire for union can contradict the beloved's will, and the beloved's will can contradict the dictates of love. Here Ibn 'Arabi makes explicit the connection between these contradictories and the perplexity (*hayrah*) that besets the lover. This accurate description of the effects of love should not be considered exclusive to the gnostics. In fact, perplexity as a characteristic shared by gnostic and nongnostic love bestows this poem with sacred and profane veracity simultaneously. In this passage Ibn 'Arabi also outlines the ascending stages of love, from capricious love (*hawa*), to pure love (*hubb*), to firm love (*wadd*), and lastly to passionate love (*'ishq*).

In another poem, Ibn 'Arabi focuses—in the first fifteen double lines—on the pain of separation. The persona, accompanied by two companions, weeps at the abandoned encampments, and only tears and the poetic tales of famous lovers in the Arabic tradition bring him comfort. An important contradiction arises; the lover enkindles and furthers his pain by remembering the beloved, and yet the mention of the beloved also somehow brings him relief. The final ten double lines of this poem (beginning "Long has been my yearning . . ."), which are my focus, more directly involve the theme of contradiction. The details Ibn 'Arabi reveals there, moreover, leave no doubt that the poet specifies Nizam as his human beloved. Nevertheless, the poem as a whole best displays the main theme of overpowering love, one that tortures the lover, yet one he seeks out actively:

My malady comes from one with malady in her eyelids,
Distract me by mentioning her! Distract me!
Suddenly flapping wings, the ashen birds in grasslands cry—
the grief of these pigeons comes from what has grieved me.
My father be the ransom for a tender one, playful, from the girls
draped in litters, who saunters among satisfied women.
She rose out in the open like the sun, and when then
she set, she radiated in the hidden horizon of my heart.
Oh desert ruins at Ramah, near completely vanished!
How many girls they saw with just-blossomed breasts and beauty!
My father, then myself, be ransomed for a young, nourished gazelle,
who pastures within my ribcage in invulnerability;
the fires therein do not hurt it—for it is light.
In such a manner is light an extinguisher of fires.
My two companions! Bind up my bridle-straps,
for I must see the trace of her abode with my eyesight!
Hence, once you have reached the abode, there dismount
and at that place, my two fellow travelers, weep for me.
Linger, for a little while, with me at those ruins.
We will try to weep. No, I will weep for what has undone me.
Love-longing it is who shoots me without arrows;
Love-longing it is who kills me without spear.
Tell me, when I am weeping on her account,
will you help me in tear-shedding, will you help me?
And recount for me the tale of Hind and of Lubna
and Sulayma, Zaynab, and of 'Inan.
Then add to it accounts of Hajir and Zarud,
reporting on the pastures in which graze the gazelles.
Moan because of me with the poetry of Qays and Layla,
and Mayya and the trouble-stricken Ghaylan.
Long has been my yearning for that young one versed in prose
and in verse, with her own pulpit, and with clarity of expression,
from the daughters of kings from the land of Persia,
from the most glorious of cities: from Isfahan.
She is the daughter of 'Iraq, the daughter of my imam;[59]
I am her contrasting opposite: a Yemeni son.
Have you ever seen, oh my masters, or ever heard

of two contrasting opposites undergoing combination?
If you could only see us in Ramah offering back and forth
winecups of love-longing without the use of fingers,
when love-longing between us drives to further chatter,
sweet and heart-arousing, but without the use of tongue,
then you would see that in which reason becomes lost,
Yemen and 'Iraq, pressed close together embracing.
He spoke a lie, the poet who had said prior to my age,
hurling at me the rocks of his faculty of reason,
"Oh you who seek to wed Canopus to the Pleiades,
may God grant you life, how will these two ever meet?[60]
They, the Pleiades, are northerly when they rise toward Syria,
and Canopus, when he rises, is southerly toward Yemen."[61]

The contrast between these two lovers, one Arab the other Persian, one male the other female, represents a vital contrast and even contradiction in existence itself: similitude and transcendence. This becomes apparent in Ibn 'Arabi's discussion of the manner in which these lovers offer cups of wine without fingers and speak without tongues. Such imagery refers to the actions that lovers take even when inactive; in the realm of imagination, lovers share the intoxicating wine of love merely through glancing, speak even when silent, and embrace even when distant. According to Ibn 'Arabi, this reference to "without the use of fingers" signifies "transcendence [*tanzih*], sanctification [*taqdis*] and a cautioning that this is a supersensory, hidden matter, removed from the sensory [*al-hiss*], the imaginal [*al-khayal*], form [*al-surah*], and representation [*mithal*]."[62] That is, there is a transcendence of love, beyond the realm of action, one that knows or needs no means to become actualized, and yet is very real. Ibn 'Arabi here compares these ungraspable and ethereal interactions of lovers to the incomparable qualities of his true Beloved, reminding us that the gnostic even loves distance and transcendence, insofar as it is the will of his Beloved. The human beloved represents not only distance but also cruelty, a point revealed in Ibn 'Arabi's commentary on his description of Nizam as "the daughter of 'Iraq." According to Ibn 'Arabi, the beloved is associated with 'Iraq because of "the harshness [*al-jafa'*], severity [*al-shiddah*], and unbelief [*al-kufr*] that can be attributed to 'Iraq."[63] One must bear in mind that the *Tarjuman al-Ashwaq* surrounds itself with the imagery of the Hajj, so that Ibn 'Arabi's association of these attributes of constraint with 'Iraq almost definitely derives from the prayer a pilgrim makes at one of the four corners of the Ka'bah, namely, the 'Iraqi Corner (*al-rukn al-'Iraqi*).[64] In chapter 72 of *al-Futuhat al-Makkiyah,* Ibn 'Arabi relates the corners of the Ka'bah to the various bestirrings (*khawatir*) that enter the heart, attributing undesirable Satanic bestirrings to the 'Iraqi Corner: "We made the Satanic bestirring pertain to the 'Iraqi Corner only because the Lawgiver has decreed that at that location be said: 'I seek refuge in God from discord [*shiqaq*], hypocrisy [*nifaq*], and evil character traits [*su' al-akhlaq*].' One can know the various grades of these corners through the formulaic remembrances decreed for them."[65]

Conversely, Ibn 'Arabi associates with Yemen the attributes of faith (*al-iman*), wisdom (*al-hikmah*), the Breath of the All Merciful (*al-nafas al-rahmani,* which in a famous tradition is associated with Yemen),[66] and tenderness of heart (*riqqat al-af'idah*). The dynamic he creates allows him to relate feminine receptive qualities to the lover (himself) and masculine qualities of dominance to the beloved (Nizam). This brings spiritual significance to a frequent phenomenon in love lyrics: the cruelty of the beloved. Ibn 'Arabi makes this point clear: "She is a beloved, so she has the traits of harsh estrangement [*al-jafa'*], distance [*al-bu'd*], roughness [*al-ghilzah*], and subjugation [*al-qahr*]. I am the lover, so I have the traits of helpfulness [*al-nusrah*], faith [*al-iman*], tenderness [*al-riqqah*], and gracefulness [*al-latafah*], beseechingly seeking the beloved's satisfaction and finding sweetness in that."[67] In other words, the polarity of God's majestic-versus-beautiful attributes presents itself not only in the male-female dichotomy, but also in the hardheartedness of the beloved and the frustrations of the delicate lover. Moreover, such attributes appear geographically as well; as has been seen, there is a complexity of association, geographic and otherwise, that occurs in the poetry and commentary of Ibn 'Arabi, one that, according to him, reflects the complex interactions that occur in the levels of existence.

Lastly, there is the matter of the faculty of reason (*al-'aql*), which has no access to contradictions and hence has no access to matters of love. As Ibn 'Arabi mentions, when these two lovers unite, they bring together contradictories. The female beloved, representing dominance (*al-qahr*), unites with the male lover, representing kindness (*al-lutf*). Love unites one who is cruel and seeks distance with one who is kind and seeks proximity; this represents the divine dilemma itself. God is, according to Ibn 'Arabi and other mystics, known as one who combines opposites.[68] Not only does he possess attributes of dominance and kindness, or glory and mercy, but he is also described by the verse quoted in Ibn 'Arabi's commentary: *he is the First and the Last, the Outer and the Inner* (57:3). The faculty of reason, in explaining this verse, would use its discerning powers to conclude that "he is First in this respect, Last in this other respect, Outer in this respect, and Inner according to something else," when this is not the case at all.[69] Reason, just like every faculty, is limited by that for which it has been created to perceive. Just as one cannot smell sights or hear smells, so too is the faculty of reason limited by the boundaries of logic. The esoteric faculty, the lordly inner heart (*al-sirr al-rabbani*) witnesses God's combining these opposites, so that the gnostic towers above a mere transcendent understanding of God through his acknowledgment and direct experience of contradictories. The gnostic sees the unseen, loves the transcendent, discovers the unbounded in forms, and, perhaps most significant here, realizes that he is both identical to and infinitely distant from the Real. Herein lies an important observation that relates human love to mysticism. The lover (even in the most profane sense of love) not only succumbs to accepting contradictories, he considers them to be a part of his existence; he lives and experiences contradictions. In this manner, the lover resembles the gnostic, and the gnostic brings to completion the spiritual dimensions of the lover as one who encounters and embodies contradictories. Although reason can never comprehend it, love itself stands as the kernel and reality of all existence, one that forces such contradictories together.

The Real's Needlessness as the Beloved's Cruel Indifference

As has been seen, one important element in the contradictions faced by the lover is the cruelty of the beloved. The lover must accept the beloved's desire for separation and, more commonly in the poetry of 'Iraqi, the beloved's indifference. It is possible that the indifference seen in the poetry of 'Iraqi in some ways stems from his emphasis on beloveds who are beardless young men. Perhaps this boy beloved—uninterested in sexual relationships, homoerotic or otherwise—captures a sense of earnest and unbreakable indifference and thus was considered a fitting model for poetic love. Nevertheless, the beloved as a representation of the cosmic force of constraint and subjugation reveals much about the experiences of gnostic lovers. Cruelty as a divine attribute is explained in some detail by 'Iraqi's predecessor, Ahmad Ghazali: "Since there has been a conjunction [of hearts] in witnessing, the love of the lover necessitates helplessness, baseness, suffering, abjectness, and submission in all forms of his behavior, while the love of the beloved necessitates tyranny, pride, and glory: 'Because of our heart-render's loveliness and beauty / We are not suitable for him, but he suits us.'"[70] Ghazali interprets the relationship between lover and beloved, one of dominion and abjectness, as a result of the polarity of attributes in a complementary relationship. The lover's share is complete passivity and helplessness, while the beloved's share is activity and tyranny; these polarities exist within a whole and comprehensive phenomenon that is love itself. The cruel beloved, then, has a theoretical role in Ghazali's (and 'Iraqi's) cosmological vision of love that demands representation in the confines of verse.

The indifference of the beloved toward his lascivious admirer provides a fitting scene for the power imbalance Ghazali describes, as can be seen in the poetry of 'Iraqi:

Many are the pains I've endured, what a shame!
My desires not fulfilled, not at all, what a shame!
In this world every door that I saw, I opened,
but no heart-holder's face I ever saw, what a shame!
I became despondent, for before this hopeful eye

no fair-cheeked beauty ever came, what a shame!
Never did I see in this world a rose-garden
that didn't scrape my eye with a thorn, what a shame!
A beloved have I who does not recollect me:
Who else has such a beloved, [so aloof]? What a shame!
He observes my sickly heart, but never does he ask,
"What ever happened to that one who was infirm?" What a shame!
One-hundred times I've been to the threshold of his intimacy—
not once did he acquiesce to grant me audience, what a shame!
To this heart of mine from lamenting for his distance
arrives a [different] sorrow every moment, what a shame!
Without your face, my days have now expired;
not much more is remaining of this life—what a shame!
Of 'Iraqi he doesn't inquire, until ['Iraqi] dies.
Thereupon says the World, "He's died. Yes, what a shame!"[71]

The *radif* of "what a shame" (*darigha*) repeated throughout the poem serves as a cry of lamentation for a beloved who simply does not care. In the final hemistich of the poem, "what a shame" might mean something slightly different; it is perhaps an ironic expression of modest grief for an 'Iraqi who has died unfulfilled. Once dead, 'Iraqi arouses nothing more than a blunt statement that "he's died" (*murd*), followed by a short pronouncement of regret. Still, whether genuinely or nonchalantly, it is the world and not the beloved who mourns, so that the beloved's indifference toward 'Iraqi ends not even with his lifespan. There is nothing blatantly or even subtly mystical about this poem, and yet there is also nothing to suggest that it lacks sacred meaning. This is actually quite an important trait in love lyrics that can function simultaneously in sacred and profane contexts: they testify to the beloved's cruelty and indifference in a sincere manner, usually devoid of conspicuous mystical language:

Each day before dawn's hour, I implore and grieve to the East Wind,
so that from me a message right to your neighborhood it brings.
I tread wind in futility and have given a lifetime to the wind,
how else could East Wind find its way to the dust before your door?
Since I have no one as confidant, with the wind I hold my discourse,
since [for this pain] I find no ointment, I ask the wind to cure me.
The fire of the heart by eye-water will not wane, so
I blow a wind on fire so it might consume me all the better.
And maybe I will turn to ash, brought high upon a wind,
liberated from this narrow suffering-place of tribulation.
Dying and becoming ash outranks this life I have with you;

much more pleasing is combustion than estrangement from your face.
Life without your face has absolutely no tranquility;
life without your face is either death or weariness.[72]

The matter of indifference and estrangement is shared by all lovers, even if it acquires cosmological significance only for the mystics. Estrangement results from the great need and attachment that the lover feels for the beloved. The beloved, then, is seen as needless in relation to the lover, even the profane lover. As 'Iraqi states, "Needlessness is an attribute of the beloved and poverty an attribute of the lover."[73] Yet when the beloved is the Supremely Needless (*al-ghani*), one can imagine the annihilating sense of estrangement experienced, as it is by the gnostic lover. The sentiment becomes magnified when one faces a divine beloved who is not indifferent on account of caprice or whim but rather is Needless (and perceived as indifferent) by his eternal essence. The mystical ramifications of the needless beloved are alluded to in the *Istilahat-i Sufiyah* attributed to 'Iraqi, where, for example, the author defines harsh estrangement (*jafa*) as "what they call the covering of the wayfarer's heart from gnostic realizations [*ma'arif*] and from witnessings [*mushahadat*]."[74] Just as the incognizant lover senses that he needs physical union, the gnostic lover senses that he needs spiritual proximity and witnessing, and suffers when the beloved denies him such.

One must bear in mind that, without the beloved's seeming indifference and demand for separation, the lover would have no need to lament or, for example, sing out in poetry. The spiritual wisdom in the divine beloved's decree of separation becomes apparent in the *Istilahat-i Sufiyah*'s definition of "the lover's groan" (*nalah*) as "whispered prayers" (*munajat*).[75] With separation, the soul cries out, searches, and discovers its own intrinsic poverty. This decree is not a matter of indifference, even if the lover's frustrated pleas depict it as such; rather, separation is divinely ordained and an essential part of the path to self-perfection. 'Iraqi clarifies this matter most explicitly in chapter 22 of the *Lama'at,* where to some extent he repeats the observations made by Ibn 'Arabi: "A requirement for the lover is to love that which the beloved loves, even if it be constant distance and separation. Usually, moreover, the beloved desires the separation and distance of the lover." Here 'Iraqi adds one important point: "This is the case, so that the lover will seek refuge from the beloved's harsh estrangement in desirous love."[76]

This important addition to Ibn 'Arabi's observation tells us that desirous love (*'ishq*), and not the beloved, should be the lover's goal. In desirous love, the lover loses himself and becomes a pauper, and ultimately "the pauper relinquishes existence and tolerates his own nonexistence."[77] 'Iraqi tells us that estrangement is more beneficial for the lover than union because "in proximity and union, the lover retains the attribute of his own will, while in distance and separation he takes on the attribute of the beloved's will."[78] Love effaces the self and (as the true motivating actor behind both lover and beloved) owns the power of abasement that the lover initially attributes to the beloved. As 'Iraqi observes, the "lover suffers abasement because of desirous love, not because of the beloved."[79] Just as love has endowed the beloved with attributes of harshness and dominance, it is love that has endowed the lover with attributes of mildness and abasement.

This abasement and relinquishment of will is, of course, not merely an effect of love, but is also the end of the spiritual wayfarer's path more generally. Thus one should not be surprised that gnostics, who were often unwilling to revere the uninitiated, would admire true lovers, even those who loved benightedly. After all, such lovers lost their very selves in pursuing the unattained and became subject to the destructive demands and contradictions of love.

Poetry: A Medium Receptive to Imagination's Forms

One final factor that renders poetry suitable to express the gnostic's visionary experience is one mentioned by Muhyi al-Din himself: its ability to evoke forms. Imagination, vision in forms, and poetry are bound together in an astrological sense in the writings of Ibn 'Arabi. According to Ibn 'Arabi's understanding of astrology, the third celestial sphere bears three important characteristics which relate directly to poetic composition: it is the sphere of the prophet Joseph, it is the sphere of the divine name "the Form-giver" (*al-musawwir*), and it is the sphere of Venus.[80] At this sphere the gnostic encounters the sciences particular to the prophet Joseph, those "related to representational forms and forms of the imagination."[81] It should be no surprise, since this sphere projects from the divine name "the Form-giver," that it includes that which pertains to forms and the form-giving abilities of the human soul. It should also be no surprise that this is the sphere of the prophet Joseph, who is known to have been a master dream interpreter; as Ibn 'Arabi mentions, since a dreamer encounters the supersensory in imaginal forms, the dream interpreter must revert such images to the meanings which they represent. He must recognize, to use a common example, milk as the form of knowledge. This is the process of interpretation or *al-ta'bir* (literally, "crossing over"), a method by which one returns from form to meaning. The opposite of this, the process of capturing meaning in form, is not unique to the mystics, who capture meaning in form through the process of witnessing. Rather, Ibn 'Arabi recognizes a number of phenomena, generally experienced in the human world, that bring meaning into the limits of form: "This is the celestial sphere of complete form-giving and harmonious arrangement [*nizam*]. From this sphere is derived assistance for poets. From it also arrive arrangement, proper fashioning, and geometrical forms within corporeal bodies. . . . From this sphere is known the meaning of proper fashioning, correct making, the beauty whose existence comprises wisdom, and the beauty that is desired by and is agreeable to a specific human constitution."[82]

Two important observations must be made here. First, this sphere provides assistance to those able to envision meaning in the forms of words and create thereby forms that evoke meaningful forms in the imaginations of others: the poets. Moreover, Ibn 'Arabi associates this sphere not only with poets but also with poetry itself as versified speech; in using the word *nizam* (which means "harmonious arrangement" and is thus cognate with the word for "verse," *nazm*), Ibn 'Arabi points to poetry as metered and rhymed language. Poetry gives artful form to meaning and constantly reminds its audience of the beauty of its form. Ibn 'Arabi assigns other modes of language—writing and speech—to the second sphere, that which pertains to knowledge. This is because in relaying knowledge, writers and speakers aim for clarity of expression; the Prophet Muhammad too was sent to clarify (*mubayyinan*) and present in detail (*mufassilan*), so that he was divinely withheld from composing poetry. Poetry, after all, is not about breaking knowledge down for clear understanding but about capturing it into an evocative image or form; in the words of Ibn 'Arabi, "poetry [*al-shi'r*] comes from perceptiveness [*al-shu'ur*], so that its locus is summation, rather than breaking [meaning] apart in explication [*al-ijmal la al-tafsil*]."[83]

One might say, then, that while other modes of speech must answer to reason, poetry is born from imagination and bears its traits. While other modes of speech unravel meaning, poetry localizes it.[84] Second, the third sphere, the sphere of poets, is also the sphere of human beauty (*al-husn*), which relates not only to Joseph, renowned for his miraculous physical beauty, but also to harmonious forms, that is, forms that suit the meanings they embody. In discussing this sphere, Ibn 'Arabi outlines a general pattern in existence. God as the form giver has brought meaning into form. These forms are considered beautiful because they allow an encounter with meaning in a manner that accords with the limits of that perceiver. Every perceiver also has the ability to create forms within his imagination, using the human form-giving faculty. The poet's role therefore is one both receptive and active. The poet receives meaning in forms within his imagination. He then creates forms, through words, forms that are able to stimulate forms within the imagination of his audience. Of course, what the gnostic *receives* from poetry is emphatically more profound than what others receive. Moreover, the poet that produces such forms need not be a gnostic. Since stimuli provoke various forms in the imaginations of various perceivers, form-giving poetry, whether by a gnostic or not, will arouse spiritually meaningful forms in the imagination of the gnostic perceiver.

Such intimations are fascinating, in part because of the extent to which they parallel statements made by the great Islamic peripatetic philosopher Abu 'Ali al-Husayn ibn Sina (d. 428/1037), known in the Latinate version of his name as "Avicenna." According to Salim Kemal, Ibn Sina posits a link between imagination and poetry: "Avicenna defines poetry as imaginative speech, pointing to an etymological relation between 'imagination' and 'imaginative representations' to explain the nature of poetic discourse. He explains that imagination is the ability to reproduce sensory experiences as mental images, even in the absence of the objects which caused these experiences. The imagination is able to combine these images and part of images in forms that differ from the original experience. This activity is crucial to human thought and present in thinking, imagining, calculating, dreaming, remembering, wishing, and so on."[85] Ibn 'Arabi's concern extends beyond the boundaries of the mental faculty of imagination shared by all human beings. One must bear in mind that the cosmos parallels the human soul in Ibn 'Arabi's cosmology, so that, just as the human being has an imagination, the cosmos has an imagination—or an imaginal realm (*'alam al-khayal*). Encounters that occur here are no less real than that which occurs in the sensory realm, but they are not subject to every limitation of physical matter. Both the subjective and objective imaginations are conducive to forms and unrestrained by the boundaries of logic.

It is, in fact, imagination that makes contradictories accessible and perceivable, as noted by a contemporary scholar, Khalid Bilqasim.[86] In discussing imagination's relationship to composition in the thought of Ibn 'Arabi, Bilqasim makes use of chapter 177 of *al-Futuhat al-Makkiyah,* in which Ibn 'Arabi discusses gnosis of the station of gnosis, including the manner in which gnosis of imagination (both subjective and objective) aids in gnosis of gnosis. Imagination can make the impossible manifest in forms, allow vision of one object in two places simultaneously, and grant the reception of an object in its state of transformation and fluctuation, among other things.[87] Sensory meets supersensory, which we have seen so often in Ibn 'Arabi's discussions of beauty; this meeting of sensory and supersensory within imagination allows for the sacred-profane ambiguity in his poetry. This meeting allows the gnostic to experience two things at once: first, the love acquired by means of the sensory realm, and second, the limitlessness of the supersensory. So too does amorous poetry celebrate the sensual, but—in evoking forms suited to the unimpaired and nearly flawless realm of imagination—intimates something more ideal than pure physicality.

Much like poetic images, imaginal forms, freely changing and enamoring, become the medium of the gnostic's vision of love; they show him what he seeks, but in a limited fashion, arousing in him an uncontrollable desire for the limitless. Love poetry is thus the most fitting medium to convey the gnostic's amorous conflict with the *shahid:*

Peace be upon Salma and whoever settles in that private pasture,
and it is the duty of one like me, so tender-hearted, to give greetings.
And what would she lose if she were to return these salutations
to us? But one cannot pass judgment against beautiful idols.

They set off, when the tenebrousness of night let down its curtains,
and I said to her, "Uncontrollably in love! Stranded! Enslaved by love!
Yearnings surrounding him jealously! Ready to unleash
upon him are racing arrows, no matter where he turns."
She smiled revealing her teeth. A flash of lightning struck.
I do not know which of the two broke the sheer night darkness.
She said, "Doesn't it suffice him, concerning me, that with his heart
he witnesses me in every single moment? Doesn't it? Doesn't it?"[88]

Of course, the irony in the final double line is that the vision of the beloved that remains in the heart, despite its permanence, does *not* suffice. This is the paradox of a beloved who perseveres in the imagination; while she is ubiquitous, it is that very ubiquity that tortures the lover, for she is never attained. In this very manner, for the gnostic, love for the *shahid* that remains in the heart from unveiling is an agonizing pleasure. Ibn 'Arabi's commentary describes this experience as witnessing the divine self-disclosures in ever-changing moments through the beautiful forms of the imaginal realm; wherever the gnostic lover turns, *there is the face of God* (2:115).[89] While the gnostic's experience is unfathomable for the uninitiated, the gnostic is still human and undergoes that experience through the faculties common to all humans. Only imagination, a human faculty employed by all who hear or write poetry, can bring the contradictions of witnessing, the allures of beauty, and the images of love together. Therefore not only lovers in the world of human affairs but also lovers of spiritual realities found the artistic medium of poetic expression most suited for the ordeal of love.

Conclusions

Extending beyond Ibn 'Arabi and 'Iraqi, and even beyond Sufi love poetry, the aesthetic outlook studied here matters because it increasingly altered the way poetry was written and read, for all love poetry fell within its purview. Unfortunately research concerning the topics of beauty and the human form in Islamic mysticism has been often plagued by either vague generalizations or mistaken analogies. The method here, however, has been first to analyze perception according to the mystics at hand, with particular emphasis on the vision of similitude (*tashbih*) and its relationship to love. Second, the method used here has considered beauty, especially human beauty, through the writings of Akbari mystics, as well as a number of mystics unaffiliated with Ibn 'Arabi or his teachings. Lastly, by means of this informed perspective on gnostic witnessing and love, this study has analyzed the often misunderstood amorous lyric poetry of these two mystics, which, as we have seen, is neither mere allegory nor false in its claims to have spiritual significance. Rather, as argued, gnostic amorous lyric verse results from a complex and even confounding experience in which the sensory and the supersensory collaborate to yield something more comprehensive than either alone. The sensory serves as a form for encountering the supersensory, which can also be called "meaning" or even a "divine self-disclosure." In other words, the divine interacts with the gnostic not only in spiritual unveilings but also through the two worlds of form, the physical and the representational.

This final point has significant applications for the Islamic tradition well beyond simply Islamic mysticism. Western scholarship and popular culture have often failed to understand the sensual in Islamic thought and have claimed to discern clandestine (or even blatant) erotic-misogynistic undercurrents in Islamic conceptions of marriage, paradise, and even modes of dress. One example of this can be found in the writings of Miguel Asín Palacios (d. 1944), a Spanish scholar of Arabic literature. Asín seems, in many ways, to have been a sensitive and insightful researcher of Ibn 'Arabi, but one burdened by unfavorable assumptions held vis-à-vis Islam. Such assumptions can be seen in the very title of his study of Sufism through an analysis of the writings of Ibn 'Arabi, *El islam cristianizado.*[1] As another example, in a separate study concerning Dante Alighieri (d. 1321), Asín states that "Islam, be it once more said, is but the bastard offspring of the Gospel and the Mosaic Law, part of whose doctrines on the after-life it adopted."[2] Asín holds that the Islamic version of paradise (*al-jannah*) in the hereafter resulted from a lack of "the restraining influence of an infallible authority whereby the fancy of its believers might have been checked," which allowed it to assimilate "elements from other Eastern sources," elements that allowed the introduction of sensual and imaginative imagery to what had been a restrained and moralistic afterlife in its original Judeo-Christian context.[3]

While such a view might seem specific to the author's time and cultural surroundings, Asín's observations concerning the Islamic conception of paradise have their parallel in a contemporary American and European fascination with the sensuality of the afterlife as depicted in the Qur'an. Asín's view is important here, however, because it springs from his attempt to understand the poetically revered beloved in Islamic literature through what he deems to be the historical development of Islamic mystical thought:

> We are thus still far from the Platonic conception of woman, idealised as an angel and a symbol of philosophy. The origin of this strange conception would seem to be due to an attempt to idealise the sensual coarseness of the Koranic paradise. The houris of the Koran, although celestial, are intended solely to be instruments of carnal delight. This idea was incompatible with the spiritual longings of the later Moslem mystics, who had been profoundly influenced by the asceticism preached and practiced by the Christian monks. But it was impossible to eliminate from the Koran the verses proclaiming these sensual joys. The mystics therefore, in their legends of the afterlife, replaced the houris by one celestial bride, a spiritual being whose love is chaste and whom God has appointed to each of the blessed.[4]

Clearly, Asín sees Islamic mystics as sharing almost completely the outlook of classical Christian asceticism and being forced to reconcile passages in the Qur'an with a religious temperament that instinctively rejects sexual pleasure and physical human beauty. This is emphatically untrue. As this study has illustrated, not only human beauty but also sexual pleasure hold an important position in Ibn 'Arabi's cosmological vision and aesthetic values. While Asín was doubtless aware of this position, he does not seem to have regarded it as a genuinely mystical experience, despite Ibn 'Arabi's detailed descriptions indicating otherwise.

Moreover, Asín overlooks indications that a profound understanding of human beauty among Muslim mystics was a natural outgrowth of the Islamic sources, the Qur'an and the *ahadith*. Ibn 'Arabi, for example, uses traditions from canonical sources to illustrate the phenomenon of witnessing the divine in forms. In fact, a narration from one of six authoritative Sunni hadith collections serves as the source for his term *tahawwul*/state-changing, used to describe the mystic's envisioning of

God in infinite and constantly changing displays: *"You will not strain yourselves to see God—Blessed and Exalted—on the Day of Resurrection. . . . The Lord of the Worlds will come to them, Glorified and Exalted, according to the lowest form [adna surah] in which they had seen him. . . . He will change [tahawwala] into his form in which they saw him the first time."*[5] When one considers Ibn 'Arabi's analyses of the foundational Islamic sources, as well as an enthusiastic acknowledgment of his veracity by other mystics such as 'Iraqi, these very sources of Islamic spirituality appear in a different light. While one might argue that envisioning the divine is an exclusively mystical affair, this is only the case insofar as it is applied to the present physical world, since foundational Islamic texts unequivocally attribute this phenomenon to the hereafter.

In other words, some sort of intimate visionary encounter with God is clearly not only part of the Islamic tradition but also part of the Qur'an's depictions of sensual pleasures in the afterlife. One should remember that, while the Qur'an does describe the delights of beautiful maidens and gardens, it also refers to otherworldly recompense for good as the attainment of God's satisfaction with his servants and the encountering of God's face—all achievements that cannot be unrelated to one another.[6] Islam's mystics differed from their uninitiated counterparts mainly in announcing that their vision of these realities occurred *before* physical death. As for that which comes *after* death and resurrection, even one moderately acquainted with the Qur'an might consider it fair to describe the images of Islam's paradise as "spiritual significance in sensory forms." In fact, this seems to correspond to Ibn 'Arabi's understanding of paradise.

Thus, in discussing otherworldly pleasures, Ibn 'Arabi makes use of a principle from the same aesthetic approach proposed in this study. According to Muhyi al-Din, the sensual delights and pains of the next life are manifestations of existence that correspond to the individual human constitution. Bliss must present itself in a manner pleasurable for the receiver:

> Punitive requital in the next life involves torment in a manner proportional to the period that that person has lived in polytheism in this lower life. When that period has ended, bliss becomes situated in the Hellfire for them. This is because, were they to enter Paradise, they would suffer pain on account of the lack of correspondence to the constitution upon which God has constructed them. Thus they enjoy the pleasures of that which they experience: fire, severe cold, and that which Hellfire offers of the biting of snakes and scorpions. They enjoy it, just as the people of Paradise take pleasure in shades, light, and kissing beautiful houris, because their constitutions decree such. Do you not see that the dung beetle of this world has been created with a constitution that suffers from the fragrance of the rose, and instead delights

> in malodorous smells? So too is the case for whomever has been created according to the dung beetle's constitution. . . . Thus every constitution in the cosmos derives pleasure from that which accords with it and experiences a lack of pleasure in that which conflicts with it.[7]

It is true that Ibn 'Arabi's reliance on a notion of the human constitution and his supposition of the eventual pleasures of hellfire are external to the traditional descriptions he analyses. Moreover, this passage reflects his mystically informed (yet philosophically justifiable) notion of the relativity and lack of true existence for the ugly, the undesirable, and even the evil. Nevertheless, Ibn 'Arabi's central argument is that constitution determines one's reception of the spiritual. This general perceptive approach echoes the hereafter of the Islamic sources, described as a result and unfathomable intensification of earthly human life. Paradise is not unrelated to the human experience; rather, it is a sublime fulfillment filtered through what has been acquired from sensory existence. After all, sensory perception is, according to medieval Muslim thought, humankind's first and basic manner of having some grasp of the supersensory.

Ibn 'Arabi and other Muslim mystics who beheld divinity in the physical presented their audience with that which many uninitiated Muslims saw and still see in the Qur'an, that God is not found elsewhere, not in the sublimity of immateriality unknown by humans but in the world that surrounds those poised to perceive him. When the divine breath lodged the human spirit in the confines of dark claylike human flesh, a new way of being, perceiving, and knowing arose. Purely spiritual entities—the angels themselves—were commanded to prostrate before this admixture, a command difficult to understand for one worshipper who had been created of higher substance. Yet the human capacity for knowledge, the names taught to Adam, served as a proof that this combination of base and divine had something that even purely spiritual beings did not have. The story of Adam in the Qur'an serves to teach human beings that their inherited humanity, even and especially their strange combination of body and spirit, is most purposeful. Having been put at a distance, exiled to the lowness of the earthly, human beings can return to their divine source with a knowledge unique to them, a comprehensive knowledge that accompanies them and defines them. In encountering the physical world and its beauties, Ibn 'Arabi and 'Iraqi proclaim, one must only recognize the true divine face behind all things, or else risk engaging in meaningless action, devoid of insight. The physical world must serve as a reminder of God, not as a means for forgetting him. Seen from this perspective, Qur'anic afterlife imagery can reintroduce itself to us as an intensely spiritual depiction. After all, whether houris and wine are realized forms of satisfaction and knowledge, or whether such enjoyments are merely enjoyments, it would seem to matter little in an abode where God cannot be forgotten.

In this book, I have also aimed to confront an unfortunate albeit very different trend in the study of Sufism: an idealization of medieval Sufi writers. While Sufism should not be relegated to mere historical circumstances, one cannot undervalue the context of history. One must concede that Sufis did engage in the Islamic societies that surrounded them, bearing quite often views and even indulgent inclinations that reflected their time. A striking example, *shahidbazi,* stands out as a reminder that gnostic conceptions of beauty and love cannot be reduced to poetic practices. The use of young men, even boys, by Sufis to achieve mystical ecstasy, even if not common, had a debilitating effect on public regard for their own tradition. One would expect saints to speak out on the matter, serving as paragons of ethical responsibility. Instead, their proclamations made it seem that such saints treated lightly a matter that was, when practiced in the social circles around them, reprehensibly grave. Attempts were made to justify this aesthetic practice, as has been seen, through unverifiable esoteric interpretations of Islam's sources as well as a circular emphasis on the precedent of Sufism's saints. In the case of *shahidbazi,* one notices that the sober Muslim jurisprudents held what might be considered a more contemporary perspective, if indeed time can serve as a judge.

Such interpretive differences are not irresolvable. On one hand, postresurrection life, interpreted perhaps too superficially and in terms too unimaginatively identical to the life of this world by certain exoterically minded Muslims, benefits from the scripturally profound insights of Sufi saints. On the other hand, "applied" *shahidbazi,* falsely justified by an excessively esoteric and insular interpretive proclivity among certain Sufis, would have benefited greatly by the sobriety and juridical rigor of those who valued the *sunnah* or "way" of the Prophet above the *sunnah* of like-minded saints. They need not have looked far, for prominent Sufi figures can be found criticizing the practice. In both cases, a sort of Islamic legitimacy can be determined by deeming which party held a more careful and scrutinizing perspective toward the Islamic sources and refrained from capitulating to simplistic thought, false methods, and self-serving analogies. In other words, medieval (as well as contemporary) Muslim writers can always be held accountable by the sources that they themselves deem ultimate standards of interpretation.

Of course, the central concern of this study has been to establish an aesthetic view common to certain mystics in the sixth/twelfth to seventh/thirteenth centuries, an aesthetic view related intrinsically to their cosmological theories and one that blossomed organically in their poetry. It is hoped that this study has contributed to the idea that, wherever an artistic tradition thrives, there are inherent aesthetic values behind it, even if they are not presented or even realized in a systematic matter. In the case of the gnostics, their unique perceptive experience and concept of beauty has yielded a tradition of love poetry with profound intimations. Considering the comprehensive nature of their theories, based on a comprehensive vision that they experienced, it should be expected that human beauty acquired cosmological and even divine significance. While their vision included other realms of existence, they often encountered those realms within the natural realm shared by their contemporaries. While the esoteric knowledge they acquired outstripped that to which uninitiated humans have access, never did such mystics claim to be anything other than human.

Notes

Introduction

1. 'Abd al-Rahman Jami, *Nafahat al-Uns min Hadarat al-Quds,* ed. Mahdi Tawhidipur (Tehran: Kitabfurushi-i Mahmudi, 1336 *hijri-shamsi*), 614. This is my translation; henceforth translations lacking attribution are my own.

2. Ibn 'Arabi, *Tarjuman al-Ashwaq* (Beirut: Dar Sadir, 1961) (hereafter cited as *Tarjuman al-Ashwaq*), 189–90; Ibn 'Arabi, *Dhakha'ir al-A'laq, Sharh Tarjuman al-Ashwaq,* ed. Muhammad 'Abd al-Rahman Najm al-Din al-Kurdi (Cairo: College of Arabic, al-Azhar University, 1968) (hereafter cited as *Dhakha'ir*), 250–53. Reynold A. Nicholson's edition of the Arabic text has *janib al-suwa* instead of *janib al-dawa* in the fifth hemistich; this accords well with Ibn 'Arabi's explanation in the commentary and, unlike its alternative, makes sense. See Reynold A. Nicholson, *The Tarjuman al-ashwaq: A Collection of Mystical Odes* (London: Royal Asiatic Society, 1911) (hereafter cited as *Mystical Odes*), 44.

3. Saint John of the Cross (1542–1591), *John of the Cross: Selected Writings,* trans. Kieran Kavanaugh (New York: Paulist Press, 1987), 220.

Chapter 1: Perception according to Ibn 'Arabi

1. Ibn 'Arabi, *Fusus al-Hikam* (Tehran: Intisharat al-Zahra, 1380 *hijri-shamsi*) (hereafter cited as *Fusus al-Hikam*), 107. Here some commentators have read the final word as *haqq,* but 'Afifi, as well as Qaysari, read it as *huqq* (singular *huqqah*), referring to a receptacle of wood or ivory in which often perfume or wine is held. See Edward William Lane, *An Arabic-English Lexicon* (London: Williams and Norgate, 1863–93), 2:608. See also Ibn 'Arabi, *The Bezels of Wisdom,* trans. R. W. J. Austin (Mahwah, N.J.: Paulist Press, 1980) (hereafter cited as *Bezels of Wisdom*), 130.

2. William C. Chittick has rightly differentiated between the "received wisdom" that had developed concerning Ibn 'Arabi and *wahdat al-wujud* and the actual teachings of the Great Shaykh. As Chittick mentions, in debates concerning the Oneness of Being, Ibn 'Arabi's own position "was not the real issue." See Chittick, *The Sufi Path of Knowledge* (Albany: State University of New York Press, 1989) (hereafter cited as *SPK*), 226.

3. See Ibn 'Arabi's *al-Futuhat al-Makkiyah* (Beirut: Dar Ihya' al-Turath al-'Arabi, 1997) (hereafter cited as *FM,* followed by volume, chapter, page, and line numbers),

vol. 3, ch. 362, p. 298, line 29. See also the Dar Sadir edition (Beirut, 1968), vol. 3, p. 306, line 8 (which will hereafter be cited by a page number in parentheses; volume and chapter numbers correspond). See also *SPK,* 227.

4. *Fusus al-Hikam,* 48.

5. This narration is another one cited throughout the works of Ibn 'Arabi and his students, one that in many ways forms the basis of Ibn 'Arabi's cosmology (it is a *hadith qudsi,* that is, God speaks in the first person). This is the version found throughout *al-Futuhat al-Makkiyah,* which differs slightly from the more popular version ("I was a *Hidden* Treasure . . . *so that I might be known*"). As Chittick points out, the "scholars of Hadith consider it a forgery, as the Shaykh is well aware. However, in his view its authenticity has been proven by unveiling (*kashf*), or vision of the Prophet in the imaginal world. Hence he writes that this hadith 'is sound on the basis of unveiling, but not established by way of transmission (*naql*).'" See *SPK,* 391n.14, 66. This version can be found throughout *al-Futuhat al-Makkiyah,* including *FM,* vol. 2, ch. 198, p. 198.30 (p. 399); *FM,* vol. 3, ch. 358, p. 260.26 (p. 267); and *FM,* vol. 4, ch. 559, p. 426.6 (p. 428).

6. *FM,* vol. 3, ch. 369, p. 352.23 (p. 362). Translation from William Chittick, *The Self-Disclosure of God* (Albany: State University of New York Press, 1998) (hereafter cited as *SDG*), 232. I have made the minor addition of "he" to reflect the possibility that the subject of the verb "to be" is deliberately ambiguous so that it can refer simultaneously to "the Real" and/or to "creation." Such deliberate ambiguity is not uncommon in Ibn 'Arabi's writings.

7. Perhaps because of later emphasis on the phrase *wahdat al-wujud,* often the philosophical implications of Ibn 'Arabi's presentation of *wujud*/existence overshadow the visionary significance of his statements. This can be seen, for example, when the Naqshbandi shaykh and theorist Ahmad Sirhindi (d. 1034/1624) added his own insight to assertions made by adherents to the Oneness of Being and offered a modified understanding of oneness, namely, the Oneness of Witnessing, or *wahdat al-shuhud,* such that an exaggerated distinction between the two phrases arose. Nevertheless two important differences cannot be ignored. First, it is clear from his writings that Sirhindi differentiated between existence and the divine essence. Second, Sirhindi's reconsideration of this doctrine rests on the possible subjectivity of a cosmology founded in mystical experience. See Ahmad Sirhindi, *Intikhab-i Maktubat-i Shaykh Ahmad Sirhindi,* ed. Fazlur Rahman (Karachi: Iqbal Academy, 1968), 120 and 174. See also William Chittick, "Wahdat al-Shuhud," *Encyclopaedia of Islam,* 2nd ed., ed. P. J. Bearman, Th. Bianquis, C. E. Bosworth, E. van Donzel, W. P. Heinrichs, and G. Lecomte (Leiden: Brill, 1960–2002), 11:37–39. Hereafter cited as EI2.

8. *FM,* vol. 2, ch. 209, p. 484.10 (p. 494–95). Ascertainment (*al-tahaqquq*) refers here to certainty acquired through witnessing the Real. Peace results from such certainty.

9. *FM,* vol. 2, ch. 209, p. 484.15 (p. 495).

10. Ibid.

11. Such a definition can be found in the manual on logic *al-Mantiq* by Muhammad Rida al-Muzaffar (d. 1322/1904), commenting on which Ra'id al-Haydari mentions a number of other definitions of knowledge from classic Islamic philosophers, all of which describe knowledge as a trace, reception, or acceptance of a "form" in the "intellect." See al-Muzaffar, *al-Mantiq* (Beirut: Mu'assasat al-Tarikh al-'Arabi, 2004), 16.

12. This is clear from Ibn 'Arabi's description of the *shahid* in chapter 266 of *FM*, where he states that "since the *shahid* is the obtainment of the form of the witnessed in the soul (*al-nafs*) during *shuhud,* it bestows other than that which is bestowed by *ru'yah." FM,* vol. 2, ch. 266, p. 557.3 (p. 567).

13. Compare the previous note to the heading of chapter 266, where Ibn 'Arabi describes the *shahid* as "the form of the witnessed in the heart," not the soul. It is likely that Ibn 'Arabi uses the two terms loosely and interchangeably here. *FM,* vol. 2, ch. 266, p. 556.32 (p. 567).

14. Such accords with Ibn Sina's definition of "thought" as "that which a human being has, at the point of resolving, to move from things present in his mind—conceptions or assents—to things not present in it." See Abu 'Ali ibn Sina, *Remarks and Admonitions, Part One: Logic,* trans. Shams Constantine Inati (Toronto: Pontifical Institute of Mediaeval Studies, 1984), 47.

15. *FM,* vol. 2, ch. 266, p. 557.3 (p. 567).

16. See *FM,* vol. 2, ch. 209/210, pp. 484.37 and 486.31 (pp. 495 and 497).

17. Abu Hamid Muhammad al-Ghazali, *Kitab al-Imla' fi Ishkalat al-Ihya',* appended to Abu Hamid Muhammad al-Ghazali, *Ihya' 'Ulum al-Din* (Beirut: Dar al-Kutub al-'Ilmiyyah, 1424/2004), 5:16. Gerhard Böwering refers to this text as *al-Imla' 'ala Mushkil al-Ihya'* in "al-Ghazali, Abu Hamed Mohammad, Biography," *Encyclopaedia Iranica,* vol. 10 (London: Routledge and Kegan Paul,1982–). It should be added that Ibn 'Arabi's definitions of these terms in his *Istilahat al-Sufiyyah* also parallel those of al-Ghazali in the *Kitab al-Imla'* almost identically; see Ibn 'Arabi, *Istilahat al-Shaykh Muhyi al-Din Ibn 'Arabi* (Beirut: Dar al-Imam Muslim, 1990), 64.

18. Abu al-Qasim 'Abd al-Karim ibn Hawazin al-Qushayri (d. 465/1072) holds this position, as does Khwajah Abu Isma'il 'Abdallah ibn Muhammad al-Ansari al-Harawi (d. 481/1089). Ansari also includes stages of perception higher than *mushahadah*/witnessing. For the first, see *al-Risalah al-Qushayriyah fi 'Ilm al-Tasawwuf,* ed. Ma'ruf Zurayq and 'Ali 'Abd al-Hamid Balta-ji (Beirut: Dar al-Jil, 1990), 75. For the second, see *Manazil al-Sa'irin,* ed. Muhammad Khwajawi (Tehran: Dar al-'Ilm, 1417 *hijri-qamari*), 124–25 and 133–44. I discuss the development of terms related to unveiling and witnessing in, "Kashf o Shohud," *Encyclopaedia Iranica.*

19. *FM,* vol. 2, ch. 210, p. 486.10 (p. 497).

20. This is my interpretation of Ibn 'Arabi's use of *dhat*/*dhawat* here, which cannot be translated as "essences" because of the ambiguity involved. It seems that Ibn 'Arabi is referring to the grammatical distinction between *ism dhat* (a real or concrete substantive,

which is also known as *ism 'ayn*) and *ism ma'na* (an ideal substantive). In the case of *ism dhat*, a specific referent in the outer world is indicated, for example, a man or tree. In the case of *ism ma'na*, an abstract concept—what Ibn 'Arabi sometimes calls *al-sifah* (attribute)—is intended, for example, knowledge or power, although most likely Ibn 'Arabi's reference to "meanings" is self-disclosures divorced from all form and matter. It is not at all unusual for Ibn 'Arabi to use terms in an unexpected context, suddenly and without notice.

21. *FM*, vol. 2, ch. 210, p. 486.3 (p. 496).

22. What exactly is "self-disclosure" (*al-tajalli*)? As Su'ad al-Hakim remarks, self-disclosure forms the basis of Ibn 'Arabi's cosmological system, for it is through self-disclosure that creation comes to be and yet still remains indistinguishable from its Creator. Self-disclosure corresponds to manifestation, unveiling, revelation, opening, in other words, God's allowing himself to be known and witnessed in receptacles, according to the receptive ability of those receptacles. By revealing himself throughout the levels of existence, the Real brings about multiplicity from Absolute Oneness. As indicated by al-Hakim, there are two major divisions of self-disclosure: existential (*al-wujudi*) and witnessed (*al-shuhudi*). Existential self-disclosure describes the Real's constant manifestation in loci, that which effects the existence of the cosmos. Witnessed self-disclosure describes the unveiling that occurs for the mystic, where the Real makes manifest some reality from himself in the heart of the gnostic. Considering the significance of this term in the thought of Ibn 'Arabi, there are numerous divisions and specifications involved, for which one can refer to al-Hakim's commendable study, *al-Mu'jam al-Sufi: al-Hikmah fi Hudud al-Kalimah* (Beirut: Dandarah, 1981), 257–66.

23. See, for example, *FM*, vol. 2, ch. 260, p. 549.29 (p. 560), where he lays out these terms expressly.

24. *FM*, vol. 4, ch. 418, p. 28.19 (p. 25). See also *SDG*, 316. Still, it seems that Ibn 'Arabi's use of the term *maddah* does often correspond to the philosophical definition of the term as a substance bearing preparedness (*isti'dad*); in fact, Ibn 'Arabi even refers to matter in its plural form as "matter of possibility" (*al-mawadd al-imkaniyah*), intimating that matter is potentiality. See *FM*, vol. 1, ch. 70, p. 704.11 (p. 582). Chittick is right to notice that Ibn 'Arabi "rarely if ever speaks of 'form' as juxtaposed with 'matter,' as was done by the Muslim philosophers, following the Greek tradition," but he often uses the term matter as corresponding to that which is subject to form, as well as, in Chittick's words, that in which pure meaning or spirit "displays its traces and exercises its properties." *SDG*, 280.

25. *FM*, vol. 2, ch. 198, p. 394.25 (p. 400).

26. *FM*, vol. 2, ch. 262, p. 551.10 (p. 561).

27. *FM*, vol. 3, ch. 369, p. 383.20 (p. 395).

28. *FM*, vol. 3, ch. 352, p. 230.3 (p. 235). The process by which meaning divorced from matter descends and becomes "dressed" in matter is called "transference"

(*intiqal*), which includes the manifestation of "the Real in the forms of bodies (*suwar al-ajsam*)." See *FM,* vol. 2, ch. 188, p. 374.15 (p. 379).

29. *FM,* vol. 3, ch. 352, 229–30 (pp. 234–35). One must of course bear in mind that matter is not necessarily physical; in fact, Ibn 'Arabi makes reference to "luminary matter" in *FM,* vol. 2, ch. 198, p. 394.26 (p. 400).

30. See *SDG,* 290. The transfer of information or matter between these faculties is discussed in *FM,* vol. 1, ch. 7, p. 176.22 (pp. 125–26).

31. Ibn 'Arabi discusses the differences in knowledge in his advice to those undertaking retreat (*khalwah*): "The person undertaking retreat should not wait expectantly for an inrush (*warid*), a form (*surah*), or a witnessing (*shuhud*), but rather should seek only knowledge of his Lord; sometimes he will give him such knowledge outside of matter and sometimes he will give it to him in matter. [In the case of the latter,] he will give him knowledge indicated by that matter." *FM,* vol. 2, ch. 78, p. 149.5 (p. 152).

32. For this description of *ilham,* see *FM,* vol. 1, ch. 57, p. 361.6 (p. 287). For this description of *shuhud,* see *Fusus al-Hikam,* 217.

33. Chittick distinguishes *shuhud* from *mushahadah* as well, describing *shuhud* as "a synonym for seeing and vision on any level of existence" and *mushahadah* as "a synonym for unveiling." It is not exactly clear how consistent Ibn 'Arabi is with these terms, but in most of the examples encountered here, *shuhud* and *mushahadah* differ from unveiling insofar as unveiling is a disclosure of meaning, while the other two terms (*shuhud* and *mushahadah*) usually relate to the mystic's interaction with meaningful forms. See *SPK,* 227.

34. As Ibn 'Arabi states, "Using the power of fantasy every person can create in the faculty of imagination that which has no external existence, and this is a general rule." *Fusus al-Hikam,* 88.

35. Ibn 'Arabi discusses human imaginal powers in his chapter concerning Abraham in the *Fusus al-Hikam,* where he asserts that the Real "never becomes disregardful, though the servant without fail becomes disregardful of one thing for another." *Fusus al-Hikam,* p. 89. See also *Bezels of Wisdom,* 102.

36. *Fusus al-Hikam,* 104. See also al-Hakim, *al-Mu'jam al-Sufi,* 451–52.

37. *Fusus al-Hikam,* 104.

38. This summary touches on some of the most basic teachings of Ibn 'Arabi regarding the imagination (*khayal*), the details of which have been analyzed elsewhere. Su'ad al-Hakim outlines *khayal* in the vocabulary of Ibn 'Arabi as having four different categories: (1) *al-khayal al-mutlaq* (the purely receptive presence that Ibn 'Arabi labels *al-'ama',* that is, the cloud that was the first locus of manifestation for the Real), (2) *al-khayal al-muhaqqaq* (the cloud after having received all the forms of created things), (3) *al-khayal al-munfasil* (the imaginal realm wherein spiritual forms take on sensory forms, forms that are independent of the viewer—what might be called "objective" imagination), and (4) *al-khayal al-muttasil* (the human imaginal faculty and its ability

to create and maintain forms—what might be called "subjective" imagination). See al-Hakim, *al-Mu'jam al-Sufi,* 449. Chittick discusses the difference between the latter two types of imagination in *SPK,* 117.

39. Henry Corbin, *Alone with the Alone: Creative Imagination in the Sufism of Ibn 'Arabi,* trans. Ralph Manheim, Mythos: Princeton/Bollingen Series in World Mythology (1969; reprint, Princeton, N.J.: Princeton University Press, 1998), 189; *SPK,* 117–18; *FM,* vol. 1, ch. 63, p. 380.22 (p. 304).

40. According to Ibn 'Arabi the imagination *bestows* form on meaning, but in order to do that *receives* meaning through matter. Imagination is incapable of "accepting meanings divorced from matter as they are in themselves," and thus it is "narrow" in one regard, but—since it gives form to that which logically cannot have form—it is also the "widest of known things" and thus can present something as abstract as religion (*din*) in the form of fetters (*qayd*) or something as limitless as the Real in the form of a human or light. See *FM,* vol. 1, ch. 63, p. 382.27 (p. 306). For a well-evidenced and detailed discussion of imagination, see *SDG,* 332–39.

41. *FM,* vol. 3, ch. 369, p. 354.25 (p. 364).

42. See, for example, *FM,* vol. 2, ch. 73, question 12, p. 50.11 (p. 48). "Treasury of the Imagination" is a phrase I borrow from Chittick's informed discussion and translation of passages related to this topic in *SPK,* 118–21, which includes passages relating dreaming and the imagination. The "tax" imagery can also be found in *FM,* vol. 3, ch. 369, p. 354.25 (p. 364).

43. A dream attributed to the Prophet Muhammad in which he sees knowledge in the form of milk, drinks it, and shares the remaining portion with 'Umar ibn al-Khattab is often cited by Ibn 'Arabi. See, for example, *Fusus al-Hikam,* 100 and 159.

44. See *FM,* vol. 3, ch. 311, p. 43.24 (p. 42).

45. *Dhakha'ir,* 27. See also *Fusus al-Hikam,* 159. Elsewhere Ibn 'Arabi mentions Dihyah al-Kalbi and Mary's encounter with Gabriel together as examples of similar phenomena occurring in the World of Imagination; see, again, *FM,* vol. 3, ch. 311, p. 43.16 (p. 42).

46. Imagination, forms, and interpretation are major points of focus in Ibn 'Arabi's chapter on Joseph in *Fusus al-Hikam;* see especially p. 100.

47. For example, commenting on one of his poems, Ibn 'Arabi describes a main type of witnessing as occurring when "divine self-disclosures of various moments occur in beautiful and comely forms in the world of image-representations (*'alam al-tamthil*)." See *Dhakha'ir,* 26–27.

48. *FM,* vol. 3, ch. 311, p. 43.17 (p. 42).

49. "There is no proximity more proximate than when his ipseity is the servant's members and faculties, for the servant is nothing more than these members and faculties. The Real, then, is a reality witnessed in a surmised creation. For the believers and the People of Unveiling and Finding, creation is known abstractly (*ma'qul*), while the Real is perceived by the senses and witnessed. For everyone else, the Real is known abstractly and creation is witnessed." *Fusus al-Hikam,* 108.

50. "The gnostic says that the hearing [of Zayd] is identical to the Real," an observation that Ibn 'Arabi applies to all senses, faculties and parts of the body. *Fusus al-Hikam,* 110.

51. A partial translation of one version of this hadith. This translation (with "grasps" instead of "seizes") can be found in *SPK,* 325, along with a number of commentaries on the narration by Ibn 'Arabi, 325–31. The full text of this narration can be found in Muhammad ibn Isma'il al-Bukhari (d. 256/870), *Sahih al-Bukhari* (Damascus: Dar Ibn Kathir, 1423/2002) (hereafter cited as *Sahih al-Bukhari*), *Kitab al-Riqaq* (81/38), #6502, p. 1617.

52. *Fusus al-Hikam,* 107.

53. The Qur'an, 25:53, 35:12.

54. "Every organ has one sort of knowledge—from among the sorts of knowledge of taste—that is specific to that organ; although the sorts of knowledge are from one source, they differ in accordance with the organs." *Fusus al-Hikam,* 107.

55. The following discussion is taken from Jandi's *Nafhat al-Ruh wa Tuhfat al-Futuh* (The Scented Breeze of the Spirit and the Gift of Inspirational Openings), a treatise that deserves greater notice. Section 1 of this manual describes the "beneficial sciences and the practical gnoses of certainty," which includes two parts—one on knowing God, the other on knowing the Perfect Man. Section Two outlines the "deeds of the Lords of the Way and the states of the People of Verification," which has as its first part a discussion of watching over one's deeds (*nazar dar a'mal*), the section that concerns us presently. See Mu'ayyid al-Din Jandi, *Nafhat al-Ruh wa Tuhfat al-Futuh,* ed. Najib Mayil Hirawi (Tehran: Intisharat-i Mawla, 1362 *hijri-shamsi,* 1403 *hijri-qamari*) (hereafter cited as *Nafhat al-Ruh*).

56. Although Jandi mentions Ibn 'Arabi and the Sufis of the west as particularly concerned with reckoning the actions of the body parts, his emphasis on the senses as gateways to the heart can be found in earlier Sufi manuals of Khurasani, that is, "eastern," Sufi figures, including—perhaps most famously—that of Abu Hamid al-Ghazali (d. 505/1111). Al-Ghazali makes clear, in *Kimiya-i Sa'adat* and elsewhere, that what one observes with the senses directly affects the heart. Abu Hamid al-Ghazali, *Kimiya-i Sa'adat,* vol. 1, ed. Husayn Khadivjam (Tehran: Shirkat-i Intisharat-i 'Ilmi wa Farhangi, 1382 *hijri-shamsi*), 20–21.

57. *Nafhat al-Ruh,* 104–5.

58. *FM,* vol. 1, ch. 33, p. 274.17 (p. 211). Claude Addas places this passage in a biographical context; see her *Quest for the Red Sulphur: The Life of Ibn 'Arabi,* trans. Peter Kingsley (Cambridge: Islamic Texts Society, 1993), 71, where she also refers to *FM,* vol. 2, ch. 284, p. 616.25 (p. 628) on the topic of bestirrings.

59. *FM,* vol. 1, ch. 33, p. 274.18 (pp. 211–12).

60. *Nafhat al-Ruh,* 105. This passage also reminds us that Ibn 'Arabi's influence was far more expansive than merely introducing his students to his vision of unity.

61. Ibid., 108.

62. This and the following quotations lacking citation come from ibid., 108–9.

63. Ibid., 109. I translate the difficult term *'ayn* (plural *a'yan*) as "identity." Caner K. Dagli presents a convincing argument for doing so in the introduction to his translation of *Fusus al-Hikam, The Ringstones of Wisdom* (Chicago: Great Books of the Islamic World, 2004), xvi-xix.

64. Ibid., 115.

65. Ibid., 114.

66. From *FM*, vol. 4, ch. 558, pp. 259–61 (pp. 259–61); Pablo Beneito, trans., "The Servant of the Loving One: On the Adoption of the Character Traits of *al-Wadud*," *Journal of the Muhyiddin Ibn 'Arabi Society* 32 (2002): 1–24, here 10.

67. *Nafhat al-Ruh*, 114–16. All subsequent Jandi quotations are from these pages.

68. *FM*, vol. 2, ch. 178, p. 319.22 (p. 323).

69. *FM*, vol. 3, ch. 375, p. 456.7 (pp. 470–71); *SPK*, 362. Chittick's translation has been modified here.

70. See Ibn 'Arabi's comment that "reason asserts God's *tanzih* and eliminates correspondence [between him and creation] in every respect. The Real comes and declares it truthful in that with *Nothing is as his likeness* [42:11]. He says to us: 'Reason speaks the truth, since it has given what is within its own capacity. It knows nothing other than that. For I have *given each thing its creation* [20:50], and reason is one of the things, so We have given it its creation.' Then he completed the verse with his words, *Then guided* [20:50], that is, clarified. He clarified something not given by reason nor by any of the other faculties. . . . The perfect among the Folk of God are those who consider each affair separately in order to see its creation that God has given to it and that he has given fully." See *SDG*, 95–96, and *FM*, vol. 2, ch. 177, p. 295.23 (p. 299).

71. *FM*, vol. 2, ch. 178, p. 322.3 (p. 326).

72. *Fusus al-Hikam*, 68. Translation from *Bezels of Wisdom*, 73.

73. It is important to note here that, in Ibn 'Arabi's reading, these idol-worshippers epitomize a broader religious tendency. Ibn 'Arabi offers a profound peek into the *meaning* of idol worship, not, as should be obvious, an endorsement of actual idol worship.

74. *Fusus al-Hikam*, 68. For such a gnostic, the Real is "manifest in every created being and in every concept," and he is manifest in the human being in an even more comprehensive sense, since the human is the Real's form and the Real is the human's spirit. Commenting on Ibn 'Arabi's statement that these idol worshippers / gnostics "make manifest that which was veiled, and then veil it after its manifestation, so that the onlooker is perplexed, not knowing what the *fajir* [that is, the one who cleaves, or the one makes manifest] intends by his action, nor what the *kaffar* [that is, the one who covers, or the one who hides] intends by his action, though they are one," Sharaf al-Din Dawud al-Qaysari (d. 751/1350) notes that such gnostics hide this manifestation, either fearing those too ignorant to understand or protecting the absolute lordship of God. The gnostic makes the Real manifest through self-annihilation, then—in some instances—covers this manifestation. The gnostic covers this manifestation either, like

al-Junayd, by veiling the manifestation of Lord-in-servant and publicly recognizing the individualized self, or, like Mansur al-Hallaj and Abu Yazid al-Bistami, by veiling his individual existence, denying any separations between self and Lord, and speaking in the divine first person. The difference between them is merely one of emphasis and perspective, so that both al-Junayd and al-Hallaj deserve praise, as epitomized by Qaysari's invocation of "may God be pleased with both of them," that is, both al-Junayd and al-Hallaj. By mentioning the complicated case of al-Hallaj, who deserves both praise and blame, Qaysari underscores the ambiguous way in which Ibn 'Arabi describes the "polytheists" or adherents to similitude. See al-Qaysari, *Sharh Fusus al-Hikam,* ed. Sayyid Jalal al-Din Ashtiyani (Tehran: Shirkat-i Intisharat-i 'Ilmi wa Farhangi, 1996), 536.

75. *FM,* vol. 2, ch. 177, 294.18 (p. 298). The gnostic "knows God through God and all things through God" since God has become "all of [his] senses."

76. *FM,* vol. 3, ch. 388, 524.7 (p. 541).

77. Thus the polytheists rejecting Noah are in perplexity because they are "drowned in the seas of the knowledge of God" (*ghariqu fi bihar al-'ilm bi-llah*), knowledge obtained through their being "annihilated in him forever." *Fusus al-Hikam,* 73. Translation from *Bezels of Wisdom,* 79–80. In fact, the very term used here, "gnostic" or *'arif* signifies knowledge of God, which, like all other types of knowledge, is first made possible through sensory perception, as has been stated. Since such knowledge associates abstract meanings with things known in the concrete sensory world, one can say that in fact all knowledge is based on some sort of *tashbih*/similitude, whether in the rational sense or, in this case, in the visionary sense.

78. Ibn 'Arabi here and elsewhere describes *al-hayrah,* the eradication of which was the stated goal of classical Islamic philosophy and theology, in a positive manner. The philosophers and theologians saw their rational proofs as a means to solve the perplexity caused by lingering questions or doubts regarding beliefs. Ibn 'Arabi, as Michael A. Sells has indicated, "pushed the theological arguments to their extreme to reveal the essential irresolvability of the dilemma [that is, any one of the theological dilemmas at hand] outside of mystical union. . . . [Ibn 'Arabi] suggests a higher knowledge that is a form of bewilderment [*al-hayrah*]." See Michael A. Sells, *Mystical Languages of Unsaying* (Chicago: University of Chicago Press, 1994), 102.

79. *FM,* vol. 2, ch. 178, p. 332.32 (p. 338).

80. *FM,* vol. 2, ch. 178, p. 321.22 (p. 325).

81. From *FM,* vol. 4, ch. 558, 259–61 (pp. 259–61). Beneito, "Servant of the Loving One," 10. The passage has been modified in order to be consistent with my translation of the terms *shuhud* and *surah.*

82. Su'ad al-Hakim rightly offers "justice" or "equity," that is, *al-'adl* or *al-insaf,* as one of the definitions for *haqq* in Ibn 'Arabi's usage, in her *al-Mu'jam al-Sufi,* 339–40. See, for example, *FM,* vol. 3, ch. 369, p. 386.26 (p. 398), which al-Hakim also cites as an instance of this application of the word *haqq,* an application quite common in

the writings of Ibn 'Arabi. William C. Chittick notes that this practice of *tahqiq* ("giving dues") means that the achieved gnostic sees each created thing "as a unique self-disclosure (*tajalli*) of the absolute *Ḥaqq*." See William C. Chittick, "The Central Point: Qunawi's Role in the School of Ibn 'Arabi," *Journal of the Muhyiddin Ibn 'Arabi Society* 35 (2004): 25–45, here 34.

83. The concept of *adab* or "courtesy" in the writings of Ibn 'Arabi demands that the gnostic observes certain parameters of decorum established by observing the relationships laid out in creation and observing the revealed law. For a more detailed discussion, see *SPK*, 174–79.

84. *FM*, vol. 2, ch. 178, p. 341.12 (p. 346). Translation by Claude Addas, "The Experience and Doctrine of Love in Ibn 'Arabi," *Journal of the Muhyiddin Ibn 'Arabi Society* 32 (2002): 25–44, here 27.

Chapter 2: Perception according to 'Iraqi

1. In other words, the existential breath that creates the cosmos, the word *kun*, or "be," begins a process whereby God's words become the existent things. In these words God makes mention of himself to himself, and the outcome is a unified remembrance of him which we perceive to be creation.

2. Fakhr al-Din Ibrahim Hamadani 'Iraqi, *Lama'at-i Fakhr al-Din 'Iraqi*, ed. Muhammad Khwajawi (Tehran: Intisharat-i Mawla, 1371), 49 (hereafter cited as *Lama'at*); modified translation based on William C. Chittick and Peter Lamborn Wilson, trans., *Divine Flashes*, with an introduction by Chittick and Wilson (New York: Paulist Press, 1982), 73 (hereafter cited as *Divine Flashes*). Some sources offer the word *yaqin* instead of *ta'ayyun* in the first line, such that it might be translated "but Love upon Its mighty Throne escapes all certain knowledge." The Khwajawi edition of the *Lama'at*, however, does offer *ta'ayyun*, much like the Nurbakhsh edition used by Chittick and Wilson, *Risalah-i Lama'at wa Risalah-i Istilahat*, ed. Jawad Nurbakhsh (Tehran, 1353/1974). A second source for the *Lama'at* is *Majmu'ah-i Athar-i Fakhr al-Din 'Iraqi*, edited with notes by Nasrin Muhtasham (Tehran: Intisharat-i Zawwar, 1382 *hijri-shamsi*) (hereafter cited as *Kulliyat*), 457. The *Kulliyat* here supports Khwajawi's edition. For citations from the *Lama'at*, the Khwajawi and Muhtasham editions are cited. For citations from 'Iraqi's other writings, especially his poetry, the *Kulliyat* is cited, along with Sa'id Nafisi's edition of 'Iraqi's collected works, *Kulliyat-i Diwan-i Shaykh Fakhr al-Din Ibrahim Hamadani mutakhallis bi-'Iraqi*, with notes by Mahmud 'Alami (Tehran: Intisharat-i Jawidan, 1377 *hijri-shamsi*/1998–99) (hereafter cited as *Diwan*).

3. *Lama'at* (Khwajawi), 60; *Kulliyat* (Muhtasham), 465 (ch. 4).

4. Of course, that which is translated as "securer" (*mu'min*) has two varying meanings depending on whether it applies to God or to humans and jinn. God is *al-Mu'min* (59:23) in the sense that he is the Guardian or Giver of Security. The human or jinn *mu'min* guards or protects his belief and is thus a "believer." The more common interpretation of this hadith would thus be "The believer is a mirror for another believer."

'Iraqi's interpretation, much like that seen in Ibn 'Arabi, finds esoteric meaning in lexical possibilities of the revealed texts. Modified translation from *Divine Flashes,* 86; *Lama'at,* 71; *Kulliyat,* 476 (ch. 7).

5. Using the terms provided by Ibn 'Arabi helps in this regard because he has defined and explained them in an apparently discursive manner in his prose works. On the other hand, looking at these terms from the perspective of 'Iraqi's metaphorical language reminds us that we are dealing not with a rational philosophy but with direct vision and insight, which is beyond the reach of any language. Thus mystical experience is often worded in the meta-language of poetic metaphor, that is, words that do not attempt to define but rather approximate mystical experience through drawing parallels (often relating such experiences to what is commonly accepted as overwhelming, infinite, or intoxicating). Why is poetic language deemed best for describing the indescribable? Clearly such is not necessarily the case, since Ibn 'Arabi often uses philosophical or theological language to delve into the details of his comprehensive vision. Yet what I argue is that the vision of unity, which provokes an intoxicating love in the mystic, is predominately expressed in amorous poetry because amorous poetry best captures the sense of the sensual-spiritual ambiguity, self-loss, yearning, and form-bestowing quality of that vision.

6. One possible reason for this might be that 'Iraqi's *Lama'at* might have been written in response to Ibn 'Arabi's *Fusus al-Hikam,* which is itself a bafflingly laconic work, although passages from *al-Futuhat al-Makkiyah* (especially chapter 178) are clearly paralleled in *Lama'at,* often more so than passages from the *Fusus.*

7. R. Julian Baldick argues that similarities between the vision of Ibn 'Arabi and 'Iraqi are especially the case if one takes into consideration the poetry of 'Iraqi written after his becoming a disciple of the great Akbari teacher Sadr al-Din Qunawi. In fact, one of the criteria used by Baldick in his doctoral thesis to determine 'Iraqi's post-Qunawi poems is this very similarity in vision. See R. Julian Baldick, "The Poems of Fakhr al-Din 'Iraqi" (Ph.D. diss., University of Oxford, 1981), 3. Unfortunately Akbari doctrine does not always present itself in an apparent fashion, nor does amorous mystical verse, which is a genre marked by ambiguity, require any formal change to be adopted into a contemplative school that emphasizes the *interpretation* of poetry and not necessarily changes in composition.

8. William C. Chittick translates *tahawwul* as "transmutation," while, because the gnostic sees the cosmos as constantly changing states (and "state" is the meaning of *sha'n* to which Ibn 'Arabi refers), I have chosen to translate the term as "state-changing." See *SPK,* 38. It is important to add that in the next life, those who have known God merely through reason and rational proofs will be bewildered because they will see him in a form other than the form in which they have always known him, since they have known him only as the object of their rational or limited spiritual abilities. The true gnostics, however, are bewildered here and now, bewildered in a praiseworthy sense, because God constantly appears to them in varying forms. This theme—

confusion concerning the forms of God on the Day of Resurrection (or in this world for the gnostics)—can be traced to a narration in *Sahih Muslim,* which serves as the source for Ibn 'Arabi's term *tahawwul.* See *SPK,* 38 and 100. This hadith can be found in Muslim ibn al-Hajjaj al-Qushayri al-Naysaburi (d. 261/875), *Sahih Muslim* (Riyadh: Dar al-Mughni, 1998), *Kitab al-Iman* (1/81), #183, pp. 112–35.

9. While it must be admitted that Chittick and Wilson's translation of this section in *Divine Flashes* is much more readable, still, because of the technical nature of this discussion, I have offered a more literal rendition of the introduction to this *lam'ah. Lama'at,* 62; *Kulliyat,* 467 (ch. 5).

10. The phrase "indivisible moment" is Chittick's translation of *an,* which is Ibn 'Arabi's understanding of the word "day," or *yawm,* in the verse cited below. According to Ibn 'Arabi, this verse indicates that in every indivisible moment, the Real can be witnessed in a different form, since the cosmos is constantly re-created. See *SPK,* 18.

11. Accordingly, in chapter 192 of *al-Futuhat al-Makkiyah,* by commenting on the Qur'anic phrase mentioned above ("He is upon a different affair every day," 55:29), Ibn 'Arabi presents this concept from two perspectives. In the first, the focus is on the cosmos as subject to change. The cosmos is every instant subject to countless affairs, that is, subject to the re-creations of all engendered things. In this smallest unit of time, God re-creates all the engendered things in a new way: "In each [moment] he is engaged in as many affairs as there are indivisible parts of the cosmos in existence." From this perspective, the verse alludes to God's active changing of the cosmos in his unending role as Creator. Each instant, he gives the created things that which they need to be, but not that which allow them to come to be on their own, reserving this quality for himself and thus prohibiting them from being self-sufficient. From the second perspective, however, the focus is not on the cosmos as subject to change, but rather on God as manifested in the constantly changing cosmos, so that he seems to have infinite and infinitely changing forms. See *FM,* vol. 2, ch. 192, p. 379.18 (pp. 384–85).

12. One might say that God is every instant in a different "condition" or "state," a secondary sense of the word *sha'n* that can be found, for example, in *Lisan al-'Arab,* where one definition given for the word is *hal,* or "state." (See *sh-'-n* in Ibn Manzur, *Lisan al-'Arab* [Qum, Iran: Nashr Adab al-Hawzah, 1984], 13:230; and Lane, *Arabic-English Lexicon* 4:1491, where he offers definitions for *sha'n* that include "state, condition, case, quality, or manner of being.") Here the gnostic perceives not the multiplicity of engendered things undergoing constant re-creation, but rather perceives God as constantly disclosing a new form of himself, as Ibn 'Arabi observes: "The Real has informed us of himself that he changes states (*yatahawwal*) within forms, for he creates every affair as a divine form." Perhaps anticipating charges that God's changing states has potentially blasphemous implications, Ibn 'Arabi clarifies that the "state (*al-hal*) is a divine characteristic with respect to his actions and his directing of attention variously to his engendered things." See *FM,* vol. 2, ch. 192, p. 379.29 (p. 385).

13. *Lama'at,* 64–65; *Kulliyat,* 470 (ch. 5).

14. *FM,* vol. 2, ch. 73, question #116, p. 108.29 (p. 111). Also, in classical Arabic poetry the sparkling wine in a goblet possesses mirror-like qualities and is of course intoxicating and thus suited to erotic love.

15. See *FM,* vol. 2, ch. 73, question #117, p. 111.22 (p. 113). The text has *lawn al-hubb lawn mahbubihi,* which makes less sense and could result easily from a displaced *mim.* The above quotation is also from this passage.

16. This narration is cited very often in Ibn 'Arabi's works, sometimes referring to "My servant" (*'abdi*) and sometimes to "My believing servant" (*'abdi al-mu'min*). For the first see *FM,* vol. 1, ch. 34, p. 279.11 (p. 216), and for the second, see the same volume and page, line 28, both instances occurring in a discussion of the human heart as the true throne of God. A full discussion of the credibility of this *hadith qudsi* occurs in the *Kashf al-Khafa'* of Isma'il ibn Muhammad Jarrah al-'Ajluni al-Jarrahi (d. 1162/1749), a Sufi hadith commentator. As evident from al-Jarrahi's discussion, although reputable names including Abu Hamid al-Ghazali have cited it, most Sunni commentators considered this hadith to be untrustworthy; see *Kashf al-Khafa' wa Muzil al-Albas,* 2nd ed. (Beirut: Dar al-Kutub al-'ilmiyah, 1408 *hijri*), vol. 2, #2256, pp. 195–96.

17. *Dhakha'ir,* 49. That Ibn 'Arabi's commentary on the line where this occurs, *bayt* 13 of the poem (see p. 179n.16), offers a passage parallel to that which has been translated (see p. 35) from *al-Futuhat al-Makkiyah.*

18. This is supported by Barzishabadi's statement, for example, that "the divine essence through its attributes is never-endingly undergoing self-disclosure, from eternity without beginning to eternity without end; the variations among expressions (*'ibarat*) and allusions (*isharat*) is due to the variations of capabilities (*qabiliyat*) and capacity (*isti'dad*)." Barzishabadi, *Sharh-i Lama'at-i 'Iraqi,* ed. Ahmad Qadasi (Tehran: Intisharat-i Mawla, 2000), 200–201.

19. "Truly the hearts of the sons of Adam are all between two fingers from among the fingers of the All-Merciful, like one heart. He turns it [this heart] however he wishes." See *Sahih Muslim, Kitab al-Qadar* (46/3), #2654, p. 1427.

20. With respect to creation, it is well known in Sufi discourse that God exhibits attributes of beauty (*jamal*), such as mercy, gentleness, and satisfaction, while also exhibiting attributes of splendor (*jalal*), such as inaccessibility, severity, and wrath.

21. Barzishabadi, *Sharh-i Lama'at-i 'Iraqi,* 202.

22. Ibid.

23. See *Diwan* (Nafisi), 254. Muhtasham has not included this poem (the refrain of which ends in the word *nist*) in her edition, although in theme, style and word choice it closely resembles one she has included (the refrain of which ends in the word *baqi*) on 281–89.

24. *Diwan,* 256.

25. A *bayt* corresponds to what we might call a "line" in English verse, except that a caesura divides the *bayt* into two halves, each of which is a *misra'* or half-line. In

my translations, the *bayt* appears as a couplet. Henceforth the *bayt* is referred to as a double line, and the *misra'* is referred to as a hemistich.

26. *Kulliyat,* 262; *Diwan,* 166–67. The final word of the first double line of this *ghazal* is *awwal.*

27. See *Kulliyat,* 562–53, and *Diwan,* 424, 428–49, for the corresponding pages of these definitions.

28. See the editor's (i.e., Hirawi's) notes, Sharaf al-Din Husayn ibn Ahmad Ulfati Tabrizi, *Rashf al-Alhaz fi Kashf al-Alfaz,* ed. Najib Mayil Hirawi (Tehran: Mawla, 1362/1983; (hereafter cited as *Rashf al-Alhaz*), 26. See also William C. Chittick, "'Eraqi, Fakhr-al-Din Ebrahim," *Encyclopaedia Iranica,* vol. 8, 1998.

29. The structure is indeed too specific to be coincidentally similar, divided into (1) terms describing the beloved, (2) terms applied to both lover and beloved, and (3) terms specific to the lover and his states, while in some cases applying to the beloved. The glossary attributed to 'Iraqi contains 385 terms, in Muhtasham's edition. Tabrizi's contains 300 terms, of which 271 can be found in the 'Iraqi version, a correspondence of about 90 percent. When the definitions do not accord exactly, usually Tabrizi's version includes more detail, often an added phrase. While 'Iraqi's glossary has a simple and very brief introduction, Tabrizi's glossary begins with a detailed argument for the spiritual depths hidden in Sufi poetic terms. Lastly, while many of the terms discussed in both glossaries do indeed appear noticeably in Persian erotic poetry, Sufi or otherwise, some do not appear noticeably in the poetry of 'Iraqi himself. None of this, of course, proves that Tabrizi is the author, but considering that the case for 'Iraqi's attribution is already not strong, it supports the possibility that the version attributed to 'Iraqi derives from Tabrizi's more identifiable glossary.

30. *Rashf al-Alhaz,* 61.

31. Ibid., 37. Tabrizi mentions Rumi and 'Attar specifically (p. 35) as poets who packed spiritual meaning into the forms of words, although his discussion (p. 36) cites without attribution a double line found in 'Iraqi's *Diwan. Diwan* (Nafisi), 364.

32. According to 'Ali Akbar Dihkhuda (d. 1955), one possible definition of the *chaghanah* is "a stringed instrument played by use of a plectrum or bow." See *chaghanah* in 'Ali Akbar Dihkhuda, *Lughatnamah* (Tehran: Mu'assasah-i Lughatnamah-i Dihkhuda, Mu'assasah-i Intisharat wa Chap-i Danishgah-i Tehran, 1993–94). In his notes on the *Diwan* of 'Iraqi, Mahmud 'Alami Darvish describes the *chaghanah* as a musical instrument that "resembles a spoon attached to which are bells, and it is moved by the hand" (212).

33. *Kulliyat,* 246–47; *Diwan,* 212. The final word in the first hemistich is *sharabkhanah.* Baldick comments that the last line of this poem might show the influence of Ibn 'Arabi, but the evidence is not sufficient, since "a vision of unity is not the same as a clear statement of the doctrine of the 'unity of existence.'" Certainly Baldick is right that this poem expresses a vision of unity. Baldick, "Poems of Fakhr al-Din 'Iraqi," 195.

34. There is an interesting discrepancy in this passage of the *Lama'at* that would account for a subtle but perhaps important difference of interpretation. Both the Khwajawi edition of the *Lama'at* and Muhtasham's edition in the *Kulliyat* describe *sharab-i hasti* (wine of existence) and *jam-i nisti* (cup of nonexistence), which is the reading I have used above. The version in Nafisi's edition (*Diwan*), however, describes a *sharab-i nisti* (wine of nonexistence) and *jam-i hasti* (cup of existence), which—while ultimately conveying the same general idea—is much less consistent with other instances of 'Iraqi's use of these terms. (Of course, very often in Sufi discourse, the goblet, possessing form, would be existence, and wine, as the agent dissolving form, would be nonexistence.) My translation is thus based on the *Lama'at* (Khwajawi), 54. See also *Kulliyat*, 460; *Diwan*, 386 (ch. 2).

35. *FM*, vol 2, ch. 209, p. 485.23 (p. 496), translated in *SPK*, 225.

36. *Kulliyat*, 319; *Diwan*, 71. This double line is from the *qasidah* concerning *tawhid* quoted above.

37. *Lama'at*, 73–74; *Kulliyat*, 477–79 (ch. 8); *Divine Flashes*, 87–89.

38. Barzishabadi, *Sharh-i Lama'at*, 219–220; Mawlana 'Abd al-Rahman Jami, *Ashi''at al-Lama'at*, ed. Hadi Rastigar Muqaddam Gawhari (Qum, Iran: Daftar-i Tablighat-i Islami, Shu'bah-i Khurasan, Bustan-i Kitab-i Qum, 1383 *hijri-shamsi*), 119–21.

39. *Kulliyat*, 318–20; *Diwan*, 71–72. The final word of the first double line of this *qasidah* is *andakhtah*.

40. See *FM*, vol. 2, ch. 209, p. 484.15/37 (p. 495).

41. Mawlana 'Abd al-Rahman Jami, in commenting on chapter 8 of the *Lama'at*, mentions four mystically perceived self-disclosures that more or less correspond to this paradigm. See Jami, *Ashi''at al-Lama'at*, 119, or the edition of Hamid Rabbani (Tehran, 1973), which numbers them as three while still listing four (72). For *tafriqah, jam'*, and *jam' al-jam'*, see, for example, Sa'id al-Din Farghani, *Mashariq al-Darari: Sharh-i Ta'iyah-i Ibn-i Farid*, 2nd ed., ed. Jalal al-Din Ashtiyani (Qum, Iran: Daftar-i Tablighat-i Islami-i Hawzah-i 'Ilmiyah-i Qum, 1379 *hijri-shamsi*), p. 376, line 8.

42. 'Abd al-Razzaq al-Qashani studied the *Fusus al-Hikam* with Mu'ayyid al-Din Jandi (d. ca. 700/1300), who studied the book with Ibn 'Arabi's own stepson and disciple, Sadr al-Din al-Qunawi (d. 673/1274).

43. See al-Qashani, *Istilahat al-Sufiyah*, ed. 'Asim Ibrahim al-Kayyali (Beirut: Dar al-Kutub al-'Ilmiyah, 2005), p. 37.

44. *Lama'at*, 74; *Kulliyat*, 479 (ch. 8).

45. See the eleventh chapter of *Lama'at*, 81–82; *Kulliyat*, 485–86.

Chapter 3: Beauty according to Ibn 'Arabi and 'Iraqi

1. This phrase occurs as an answer to a question raised in the Prophet's presence: Is it a sign of arrogance to enjoy wearing good clothing and sandals? The Prophet responds that "indeed, God is beautiful and loves beauty (*inna-Allah jamil yuhibb*

al-jamal)" and that "arrogance means vainly disregarding the truth and holding others in contempt." *Sahih Muslim, Kitab al-Iman* (1/39), #91, pp. 60–61.

2. *FM*, vol. 2, ch. 178, p. 322.14 (p. 326).

3. Ibid.

4. Ibn 'Arabi makes this observation in *Dhakha'ir*, 103. Concerning *al-ihsan*, Sachiko Murata and William Chittick translate the term as "doing what is beautiful" and discuss the interconnectedness of ethical perfection and inherent beauty in *The Vision of Islam* (New York: Paragon House, 1994), 267–82.

5. According to this image of turning, God turns to humans initially to awaken their hearts in regret, which brings them to turn to him in repentance, which brings him to turn to them in forgiveness (9:118). See *FM*, vol. 2, ch. 178, p. 336.23 (pp. 341–42).

6. Ibn 'Arabi quotes this hadith on *FM*, vol. 2, ch. 178, p. 338.29/33 (p. 344). It can also be found in *Sahih Muslim, Kitab al-Iman* (1/1), #8 and #9, pp. 21–23, and in *Sahih al-Bukhari, Kitab al-Iman* (2/37), #50, p. 23.

7. *FM*, vol. 2, ch. 178, p. 338.29 (p. 344).

8. See the Qur'an 17:110 and 7:180. Citing this Qur'anic phrase, Ibn 'Arabi clarifies elsewhere that the beautiful names are divine presences sought and defined by external forms. Moreover, the inherent beauty and goodness of those names means that all names and actions, that is, all created things, are beautiful. See *FM*, vol. 4, ch. 558, p. 198.21 (p. 196), as well as *FM*, vol. 4, ch. 558, p. 251.14 (p. 250).

9. This is one of the unique and profound observations of Ibn 'Arabi, namely, that human beings have absolutely no access to the true *jalal* of God, for God's "majesty is a relation that proceeds from him to him" and his beauty "is a relation that proceeds from him to us." Thus the majesty that humans encounter is in fact the "majesty of beauty," not directly related to God's actual majesty. See a translation of Ibn 'Arabi's short treatise *Kitab al-Jalal wa-l-Jamal* by Rabia Terra Harris, "On Majesty and Beauty: The *Kitab al-Jalal wa-l Jamal* of Muhyiddin Ibn 'Arabi," *Journal of the Muhyiddin Ibn 'Arabi Society* 8 (1989): 5–32, here 7. Pablo Beneito has also published an article on this subject; see his "On the Divine Love of Beauty," *Journal of the Muhyiddin Ibn 'Arabi Society* 18 (1995): 1–22.

10. *FM*, vol. 2, ch. 178, p. 338.32 (p. 344). Just as all beauty derives from the Beautiful (*al-jamil*), all excellent action—that is, the constant admiration of divine beauty—derives from the Excellent Actor (*al-muhsin*); see *FM*, vol. 2, ch. 178, p. 322.14 (p. 326).

11. Abu 'Abdallah Muhammad ibn 'Ali al-Tirmidhi, known as "al-Hakim," lived in the third/ninth century (from about 204/820 to about 297/905). A number of his esoteric doctrines resemble those of Ibn 'Arabi and clearly had an influence on the Great Shaykh, as seen in Ibn 'Arabi's placement of 157 questions posed to the "Seal of the Saints" in Tirmidhi's *Sirat al-Awliya'* (sometimes called *Khatm al-Awliya'*) in *al-Futuhat al-Makkiyah*. These questions, answered by Ibn 'Arabi, constitute the first *wasl*

of chapter 73. Concerning the resemblances between the writings of Tirmidhi and Ibn 'Arabi, see Bernd Radtke, "A Forerunner of Ibn al-'Arabi: Hakim Tirmidhi on Sainthood," *Journal of Muhyiddin Ibn 'Arabi Society* 8 (1989), 42–49.

12. *FM*, vol. 2, ch. 73, question #118, p. 111.31 (p. 114).

13. *FM*, vol. 2, ch. 73, question #116, p. 110.27 (p. 113).

14. *FM*, vol. 2, ch. 73, question #116, p. 110.32 (p. 113). One can also see from the first sentence in this passage that it is through *shuhud* that existents come into being, and, as implied in the subsequent sentences, *shuhud* causes them to remain in existence.

15. *FM*, vol. 4, ch. 472, pp. 107–9 (pp. 104–6). See *SDG*, 216–18. Until otherwise noted, all quotations are from this page, although Chittick's translation has been modified.

16. What is the constitution (*al-mizaj*)? Ibn 'Arabi defines *al-mizaj* as "that through which the entity of the element has existence. It is what is called 'the nature.' Thus it is said that the nature of water or the constitution of water is cold and wet; that of fire is hot and dry, of air hot and wet, and of earth cold and dry." More specifically, the human constitution depends on the balance of the four humors (black bile, yellow bile, phlegm, and blood) much as the natural world is an admixture of the four elements (earth, fire, water, and air). Ibn 'Arabi reminds his reader that just as the natural world—and thus the microcosmic human body—results from the opposition of these elements, so too do the divine names result from a differing in excellence. For example, the divine name "the One who harms" is less excellent than the divine name "the One who brings benefit." The differences in excellence that result in the natural realm have their origins in the hierarchy or "differences in excellence" of the divine names. The constitution, then, is a result of the divine ranking and ordering; as such, it is removed from the absolute, undifferentiated divine breath. See *FM*, vol. 2, ch. 178, p. 330.13 (p. 335). For the quotation defining *al-mizaj*, see *FM*, vol. 2, ch. 198, p. 447.13 (p. 456), translated by Chittick in *SDG*, 322. Also important here is Ronald L. Nettler's discussion of the divine inbreathing as a divine fire that serves as a unique part of the human constitution. See Ronald L. Nettler, *Sufi Metaphysics and Qur'anic Prophets: Ibn 'Arabi's Thought and Method in the Fusus al-hikam* (Cambridge: Islamic Texts Society, 2003), 185–86.

17. Chittick translates *su'* as "ugly" but only to provide a consistent antonym for the word "beautiful," or *husn*.

18. For *khabith*, see Lane, *Arabic-English Lexicon* 2:694, and for *tayyib*, see Lane, *Arabic-English Lexicon* 5:1902.

19. Verse 39:18 praises those who listen to the word (*al-qawl*), namely, the Qur'an, and follow the best or most beautiful in it (*ahsanah*). Verse 4:148 declares that God dislikes clamorous, vile speech (*al-jahr bi-l-su' min al-qawl*) while also clarifying that loud and public speech receives the divine pleasure when undertaken by those suffering under oppression.

20. See, for example, 2:267 and 4:2. It should be mentioned that the term *tayyib* is also used in the Qur'an to describe offspring, specific children, words, cities, wind, habitats, angels, trees, and greetings.

21. This translation accords with Ibn 'Arabi's somewhat unusual interpretation of this verse.

22. The wife in question is usually said to be 'A'ishah (a position Ibn 'Arabi holds).

23. "He describes their odors as 'goodly,' since speech is breath, and breath is the source of odor which issues forth in either a goodly or a foul manner, in accordance with that which appears from it in the form of utterance." *Fusus al-Hikam,* 221.

24. Ibid. See also *Sharh Qaysari,* 1182–83, which clarifies the meaning of this passage.

25. *Fusus al-Hikam,* 221. This *hadith* can be found in *Sahih Muslim, Kitab al-Masajid* (5/17) #565, p. 283, as part of a series of narrations discouraging attendance in mosques with the smell of garlic or onion on one's breath.

26. *Fusus al-Hikam,* 221.

27. Ibid.

28. This citation refers to 'Abd al-Razzaq al-Qashani's commentary on *Fusus al-Hikam: Sharh Fusus al-Hikam,* ed. Majid Hadi-zadah (Tehran: University of Tehran, Silsilah Intisharat-i Anjuman-i Athar wa Mafakhir-i Farhangi, 2004), 558.

29. In fact, as noted above, the original context of the hadith concerning the Prophet's aversion to the smell of garlic concerns attendees of mosques.

30. *Fusus al-Hikam,* 221.

31. Ibid., 221–22. For my interpretation of this passage, see 'Abd al-Rahman Jami (d. 898/1492), *Sharh al-Jami 'ala Fusus al-Hikam,* ed. 'Asim Ibrahim al-Kayyali al-Husayni al-Shadhili al-Darqawi (Beirut: Dar al-Kutub al-'Ilmiyah, 2004), 524. "Meaning" here refers to that which Chittick defines as "a reality of the world of intelligible things without any outward form." See *SPK,* 115.

32. *Fusus al-Hikam,* 222.

33. It should be noted that attraction does not need to be sexual—if one considers attraction to be a sort of interested or compelling fascination. In such a manner, for example, toddlers tend to be "attracted" to other toddlers.

34. *Lama'at,* 69; *Kulliyat,* 474–75 (ch. 7).

35. *Lama'at,* 68; *Kulliyat,* 474 (ch. 7). Muhtasham's edition differs slightly in wording. Clearly there is an allusion here to the verse "So wherever you turn, there is the face of God" from the Qur'an, 2:115.

36. The following quotations are from *Lama'at,* 70; *Kulliyat,* 475 (ch. 7). "Layli" is more common to 'Iraqi's poetry (and Persian poetry in general) than "Layla."

37. See note 1.

38. As noted before, Ibn 'Arabi's comment that God's beauty causes him to love himself and that beauty is "beloved by its very essence" can be found in *FM,* vol. 2, ch. 178, p. 322.13 (p. 326).

39. Declaring the hadith's status as verified as authentic by unveiling, not by transmission, Ibn 'Arabi seems unsure about this *version* of the hadith (the "Treasure Unknown"), the one he repeatedly cites, calling it a narration "the meaning of which is as follows," which seems to recognize a possibility of imprecision or at least the legitimacy of other versions, whether current or not. In this discussion, he also makes the connection between this narration and a genesis of love. See *FM*, vol. 2, ch. 198, p. 393.30 (p. 399).

40. *Lama'at,* 60; *Kulliyat,* 464 (ch. 4). For Ibn 'Arabi's statement that "every thing is created with a disposition (*majbul*) to the love of itself," see *FM*, vol. 2, ch. 73, question #116, p. 110.27 (p. 113).

41. *Lama'at,* 66; *Kulliyat,* 471 (ch. 6).

42. *Kulliyat,* 286–87; *Diwan,* 268. The version in the *Diwan* (Nafisi) shows some dissimilarities.

43. *Kulliyat,* 287; *Diwan,* 268.

44. See *Kulliyat,* 286, which is translated here, and a slightly variant version in *Diwan,* 267.

45. *Diwan* (Nafisi), 144. This *ghazal* displays the style, thematic content, and *takhallus* of 'Iraqi, but is missing from Muhtasham's *Kulliyat.*

46. *Kulliyat,* 99; *Diwan,* 105.

47. See *Fusus al-Hikam,* p. 219.

48. This *ruba'i* closely parallels and is probably based on another *ruba'i* by Awhad al-Din Kirmani, as can be seen in chapter 5, p. 101, in the subsection concerning Kirmani. *Kulliyat,* p. 365, #186; *Diwan,* 376.

49. *Lama'at,* 69; *Kulliyat,* 475 (ch. 7). The subject of this sentence is somewhat ambiguous; this interpretation—that the missing subject refers to the qualities of beauty and excellent action that 'Iraqi has previously mentioned—can be attributed to Jami, *Ashi''at al-Lama'at,* 112. See also *Divine Flashes,* 85.

50. *Lama'at,* 71; *Kulliyat,* 476 (ch. 7). Muhtasham's *Kulliyat* and the text used by Chittick and Lamborn in their *Divine Flashes* (ed. Jawad Nurbaksh, Tehran, 1353/1974) both have the word "city" (*shahr*) in place of the word "lion" (*shir*). The word *shahr* also appears in the commentaries of Jami and Barzishabadi. Still, the version of this double line found in Muhammad Khwajawi's edition of the *Lama'at,* which uses *shir* instead of *shahr,* also makes a good deal of sense, since pure love devours the one attempting to approach it with its awesomeness, like a lion.

51. *Kulliyat* (Muhtasham), 228; *Diwan* (Nafisi), 260.

52. *Diwan* (Nafisi), 364. This *ruba'i* has not been included in Muhtasham's *Kulliyat.* Interestingly, one finds it in Tabrizi's *Rashf al-Alhaz* with anonymous attribution (*sha'ir guyad*) on 36.

53. Of course, the parallels with Ibn 'Arabi need not be a result of influence, since 'Iraqi's predecessors in Persian Sufism, especially Ahmad Ghazali and Ruzbihan Baqli, expressed a similar idea.

54. A Turkic-inhabited city in central Asia, the residents of which were renowned in Persian literature for their beauty. The features that poets associated with the Yaghma'i people, as well as the Turkic people in general, especially fair skin, round faces, and small mouths, can be seen as standards of physical attractiveness in the medieval Persian-speaking world.

55. Here begins a series of puns, describing the beauty of the beloved as a bride.

56. *Kulliyat,* 240; *Diwan,* 243–44. One subtle difference in Nafisi's *Diwan* is the use of *chih* instead of *kih* so that the first hemistich of the fifth double line would read, "I see your visage in anything I observe." Baldick places this profound poem among those written after Fakhr al-Din's acquaintance with al-Qunawi and the Akbari contemplative school. (See Baldick, "Poems of Fakhr al-Din 'Iraqi," 225, where the author raises the possibility that this poem is influenced by the teachings of Ibn 'Arabi's "doctrine of the 'unity of existence.'") One sees reference here to a oneness of witnessing, divine self-admiration, state-changing, and the divine jealousy, all themes prevalent in Ibn 'Arabi's teachings. Nevertheless, because of 'Iraqi's focus on the *experience* of witnessing unity, it would not be impossible for the composition of this poem to precede 'Iraqi's move to Konya. In other words, 'Iraqi's concern here is with what he as a mystic sees and undergoes—beholding the Beloved in all things, for example, or constant change in the cosmos. Observations such as these can be found in Sufis well before Ibn 'Arabi.

57. *Kulliyat,* 79–80; *Diwan,* 91–92.

58. In al-Qushayri's presentation of the *shahid,* an imprint in the heart affects the perception of the mystic. Moreover, this imprint that takes possession of the mystic's heart is God's sign—a phenomenon that the Akbari school would equate with divine self-disclosure. Not only does al-Qushayri then proceed to relate the *shahid* to the act of witnessing, but he also comments on two different types of witnessing human beauty—one absolved of the lower self as opposed to one that testifies to the dogged perseverance of the lower self. Thus the *shahid* is more a witness for or against the contemplator than a witness to the divine beauty. In this regard, al-Qushayri's analysis of the *shahid* vies with Ibn 'Arabi's discussions of the *shahid* in terms of exactitude and profundity. While al-Qushayri might seem to shy away from identifying the *shahid* as a human medium for divine beauty, rather, such hesitancy reflects his desire to be precise; after all, the *shahid* is not merely human, for any object in the external world that allows the contemplator to witness his own *dhikr,* according to al-Qushayri, is a *shahid.* Nevertheless, it is significant that the singular example he cites is the form of a beautiful person. See al-Qushayri, *al-Risalah al-Qushayriyah fi 'Ilm al-Tasawwuf,* 86. This corresponds to the translation by Alexander D. Knysh, *Al-Qushayri's Epistle on Sufism* (*al-risala al-qushayriyya fi 'ilm al-tasawwuf*) (Reading, UK: Garnet, Center for Muslim Contribution to Civilization, 2007), 108–9.

59. Beauty occupies an axial position in al-Daylami's theory of love, one almost as significant as love itself. Even before beginning his discussion of love, al-Daylami deems it necessary to establish love's primary cause, namely, beauty (*husn*), which the

author describes as a "supersensory thing (*ma'na*) that God displayed to this world." For al-Daylami, love is a relationship caused by beauty, a relationship between the one endowed with beauty (the beloved) and the perceiver of that beauty (the lover). In other words, while most Sufi treatises leave the matter of beauty either unclear or secondary to discussions of love, in al-Daylami's treatise, beauty is the reality that induces love. Beauty, far from being simply an outcome of perception or "in the eyes of the beholder," is a *meaning* which God brings to actualize in the *form* of beloved entities. Quoting an unnamed philosopher, al-Daylami summarizes this concept of beauty, commenting that "beauty is the breaking forth of the light of the rational soul on the physical form." Thus beauty, in al-Daylami's analysis, is a quality of spirit; physical forms come to display beauty in a depreciated manner. The concept that beauty is a matter of descending perfections impels al-Daylami to divide his discussion of beauty into three main categories: the excellence of beauty (*al-husn*), the excellence of the beautiful (*al-hasan*), and the excellence of that which is perceived as beautiful (*al-mustahsan*). In his discussion of the first in this series, beauty itself, al-Daylami outlines God's creation of sources of beauty. All beautiful entities in the perceivable world around us have their source in one of two *shahid*s: either Adam, whom God created in his own image, or Paradise, which God adorned with his own beauty. The beauty of these two testimonies to divine perfection then descended on all things, resulting in two beauties, "one being animal, corporeal, and spiritual, and the other being inanimate and vegetable." Any lack of beauty seen in the world around us results from deterioration; that is, entities in this world lack beauty to the extent that they are removed from God's two original *shahid*s. The subchapter on the second term in this series, the beautiful, is devoted entirely to human beings, describing beauty as an excellence (*al-fadilah*) that has been bestowed on certain people while inside the womb through God's power. Those who have been blessed with innate beauty coupled with good character enjoy protection from hellfire. The categorization of human beauty as the "beautiful" as opposed to "that which is perceived as beautiful" indicates that, for al-Daylami, human beauty is real and innate beyond mere perception. See 'Ali ibn Muhammad al-Daylami, *'Atf al-Alif al-Ma'luf 'ala al-Lam al-Ma'tuf*, ed. Joseph Norment Bell and Hassan Mahmood Abdul Latif Al Shafie (Cairo: Dar al-Kitab al-Misri, 2007), 12–15.

60. *Kulliyat*, 332–33; *Diwan*, 234. See Baldick, "Poems of Fakhr al-Din 'Iraqi," 210, for Baldick's discussion of this poem. For the varied and often inconsistent meanings of *lahut* and *nasut* see Jamal J. Elias *The Throne Carrier of God* (Albany: State University of New York Press, 1995), 154–157.

61. *Kulliyat*, 565; *Diwan*, 423.

62. In addition to his fatherless birth and well-known asceticism, Jesus' being associated with spirit can be found in the text of the Qur'an, which describes him as "God's messenger, his word that he dispatched to Mary, and a spirit from him." See 4:171.

63. *Kulliyat*, 243–44; *Diwan*, 88. See Baldick, "Poems of Fakhr al-Din 'Iraqi," 212, for Baldick's discussion of this poem.

Chapter 4: Ibn 'Arabi and Human Beauty

1. As Omid Safi describes it, "The Path of Love may be described as a loosely affiliated group of Sufi mystics and poets who throughout the centuries have propagated a highly nuanced teaching focused on passionate love (*'ishq*)." See Omid Safi, "The Path of Sufi Love in Iran and India," in *A Pearl in Wine: Essays on the Life, Music, and Sufism of Hazrat Inayat Khan,* ed. Pirzade Zia Inayat Khan (New Lebanon, N.Y.: Omega, 2001), 221–266, 244.

2. 'Ayn al-Qudat's use of this phrase has been quoted in Carl W. Ernst, *Words of Ecstasy in Sufism* (Albany, N.Y.: State University of New York Press, 1985), 74.

3. Th. Emil Homerin describes this section as telling "the seeker to become sensitive to the divine beauty within all of existence and its shifting self-manifestation among lovers." See Th. Emil Homerin, *'Umar Ibn al-Farid: Sufi Verse, Saintly Life* (Mahwah, N.J.: Paulist Press, 2001), 68.

4. Ibn al-Farid, *Diwan Ibn al-Farid,* ed. Mahdi Muhammad Nasir al-Din (Beirut: Dar al-Kutub al-'Ilmiyah, 1423/2002) (hereafter cited as *Diwan Ibn al-Farid*), p. 32, line 83.

5. *Diwan Ibn al-Farid,* p. 31, line 64.

6. Farghani, *Mashariq al-Darari,* p. 234, line 3. William C. Chittick discusses the various possibilities for Farghani's death dates in "Sa'id al- Din Muhammad b. Ahmad Farghani," *EI2,* 8:860–61.

7. Farghani, *Mashariq al-Darari,* 440. Farghani describes the station of passionate love for the witness/testimony as a "lower station," presumably lower than the rank of the most achieved gnostic.

8. Baqli, *Kitab 'Abhar al-'Ashiqin,* ed. Henry Corbin and Muhammad Mu'in (Tehran: Dep. d'iranologie de l'Institut francoiranien, 1337/1958) (hereafter cited as *Kitab 'Abhar al-'Ashiqin*), p. 16, #33.

9. See the Persian text in *Heart's Witness: The Sufi Quatrains of Awhaduddin Kirmani,* edited with introduction and notes by Bernd Manuel Weischer, trans. Peter Lamborn Wilson and Bernd Manuel Weischer (Tehran: Imperial Iranian Academy of Philosophy, 1978), p. 98, #62. This *ruba'i* is missing from the *Diwan-i Ruba'iyat,* which are cited later.

10. Jami, *Nafahat al-Uns,* 591. The second name included is Awhad al-Din 'Iraqi, although surrounding context clarifies that Kirmani is meant.

11. Omid Safi highlights the "fresh, dynamic, and ever transforming understanding of themselves" that characterized adherents to the School of Love. See Omid Safi, "On the Path of Love Towards the Divine: A Journey with Muslim Mystics," *Sufi* 78 (Winter 09/Spring 10): 22–38, here 28, reprinted from the *Journal of Scriptural Reasoning* 3, no. 2 (August 2003).

12. See William C. Chittick, *The Sufi Path of Love: The Spiritual Teachings of Rumi* (Albany: State University of New York Press, 1983), 168–69, 212–20, and 288–94, which clarify the importance of human beauty (and the term *shahid*) in Rumi's poetry.

13. Hellmut Ritter, *Das Meer der Seele,* translated as *The Ocean of the Soul: Men, the World and God in the Stories of Farid al-Din 'Attar,* trans. John O'Kane (Leiden: Brill, 2003) (hereafter cited as *Ocean of the Soul*), 471. Ritter cites the *Kashf al-Mahjub.*

14. See Cyrus Ali Zargar, "The Satiric Method of Ibn Daniyal: Morality and Anti-Morality in *Tayf al-Khayal,*" *Journal of Arabic Literature* 37, no. 1 (2006): 68–108, here 90–92.

15. *FM,* vol. 2, ch. 177, p. 311.18 (p. 315). Translation taken from Carl W. Ernst, *Ruzbihan Baqli: Mysticism and the Rhetoric of Sainthood in Persian Sufism* (Surrey, UK: Curzon Press, 1996), 3–4, with some slight modifications. The story is also narrated by Jami in his *Nafahat al-Uns,* 257. It seems that Louis Massignon considered the protagonist of this episode to be Ruzbihan Misri, not Ruzbihan al-Baqli (the text of *FM* has the name as "al-Shaykh Ruzbahar"). However, Henry Corbin, Muhammad Mu'in (Mo'in), and Ghulam 'Ali Ariya confirm that the protagonist is indeed Ruzbihan al-Baqli. See Masataka Takeshita, "Continuity and Change in the Tradition of Shirazi Love Mysticism: A Comparison between al-Daylami's *'Atf al-alif* and Ruzbihan Baqli's *'Abhar al-'Ashiqin,*" *Orient: Report of the Society for Near Eastern Studies in Japan* 23 (1987): 113–31, here 129n.4.

16. *Tarjuman ạl-Ashwaq,* 43–44. For the entirety of the poem, translated stunningly with a commentary elucidating the poem's literary and mystical context, see Michael Sells, "Love," in *The Literature of al-Andalus,* ed. María Rosa Menocal, Raymond P. Scheindlin, and Michael Sells (Cambridge University Press, Cambridge, 2000), 126–58, especially 150–55. Since I mention the poem on a few occasions throughout the book, and since endnote formatting will not do justice to Sells' lyrical use of line breaks, I will here cite Nicholson's translation (*Mystical Odes,* 66–67) with very minor adjustments:

> O doves that haunt the *arak* and *ban* trees, have pity! Do not double my woes by your lamentation!
> Have pity! Do not reveal, by wailing and weeping, my hidden desires and my secret sorrows!
> I respond to her, at eve and morn, with the plaintive cry of a longing man and the moan of an impassioned lover.
> The spirits faced one another in the thicket of *ghada* trees and bent their branches towards me, and it (the bending) annihilated me;
> And they brought me divers sorts of tormenting desire and passion and untried affliction
> Who will give me sure promise of Jam' and al-Muhassab of Mina? Who of Dhat al-Athl? Who of Na'man?
> They encompass my heart moment after moment, for the sake of love and anguish, and kiss my pillars,
> Even as the best of mankind encompassed the Ka'ba, which the evidence of reason proclaims to be imperfect,

And kissed stones therein, although he possessed reason. And what is the rank of the Temple in comparison with the dignity of a human?
How often did they vow and swear that they would not change, but one dyed with henna does not keep oaths.
And one of the most wonderful things is a veiled gazelle, who points with red finger-tip and winks with eyelids,
A gazelle whose pasture is between the breast-bones and the bowels. O marvel! a garden amidst fires!
My heart has become receptive to every form: it is a pasture for gazelles and a convent for Christian monks,
And a temple for idols and the pilgrim's Ka'ba and the tables of the Torah and the Book of the Qur'an.
I follow the Religion of Love: whatever way Love's camels take, that is my religion and my faith.
Ours is a model in Hind's lover Bishr and in their counterparts and in Qays and Layla, and in Mayya and Ghaylan.

17. *FM*, vol. 2, ch. 178, p. 321.15 (p. 325). While this quotation acknowledges homoerotic love for young boys, prevalent in the author's time, it should not be taken as a sanctioning of *concupiscent* gazing at beardless youths, a practice that Ibn 'Arabi explicitly declares forbidden in his 108th chapter of *al-Futuhat,* an interesting point to which we will return (gazing without sexual desire, though, he clearly does allow for the elite). In at least one other instance, Ibn 'Arabi names the love for a *jariyah* or *ghulam* to be the peak of human love; see *FM*, vol. 2, ch. 108, p. 186.17 (p. 189). It is also interesting that both terms used here are commonly used to describe a female and male slave respectively.

18. *FM* (Ihya'), vol. 4, ch. 558, p. 260.33 (p. 260). See also William C. Chittick, "The Divine Roots of Human Love," *Journal of the Muhyiddin Ibn 'Arabi Society* 17 (1995): 55–78, here 76–77, where this passage along with much of the subchapter discussing the Presence of Love (*hadrat al-wudd*) has been translated.

19. *FM*, vol. 3, ch. 358, p. 260.26 (p. 267).

20. *Fusus al-Hikam,* 217. For a lucid analysis of this chapter, see Nettler, *Sufi Metaphysics and Qur'anic Prophets,* 176–203.

21. *Fusus al-Hikam,* 217.

22. Ibid.

23. Numerous passages on Ibn 'Arabi's cosmological approach to sexual intercourse and male-female love have been translated and analyzed insightfully by Sachiko Murata in chapter 6 of *The Tao of Islam: A Sourcebook on Gender Relationships in Islamic Thought* (Albany: State University of New York Press, 1992), 171–202.

24. See, for example, *FM*, vol. 3, ch. 380, p. 485.19 (p. 501). Ahmad ibn Hanbal (d. 241/855) narrates this hadith from Anas ibn Malik in *Musnad Ahmad ibn Hanbal*

(Riyadh: Bayt al-Afkar al-Duwaliyah, 1419/1998), #12318/9, p. 868. This hadith is also narrated from Anas ibn Malik by Abu 'Abd al-Rahman Ahmad (ibn 'Ali) ibn Shu'ayb al-Nasa'i (d. 303/915), in *al-Mujtaba min al-Sunan, al-mashhur bi-Sunan al-Nasa'i* (Riyadh: Bayt al-Afkar al-Duwaliyah, 1420/1999), *Kitab 'Ishrat al-Nisa'* (36/1), #3939/3940, p. 416. All versions in these two collections are missing the word *thalath* found in Ibn 'Arabi's citation, and all have either *al-dunya* or no prepositional phrase instead of *dunyakum*.

25. *FM*, vol. 3, ch. 380, p. 488.22 (p. 504).

26. Commenting on the hadith "He who knows his soul (or self) knows his Lord," Ibn 'Arabi states that "a human's gnosis of himself is a precursor to gnosis of his Lord." *Fusus al-Hikam*, 215. As William Chittick comments, it is a hadith "not accepted by the specialists," that is, the specialists in Sunni narrations. See *SPK*, 396n.22.

27. Again this comes from a *hadith qudsi*, "Oh David! I long for them [i.e., those who long for me] much more intensely!" See *Fusus al-Hikam*, 215. I have not been able to locate this narration with the wording that Ibn 'Arabi uses in any of the traditional hadith collections.

28. In Ibn 'Arabi's thought, the cosmos is the Great Man (*al-insan al-kabir*), such that man and cosmos share formal similarities (e.g., being made up of four elements or humors, making use of faculties or angels, and of course, having the ability to serve as a divine mirror). In more familiar terminology, man is a "microcosm." Still, the human being has a comprehensiveness not possessed by the cosmos. See *Fusus al-Hikam*, 49.

29. Ibid., 215. While Ibn 'Arabi's understanding of gender and creation can arguably be described as "patriarchal," he also does not hesitate to take stances on spiritual and even jurisprudential matters that oppose traditional views of women. See Sa'diyya Shaikh, "In Search of 'Al-Insan': Sufism, Islamic Law, and Gender," *Journal of the American Academy of Religion* 77, no. 4 (December 2009): 781–822.

30. See narrations describing women as "created from a rib" in *Sahih al-Bukhari, Kitab Ahadith al-Anbiya'* (60/1), #3331, p. 819, as well as *Kitab al-Nikah* (67/80), #5185, p. 1321. Also see *Sahih Muslim, Kitab al-Rada'* (17/18), #1468, p. 775. This account of Eve's creation is rejected in certain Shi'i narrations (which indicate that Eve was made from clay like Adam) and, hence, in Shi'i scholarly circles as well; see 'Allamah Muhammad Husayn Tabataba'i (1402/1981), *al-Mizan fi Tafsir al-Qur'an* (Beirut: Mu'assasat al-A'lami li-l-Matbu'at, 1418/1997), 4:136, 146, and especially 151.

31. *FM*, vol. 1, ch. 7, p. 175.12 (p. 124).

32. Ibid.

33. *Fusus al-Hikam*, 216.

34. Ibn 'Arabi states this explicitly: "Man, that is, Adam, was created according to his form and Eve was created according to the form of Adam." See *FM*, vol. 1, ch. 72, p. 811.4 (p. 679). This hadith is cited often in the works of Ibn 'Arabi; he considers it fully in a series of answers to questions posed to him. See *FM* (Ihya'), vol. 2, ch. 73,

question #143, p. 121.6 (p. 124). This hadith can also be found in *Sahih al-Bukhari, Kitab al-Isti'dhan* (79/1), #6227, p. 1554, and *Sahih Muslim, Kitab al-Birr* (45/32), #2612, p. 1408, *Kitab al-Jannah* (51/11), #2841, p. 1523.

35. *FM*, vol. 1, ch. 7, p. 175.17 (p. 124)

36. Ibid.

37. Ibid.

38. Ibid.

39. *Fusus al-Hikam*, 220. As Ibn 'Arabi mentions, this proverb was still current in his day.

40. Ibid.

41. That is, the word for "prayer" is not actually female in terms of sex. Arab grammarians have divided feminine words into "real" (*haqiqi*) and "lexical" (*lafzi*). Real feminine words are those the referents of which possess female reproductive organs; all other words are lexically feminine. See, for example, an introductory treatise on Arabic grammar by Baha' al-Din Muhammad ibn Husayn 'Amuli, that is, Shaykh al-Baha'i (d. 1030/1621), *al-Fawa'id al-Samadiyah* (Qum, Iran: Intisharat-i Nahawandi, 2006), 11.

42. While each set of words (the Intellect and the Soul, the Cloud and the Breath, and the Pen and the Tablet) has its own specific function in the vision of Ibn 'Arabi, sometimes certain parallel terms are in fact treated as synonyms.

43. Ibn 'Arabi tells us that in the creation of the cosmos an existent (*mawjud*) allows for the coming to being of that which is "detached" or derived (*munfasil*) from that existent. The first existent is the Primary Intellect, and the first derivative or detachment is the Universal Soul. In parallel fashion, the last existent is Adam, and the last derivative is Eve. See *FM*, vol. 1, ch. 10, p. 188.28 (p. 137). Elsewhere Ibn 'Arabi explains that the Primary Intellect is "a precondition for the existence of the [Universal] Soul," and that the process of active-receptive creation continues with the Dust Cloud (*al-haba'*) and the Universal Body (*al-jism al-kull*) acting as receptive counterparts to that which results from the marriage of the Intellect and the Soul, resulting in the created forms. See *FM*, vol. 1, ch. 60, p. 367.17 (p. 293). More often, as the process of receptivity continues, Ibn 'Arabi describes the Universal Nature (*al-tabi'ah al-kulliyah*) as being receptive vis-à-vis the Universal Soul.

44. Ibn 'Arabi never clearly lays out these three components as one set but speaks of the relationship between the essential light and the Cloud in one instance, *FM*, vol. 1, ch. 13, p. 201.11 (p. 148), and the relationship between the Cloud and the Breath of the All-Merciful in another, *FM*, vol. 2, ch. 198, p. 394.7 (p. 400). Chittick has translated the latter passage, wherein Ibn 'Arabi clearly describes the Cloud as "an All-Merciful Breath receptive to the forms of the letters and words of the cosmos." See *SDG*, 70. In other words, the Cloud and the Breath are one reality, a reality described using different terms in accordance with its function as receptive or active.

45. Su'ad al-Hakim discusses in detail the concept of *al-nikah* in the writings of Ibn 'Arabi, which she defines as the "marriage of two things resulting in a third, on

whatever level it might be" and identifies as the concept of triplicity (*al-tathlith*). See al-Hakim, *al-Mu'jam al-Sufi,* 1069–71. Among later Akbari commentators, Ibn 'Arabi's use of the term developed into the "five conjugal unions" (*al-nikahat al-khamsah*), a more complex hierarchy of unions begetting the Five Presences or Five "Worlds": the World of Meanings (*'alam al-ma'ani*), the World of Pure Spirits (*'alam al-arwah al-mujarradah*), the World of Rational Souls (*'alam al-nufus al-natiqah*), the World of Representations (*'alam al-mithal*), and, last, the World of Sensory Perception (*'alam al-hiss*) or the Visible World (*'alam al-shahadah*). The conjugal unions that beget the Five Presences (sometimes four), which differ in name and distinction among various Akbari commentators, are discussed ably by 'Abd al-Razzaq al-Qashani in his *Sharh Fusus al-Hikam,* 549–50. See also chapter 5 (143–69) of Murata's *Tao of Islam* for a clear discussion in English of "macrocosmic marriage."

46. In a chapter concerning cosmological "fathers" and "mothers," Ibn 'Arabi discusses the marriage of the Pen and the Tablet, terms taken from Qur'anic usage (68:1 and 85:22). According to Ibn 'Arabi, "the Pen and Tablet have a conjugal union that is suprasensory (*ma'nawi*) and abstracted but an effect that is sensory and witnessed." *FM,* vol. 1, ch. 11, p. 191.25 (p. 139).

47. Ibn 'Arabi sometimes equates the Muhammadan Reality with the Highest Pen (*al-qalam al-a'la*) and mentions that in the terminology of others it is called the Primary Intellect (*al-'aql al-awwal*); he consistently refers to the comprehensiveness of this Reality, its precedence over all creation, and its being the first receptive (and thus, other than the Real, the first active) agent. See *FM,* vol. 1, ch. 3, p. 140.29 (p. 94). Su'ad al-Hakim defines the Muhammadan Reality as the "most perfect created locus of self-disclosure in which the Real becomes manifest; rather, this reality is the Perfect Man in the truest sense. Although every existent is a particular locus of self-disclosure for a divine name, Muhammad is unique in being a locus of self-disclosure for the Comprehensive Name (*al-ism al-jami'*), which is also the Greatest Name (*al-ism al-a'zam*); thus his is the rank of utter comprehensiveness (*al-jam'iyah al-mutlaqah*)." After listing the creative functions of the Muhammadan Reality, al-Hakim provides textual proof for her claims, which—due to the discussion of the Muhammadan Reality in the coming paragraph—need not be cited here. See al-Hakim, *al-Mu'jam al-Sufi,* 347–52.

48. It is also a precedence and proximity that is ceaseless: The continued maintenance of those things depends upon the Perfect Man (*al-insan al-kamil*), who acquires the inner Muhammadan perfections and embodies the Muhammadan Reality (*al-haqiqah al-Muhammadiyah*).

49. *Fusus al-Hikam,* 49. See also Sells, *Mystical Languages of Unsaying,* 72–73, where Sells translates this passage powerfully in free verse; the phrase "very polishing" can be found in his translation.

50. Ibn 'Arabi makes this clear: "When the Real (may he be exalted), because of his innumerable Beautiful Names, wanted to see the essences of those Names, or, if you prefer, wanted to see his own essence, in a comprehensive being (*kawn jami'*) that,

upon having the attribute of existence, would encompass the affair in its entirety and through which he would make manifest his own mystery to himself, [he created Adam.] . . . All of those Names which are in the Divine Form are made manifest in this human configuration, such that—through this [external] existence—it has obtained the rank of comprehending (*al-jam'*) and encompassment (*al-ihatah*). . . . Angels do not possess the comprehensiveness (*jam'iyah*) of Adam and only understand the divine names particular to them, those names by which they declare the transcendence of the Real and glorify him; they do not know that God has certain names the knowledge of which does not reach them, names by which they do not declare his transcendence [like Adam] and do not glorify him with the glorification of Adam." *Fusus al-Hikam,* 48 and 50. My translation of "Divine Form" (*al-surah al-ilahiyah*) instead of the plural "Divine Forms" (*al-suwar al-ilahiyah*) is a correction of the text based on Qaysari's quotation of the *Fusus al-Hikam* in his commentary, 363.

51. *FM,* vol. 4, ch. 463, p. 88.12 (p. 84).

52. Muhammad's combination of two polar perspectives, receptive and active, enjoys a higher degree of perfection than one alone; as Ibn 'Arabi states elsewhere, the offspring of the male-female relationship combines the perfection and preparedness (*isti'dad*) of both male and female, such that "the perfection of the Perfect Son is greater than the perfection of the [Perfect] Father," which is why Muhammad—as a "son" or a merging of male and female—is "distinguished by the most complete perfection." Adam, on the other hand, while having male qualities, had no mother and so lacks comprehensiveness. In the present context the offspring discussed is not a human child but the very *act* of attraction and union. By bringing together male activity and female receptivity, the phenomenon of male-female attraction and the act of male-female union has a comprehensiveness that parallels the essential nature of the Muhammadan Reality. Thus one might say that the witnessing that man experiences in woman, by reenacting the original triplicity of the cosmos, parallels that of existence's greatest witness, Muhammad. See *FM,* vol. 1, ch. 72, p. 811.4 (p. 679).

53. *Fusus al-Hikam,* 220.

54. In distinguishing Muhammad from Adam, Ibn 'Arabi depicts Adam as the male prototype or "father" of mankind while attributing to Muhammad—as has been said—the attributes of the first entification, that which God created from nothing else. While Adam as the first man represents primacy, Muhammad as the first light represents completion, totally, and comprehensiveness. In other words, Ibn 'Arabi uses "Adam" to discuss human origins, nature, and potential but relates "Muhammad" to the comprehensive creative faculty, for Muhammad represents the ambiguity that lies between the Perfect Man and pure divine action.

55. *Fusus al-Hikam,* 217. The word here translated as "completeness," *kamal,* can also mean "perfection" and has been translated as such in a number of instances throughout this chapter. In the case of witnessing in women, however, Ibn 'Arabi does seem to refer to witnessing in a locus that allows for comprehensiveness, wholeness, or "completeness," as has been discussed.

56. This is implied in Ibn 'Arabi's statement that the one who enjoys women as a locus of pleasure does not know "through Whom he has pleasure and Who [in reality] has pleasure," implying—as he has throughout this chapter—that comprehensive witnessing is the Real's witnessing of himself as cosmos and as God simultaneously through man. See *Fusus al-Hikam,* 219.

57. *FM,* vol. 4, ch. 463, p. 88.21 (p. 84).

58. Ibid.

59. *Fusus al-Hikam,* 218.

60. Hellmut Ritter states such in *Ocean of the Soul,* 494. Joseph Norment Bell makes this assertion in his *Love Theory in Later Hanbalite Islam* (Albany: State University of New York Press, 1979), 140.

61. For the matter of rain, see note 64, which refers to a hadith from *Sahih Muslim.* As for the phrase *maqam al-tajrid,* it refers to the wayfarer's setting aside all things, including the entire cosmos and even his own heart; it is precursory to *maqam al-tafrid,* in which the wayfarer experiences an even purer oneness with God. See al-Hakim, *al-Mu'jam al-Sufi,* 878–80, wherein al-Hakim cites Ibn 'Arabi's *al-Istilahat.* A concise but clear explanation of these two stations can also be found in Shihab al-Din 'Umar al-Suhrawardi (d. 632/1234), *'Awarif al-Ma'arif,* appended to Abu Hamid al-Ghazali, *Ihya' 'Ulum al-Din* (Beirut: Dar al-Kutub al-'Ilmiyah, 2004), 5:42–250, here 243.

62. *FM,* vol. 2, ch. 108, p. 186.24 (p. 190).

63. Ibn 'Arabi also discusses the recentness of the young in his discussion of the child Moses' power of subjection (*taskhir*) over the adult Pharoah in the chapter concerning Moses of *Fusus al-Hikam.* The subjugating force that the young have over the old comes from being newer in terms of creation (*hadith al-takwin*). See *Fusus al-Hikam,* 197–98.

64. *Sahih Muslim, Kitab Salat al-Istisqa'* (9/2), #898, p. 446. See also *Fusus al-Hikam,* 198, as well as al-Daylami, *'Atf al-Alif,* 23.

65. See *Fusus al-Hikam,* 198.

66. Shams al-Din Ahmad-i Aflaki (fl. 754/1354), *Manaqib al-'Arifin,* ed. Tahsin Yazici (Tehran: Dunya-i Kitab, 1362 *hijri-shamsi*) (hereafter cited as *Manaqib al-'Arifin*), trans. in John O'Kane, *The Feats of the Knowers of God: Manaqeb al-'Arefin* (Leiden: Brill, 2002), xvi–xvii.

67. *Sahih Muslim, Kitab al-Zakah* (12/20), #1017, p. 508, for this and the following portion of the hadith. It is interesting to note the possibility raised by Franklin D. Lewis that the person mentioned as "Shaykh Muhammad" might be Ibn 'Arabi. Important here is that while Shams generally admires "Shaykh Muhammad," he disapproves of his "failure to follow in the way of the Prophet and observe the law." See Franklin D. Lewis, *Rumi: Past and Present, East and West: The Life, Teachings and Poetry of Jalal al-Din Rumi* (Oxford: Oneworld, 2000), 149–51, here 151.

68. *Manaqib al-'Arifin,* vol. 2, p. 578, translation from O'Kane, *Feats of the Knowers of God,* p. 397, #564.

69. See Al-Ghazali, *Kimiya-i Sa'adat,* vol. 1, 19–20.

70. Chittick discusses the useful opposition of desire and intellect (or, in his translation, passion and reason) in Ibn 'Arabi's thought in *SPK,* 159–62.

71. See *FM,* vol. 2, ch. 108, p. 186.17 (p. 189) as well as *FM,* vol. 2, ch. 178, p. 321.15 (p. 325). The equivalence suggested here between the lovability of young women and young men is worth mentioning.

72. *FM,* vol. 2, ch. 108, p. 188.5 (p. 191).

73. As quoted and discussed in the first chapter of this book, this hadith is narrated in the divine first-person: "My servant draws near to Me through nothing I love more than that which I have made obligatory for him. My servant never ceases drawing near to Me through supererogatory works until I love him. Then, when I love him, I am his hearing through which he hears, his sight through which he sees, his hand through which he seizes, and his foot through which he walks." There are other versions of this hadith that Ibn 'Arabi cites. For this version, see *SPK,* 325, and al-Bukhari, *Kitab al-Riqaq* (81/38), #6502, p. 1617.

74. *FM,* vol. 2, ch. 178, p. 322.18–19 (p. 326).

75. *FM,* vol. 2, ch. 178, p. 329.13 (p. 334).

76. *FM,* vol. 2, ch. 178, p. 328.16 (p. 333).

77. Ibid.

78. *FM,* vol. 2, ch. 178, p. 323.21 (p. 327).

79. Ibid.

80. *FM,* vol. 2, ch. 178, p. 316.2 (p. 320).

81. *FM,* vol. 2, ch. 73, question #116, p. 111.13 (p. 113).

82. Ibid.

83. *FM,* vol. 2, ch. 73, question #116, p. 108.34 (p. 111).

84. *FM,* vol. 2, ch. 178, p. 329.36 (p. 334).

85. *FM,* vol. 2, ch. 73, question #116, p. 108.34 (p. 111). As Ibn 'Arabi indicates, a desire for union is the natural result of love on every level of existence—on the level of sensory or material existence, this union is called "sexual." But in the "elemental configuration" (*al-nash'ah al-'unsuriyah*), the most complete union is conjugal or sexual union (*nikah*). See *Fusus al-Hikam,* p. 217, line 5. Whether in an embrace, time spent together, or sexual relations, all lovers seek some sort of union; see *FM,* vol. 2, ch. 178, p. 322.31 (p. 327).

86. Thus Ibn 'Arabi tells us that the ultimate result of spiritual love is for "the essence of the beloved to become identical with the essence of the lover, and the essence of the lover to be identical with the essence of the beloved, which is what the School of Incarnation (*al-Huluiliyah*) suggests, though they have no knowledge of it in its true sense." *FM,* vol. 2, ch. 178, p. 329.11 (p. 334).

87. *FM,* vol. 2, ch. 73, question #116, p. 110.16 (p. 112).

88. *FM,* vol. 2, ch. 73, question #116, p. 110.35 (p. 113).

89. *FM,* vol. 2, ch. 178, p. 324.26 (p. 329).

90. *FM,* vol. 2, ch. 73, question #116, p. 110.32 (p. 113).

91. *FM*, vol. 2, ch. 178, 315.33 (p. 320).

92. *FM*, vol. 2, ch. 178, p. 325.3 (p. 329).

93. *FM*, vol. 2, ch. 178, p. 325.22 (p. 330).

94. Al-Qurashi, *Hayat al-Imam al-Rida* (Tehran: Manshurat Sa'id ibn Jubayr, 1412/1992), 2:225. Al-Hafiz Abu al-Fida' Isma'il ibn 'Umar ibn Kathir (d. 774/1373), the famous historian and student of the vehement Ibn 'Arabi critic Ahmad ibn Taymiyah (d. 728/1328), reports after citing this poem that singing girls performed for Harun al-Rashid, whereupon, having become overexcited by their music, he lavished money upon them, no less than three thousand dirhams for each performer. See Ibn Kathir, *al-Badayah wa-l-Nahayah*, ed. 'Ali Shiri (Beirut: Dar Ihya' al-Turath al-'Arabi, 1408 *hijri*), 10:238–39.

95. The three double lines quoted here appear in *FM*, vol. 2, ch. 73, question #116, p. 111.3 (p. 113), while the first double line also appears in *FM*, vol. 2, ch. 178, p. 325.17 (p. 329).

96. See *FM*, vol. 2, ch. 178, p. 325.18 (p. 330) for this and the following quotation.

97. Ibid.

98. *FM*, vol. 2, ch. 73, question #116, p. 110.36 (p. 113).

99. *FM*, vol. 2, ch. 178, p. 322.14 (p. 326). See p. 45.

Chapter 5: 'Iraqi and the Tradition of Love, Witnessing, and *Shahidbazi*

1. Of course, genre must be considered as well. For Sufi authors, the word seems to have carried its many connotations in disparate contexts, even when one connotation was highlighted. While in poetry, the human *shahid* was emphasized, in prose, authors tended to focus on cosmological aspects of the word. Thus the glossaries attributed to 'Iraqi and authored by Tabrizi define the *shahid* rather simply as "what they call the self-disclosure (*tajalli*)." See *Kulliyat*, 564; *Diwan*, 430; *Rashf al-Alhaz*, 64. 'Abd al-Razzaq al-Qashani offers a more detailed definition of *shahid* in his glossary of Sufi terms, a definition that still includes *tajallin* as a factor; see his *Istilahat al-Sufiyah*, 37.

2. See Bell, *Love Theory*, 125–47.

3. The use of the word *baz*, an active participle derived from *bazi* (playing), carries a negative sense in many of the compound words where it occurs, such as *qumarbaz* (a gambler) or *nazarbaz* (a profligate gazer). The word often conveys a sense of hedonism. Yet since *bazi* also implies playfulness, in the case of *shahidbazi*, there might also exist a sense of harmlessness, something stopping short of carnal conduct. See Dihkhuda, *Lughatnamah*, under *shahidbazi*.

4. See the Qur'an, 11:90, 85:14, 3:31, 60:8, 61:4, 3:76, 3:148, 3:159, 20:39, and so on.

5. A number of medieval Muslim commentators have noted the differences in the various terms meaning "love," including Ibn 'Arabi. In chapter 178 of *al-Futuhat al-Makkiyah*, Ibn 'Arabi, always sensitive to etymologies, outlines the implications of four such words: (1) *hubb*, from a root related to the seed and thus indicating "germinal,

seminal or original love, whose purity penetrates the heart and whose limpidity is not subject to accidental changes"; (2) *wadd,* from a root indicating a peg, such that the word indicates "the faithful attachment of love" and "the constantly lovable and loving"; (3) *'ishq,* a word that shares the same root as the bindweed, a plant that twists around and seems to suffocate other plants, thus indicating this love's overwhelming nature; and (4) *hawa,* a word that—perhaps because it indicates a sudden drop—is associated with "the sudden inclination of love" or, in accordance with its literal meaning, "unexpected passion." The above translations and further commentary on Ibn 'Arabi's analysis of these terms can be found in Maurice Gloton, "The Quranic Inspiration of Ibn 'Arabi's Vocabulary of Love," trans. Cecilia Twinch, *Journal of the Muhyiddin Ibn 'Arabi Society* 27 (2000): 37–52, here 41.

6. Lane, *Arabic-English Lexicon* 5:2054.

7. One sees, for example, that according to the writer Abu 'Uthman al-Jahiz (d. ca. 255/868–69), in the words of Lois Anita Giffen, *'ishq* is "a feeling evoked in men by women and by nothing else." See Lois Anita Giffen, *Theory of Profane Love among the Arabs: The Development of the Genre,* Studies in Near Eastern Civilization 3 (New York: New York University Press, 1971), 86. It seems that later al-Jahiz modified this definition to include sexually desirous love between men, 86n.10.

8. See Khaled El-Rouayheb, *Before Homosexuality in the Arab-Islamic World, 1500–1800* (Chicago and London: The University of Chicago Press, 2005), especially the second and third chapters. Of use also is the anthology *Islamic Homosexualities: Culture, History, and Literature,* the most relevant article of which is by Jim Wafer; see "Vision and Passion: The Symbolism of Male Love in Islamic Mystical Literature," *Islamic Homosexualities: Culture, History, and Literature,* ed. Stephen O. Murray and Will Roscoe (New York: New York University Press, 1997), pp. 107–31.

9. Sirus Shamisa, *Shahidbazi dar Adabiyat-i Farsi* (Tehran: Intisharat-i Firdaws, 1381 *hjri-shamsi*), 95–140.

10. Hellmut Ritter, *Das Meer der Seele: Mensch, Welt und Gott in den Geschichten des Fariduddin 'Attar* (Leiden: Brill, 1978); see ch. 26. This study has been translated by John O'Kane as *The Ocean of the Soul.*

11. An interesting observation made by Ritter concerning *shahidbazi* illustrates the far-reaching effects of this practice and its existence even in the twentieth century. Ritter notes that an Albanian newspaper dated June 21, 1936, describes fifty to sixty people enamored with a young man whom, upon acquiring the permission of the young man's father, they dress as one would a girl and gaze at for hours. Not only do they refrain from harming him, but the practice seems to be a source of prestige for the young man within the community. See *Ocean of the Soul,* 516.

12. Considering some of the parallels seen in the *Sawanih* and chapter 178 of *al-Futuhat al-Makkiyah,* it is not impossible that Ibn 'Arabi had some familiarity with Ghazali's work. To protest that the treatise is in Persian is to overemphasize texts in a world where a living and oral pedagogical tradition thrived. Ibn 'Arabi associated with

shaykhs fluent in Persian (such as Awhad al-Din Kirmani, and Abu Shuja' Zahir ibn Rustam al-Isfahani, d. 609/1212, whom he famously mentions in the *Tarjuman*), so his exposure to Ghazali's observations—if not his approximate words—is a possibility that must be considered. Certainly the plethora of references one finds to Abu Hamid al-Ghazali's writings in the works of Ibn 'Arabi suggests that Muhyi al-Din would have some interest in the writings of Abu Hamid's well-known brother Ahmad.

13. References to Ahmad Ghazali's treatise correspond to *Sawanih* from *Ganjinah-i 'Irfan: Ashi''at al-Lama'at-i Jami / Sawanih-i Ghazali*, ed. Hamid Rabbani. The translation used here is that of Nasrollah Pourjavady, *Sawanih: Inspirations from the World of Pure Spirits (The Oldest Persian Sufi Treatise on Love)*, with commentary by Nasrollah Pourjavady (London: KPI, 1986). Pourjavady's translation of genderless third-person pronouns referring to the beloved as "she" has been changed.

14. My translation of this sentence corresponds to Khwajawi's *Lama'at*, 45, as opposed to Muhtasham's *Kulliyat*, 452–53, which is less coherent. A passage-by-passage comparison of the *Lama'at* and the *Sawanih* can be found in Muhammad Akhtar Chimah, *Maqam-i Shaykh Fakhr al-Din Ibrahim 'Iraqi dar Tasawwuf-i Islami* (Islamabad: Markaz-i Tahqiqat-i Farsi-i Iran wa Pakistan, 1994), 242–44.

15. I estimate the age of 'Iraqi to be between fifty-five and sixty based on Shaykh Baha' al-Din's death in 666/1267, at which point 'Iraqi was roughly fifty-four years old. After Baha' al-Din's passing, 'Iraqi undertook a trip that included Mecca, Medina, Oman, Syria, and, finally, Anatolia, where he began his study with al-Qunawi. *Diwan*, 25–27.

16. A similar point is made by William Chittick and Peter Lamborn Wilson, who see 'Iraqi's work as fundamentally based on the teachings of Sadr al-Din al-Qunawi, except that 'Iraqi "follows Ghazali calling Ultimate Reality 'Love,' and thus he neglects the terminology relating to the discussion of Being preferred by most of the other members of Ibn al-'Arabi's school." See *Divine Flashes*, 6.

17. Moreover, it is not unlikely that Fakhr al-Din was attempting to make explicit the centrality of love in the cosmology of Ibn 'Arabi, a centrality expressed in, for example, chapter 178 of *al-Futuhat*, but never as clearly as in 'Iraqi's writings.

18. One contemporary scholar, Nasrollah Pourjavady, has seen 'Iraqi's *Lama'at* as an attempt to "bridge the gap between Ibn 'Arabi and Ghazali by expressing the semi-philosophical teachings of the *Fusus* according to the poetic non-philosophical Sufism of the *Sawanih*" If such indeed was 'Iraqi's intention, then he certainly seems to have succeeded. See Pourjavady, introduction to *Sawanih*, 9.

19. Ghazali indicates that the divine essence is Love through metaphor. See *Sawanih*, 163–64; translation by Pourjavady, *Sawanih*, 30–31.

20. See *Sawanih*, 189; translation by Pourjavady, *Sawanih*, 62. Where Pourjavady has used the feminine pronoun "she" to translate the genderless pronoun representing the beloved, I have put "beloved" in brackets. This is mainly because our present topic demands that one avoid thinking of the beloved—who in the case of many practitioners of *shahidbazi* was a beardless young man—as female.

21. If the physical eye were not intended here, then Ghazali's association of tears with that eye would be incongruous: "Those tears that the heart sends to the eye are the scouts of its quest; they are sent forth in order to bring back some information about the beloved. This is because love starts from the eye. The heart sends its agent to the eye to claim that 'this affliction has come to me through you, so my nutriment must come through you too.'" See *Sawanih,* 185–86; translation by Pourjavady, *Sawanih,* 63.

22. Ghazali narrates two stories concerning Mahmud and Ayaz in the *Sawanih,* on 181–82 and 191–92; see also Pourjavady, *Sawanih,* 55–57 and 70–71.

23. See *Sawanih,* 157; translation by Pourjavady, *Sawanih,* 19.

24. See *Sawanih,* 188; translation by Pourjavady, *Sawanih,* 67. I have made the hadith's translation match my own translations in the previous chapter.

25. For example, Shams-i Tabrizi reports that when one of Ghazali's disciples begins to doubt his master's pious intentions, on account of Ghazali's interactions with young men, Ghazali not only persists in his actions but also seems to be using his influence over the heart of his disciple to create doubt, so that the disciple becomes—in the words of Shams—"like a child who is made to cry one moment and to laugh the next." In this example, Shams also describes Ghazali playing chess with young boys—despite the fact that, as Nasrollah Pourjavady describes it, chess in Islamic law is either "not permitted especially when played with an attractive young man" or "not forbidden but . . . not meritorious in the pious." To do so publicly would seem to be either a complete disregard for reputation or an intentional effort to damage one's own reputation. Nasrollah Pourjavady, "Stories of Ahmad al-Ghazali 'Playing the Witness' in Tabriz (Shams-i Tabrizi's Interest in *shahid-bazi*)," trans. Scott Kugle, in *Reason and Inspiration in Islam: Theology, Philosophy and Mysticism in Muslim Thought, Essays in Honour of Hermann Landolt,* ed. Todd Lawson (New York: I. B. Taurus and the Institute of Ismaili Studies, 2005), 200–221. See 206–68 for the first citation and 208–89 for the second. Shams reports that one of Ghazali's devotees was so torn between suspicion and allegiance when faced with the saint's actions that he "affirmed [Ghazali's] guilt 100 times and denied it 100 times." See Shams-i Tabrizi, *Maqalat-i Shams-i Tabrizi,* ed. Muhammad 'Ali Muwahhid (Tehran: Diba, 1990), 324, line 22 (hereafter cited as *Maqalat*).

26. Pourjavady writes that "the issue of Ahmad al-Ghazali 'playing [with] the witness' comes as no surprise, for it was previously well known. Authors of *tadhkirah* literature and Sufi biographies (*tarajim*) agree on this, and there are many stories about it set in other cities, including a particular story of Ahmad al-Ghazali practicing the loving gaze with a son of Sultan Malikshah, namely, Sanjar, and kissing his cheek. Because there are so many accounts we know that al-Ghazali made no effort to conceal these practices. Even in the middle of a sermon, he acknowledged it openly." See Pourjavady, "Stories of Ahmad al-Ghazali," 216.

27. Ibn al-Jawzi's account describes Ghazali's action as a response to a letter critical of his behavior. See Ibn al-Jawzi, *Talbis Iblis,* ed. Adam Abu Sunaynah (Amman: Dar al-Fikr li-l-Nashr wa-l-Tawzi', 1986[?]) (hereafter cited as *Talbis Iblis*), 303. I discuss this incident, along with Ibn al-Jawzi's response, on p. 117.

28. Shams al-Din Muhammad ibn 'Ali ibn Malik-dad al-Tabrizi, the famously eccentric and charismatic teacher, student, and companion of Mawlana Jalal al-Din Rumi/Balkhi (d. 672/1273), despite his antinomian behavior, is often described as an opponent of gazing at young men in Mevlevi literature. Nevertheless, some evidence indicates otherwise. To see the manner in which Sufis themselves depicted and remembered Shams, see Jami's *Nafahat al-Uns,* 464–48. Also see Annemarie Schimmel, "Shams-i Tabriz(i)," *EI2,* 9:298.

29. Shams' hesitations about the topic of *shahidbazi* are seen in his statement describing Ghazali: "It is not pleasant to say: he had an inclination to such pretty faces, [but] not lustfully so." Yet as Shams' account of Ghazali's *shahidbazi* continues, the arguments more apparently defend Ghazali's actions: "That which he saw no one else saw. If they were to tear him to shreds, not one atom of sexual desire was in him. But, because of that manner of action, the people would continually affirm [his] guilt and deny it." This last statement indicating that the controversy of Ghazali's actions created suspicion is not a criticism. Rather, it is part of a larger argument Shams makes concerning the incontestability of saints and the unwavering faith others must have in them. See *Maqalat,* 1:324.

30. See Pourjavady, "Stories of Ahmad al-Ghazali," 213. This passage from Aflaki's Mevlevi chronicle comes from O'Kane, *Feats of the Knowers of God,* 427, which corresponds to the original text, *Manaqib al-'Arifin,* vol. 2, p. 621, #11.

31. Pourjavady, "Stories of Ahmad al-Ghazali," 213, who cites *Manaqib al-'Arifin* 2:622. See also Lewis, *Rumi,* 151.

32. For an account of Shams playing backgammon with a Frankish boy, see Pourjavady, "Stories of Ahmad al-Ghazali," 214, wherein he cites *Manaqib al-'Arifin* 2:695, as well as O'Kane's translation, *Feats of the Knowers of God,* 427. For an account of Ghazali playing chess, as has been discussed already, see 208, wherein he cites the *Maqalat* 2:19, as well as the edition of the *Maqalat* edited by Khushnivis, 156. For an account of Ghazali in the *hamam* with a young boy (and the miracle that preserves his reputation) see Pourjavady, "Stories of Ahmad al-Ghazali," 205, wherein he cites the *Maqalat* 1:325.

33. This quotation from the treatise *Fatawa al-Sufiyah fi al-Tariqah al-Baha'iyah* is cited and translated by Baldick in "Poems of Fakhr al-Din 'Iraqi," 55.

34. For the first instance, see Pourjavady, "Stories of Ahmad al-Ghazali," 209, where Ghazali also reproduces a tray filled with nuts and raisins carried by the Prophet Muhammad in the disciple's dream. For the second instance, see 205.

35. Ibid., 210. Shams' account of this episode describes Ghazali publicly reciting a poem in praise of the young man's beauty (*jamal*), height (*sarwist bulandi*), and stature

(*qamat*), removing any doubts that Ghazali's request was aimed at gazing upon the boy. Pourjavady identifies this boy as the son of the Atabeg. See *Maqalat* 2:20.

36. Biographer and historian Muhammad 'Ali Mudarris (d. 1954) expresses the probability that 'Ayn al-Qudat al-Hamadhani has composed the *Sawanih* and later attributed the work to his teacher and master Ahmad Ghazali, in a manner analogous to Mawlana Rumi's attribution of his *diwan* to Shams-i Tabrizi. *Rayhanat al-Adab* (Tehran: Chapkhanah-i Shirkat Sihami, 1948), 4:225. See also *Kulliyat*, 452, where Muhtasham, in her footnotes, cites Mudarris' opinion.

37. Al-Hamadhani, *Zubdat al-Haqa'iq*, ed. 'Afif 'Usayran (Tehran: University of Tehran, 1341 *hijri-shamsi*), 7. This statement is also recorded by Jami, although in Persian, in *Nafahat al-Uns*, 415.

38. Al-Hamadhani, *Tamhidat*, ed. 'Afif 'Usayran (Tehran: University of Tehran, 1341 *hijri-shamsi*) (hereafter cited as *Tamhidat*), #389, p. 297.

39. Ibid., #143, pp. 101–2.

40. The charges brought against 'Ayn al-Qudat involved his statements that prophecy transcends reason, that a guide or shaykh is necessary (which was said to resonate with *ta'limi*/Ismaili beliefs), and that the cosmos is eternal (which he seems to have never stated). The details of this event can be found in Ernst, *Words of Ecstasy in Sufism*, 110–15. A masterful analysis of the political dimensions of sainthood under Saljuq rule, especially in relation to 'Ayn al-Qudat, can be found in Omid Safi's *The Politics of Knowledge in Premodern Islam: Negotiating Ideology and Religious Inquiry* (Chapel Hill: University of North Carolina Press, 2006), especially 158–200.

41. This hadith is both sourceless and highly suspect. One narration comes somewhat close to it, in which Abu Hurayrah reports that "God's Messenger, the blessings and peace of God be upon him, used to forbid a man from staring at a beardless youth (*al-ghulam al-amrad*)." The report rests on al-Wazi' ibn Nafi', a markedly untrustworthy narrator. See Abu Ahmad 'Abdallah ibn 'Adi al-Jurjani, *al-Kamil fi Du'afa' al-Rijal*, ed. Suhayl Zakkar (Beirut: Dar al-Fikr, 1409 Hijri) (hereafter cited as *al-Kamil fi Du'afa' al-Rijal*), 7:94, 96. The version quoted by al-Hamadhani is even more dubious, since it assumes an anachronistic, aesthetic-contemplative perspective on young male beauty. Ritter points out that "contemplating the beauty of God in a beautiful youth or boy is an alien element within the Semitic cultural sphere. Neither ancient Arabian paganism, nor Judeo-Christian monotheism, nor the social structure of the Semitic peoples who thought in terms of family connections, could have been favorable to the emergence of such attitudes. They only arose once Muslims had come into contact with Indo-European peoples." See *Ocean of the Soul*, 516–17. Considering this, both the Prophet's observation and his warning seem historically out of place. Sirus Shamisa hypothesizes that the trading of Turkic male slaves, especially bestowing them as rewards for panegyric poetry (a practice established well after the life of the Prophet), might have been behind the fascination with young men in the medieval Persian world. See Sirus Shamisa, *Sayr-i Ghazal dar Shi'r-i Farsi* (Tehran: Ramin, 1376 *hijri-shamsi*), 50.

42. This hadith, while cited often by advocates of *shahidbazi*, is certainly not well supported. It can be found, nevertheless, in a collection by Abu Ahmad 'Abdallah ibn 'Adi al-Jurjani (d. 365/976), a collection that concerns narrators who have been considered weak—some, according to Ibn 'Adi, justifiably, others groundlessly. Ibn 'Adi echoes the opinion of Ahmad ibn Hanbal that the narrator of this hadith, Abu Salmah Hammad ibn Salmah ibn Dinar al-Basri (d. 167/784), has been falsely accused of unreliability, a judgment supported by many testimonies to his piety, trustworthiness, and earnest pursuit of knowledge. Moreover, similar *ahadith* have, according to Ibn 'Adi, been narrated elsewhere. See *al-Kamil fi Du'afa' al-Rijal* 2:254, 260–61, 266.

43. *Tamhidat*, #385, p. 294.

44. Ibid., #387, p. 295.

45. Ibid.

46. Discussion of the narrator of this hadith—'Abd al-Rahman ibn 'A'ish al-Hadrami—and his possible status as a companion of the Prophet (as opposed to a "second-generation" Muslim, or *tabi'i*), as well as its text, can be found in Shihab al-Din ibn Hajar al-'Asqalani's (d. 852/1449) *Tahdhib al-Tahdhib* (Dar al-Fikr, Beirut, 1404 Hijri), 6:185–86. As with the hadith mentioned above, the phrase "on the Night of Mi'raj" does not exist in the text and is possibly an exegetical addition made by al-Hamadhani.

47. The phrase "and his children" does not appear in the sources I have encountered and might again be an exegetical addition highlighting the commonly acknowledged truth that the human race has inherited the beautiful form of Adam. A hadith resembling that quoted here reads, "Do not disfigure the face, for truly the son of Adam was created upon the form of the All-Merciful." This version is cited as based on suspect sources in the massive "Biographies of Noble Personalities" by Muhammad ibn Ahmad al-Dhahabi (d. 748/1347–48); see *Siyar A'lam al-Nubala'*, ed. Akram al-Bushi (Mu'assasah al-Risalah, Beirut, 1413 *hijri*), 14:375. Ibn Hajar al-'Asqalani presents a shorter version, "Truly God created Adam upon the form of the All-Merciful," more favorably in his *Fath al-Bari bi-Sharh Sahih al-Bukhari*, ed. Muhibb al-Din al-Khatib (Cairo: al-Maktabah al-Salafiyah, 1407 Hijri), 5:217. Of course, if "the All-Merciful" is replaced by a possessive pronoun ("God created Adam according to his form"), then the hadith can be found in both Bukhari (*Kitab al-Isti'dhan*, 79:1, #6227, p. 1554) and Muslim (*Kitab al-Birr*, 45:32, #2612, p. 1408; *Kitab al-Jannah*, 51:11, #2841, p. 1523).

48. A hadith very similar to this is narrated by Ahmad ibn Hanbal from 'Ali ibn Abi Talib: "In Paradise there is a bazaar (*suqan*) in which the only things sold and bought are the forms of women and men; so, when a man craves a form, he enters it [this bazaar], and in it is a gathering place for houris who raise their voices, whose likes the creatures have not seen, saying, 'We are the eternal ones, so we do not perish; we are the satisfied ones, so we do not grow displeased; we are the gentle ones, so we do not grow wicked—so good news for him who belongs to us and to whom we belong!'" See Ahmad ibn Hanbal, *Musnad Ahmad ibn Hanbal*, #1343/4, p. 145.

49. *Tamhidat,* #387–88, p. 296.

50. Ibid., #397–98, p. 303.

51. See Ruzbihan Baqli's *Kashf al-Asrar,* ed. Firoozeh Papan-Matin with Michael Fishbein (Leiden: Brill, 2006), p. 45, #89, for the reference to Adam; pp. 41–42, #82–83, for the first mention of the form of the Turks; and p. 99, #176, for the second mention of the form of the Turks. For a discussion of these images, see Ernst, *Ruzbihan Baqli,* 69–70.

52. Like the story told below of Ruzbihan, one story (of two) told concerning Ahmad Ghazali also parallels an account in Shams-i Tabriz's *Maqalat.* The *'Ushshaqnamah* describes Ghazali's visit to Tabriz to witness a *shahid,* the suspicions that arise, the miraculous dream of the Prophet and raisins absolving Ghazali, and Ghazali's request for his *shahid* from the pulpit. See the final story of the sixth *fasl* (of ten) in *Kulliyat,* 419–22, and *Diwan,* 335–36.

53. Baldick presents weighty evidence that the *'Ushshaqnamah* was probably written by a certain erudite mystic and merchant known as 'Ata'i, who was a contemporary of 'Iraqi and his admirer. 'Ata'i's use of the *takhallus* "'Iraqi" and his attribution of this *mathnawi* to 'Iraqi is either a case of the same sort of intentional identity confusion inspired by veneration found between Rumi and Shams, or an attempt to bestow on the work the esteem accorded by 'Iraqi's name. Baldick's evidence that this poem does not belong to 'Iraqi includes a note on a ninth/fifteenth-century manuscript of 'Iraqi's *diwan* mentioning 'Ata'i as the author; historical evidence that the dedication of the poem does not correspond to 'Iraqi's political inclinations; and, most convincingly, that the style of the *ghazal*s embedded is both inferior and markedly dissimilar to that of 'Iraqi. See R. Julian Baldick, "The Authenticity of 'Iraqi's 'Ushshaq-nama," *Studia Iranica,* Tome 2, 1973, fascicule 1, ed. J. Aubin and Ph. Gignoux (Leiden: Brill, 1973), 67–78.

54. This corresponds to the first story of the ninth *fasl;* see *Kulliyat,* 437–38, and *Diwan,* 347–48.

55. Another possible example of this occurs when the *Nafahat al-Uns* mentions great saints who witness the divine in forms as "Shaykh Ahmad Ghazali and Shaykh Awhad al-Din 'Iraqi," seemingly combining the names of Awhad al-Din Kirmani and Fakhr al-Din 'Iraqi. See Jami, *Nafahat al-Uns,* 591.

56. Ruzbihan's praise for beautiful *qawwali* singers and his famous statement that the three necessities for refreshing the gnostics' hearts in *sama'* are "pleasant fragrances, a pretty face, and a beautiful voice" can be found in Jami's *Nafahat al-Uns,* 256. Of course, considering descriptions in other accounts of the time, it would be likely for the pretty faces present at such *sama'* sessions to be male.

57. Jami, *Nafahat al-Uns,* 256.

58. *Kitab 'Abhar al-'Ashiqin,* p. 3, #4.

59. In the introduction to his translation of the first chapter, Henry Corbin notes that "il est frappant de constater combien la situation qu'expose le chapitre Ier du Jasmin

s'accorde aux péripéties du drame intérieur advenu à La Mekke," raising the possibility that the female beloved in the dialogue of this first chapter is the reformed singing girl from Ibn 'Arabi's account. It seems quite possible, however, that the presence of a female inquirer in this first chapter is an imaginal event. See Corbin's introduction to ibid., 110.

60. Ibid., p. 8, #19, and p. 12, #27.

61. Interestingly, as this female speaker poses an inquiry into the legitimacy of *'ishq* as a term applicable to God, she immediately shifts to speaking in Arabic, using terms common to Islamic law, for example, *hal yajuz* (is it permissible). See ibid., p. 9, #21.

62. For a more detailed discussion, see Joseph E. B. Lumbard, "From Hubb to 'Ishq: the Development of Love in Early Sufism," *Journal of Islamic Studies* 18, no. 3 (2007): 345–85.

63. *Kitab 'Abhar al-'Ashiqin*, p. 17, #35. Ruzbihan discusses the "wayfarers whose first step is not human love within divine love" elsewhere, noting that they tend to be practitioners of asceticism, affected more by the names of splendor (*jalal*) than beauty (*jamal*). See pp. 49–51, #107–11.

64. Ibid., p. 99, #203.

65. Discussion of the unreliability of this hadith (*man 'ashiqa . . .*), one often cited by proponents of *nazar*, can be found in Joseph Norment Bell's treatment of the Hanbali scholar Ibn Qayyim al-Jawziyah (d. 751/1350). See Bell, *Love Theory*, 133–37.

66. The term *ghalabah*, seen sometimes in discussions of love, was considered by Muslim translators to be an equivalent to a Greek term meaning "victory." According to al-Daylami's account, the Greek philosopher Empedocles deemed love (*mahabbah*) and victory (*ghalabah*) to be the first things that God created, out of which all other things were created. See the comments of translators Joseph Norment Bell and Hassan Mahmood Abdul Latif Al Shafie in 'Ali al-Daylami's *'Atf al-Alif al-Ma'luf 'ala al-Lam al-Ma'tuf, A Treatise on Mystical Love* (Edinburgh: Edinburgh University Press, 2005) (hereafter cited as *Treatise on Mystical Love*), 38, especially n. 2. Considering the absence of *alif-lam* on the word *wajh* in this untraceable tradition, it would make sense grammatically that *wajh al-hasan* would refer to the face of al-Hasan, a specific beautiful face, one mentioned in traditions as not only beautiful but also resembling the face of the Prophet Muhammad. Reports of the beauty of the Prophet's grandson's face are not limited to Shi'i narrations. For example, Ibn Kathir narrates in his *al-Badayah wa-l-Nahayah* from Muhammad ibn al-Dahhak al-Hizami that "the face of al-Hasan (*wajh al-hasan*) resembled the face of God's Messenger—may God's blessings be upon him—and the body of al-Husayn resembled God's Messenger's body, peace be upon him." See *al-Badayah wa-l-Nahayah* 8:161. Of course, Ruzbihan seems to be in the habit of dropping the *alif-lam* from *wajh* when quoting narrations about beautiful faces, for whatever reason.

67. *Kitab 'Abhar al-'Ashiqin*, p. 9, #20

68. Ibid., pp. 28–29, #61–62.

69. *'Atf al-Alif al-Ma'luf 'ala al-Lam al-Ma'tuf,* p. 11; *Treatise on Mystical Love,* p. 17. Ruzbihan has included long passages by al-Daylami in his treatise, focusing especially on four chapters: 2, 3, 4, and 5. For a detailed account, see Takeshita, "Continuity and Change in the Tradition of Shirazi Love Mysticism," 113–31.

70. *Kitab 'Abhar al-'Ashiqin,* p. 9, #19. Ruzbihan refers to the Qur'anic qualification of the tale of Joseph as *ahsan al-qasas* (12:3). It should be borne in mind that the matter of the love of Zulaykha (who remains unnamed in the Qur'an) for Joseph is a minor episode in the Qur'anic account of Joseph. Rather, if one considers the *surah* as a whole, the description of this narrative as among the most beautiful of stories is more likely to result from its themes of the realization of divine promises, ethical/moral steadfastness, or God's loving surveillance of his servants.

71. See chapter 6 of *Kitab 'Abhar al-'Ashiqin* (Concerning the particulars of human love's substance and quiddity), pp. 38–44, #85–96.

72. *FM,* vol. 1, ch. 8, p. 178.23 (p. 127).

73. In this instance, the Arabic text of al-Qunawi's will has been found in the introduction to a Persian translation of Qunawi's *al-Fukuk,* a commentary on the *Fusus al-Hikam;* see *Tarjumah-i Fukuk, ya Kilid-i Asrar-i Fusus al-hikam,* trans. Muhammad Khwajawi (Tehran: Intisharat-i Mawla, 1371 *hijri-shamsi*), 24–25.

74. Jami, *Nafahat al-Uns,* 590. It should be noted that Jami, in narrating Kirmani's practice, is in no way criticizing it.

75. Ibid., 589.

76. Ibid., 590.

77. Ibid., 589.

78. Ibid., 590. This narrative can also be found in chapter 4 of *Manaqib al-'Arifin,* vol. 2, p. 616, #4; see O'Kane, *Feats of the Knowers of God,* pp. 423–24, #4. In Aflaki's more complete version, Kirmani requests to enter into Shams' service, but, after refusing Shams' condition that he become his wine-drinking companion (which is of course Shams' test of Kirmani's attachment to reputation), Shams refuses.

79. If the moon is to represent God's beauty and the basin of water is to represent forms, then Shams' suggestion to look at the moon directly points again to the defiantly lofty claims of this saint. After all, strict opponents to *nazar* maintain that God, if seen at all, will only be witnessed after the Resurrection. Shams' suggestion to gaze directly at the moon implies that God's beauty can be seen in this life without the medium of forms. Shams might here be making a venturesome assertion that he has surpassed the need for witnessing in forms, while Kirmani has not. This is markedly different from opposing the practice altogether. Other examples from the *Manaqib al-'Arifin,* however, do seem to support Shams' opposition to *shahidbazi*—although even those might be instances where the *firasah* (cardiognosy) of Shams discloses the indecent intentions of those who should gaze only without lust.

80. Jami, *Nafahat al-Uns,* 590. Also see *Manaqib al-'Arifin,* vol. 1, p. 439, #400; *Feats of the Knowers of God,* p. 302, #399. Rumi's reply, "If only he would do it [that is, fulfill

his sexual urge] and move on," points to his skepticism about the practice of *shahid-bazi.*

81. Awhad al-Din Kirmani, *Diwan-i Ruba'iyat,* ed. Ahmad Abu Mahjub (Tehran: Surush, 1366/1987), p. 233, #1147.

82. Ibid., p. 225, #1075.

83. The *ruba'i* by 'Iraqi in question: "If, because of your heart's striving against you, / the transgressor and ascetic should seem similar to you, / arise from the lust that you hold within / so that one-thousand *shahids* sit with you." *Kulliyat,* p. 365, #186; *Diwan,* 376.

84. Kirmani, *Diwan-i Ruba'iyat,* p. 203, #886.

85. Ibid., p. 233, #1141.

86. Ibid., p. 226, #1085.

87. Ibid., p. 226, #1083. The phrase "green fuzz" refers here to the first sprouts of adolescent facial hair on beardless youths.

88. Ibid., p. 233, #1144.

89. Ibid., p. 228, #1099.

90. Ibid., p. 224, #1068.

91. Ibid., p. 233, #1142.

92. Ibid., p. 225, #1073.

93. Ibid., p. 233, #1144.

94. One should also mention here his teacher's emphasis on using amorous verse to instruct disciples, as noted by Michael Sells: "It is worth noting that, toward the end of his life, when Ibn 'Arabi was conscious of passing on his legacy to his school of disciples in Damascus, he made the reading of the *Tarjuman al-Ashwaq* a regular part of his sessions and it is the *Tarjuman* that Ibn 'Arabi, of all his works, chose to recite in person, rather than having one of his students recite it." See Michael A. Sells, *Stations of Desire: Love Elegies from Ibn 'Arabi and New Poems* (Jerusalem: Ibis Editions, 2000), 37. Sells makes use of an article by Gerald Elmore to make this assertion; see "Sadr al-Din al-Qunawi's Personal Study-List of Books by Ibn al-'Arabi," *Journal of Near Eastern Studies* 56, no. 3 (1997): 161–81, here especially 175 and 179.

95. Qunawi (attributed), *Tabsirat al-Mubtadi wa Tadhkirat al-Muntahi,* ed. Najafquli Habibi (Qum, Iran: Bakhshayish, 1381 *hijri-shamsi*), 37. This very closely resembles a *ruba'i* by Kirmani: "When my soul with the heart's eye looked into that meaning, / I saw form, but the heart saw meaning. / Do you know why I gaze at form? / Meaning cannot be seen except in form." See Kirmani, *Diwan-i Ruba'iyat,* p. 233, #1144. The poem actually attributed by the text's author to Kirmani can be found on p. 42. The treatise's author refers to this poem as part of a discussion of the gnostic's experience of seeing the outer forms of existent things as places of divine manifestation and seeing God through the medium of the cloak of grandeur (*rida'-i kibriya*).

96. The author also mentions two narrations concerning witnessing God in forms, the first of which is often cited in support of *shahidbazi.* The first: *I saw my Lord in the*

most beautiful of forms. The second (often attributed to Abu Bakr by Ibn 'Arabi): *I do not see anything without seeing God in it* (pp. 36–37). Later in the treatise, the author acknowledges another important point for the School of Passionate Love: We entities of the cosmos "are the mirror that displays God" (p. 89). The discussion of witnessing here is sober, lacking any direct reference to *shahidbazi,* while also briefly mentioning some of the basic arguments in favor of witnessing the divine in forms. There is not, however, any evidence in the *Tabsirat al-Mubtadi* that the author, Qunawi or not, necessarily supports extending this practice to gazing at the human *shahid.*

97. See William Chittick, *Faith and Practice in Islam: Three Thirteenth Century Sufi Texts* (Albany: State University of New York Press, 1992), Appendix 1, 255–59. This book includes an English translation of the *Tabsirat al-Mubtadi.*

98. As Chittick notes, Nasafi was a disciple of Qunawi's friend Sa'd al-Din Hammuyah (d. 649/1252). See Chittick, *Faith and Practice of Islam,* 255.

99. It is important to note that Ibn al-Farid's *Diwan* has a prominent place as one of seventeen books in Qunawi's own study list. See Elmore, "Sadr al-Din al-Qunawi's Personal Study-List of Books by Ibn al-'Arabi," 163–64 and 181.

100. Farghani, *Mashariq al-Darari,* 117–18. The Arabic commentary is titled *Muntaha al-Madarik,* vols. 1 and 2, ed. Wisam al-Khatawi (Qum, Iran: Matbu'at-i Dini, 1386/2007 and 1388/2010).

101. Farghani, *Mashariq al-Darari,* 111.

102. Ibid., 111–12.

103. Ibid., 377–78; *Diwan Ibn al-Farid,* p. 44, line 241.

104. Farghani, *Mashariq al-Darari,* 381; *Diwan Ibn al-Farid,* p. 45, line 251.

105. 'Iraqi, *Kulliyat,* 475; *Diwan Ibn al-Farid,* p. 44, lines 243–45. For a complete translation of Ibn al-Farid's poem, see Homerin, *'Umar Ibn al-Farid,* the lines here corresponding to p. 143.

106. *Diwan Ibn al-Farid,* p. 44, line 246. See Farghani's commentary, *Mashariq al-Darari,* 379.

107. *Diwan Ibn al-Farid,* p. 56, lines 411–12.

108. Ibid., p. 47, lines 280–83.

109. *Majalis al-'Ushshaq ba taswirat* (Kanpur, India: Munshi Nawal Kishur, 1896), see 119–23. I refer to the *Istilahat-i Sufiyah* along with the *'Ushshaqnamah,* both of which indicate 'Iraqi's prominence as an advocate of *shahidbazi,* a contemplator of absolute beauty in sensory human form who captured the strata of beauty's resonances in the tropes of Persian verse. The controversies and homoerotic context surrounding later counterparts to the aesthetes of 'Iraqi's day have been presented by El-Rouayheb in his discussion of "mystical aestheticism." See El-Rouayheb, *Before Homosexuality in the Arab-Islamic World,* 95–110.

110. See Baldick, "Poems of Fakhr al-Din 'Iraqi," 4–7; and *Diwan,* 18–19.

111. See Jami, *Nafahat al-Uns,* 601–5 and n. 1.

112. This adage can be found in many Sufi texts, including those by and attributed to 'Iraqi. The *'Ushshaqnamah* attributed to 'Iraqi alludes to it in the second *mathnawi* of the first fasl; see *Kulliyat,* 391, and *Diwan,* 313. 'Iraqi himself refers to it in a *ghazal,* the first hemistich of which ends in *saz-ast,* saying, "You will know then why reality is in the binding of the metaphorical"; see *Kulliyat,* 322, and *Diwan,* 100. See also Chimah, *Maqam-i Shaykh Fakhr al-Din Ibrahim 'Iraqi,* 235, where Chimah mentions this saying.

113. 'Attar, *Mantiq al-Tayr,* ed. Hamid Hamid, (Tehran: Nashr-i Tulu', 2000) (hereafter cited as *Mantiq al-Tayr*), 102–8.

114. Ibid., 102.

115. *Ocean of the Soul,* 399–402.

116. Ibid., 400.

117. *Mantiq al-Tayr,* 103.

118. I use the term "Qalandar" to refer to a person, as opposed to "Qalandari," despite Muhammad-Rida Shafi'i Kadkani's convincing argument that the "Qalandar" originally referred to a place of ill repute and a person associated with that place was a "Qalandari." As Kadani mentions, the term underwent changes, and by the time the hagiographical introduction cited here was written, "Qalandar" (and not only "Qalandari") was used for a person. Indeed, the anonymous author prefers to use the plural of the first (Qalandaran) and avoids the second. See Kadkani, *Qalandariyah dar Tarikh* (Tehran: Intisharat-i Sukhan, 1387 *hijri-shamsi*), 37–49.

119. *Diwan,* 20–21.

120. Ibid.

121. Ibid., 21–22. Kadkani argues that the *rah-i Qalandar* was a musical style, based on evidence from other occurrences of the phrase in Persian poetry. Not much specifically is known about the particulars of this style. See Kadkani, *Qalandariyah dar Tarikh,* 273–76.

122. *Ocean of the Soul,* 399.

123. *Lama'at,* 116–18 (ch. 22); *Kulliyat,* 516–18.

124. *Mantiq al-Tayr,* 115.

125. *Diwan,* 22.

126. Ibid.

127. Ibid., 24. Devin A. DeWeese notes that an interesting, though uncorroborated, affiliation appears in the *Jawahir al-Asrar* of Husayn al-Khwarazmi (d. 839 or 840/1435–6), a commentary on Rumi's *Mathnawi* that includes Sufi biographical material. Zakariya is said to have had 'Iraqi spend time under the guidance of Baba Kamal Jandi (d. 654/1256), the renowned disciple of Najm al-Din Kubra (d. 618/1221). Khwarazmi, a Kubrawi himself, reports that 'Iraqi was accompanied in his service of Baba Kamal by Rumi's famous intimate Shams-i Tabrizi. The account lacks feasibility, at the very least insofar as 'Iraqi supposedly reads to Baba Kamal a certain work that strikingly

resembles his *Lama'at,* when, in fact, 'Iraqi clearly composed his masterpiece after Zakariya's death, after 'Iraqi's own move westward, and after his acquaintance with Sadr al-Din al-Qunawi. See Devin A. DeWeese, *The "Kashf al-Huda" of Kamal ad-Din Husayn Khorezmi: A fifteenth-century Sufi commentary on the "Qasidat al-Burdah" in Khorezmian* (Ph.D. dissertation, Indiana University, 1985), 78. See Husayn al-Khwarazmi, *Jawahir al-Asrar wa Zawahir al-Anwar,* ed. Muhammad Jawad Shari'at (Isfahan: Mu'assasah-i Mash'al-i Isfahan, 1981), 1:131.

128. As Baldick indicates, 'Iraqi's poetry as well as other sources point to Baha' al-Din's son Sadr al-Din as being his successor, and Sadr al-Din's son Rukn al-Din succeeding him. See Baldick, "Poems of Fakhr al-Din 'Iraqi," 26.

129. Baldick contests much of the entire account, while still acknowledging the narrative's value for the study of Sufi orders in the eastern Islamic world, especially India, during the age of 'Iraqi. See Baldick, "Poems of Fakhr al-Din 'Iraqi," 23–27.

130. *Kulliyat,* 536, the first letter.

131. *Diwan,* 25.

132. Ibid., 29 (for the first reference), 28–29 (for the second reference). While Mu'in al-Din was not the ruler of the Saljuq areas in an official sense, his power far exceeded that which the title *parwanah* (the sultan's personal assistant) implies. See Carole Hillenbrand, "Mu'in al-Din Sulayman Parwana," *EI2,* 7:479–480. See also Claude Cahen, *Pre-Ottomon Turkey* (London: Sidgwick and Jackson, 1968), 276–91.

133. *Diwan,* 36.

134. This is largely the focus of Najm al-Din Abu Bakr ibn Muhammad al-Razi Dayah (d. 654/1256) in his *Mirsad al-'Ibad min al-Mabda' ila al-Ma'ad* (Tehran: Kitabfurushi-i Aqa Sayyid Muhammad Mir Kamali, 1958); see the translation of Hamid Algar, *The Path of God's Bondsmen from Origin to Return* (North Haledon, N.J.: Islamic Publications International, 1980). The theme, of course, can be found throughout the Sufi tradition.

135. Ibn 'Arabi refers to a youthful period of his life as his *jahiliyah* (Age of Ignorance), a period in which he spent time with friends dancing, listening to music, and performing prayers halfheartedly; see Addas, *Quest for the Red Sulphur,* 27–32. Of course, he emerged from this period to become one of Islam's most celebrated saints.

136. "Indeed We created the human being in the finest proportion / then We consigned him to the lowest of the low." Qur'an, 95:4–5.

137. *Maqam-i Shaykh Fakhr al-Din Ibrahim 'Iraqi dar Tasawwuf-i Islami,* 235.

138. See Tahsin Yazici, "Kalandariyya," *EI2,* 4:473–474, for a discussion of the Qalandariyah. For the image of the Qalandar in Persian poetry, see *Ocean of the Soul,* 502–6.

139. See F. de Jong, Hamid Algar, and C. H. Imber, "Malamatiyya," *EI2,* 6:223–228, as well as J. Spencer Trimingham, *The Sufi Orders in Islam* (1971; reprint, New York: Oxford University Press, 1998), 264–69.

140. An excellent source on antinomian movements in medieval Islamic mysticism is Ahmet T. Karamustafa, *God's Unruly Friends: Dervish Groups in the Islamic Later Middle Period 1200–1550* (Salt Lake City: University of Utah Press, Salt Lake City, 1994).

141. *'Awarif al-Ma'arif,* in al-Ghazali, *Ihya' 'Ulum al-Din* 5:69–72.

142. See J. T. P. De Bruijn, "The *Qalandariyyat* in Persian Mystical Poetry, from Sana'i Onwards," in *The Legacy of Mediaeval Persian Persian Sufism,* ed. Leonard Lewisohn (London: Khaniqahi Nimatullahi Publications, 1992), 75–86, here 80.

143. Ritter discusses the Qalandar theme in Sufi poetry, including that of 'Iraqi, in *Ocean of the Soul,* 502–6.

144. The word *nawa,* translated here as "tune," might also be translated as "provender."

145. Or "I saw everyone hold nothing back in gambling," according to another translation of *pakbaz.*

146. *Kulliyat,* 108–9; *Diwan,* 239–40.

147. The Nafisi edition begins, "Boy! It is befitting for you to show me the Qalandar way, / because I see as long and distant the path of asceticism and devoutness," the first hemistich of which corresponding almost identically to that which the narrator of 'Iraqi's biography recites when he joins the Qalandars. Kadkani deems it probable that Nafisi relied solely on his own poetic sensibility in adding these two hemistiches and states that they cannot be found in the earliest manuscripts. See Kadkani, *Qalandariyah dar Tarikh,* 322.

148. Drawing on initial research by literary historian 'Abd al-Husayn Zarrinkub (d. 1420/1999), Chimah discusses 'Iraqi's influence on Hafiz in Chimah, *Maqam-i Shaykh Fakhr al-Din Ibrahim 'Iraqi,* 276–81. Brief mention is also made in Shamisa's *Sayr-i Ghazal dar Shi'r-i Farsi,* 116.

149. See Kadkani, *Qalandariyah dar Tarikh,* 232–55 and 207–11, as well as Karamustafa, *God's Unruly Friends,* 19 and 37. In the pages cited here Kadkani argues that *qalandari* and *jawaliqi* are indeed synonymous; see also Kadkani, *Qalandariyah dar Tarikh,* 320–23.

150. Baldick, "Poems of Fakhr al-Din 'Iraqi," 17.

151. See Da'i Shirazi, *Kulliyat-i Da'i Shirazi,* ed. Muhammad Dabir-Siyaqi (Tehran: Kanun-i Ma'rifat, 1961), vol. 1, pp. 281–84, lines 4491–4569.

152. Baldick, "Poems of Fakhr al-Din 'Iraqi," 33. Da'i furthers the complexities between externalities and internal realities when he comments that upon meeting Baha' al-Din, "'Iraqi became Sufi inside / even if he was a Qalandar in external appearances." Elsewhere the Qalandar 'Iraqi tells Baha' al-Din, "I wish that this color were not upon me / were in my heart instead, not on my body." See Da'i, *Kulliyat-i Da'i Shirazi,* p. 282, line 4512, p. 282, line 4522, and p. 283, line 4528.

153. In this regard see the previous note as well as Da'i's description of Baha' al-Din Zakariya as free of both arrogance (*kibr*) and ostentation (*riya'*). Ibid., p. 282, line 4519. The description of Qalandars occurs on p. 284, line 4555.

154. *Diwan*, 30.

155. *Divine Flashes*, 46–49. The two manuscripts that Chittick and Wilson have used to translate this letter were not available to me, but parts of the letter, including the verse by Ibn 'Arabi, seem to correspond to the third letter (one that was, according to the editor, written to 'Iraqi's elder brother Qadi Ahmad) in Muhtasham's *Kulliyat*, 540–42. For details on the manuscript sources for the letter to Qunawi, see *Divine Flashes*, 64–65n.20.

156. *Diwan*, 25, 26, 34, and 37.

157. Ibid., 36.

158. Qur'an, 24:30.

159. Qur'an, 17:32.

160. *Sahih Muslim, Kitab al-Adab* (38/10), #2159, 1190.

161. Abu Ja'far Muhammad ibn Ya'qub al-Kulayni (d. 329/941), *al-Kafi*, ed. 'Ali Akbar Ghaffari, 3rd ed. (Tehran: Dar al-kutub al-Islamiyah,1376 *hijri-qamari*), 5:559. Abu Hamid al-Ghazali attributes the first half of this *hadith* to the Prophet Muhammad, with a slightly different word arrangement; see al-Ghazali, *Ihya' 'Ulum al-Din*, 3:92, line10.

162. See El-Rouaheyb, *Before Homosexuality in the Arab-Islamic World*, pp. 102–104. This defense of gazing at beardless youths by al-Nabulusi is titled *Ghayat al-Matlub fi Mahabbat al-Mahbub*, ed. Bakri 'Ala' al-Din and Shirin Mahmud Daquri (Damascus: Dar Shahrazad al-Sham, 2007).

163. Al-Ghazali, *Ihya' 'Ulum al-Din*, vol. 2, p. 92. Still, Abu Hamid should not be excluded from those advocating the contemplative love of beautiful (non-human) forms; see El-Rouayheb, *Before Homosexuality in the Arab-Islamic World*, 54.

164. Ibid., p. 93, line 2.

165. Ibid., p. 92, line 20.

166. *Talbis Iblis*, 303.

167. Ibid., 304.

168. Ibid., 300. A more complete discussion of the Hanbali view of *nazar* can be found in Bell, *Love Theory*, 139–44, with a discussion specifically pertaining to Ibn al-Jawzi's opinions on 21–24.

169. Rumi, *Mathnawi-i Ma'nawi*, ed. Abdolkarim Soroush (Tehran: Shirkat-i Intisharat-i 'Ilmi wa Farhangi, 1378 *hijri-shamsi*), vol. 2, bk. 5, p. 725, line 364. Also see Shamisa, *Shahidbazi*, 123.

170. *Manaqib al-'Arifin*, vol. 1, p. 440, #401; *Feats of the Knowers of God*, p. 303, #400.

171. See chapter 4, p. 75. The hadith has been translated, "Whoever leaves an exemplary established way in Islam will have its reward and the reward of all those who practice it after him, without any reduction in their reward. And whoever leaves an evil established way in Islam will bear its burden and the burden of all those who practice it after him, without any reduction in their burden." *Sahih Muslim, Kitab al-Zakah* (12/20), #1017, p. 508.

172. Shamisa, *Shahidbazi,* 124.

173. Cited and translated by Clifford Edmund Bosworth, *The Mediaeval Islamic Underworld: The Banu Sasan in Arabic Society and Literature* Part One (Leiden: E. J. Brill, 1976), 115.

174. Hafiz, *Diwan-i Hafiz,* ed. Parwiz Natil Khanluri (Tehran: Khwarazmi, 1362 *hijri-shamsi*), vol. 1, p. 230, #108.

175. Ibid., vol. 1, p. 110, #47.

176. *Kulliyat-i Sa'di,* ed. Muhammad 'Ali Furughi (Tehran: Nashr-i Tulu', 2003), *tayyibat,* 641.

177. *Talbis Iblis,* 303.

Chapter 6: The Amorous Lyric as Mystical Language

1. In Gerhard Böwering's words, "Exegesis evolved into eisegesis." See "The Light Verse: Qu'ranic Text and Sufi Interpretation," *Oriens* 36 (2001): 113–44, here 144.

2. Jaroslav Stetkevych, *The Zephyrs of Najd: the Poetics of Nostalgia in the Classical Arabic Nasib* (Chicago: University of Chicago Press, 1993), 79–92, 100–102. For an excellent example of Michael Sells work in this regard, see "'At the Way Stations, Stay' Ibn 'Arabi's Poem 18 (Qif bi l-Manazil) from the *Translation of Desires,*" *Journal of the Muhyiddin Ibn 'Arabi Society* 18 (1995), 57–65.

3. As William Chittick suggests, "Without a detailed analysis of the Shaykh's concepts and worldview, it is impossible to grasp the world of meanings behind his literary forms." See William C. Chittick, *Imaginal Worlds: Ibn al-'Arabi and the Problem of Religious Diversity* (Albany: State University of New York Press, 1994), 67.

4. *Dhakha'ir,* 4.

5. Stetkevych, *Zephyrs of Najd,* 92.

6. Ibid.

7. Ibid., 99.

8. Ibid.

9. Michael A. Sells presents Ibn 'Arabi's commentary from an informed and textually sensitive position: "Ibn 'Arabi's commentary on his love poem is not an artificial imposition of intellectualized allegory. The connections between the actual language of the poem and the expansions in the commentary are robust, and the terminological affinities between the poem and Ibn 'Arabi's philosophy are precise . . . To ask who she is, human or deity, would violate *adab.* It would be an indelicate question. The beloved, immanent within the heart-secret (*sirr*) of the poet and the Sufi, is also transcendent, beyond all delimitation, beyond any single static image." Sells, *Mystical Languages of Unsaying,* 111.

10. A reference to the Qur'an, 81:18.

11. *Where is the escape* alludes to the Qur'an, 75:10.

12. *Dhakha'ir,* 225–30; *Tarjuman al-Ashwaq,* 168–70. I have based my translation mostly on the text of the poems found in the commentary (*Dhakha'ir*), since the

commentary will occupy a prominent place in my discussion. Still, I also will cite the Dar Sadir edition of *Tarjuman al-Ashwaq,* for ease of reference. Some of the inconsistencies in the text of this poem concerning place-names have been best resolved by Nicholson, *Mystical Odes,* 39–40 (#46). I have also favored Nicholson's reading of *maghnan* instead of *ma'nan,* in the twenty-third hemistich, because it seems to follow more closely the tone and sense of the rest of the poem.

13. It is not uncommon for Ibn 'Arabi to refer to Nizam's name through allusions. In *al-Futuhat,* Ibn 'Arabi comments that "like the name of Allah in elucidation and verification / my beloved's name is based upon the form of the source." The name Allah, if taken to be derived from *al-ilah,* has the same lexical pattern or *wazn* as al-Nizam. See *FM,* vol. 2, ch. 178, p. 320.25 (p. 324). Also see a less indirect allusion in *FM,* vol. 2, ch. 178, p. 321.33 (p. 326) or *FM,* vol. 2, ch. 178, p. 316.9 (p. 320). Three other instances, all from *Tarjuman al-Ashwaq,* are cited in Nicholson's introduction to *Mystical Odes,* 8.

14. *Tarjuman al-Ashwaq,* 9.

15. Stetkevych, *Zephyrs of Najd,* 97.

16. See 68:42.

17. See Ibn 'Arabi, *Kitab al-Jalal wa-l-Jamal* from *Rasa'il Ibn al-'Arabi* (Hyderabad-Deccan: Da'irat al-Ma'arif al-'Uthmaniyah, 1948), 3–4.

18. *Dhakha'ir,* 229. Muslim records that the Prophet responds to Anas ibn Malik's inquiry, asking him why he exposes himself to being hit by the falling rain, "Because it is recent from its Lord (*hadithu 'ahdin bi-rabbihi*), may he be exalted." See *Sahih Muslim, Kitab Salat al-Istisqa'* (9/2), #898, 446. This hadith is also mentioned (and related to the beauty of the young—the child Moses in one instance, beardless youths in the latter) in *Fusus al-Hikam,* 198, and alluded to in *FM,* vol. 2, ch. 108, p. 186.24 (p. 190).

19. *Dhakha'ir,* 230.

20. Ibid., 229–30. For reference to the hadith, see chapter 2, note 16.

21. One often finds that, depending on context and function, a cosmological reality can be indicated by various names in the writing of Ibn 'Arabi.

22. *Dhakha'ir,* 5. This passage is also discussed in Chittick, *Imaginal Worlds,* 78.

23. Baldick, "Poems of Fakhr al-Din 'Iraqi," 8.

24. Ibid., 8–9.

25. Baldick refers his readers to *The Mystical Philosophy of Muhyid Din-Ibnul 'Arabi* (Cambridge: Cambridge University Press, 1939). See Baldick, "Poems of Fakhr al-Din 'Iraqi," 9.

26. Hamid ibn Fadlallah Jamali (d. 942/1536) asserts such in his *Siyar al-'Arifin,* a hagiographical account of Chishti and Indian Suhrawardi saints. In this text, Jamali presents an account of his meeting with Jami in which they disagree about the matter, Jamali proposing 'Arif and Jami proposing al-Qunawi, until Jami supposedly has a dream verifying Jamali's stance. See Baldick, "Poems of Fakhr al-Din 'Iraqi," 92.

27. Ibid., 154.

28. *Kulliyat,* 137; *Diwan,* 94.

29. *Kulliyat,* 184; *Diwan,* 116–17.

30. Baldick, "Poems of Fakhr al-Din 'Iraqi," 199.

31. *Kulliyat,* 248; *Diwan,* 116.

32. For example, the author of 'Iraqi's glossary defines *zuhd* (which literally means "asceticism") as "what they call turning away from the world (*dunya*) and that which is in it." Tabrizi's definition is similar: "turning away from excess and worldly luxuries." Nafisi's edition of 'Iraqi's *Diwan* relays a definition almost identical to Tabrizi's, adding the phrase "but only when the soul has some yearning for it." While this is an accurate description of *zuhd* as a desired ethical trait, it does not strive to capture the nuanced meaning of *zuhd* in 'Iraqi's poetry, which very often conveys the negative sense of ostentatious and hollow worship. *Kulliyat,* 565; *Diwan,* 428; *Rashf al-Alhaz,* 69.

33. *Rashf al-Alhaz,* 33–34.

34. Ibid., 34–35.

35. *Sahih al-Bukhari, Kitab al-Isti'dhan* (79/1), #6227, 1554; and *Sahih Muslim, Kitab al-Birr* (45/32), #2612, 1408 and *Kitab al-Jannah* (51/11), #2841, 1523.

36. *Rashf al-Alhaz,* 37. The phrase *A-last,* literally "Am-I-Not," refers to the Qur'an, 7:172, which is interpreted as mentioning a pre-eternal covenant in which God asks the yet unborn children of Adam to affirm that he is their Lord.

37. *Majmu'ah-i Athar-i Shaykh Mahmud Shabistari,* ed. Samad Muwahhid (Tehran: Kitabkhanah-i Tahuri, 1365/1986). The *Gulshan-i Raz* occurs on 67–108; here see p. 97, double lines 725–76. Hirawi also discusses these lines in his introduction to Tabrizi's *Rashf al-Alhaz,* 21–22.

38. *Kulliyat,* 556; *Diwan,* 425; *Rashf al-Alhaz,* 43.

39. *Kulliyat,* 556; *Diwan,* 424; *Rashf al-Alhaz,* 43.

40. *Tarjuman al-Ashwaq,* 40–44. See also the next note.

41. A summary of Ibn 'Arabi's statements in *FM,* vol. 4, ch. 558, pp. 259–61 (pp. 259–61), translated by Beneito, "Servant of the Loving One," especially 10–13.

42. *Dhakha'ir,* 51. I have changed the name "Ibn al-Durayj" in the text to "[Qays] ibn al-Dharih." A misplacement of dots easily explains the error in this text.

43. *FM,* vol. 2, ch. 178, p. 322.11 (p. 326).

44. Ibid.

45. *FM,* vol. 2, ch. 108, p. 186.20 (p. 189).

46. *Diwan,* 255. This *tarji'band* is missing from Muhtasham's edition (the *Kulliyat*), although reference to Mahmud and Ayaz can be found in a separate *tarji'band* in *Kulliyat,* 228; *Diwan,* 260. For reference to these two male lovers, also see *Lama'at,* 67; *Kulliyat,* 471 (ch. 6).

47. Anwari, *Diwan-i Anwari,* ed. Muhammad Taqi Mudarris Radawi (Tehran: Bungah-i Tarjumah wa Nashr-i Kitab, 1961), 2:769; *Lama'at,* 63; *Kulliyat,* 468 (ch. 5).

48. I refer to Hossein Mohyeddin Elahi Ghomshei, whose perspective is clearly, in many respects, influenced by Akbari thought; according to Ghomshei, the philosophical premise of his observations is that "the Being of the One precedes the being of the Many, that the existence of Unity precedes the existence of Multiplicity." See "Poetics

and Aesthetics in the Persian Sufi Literary Tradition," *Sufi* 28 (Winter 1995–96): 21–27, here especially 21, which is based on a lecture by Ghomshei given on October 18, 1994, at the Temenos Academy of Integral Studies, London.

49. *FM*, vol. 2, ch. 178, 315.34 (p. 320).

50. Of course, contradictions and paradoxes play an important role in mystical language more generally, as commented on by Lynn Charles Bauman in "The Hermeneutics of Mystical Discourse" (Ph.D. diss., University of Texas at Arlington, 1990), 44.

51. *FM*, vol. 2, ch. 178, p. 315.21 (p. 320).

52. 57:3.

53. *FM*, vol. 2, ch. 178, p. 323.4 (p. 327).

54. *FM*, vol. 2, ch. 178, p. 322.3 (p. 326).

55. *Dhakha'ir*, 7; *Tarjuman al-Ashwaq*, 11.

56. *Dhakha'ir*, 7–8 (for this entire narrative). It is interesting that this passage seems to describe actual physical contact (usually forbidden according to Islamic law), attested to by Ibn 'Arabi's description of this lady's silk-like skin and the possibility that he is here wearing the two cloths of pilgrim sanctity (*ihram*), which might leave the area on the upper back exposed. Of course, one must bear in mind that this is possibly an imaginal event.

57. *Dhakha'ir*, 9.

58. Ibid.

59. Ibn 'Arabi alludes to Nizam's father, Abu Shuja' Zahir ibn Rustam al-Isfahani (d. 609/1212), who instructed him.

60. Nicholson has located these two double lines (the four lines that here conclude Ibn 'Arabi's poem), which belong to 'Umar ibn Abi Rabi'ah; see *Mystical Odes*, 87.

61. *Dhakha'ir*, 99–115; *Tarjuman al-Ashwaq*, 78–86.

62. *Dhakha'ir*, 111.

63. Ibid., 110.

64. These four corners are the Corner of the Black Stone in the East, the 'Iraqi Corner in the North, the Shami Corner in the West, and the Yemeni Corner in the South.

65. *FM*, vol. 1, ch. 72, p. 796.27 (p. 666).

66. See, for example, chapter 15 of *al-Futuhat*, which begins by citing this hadith, "Truly the Breath of the All-Merciful comes to me from the direction of Yemen," referring to the Prophet's distant companion Uways al-Qarani, who inhabited Yemen. See *FM*, vol. 1, ch. 15, p. 205.24 (p. 152).

67. *Dhakha'ir*, 110.

68. Ibn 'Arabi mentions the Baghdadi Sufi, Abu Sa'id Ahmad ibn 'Isa al-Kharraz (d. 286/899), as also proposing this description of God. See *Dhakha'ir*, 112.

69. *Dhakha'ir*, 112–13.

70. *Sawanih*, 171, ch. 20; in the translation, ch. 21. For the translation, see Pourjavady, *Sawanih*, 41.

71. *Kulliyat,* 127–28; *Diwan,* 90. There is a slight difference in wording between these two editions in the penultimate hemistich. Nafisi's *Diwan* makes more sense in this regard, so I have translated that version.

72. *Kulliyat,* 145; *Diwan,* 88–89. In this last hemistich, Nafisi's *Diwan* has a *ba* instead of *ya* before the last word, so that it would read, "Life without your face equals death plus weariness." Nafisi's *Diwan* and alternate manuscripts recognized by Muhtasham have *qaymati* instead of *rahati* as the last word in the penultimate hemistich, so that it would read, "Life without your face has absolutely no value."

73. *Lama'at,* 110; *Kulliyat,* 511 (ch. 20).

74. *Kulliyat,* 557; *Diwan,* 424. Or to give another example, 'Iraqi defines the beloved's anger (*khashm*) as "what they call the manifestation of the attributes of dominance (*qahr*)." See *Kulliyat,* 557; *Diwan,* 425.

75. *Kulliyat,* 574; *Diwan,* 436.

76. *Lama'at,* 116; *Kulliyat,* 516.

77. *Lama'at,* 112; *Kulliyat,* 513 (ch. 20). Muhtasham's edition omits the word *wujud.*

78. *Lama'at,* 117; *Kulliyat,* 517 (ch. 22).

79. *Lama'at,* 110; *Kulliyat,* 511 (ch. 20).

80. Venus' relationship to poetry, which will not be discussed, can be seen in the planet's association with radiance, beauty, and hence the impetus for love. See *FM,* vol. 4, ch. 559, 431.6 (p. 433). For the divine name "the Form-giver" as relating to this sphere, see Titus Burckhardt, *Mystical Astrology According to Ibn 'Arabi,* trans. Bulent Rauf (Abingdon, UK: Beshara, 1977), 41.

81. *FM,* vol. 2, ch. 168, p. 272.4 (p. 275). For a translation of a portion of this chapter that pertains to this discussion, see Chittick, *Imaginal Worlds,* 80–81.

82. Chittick, *Imaginal Worlds,* 81; FM vol. 2, ch. 168, p. 272.9 (p. 275).

83. *FM,* vol. 2, ch. 168, p. 271.23 (p. 274). This is also discussed by Claude Addas, "L'œuvre poétique d'Ibn 'Arabî et sa reception," *Studia Islamica* 91 (2000): 23–38, here 35–36.

84. Ibn 'Arabi also discusses the matter of prose versus poetry in the poem mentioned on p. 141: beginning "Long has been my yearning for that young one versed in prose / and in verse, with her own pulpit, and with clarity of expression." In possessing both prose (*nathr*) and verse (*nizam,* another allusion to the beloved's name), the female beloved represents the Real's dual qualities of being unbounded in terms of his essence (*wujud al-mutlaq*) and being bound to his creation in the names that relate to creation (*wujud al-muqayyad*). The word for prose, *nathr,* relates to scattering, hence Ibn 'Arabi's association of the word to essential being, which is unbounded or pure. The word for verse, *nizam,* relates to ordering and organizing, hence its relationship to bounded existence. Yet since Ibn 'Arabi does not clarify which mode of being is represented by which mode of language, there is another possibility. Perhaps since poetry is unbounded by the restraints of reason, it represents unbounded being. See *Dhakha'ir,* 109.

85. Salim Kemal, *The Philosophical Poetics of Alfarabi, Avicenna and Averroës: The Aristotelian Reception* (New York: RoutledgeCurzon, 2003), 83.

86. See *al-Kitabah wa-l-Tasawwuf 'ind Ibn 'Arabi* (al-Dar al-Bayda', Morocco: Dar Tubqal li-l-Nashr, 2004), 149. In the third section of this study, Bilqasim undertakes an informed and careful discussion of poetic composition according to Ibn 'Arabi, including the *Tarjuman al-Ashwaq*. Especially pertinent here is his observation that Ibn 'Arabi's altering of pronouns for the beloved, making use of feminine-singular, masculine-singular, and feminine-plural third-person pronouns, indicates that he does not have in mind love merely for an individual human. See 170–74.

87. See *al-Kitabah wa-l-Tasawwuf 'ind Ibn 'Arabi*, 149–50; *FM*, vol. 2, ch. 177, p. 305.7 (p. 309).

88. *Dhakha'ir*, 24–28; *Tarjuman al-Ashwaq*, 25–27.

89. *Dhakha'ir*, 26–27.

Conclusions

1. *El islam cristianizado: Estudio del "Sufismo" a través de las obras de Abenarabi de Murcia*, 1st ed. (Madrid: Editorial Plutarco, 1931).

2. *Islam and the Divine Comedy*, trans. Harold Sunderland (Lahore: Qausain, 1977), 277.

3. Ibid.

4. *Islam and the Divine Comedy*, 274.

5. *Sahih Muslim, Kitab al-Iman* (1/80), #183, pp. 112–35.

6. Many verses illustrate this. One example: "God has promised believing men and women gardens beneath which flow rivers, [gardens] in which they will live eternally, and goodly abodes, in Gardens of Eden. And the satisfaction of God is greater—that is the mighty success" (9:72). See also examples where the end goal of a life lived morally is described as "the face of God," for example, 2:272, 13:22, 30:37, 76:9, 92:20, et al.

7. *FM*, vol. 2, ch. 289, p. 636.11 (p. 648).

Selected Bibliography

In cases where more than one edition has been cited, an asterisk (*) indicates which source has been used throughout the book for quotations or reference. This bibliography includes works that were used or useful for the writing of this book and does not at all aim to be comprehensive.

General References

Bearman, P., Th. Bianquis, C. E. Bosworth, E. van Donzel, and W. P. Heinrichs, eds. *Encyclopaedia of Islam.* Leiden: Brill, 2008. (*EI2*)

Dihkhudā, 'Alī Akbar. *Lughatnāmah.* Tehran: Mu'assasah-i Lughatnāmah-i Dihkhudā, Mu'assasah-i Intishārāt wa Chāp-i Dānishgāh-i Tehran, 1993–94.

Ibn Manẓūr, Jamāl al-Dīn. *Lisān al-'Arab.* Qum, Iran: Nashr Adab al-Ḥawzah, 1984.

Lane, Edward William. *An Arabic-English Lexicon.* Edinburgh: Williams and Norgate, 1863–93.

Yaḥyā, 'Uthmān. *Histoire et classification de l'œuvre d'Ibn 'Arabī.* Damascus: Damas, Institut français de Damas, 1964.

Yarshater, Ehsan, ed. *Encyclopaedia Iranica.* Boston: Routledge and Kegan Paul, 1982– .

Primary Sources

Aflākī, Shams al-Dīn Aḥmad. *Manāqib al-'Ārifīn.* Edited by Tahsin Yazici. Tehran: Dunyā-i Kitāb, 1362 *hijrī-shamsī.*

———. *Manāqib al-'Ārifīn.* Translated in John O'Kane, *The Feats of the Knowers of God: Manāqeb al-'Ārefīn.* Leiden: Brill, 2002.

al-Anṣārī al-Harawī, Khwājah Abū Ismā'īl 'Abdallāh ibn Muḥammad. *Manāzil al-Sā'irīn.* Edited by Muḥammad Khwājawī. Tehran: Dār al-'Ilm, 1417 *hijrī-qamarī.*

Anwarī, Awḥad al-Dīn Muḥammad. *Dīwān-i Anwarī.* Edited by Muḥammad Taqī Mudarris Raḍawī. Tehran: Bungāh-i Tarjumah wa Nashr-i Kitāb, 1961.

'Aṭṭār, Farīd al-Dīn. *Manṭiq al-Ṭayr.* Edited by Ḥamīd Ḥamīd. Tehran: Nashr-i Ṭulū', 2000.

———. *Tadhkirat al-Awliyā'.* Edited by Muḥammad Isti'lāmī. Tehran: Zawwār, 1967.

al-Bahā'ī, Shaykh Bahā' al-Dīn Muḥammad ibn Ḥusayn 'Āmulī. *al-Fawā'id al-Ṣamadīyah.* Qum, Iran: Intishārāt-i Nahāwandī, 2006.

Baqlī, Rūzbihān. *Kashf al-Asrār.* Edited by Firoozeh Papan-Matin with Michael Fishbein. Leiden: Brill, 2006.

———. *Kitāb 'Abhar al-'Āshiqīn.* Edited by Henry Corbin and Muḥammad Mu'īn. Tehran: Dep. d'iranologie de l'Institut francoiranien, 1337/1958.

al-Barzishābādī al-Mashhadī, Shihāb al-Dīn Amīr 'Abdallāh. *Sharḥi Lama'āt-i 'Irāqī.* Edited by Aḥmad Qadasī. Tehran: Intishārāt-i Mawlā, 2000.

al-Bukhārī, Muḥammad ibn Ismā'īl. *Ṣaḥiḥ al-Bukhārī.* Damascus: Dar Ibn Kathir, 1423/2002.

al-Būrīnī, Badr al-Dīn al-Ḥasan ibn Muḥammad. *Sharḥ Dīwān Ibn al-Fāriḍ.* Compiled by al-Fāḍil Rushayd ibn Ghālib al-Banānī, edited by Muḥammad 'Abd al-Karīm al-Nimrī. Beirut: Dār al-Kutub al-'Ilmīyah, 2003.

Dā'ī Shīrāzī, Shāh Sayyid Niẓām al-Dīn. *Kullīyāt-i Dā'ī Shīrāzī.* Edited by Muḥammad Dabīr-Siyāqī. Tehran: Kānūn-i Ma'rifat, 1961.

al-Daylamī, 'Alī ibn Muḥammad. *'Aṭf al-Alif al-Ma'lūf 'alā al-Lām al-Ma'ṭūf.* Edited by Joseph Norment Bell and Hassan Mahmood Abdul Latif Al Shafie. Cairo: Dār al-Kitāb al-Miṣrī, 2007.

———. *'Aṭf al-Alif al-Ma'lūf 'alā al-Lām al-Ma'ṭūf.* Translated by Joseph Norment Bell and Hassan Mahmood Abdul Latif Al Shafie, *A Treatise on Mystical Love.* Edinburgh: Edinburgh University Press, 2005.

al-Dhahabī, Muḥammad ibn Aḥmad. *Siyar A'lām al-Nubalā'.* Edited by Akram al-Būshī Beirut: Mu'assasat al-Risālah, 1413 *hijrī-qamarī.*

Farghānī, Sa'īd al-Dīn. **Mashāriq al-Darārī: Sharḥ-i Tā'īyah-i Ibn-i Fāriḍ*, 2nd ed. Edited by Jalāl al-Dīn Āshtiyānī. Qum, Iran: Daftar-i Tablīghāt-i Islāmī-i Ḥawzah-i 'Ilmīyah-i Qum, 1379 *hijrī-shamsī.*

———. *Muntahā al-Madārik.* Vols. 1 and 2. Edited by Wisām al-Khaṭāwī. Qum, Iran: Maṭbū'āt-i Dīnī, 1386/2007 and 1388/2010.

Gāzurgāhī, Kamāl al-Dīn Ḥusayn ibn Ismā'īl. *Majālis al-'Ushshāq bā taṣwīrāt.* Kanpur, India: Munshī Nawāl Kishūr, 1896.

al-Ghazālī, Abū Ḥāmid Muḥammad. *Iḥyā' 'Ulūm al-Dīn.* Beirut: Dār al-Kutub al-'Ilmīyah, 2004.

———. *Kīmīyā-i Sa'ādat.* Edited by Ḥusayn Khadīwjam. Tehran: Shirkat-i Intishārāt-i 'Ilmī wa Farhangi, 1382 *hijrī-shamsī.*

Ghazālī, Aḥmad. *Sawāniḥ.* Found in *Ganjīnah-i 'Irfān: Ashi''at al-Lama'āt-i Jāmī / Sawāniḥ-i Ghazālī,* edited by Ḥāmid Rabbānī. Tehran: Intishārāt-i Ganjīnah, 1973.

———. *Sawāniḥ: Inspirations from the World of Pure Spirits (The Oldest Persian Sufi Treatise on Love).* Translated with commentary by Nasrollah Pourjavady. London: KPI, 1986.

Ḥāfiẓ, Shams al-Dīn Muḥammad. *Dīwān-i Ḥāfiẓ.* Edited by Parwīz Nātil Khānlurī Tehran: Khwārazmī, 1362 *hijrī-shamsī.*

al-Hamadhānī, 'Ayn al-Quḍāt. *Tamhīdāt.* Edited by 'Afīf 'Usayrān. Tehran: University of Tehran, 1341 *hijrī-shamsī.*

———. *Zubdat al-Ḥaqā'iq*. Edited by 'Afīf 'Usayrān. Tehran: University of Tehran, 1341 *hijrī-shamsī*.

Ibn al-'Arabī, Muḥyī al-Dīn Muḥammad ibn 'Alī. *Dhakhā'ir al-A'lāq, Sharḥ Tarjumān al-Ashwāq*. Edited by Muḥammad 'Abd al-Raḥmān Najm al-Dīn al-Kurdī. Cairo: College of Arabic, al-Azhar University, 1968.

———. *Dīwān Ibn 'Arabī*. Beirut: Dār al-Kutub al-'Ilmīyah, 2002.

———. *Fuṣūṣ al-Ḥikam*. Edited by A. E. Affifi. Tehran: Intishārāt al-Zahrā, 1380 *hijrī-shamsī*.

———. *Fuṣūṣ al-Ḥikam*. Translated as *The Bezels of Wisdom*, trans. R. W. J. Austin. Mahwah, N.J.: Paulist Press, 1980.

———. *Fuṣūṣ al-Ḥikam*. Translated as *The Ringstones of Wisdom*, with an introduction and glosses, by Caner K. Dagli. Chicago: Great Books of the Islamic World, 2004.

———. **al-Futūḥāt al-Makkīyah*. Beirut: Dār Iḥyā' al-Turāth al-'Arabī, 1997. (*FM*)

———. *al-Futūḥāt al-Makkīyah*. Beirut: Dār Ṣādir, 1968.

———. *Iṣṭilāḥāt al-Shaykh Muḥyī al-Dīn Ibn 'Arabī*. Beirut: Dār al-Imām Muslim, 1990.

———. *Kitāb al-Jalāl wa-l-Jamāl*. From *Rasā'il Ibn al-'Arabī*. Hyderabad-Deccan: Dā'irat al-Ma'ārif al-'Uthmānīyah, 1948.

———. *Kitāb al-Jalāl wa-l-Jamāl*. Translation by Rabia Terra Harris, "On Majesty and Beauty: The *Kitāb al-Jalāl wa-l Jamāl* of Muhyiddin Ibn 'Arabī." *Journal of the Muhyiddin Ibn 'Arabi Society* 8 (1989): 5–32.

———. *Kitāb al-Isrā' ilā Maqām al-Asrā*. From *Rasā'il Ibn al-'Arabī*. Hyderabad-Deccan: Dā'irat al-Ma'ārif al-'Uthmānīyah, 1948.

———. *Kitāb al-Shāhid* from *Rasā'il Ibn al-'Arabī*. Hyderabad-Deccan: Dā'irat al-Ma'ārif al-'Uthmānīyah, 1948.

———. *Risālah fī Su'āl Ismā'īl ibn Sūdakīn*. From *Rasā'il Ibn al-'Arabī*. Hyderabad-Deccan: Dā'irat al-Ma'ārif al-'Uthmānīyah, 1948.

———. **Tarjumān al-Ashwāq*. Beirut: Dār Ṣādir li-l-Ṭibā'ah wa-l-Nashr, Dār Bayrūt li-l-Ṭibā'ah wa-l-Nashr, 1961.

———. *The Tarjumān al-ashwāq: A Collection of Mystical Odes*. Translated by Reynold A. Nicholson. Includes Arabic text. London: Royal Asiatic Society, 1911.

———. *Tarjumān al-Ashwāq*. Translated as *Ibn al-'Arabi: L'interprète des desires* (*Tarjuman al-ashwaq*), trans. Mauric Gloton. Paris: Albin Michel, 1996.

Ibn al-Fāriḍ, 'Umar. *Dīwān Ibn al-Fāriḍ*. Edited by Mahdī Muḥammad Nāṣir al-Dīn. Beirut: Dār al-Kutub al-'Ilmīyah, 2002.

Ibn Ḥajar al-'Asqalānī, Shihāb al-Dīn Abū al-Faḍl Aḥmad ibn Nūr al-Dīn 'Alī ibn Muḥammad. *Fatḥ al-Bārī bi-Sharḥ Saḥīḥ al-Bukhārī*. Edited Muḥibb al-Dīn al-Khaṭīb. Cairo: al-Maktabah al-Salafīyah, 1407 *hijrī-qamarī*.

———. *Tahdhīb al-Tahdhīb*. Beirut: Dār al-Fikr, 1404 *hijrī-qamarī*.

Ibn Ḥanbal, Aḥmad. *Musnad Aḥmad ibn Ḥanbal*. Riyadh: Bayt al-Afkār al-Duwalīyah li-l-Nashr wa-l-Tawzī', 1419/1998.

Ibn al-Jawzī, 'Abd al-Raḥmān. *Talbīs Iblīs.* Edited by Ādam Abū Sunaynah. Amman: Dār al-Fikr li-l-Nashr wa-l-Tawzī', [1986].

Ibn Kathīr, al-Ḥāfiẓ Abū al-Fidā' Ismā'īl ibn 'Umar. *al-Badāyah wa-l-Nahāyah.* Edited by 'Alī Shīrī. Beirut: Dār Iḥyā' al-Turāth al-'Arabī, 1408 *hijrī-qamarī.*

Ibn Sīnā, Abu 'Alī. *Remarks and Admonitions, Part One: Logic.* Translated by Shams Constantine Inati. Toronto: Pontifical Institute of Mediaeval Studies, 1984.

'Irāqī, Fakhr al-Dīn Ibrāhīm Hamadānī. **Kullīyāt-i Dīwān-i Shaykh Fakhr al-Dīn Ibrāhīm Hamadānī mutakhalliṣ bi-'Irāqī.* Edited by Sa'īd Nafīsī, with notes by Maḥmūd 'Alamī. Tehran: Intishārāt-i Jāwīdān, 1377 *hijrī-shamsī.* (*Dīwān*)

———. **Lama'āt-i Fakhr al-Dīn 'Irāqī.* Edited by Muḥammad Khwājawī. Tehran: Intishārāt-i Mawlā, 1371 *hijrī-shamsī.* (*Lama'āt*)

———. *Lama'āt.* Translated in *Divine Flashes,* trans. William C. Chittick and Peter Lamborn Wilson, with an introduction by William C. Chittick and Peter Lamborn Wilson. New York: Paulist Press, 1982.

———. **Majmū'ah-i Āthār-i Fakhr al-Dīn 'Irāqī.* Edited with notes by Nasrīn Muḥtasham. Tehran: Intishārāt-i Zawwār, 1382 *hijrī-shamsī.* (*Kullīyāt*)

al-Jarrāḥī, Ismā'īl ibn Muḥammad Jarrāḥ al-'Ajlūnī. *Kashf al-Khafā' wa Muzīl al-Albās.* 2nd printing. Beirut: Dār al-Kutub al-'Ilmīyah, 1408 *hijrī-qamarī.*

Jāmī, 'Abd al-Raḥmān. **Ashi''at al-Lama'āt.* Edited by Hādī Rastigār Muqaddam Gawharī. Qum, Iran: Daftar-i Tablīghāt-i Islāmī, Shu'bah-i Khurāsān, Būstān-i Kitāb-i Qum, 1383 *hijrī-shamsī.*

———. *Ashi''at al-Lama'āt.* Edited by Ḥāmid Rabbānī. Tehran: Intishārāt-i Ganjīnah, 1973.

———. *Nafaḥāt al-Uns min Ḥaḍarāt al-Quds.* Edited by Mahdī Tawḥīdīpūr. Tehran: Kitābfurūshī-i Maḥmūdī, 1336 *hijrī-shamsī.*

———. *Naqd al-Nuṣūṣ fī Sharḥ Naqsh al-Fuṣūṣ.* Edited by 'Āṣim Ibrāhīm al-Kayyālī al-Ḥusaynī al-Shādhilī al-Darqāwī. Beirut: Dār al-Kutub al-'Ilmīyah, 2005.

———. *Sharḥ al-Jāmī 'alā Fuṣūṣ al-Ḥikam.* Edited by 'Āṣim Ibrāhīm al-Kayyālī al-Ḥusaynī al-Shādhilī al-Darqāwī. Beirut: Dār al-Kutub al-'Ilmīyah, 2004.

Jandī, Mu'ayyid al-Dīn. *Nafḥat al-Rūḥ wa Tuḥfat al-Futūḥ.* Edited by Najīb Māyil Hirawī. Tehran: Intishārāt-i Mawlā, 1362 *shamsī-hijrī,* 1403 *qamarī-hijrī.*

———. *Sharḥ Fuṣūṣ al-Ḥikam.* Edited by Sayyid Jalāl al-Dīn Āshtiyānī. Qum, Iran: Būstān-i Kitāb-i Qum, 1423/1381 *hijrī.*

John of the Cross. *John of the Cross: Selected Writings.* Translated and edited by Kieran Kavanaugh. New York: Paulist Press, 1987.

al-Jurjānī, Aḥmad 'Abdallāh ibn 'Adī. *al-Kāmil fī Ḍu'afā' al-Rijāl.* Edited by Suhayl Zakkār. Beirut: Dār al-Fikr, 1409 *hijrī-qamarī.*

al-Khwārazmī, Ḥusayn. *Jawāhir al-Asrār wa Zawāhir al-Anwār: Sharḥ-i Mathnawī-i Mawlawī,* ed. Muḥammad Jawād Sharī'at. Isfahan: Mu'assasah-i Mash'al-i Iṣfahān, 1981.

al-Kirmānī, Awḥad al-Dīn. **Dīwān-i Rubā'īyāt.* Edited by Aḥmad Abū Maḥjūb. Tehran: Surūsh, 1366/1987.

———. *Heart's Witness: The Sufi Quatrains of Awḥaduddīn Kirmānī.* Edited, and with an introduction and notes by, Bernd Manuel Weischer. Translated by Peter Lamborn Wilson and Bernd Manuel Weischer. Tehran: Imperial Iranian Academy of Philosophy, 1978.

al-Kulaynī, Abū Ja'far Muḥammad ibn Ya'qūb. *al-Kāfī.* 3rd ed. Edited by 'Alī Akbar Ghaffārī. Tehran: Dār al-Kutub al-Islāmīyah, 1376 *hijrī-qamarī.*

al-Majlisī, 'Allāmah Muḥammad Bāqir. *Biḥār al-Anwār.* Beirut: Mu'assasat al-Wafā', 1983.

Muslim ibn al-Ḥajjāj al-Qushayrī al-Naysābūrī. *Ṣaḥīḥ Muslim.* Riyadh: Dar al-Mughnī, 1998.

al-Muẓaffar, Muḥammad Riḍā. *al-Manṭiq.* Beirut: Mu'assasat al-Ta'rīkh al-'Arabī, 2004.

al-Nābulusī, 'Abd al-Ghanī ibn Ismā'īl. *Ghāyat al-Maṭlūb fī Maḥabbat al-Maḥbūb,* ed. Bakrī 'Alā' al-Dīn and Shīrīn Maḥmūd Daqūrī. Damascus: Dār Shahrazād al-Shām, 2007.

———. *Sharḥ Dīwān Ibn al-Fāriḍ.* Conjoined with the commentary of Badr al-Dīn al-Ḥasan ibn Muḥammad al-Būrīnī (d. 1024/1615). Compiled by al-Fāḍil Rushayd ibn Ghālib al-Banānī and edited by Muḥammad 'Abd al-Karīm al-Nimrī. Beirut: Dār al-Kutub al-'Ilmīyah, 2003.

al-Nasā'ī, Abū 'Abd al-Raḥmān Aḥmad [ibn 'Alī] ibn Shu'ayb. *al-Mujtabā min al-Sunan, al-mashhūr bi-Sunan al-Nasā'ī.* Riyadh: Bayt al-Afkār al-Duwalīyah li-l-Nashr wa-l-Tawzī', 1420/1999.

al-Qāshānī, 'Abd al-Razzāq. *Iṣṭilāḥāt al-Ṣūfīyah, wa yalīhi Rashḥ al-Zulāl fī Sharḥ al-Alfāẓ al-Mutadāwalah bayn Arbāb al-Adhwāq wa-l-Aḥwāl,* ed. 'Āṣim Ibrāhīm al-Kayyālī. Beirut: Dār al-Kutub al-'Ilmīyah, 2005.

———. *Sharḥ Fuṣūṣ al-Ḥikam.* Edited by Majīd Hādī-zādah. Tehran: University of Tehran, Silsilah Intishārāt-i Anjuman-i Āthār wa Mafākhir-i Farhangī, 2004.

———. *Ta'wīlāt.* Published as *Tafsīr Ibn 'Arabī.* Beirut: Dār Iḥyā' al-Turāth al-'Arabī, 2001.

al-Qayṣarī, Sharaf al-Dīn Dāwūd. *Sharḥ Fuṣūṣ al-Ḥikam.* Edited by Sayyid Jalāl al-Dīn Āshtiyānī. Tehran: Shirkat-i Intishārāt-i 'Ilmī wa Farhangī, 1996.

———. *Sharḥ Tā'īyat Ibn al-Fāriḍ al-Kubrā.* Edited by Aḥmad Farīd al-Mazīdī. Beirut: Dār al-Kutub al-'Ilmīyah, 2004.

al-Qūnawī, Ṣadr al-Dīn (attributed). *Tabṣirat al-Mubtadī wa Tadhkirat al-Muntahī.* Edited by Najafqulī Ḥabībī. Qum, Iran: Bakhshāyish, 1381 *hijrī-shamsī.*

———. *Tarjumah-i Fukūk, yā Kilīd-i Asrār-i Fuṣūṣ al-Ḥikam.* Translated by Muḥammad Khwājawī. Tehran: Intishārāt-i Mawlā, 1371 *hijrī-shamsī.*

al-Qurashī, Bāqir Sharīf. *Ḥayāt al-Imām al-Riḍā.* Tehran: Manshūrāt Sa'īd ibn Jubayr, 1412/1992.

al-Qushayrī, Abū al-Qāsim. *al-Risālah al-Qushayrīyah fī 'Ilm al-Taṣawwuf.* Edited by Ma'rūf Zurayq and 'Alī 'Abd al-Ḥamīd Balṭa-jī. Beirut: Dār al-Jīl, 1990.

———. *al-Risālah al-Qushayrīyah.* Translated as *Al-Qushayrī's Epistle on Sufism* (*al-risāla al-qushayriyya fī 'ilm al-taṣawwuf*), trans. Alexander D. Knysh. Reading, UK: Garnet, Center for Muslim Contribution to Civilization, 2007.

al-Rāzī Dāyah, Najm al-Dīn Abū Bakr ibn Muḥammad. *Mirṣād al-'Ibād min al-Mabda' ilā al-Ma'ād*. Tehran: Kitābfurūshī-i Āqā Sayyid Muḥammad Mīr Kamālī, 1958.

———. *Mirṣād al-'Ibād*. Translated as *The Path of God's Bondsmen from Origin to Return*, trans. Hamid Algar. North Haledon, N.J.: Islamic Publications International, 1980.

Rūmī, Mawlānā Jalāl al-Dīn. *Mathnawī-i Ma'nawī*. Edited by Abdolkarim Soroush. Tehran: Shirkat-i Intishārāt-i 'Ilmī wa Farhangī, 1378 *hijrī-shamsī*.

Sa'dī, Abū 'Abdallāh Musharraf al-Dīn. *Kullīyāt-i Sa'dī*. Edited by Muḥammad 'Alī Furūghī. Tehran: Nashr-i Ṭulū', 2003.

Shabistarī, Maḥmūd. *Majmū'ah-i Āthār-i Shaykh Maḥmūd Shabistarī*. Edited by Ṣamad Muwaḥḥid. Tehran: Kitābkhānah-i Ṭahūrī, 1365/1986.

al-Suhrawardī, Shihāb al-Dīn 'Umar. *'Awārif al-Ma'ārif*. Appended to Abū Ḥāmid al-Ghazālī, *Iḥyā' 'Ulūm al-Dīn*. Vol. 5. Beirut: Dār al-Kutub al-'Ilmīyah, 2004.

Ṭabāṭabā'ī, 'Allāmah Muḥammad Ḥusayn. *al-Mīzān fī Tafsīr al-Qur'ān*. Beirut: Mu'assasat al-A'lamī li-l-Maṭbū'āt, 1418/1997.

Tabrīzī, Shams al-Dīn Muḥammad. **Maqālāt-i Shams-i Tabrīzī*. Edited by Muḥammad 'Alī Muwaḥḥid. Tehran: Dībā, 1990.

———. *Maqālāt-i Shams-i Tabrīzī*. Edited by Aḥmad Khūshnawīs. Tehran: Mu'assasah-i Maṭbū'ātī-i 'Aṭā'ī, 1970.

Tabrīzī, Sharaf al-Dīn Ḥusayn Ulfatī. *Rashf al-Alḥāẓ fī Kashf al-Alfāẓ*. Edited by Najīb Māyil Hirawī. Tehran: Intishārāt-i Mawlā, 1404/1362 *hijrī*.

Secondary Sources

Abdul Haq Ansari, Muhammad. *Sufism and Sharī'ah: A Study of Shaykh Aḥmad Sirhindī's Effort to Reform Sufism*. Leicester, UK: Islamic Foundation, 1986.

Abrahamov, Binyamin. *Divine Love in Islamic Mysticism: The Teachings of al-Ghazālī and al-Dabbāgh*. New York: RoutledgeCurzon, 2003.

Addas, Claude. "The Experience and Doctrine of Love in Ibn 'Arabī." *Journal of the Muhyiddin Ibn 'Arabi Society* 32 (2002): 25–44.

———. "L'œuvre poétique d'Ibn 'Arabî et sa reception." *Studia Islamica* 91 (2000): 23–38.

———. *Quest for the Red Sulphur: The Life of Ibn 'Arabī*. Translated by Peter Kingsley. Cambridge: Islamic Texts Society, 1993.

Affifi, A. E. *The Mystical Philosophy of Muhyid Din-Ibnul 'Arabi*. Cambridge: Cambridge University Press, 1939.

Ardalan, Nader, and Laleh Bakhtiar. *The Sense of Unity: The Sufi Tradition in Persian Architecture*. Chicago: University of Chicago Press, 1975.

Asín Palacios, Miguel. *Islam and the Divine Comedy*. Translated by Harold Sunderland. Lahore: Qausain, 1977.

———. *El islam cristianizado: Estudio del "Sufismo" a través de las obras de Abenarabi de Murcia*. 1st ed. Madrid: Editorial Plutarco, 1931.

———. *Saint John of the Cross and Islam.* Translated by Howard W. Yoder and Elmer H. Douglas. New York: Vantage Press, 1981.

Austin, Ralph. "The Lady Niẓām—an Image of Love and Knowledge." *Journal of the Muhyiddin Ibn 'Arabī Society* 7 (1988): 35–48.

Avery, Kenneth S. *A Psychology of Early Sufi Samā': Listening and Altered States.* New York: RoutledgeCurzon, 2004.

Bachmann, Peter. "Manifestations of the Divine as Represented in Poems by Ibn al-'Arabī." In *Representations of the Divine in Arabic Poetry,* edited by Gert Borg and Ed de Moor, 71–83. Amsterdam: Rodopi, 2001.

Baker, Patricia L. *Islam and the Religious Arts.* New York: Continuum, 2004.

Baldick, R. Julian. "The Authenticity of 'Irāqī's 'Ushshāq-nāma." *Studia Iranica.* Tome 2, 1973, fascicule 1. Edited by J. Aubin and Ph. Gignoux. Leiden: Brill, 1973.

———. "The Poems of Fakhr al-Dīn 'Irāqī." Ph.D. diss., University of Oxford, 1981.

Bauman, Lynn Charles. "The Hermeneutics of Mystical Discourse." Ph.D. diss., University of Texas at Arlington, 1990.

Bell, Joseph Norment. *Love Theory in Later Ḥanbalite Islam.* Albany: State University of New York Press, 1979.

Benaïssa, Omar. "The Diffusion of Akbarian Teaching in Iran during the 13th and 14th Centuries." Translated by Zahra Benaïssa and Cecilia Twinch. *Journal of the Muhyiddin Ibn 'Arabi Society* 26 (1999): 89–109.

Beneito, Pablo. "On the Divine Love of Beauty." *Journal of the Muhyiddin Ibn 'Arabi Society* 18 (1995): 1–22.

———, trans. "The Servant of the Loving One: On the Adoption of the Character Traits of *al-Wadūd.*" *Journal of the Muhyiddin Ibn 'Arabi Society* 32 (2002): 1–24.

Bilqāsim, Khālid. *al-Kitābah wa-l-Taṣawwuf 'ind Ibn 'Arabī.* al-Dār al-Bayḍā', Morocco: Dār Tūbqāl li-l-Nashr, 2004.

Black, Deborah L. "Aesthetics in Islamic Philosophy." In *Routledge Encyclopedia of Philosophy,* edited by E. Craig. London: Routledge, 1998.

———. *Logic and Aristotle's Rhetoric and Poetics in Medieval Arabic Philosophy.* Leiden: Brill, 1990.

Bosworth, Clifford Edmund. *The Mediaeval Islamic Underworld: The Banū Sāsān in Arabic Society and Literature.* Pt. 1. Leiden: Brill, 1976.

Böwering, Gerhard. "Ghazālī, Abū Ḥāmed Moḥammad, Biography." *Encyclopaedia Iranica.* Vol.10, Boston, 2000.

———. "The Light Verse: Qur'ānic Text and Ṣūfī Interpretation." *Oriens* 36 (2001): 113–44.

———. *The Mystical Vision of Existence in Classical Islam: The Qur'ānic Hermeneutics of the Ṣūfī Sahl al-Tustarī (d. 283/896).* New York: De Gruyter, 1979.

Burckhardt, Titus. *Art of Islam: Language and Meaning.* London: World of Islam Festival Trust, 1976.

———. *Mystical Astrology According to Ibn 'Arabi.* Translated by Bulent Rauf. Abingdon, UK: Beshara, 1977.

———. "The Spirituality of Islamic Art." In *Islamic Spirituality,* edited by Seyyed Hossein Nasr, 506–40. New York: Crossroad, 1990.

Cahen, Claude. *Pre-Ottomon Turkey.* London: Sidgwick and Jackson, 1968.

Chīmah, Muḥammad Akhtar. *Maqām-i Shaykh Fakhr al-Dīn Ibrāhīm 'Irāqī dar Taṣawwuf-i Islāmī.* Islamabad: Markaz-i Taḥqīqāt-i Fārsī-i Īrān wa Pākistān, 1994.

Chittick, William C. "The Central Point: Qūnawī's Role in the School of Ibn 'Arabī." *Journal of the Muhyiddin Ibn 'Arabī Society* 35 (2004): 25–45.

———. "The Divine Roots of Human Love." *Journal of the Muhyiddin Ibn 'Arabi Society* 17 (1995): 55–78.

———. "Ebno'l-'Arabi as Lover." *Sufi* 9 (Spring 1991): 6–9.

———. "'Erāqī, Fakhr-al-Dīn Ebrāhīm." *Encyclopædia Iranica.* Vol. 8, 1998.

———. *Faith and Practice in Islam: Three Thirteenth Century Sufi Texts.* Albany: State University of New York Press, 1992.

———. *Imaginal Worlds: Ibn al-'Arabī and the Problem of Religious Diversity.* Albany: State University of New York Press, 1994.

———. "Jami on Divine Love and the Image of Wine." *Studies in Mystical Literature* 1, no. 3 (1981): 193–209.

———. "Sa'īd al-Dīn Muḥammad b. Aḥmad Farghānī." *EI2,* vol. 8, pp. 860–861.

———. *The Self-Disclosure of God.* Albany: State University of New York Press, 1998. (*SDG*)

———. *The Sufi Path of Knowledge.* Albany: State University of New York Press, 1989. (*SPK*)

———. "Waḥdat al-Shuhūd." *EI2,* vol. 11, pp. 37–39.

Chodkiewicz, Michel. "The Diffusion of Ibn 'Arabi's Doctrine." *Journal of the Muhyiddin Ibn 'Arabi Society* 9 (1991): 36–57.

———. "The *Futūḥāt Makkiyya* and its Commentators: Some Unresolved Enigmas." Translated by Peter Kingsley. In *The Legacy of Mediaeval Persian Sufism,* edited by Leonard Lewisohn, 219–32. London: Khaniqahi Nimatullahi Publications, 1992.

———. *An Ocean without Shore: Ibn Arabi, the Book, and the Law.* Translated by David Streight. Albany: State University of New York Press, 1993.

———. *The Seal of the Saints.* Cambridge: Islamic Texts Society, 1993.

Clark, Jane. "Early Best-sellers in the Akbarian Tradition: The Dissemination of Ibn 'Arabī's Teaching Through Ṣadr al-dīn al-Qūnawī." *Journal of the Muhyiddin Ibn 'Arabi Society* 33 (2003): 22–53.

Corbin, Henry. *L'Imagination créatrice dans le soufisme d'Ibn 'Arabī.* Translated as *Alone with the Alone: Creative Imagination in the Sūfism of Ibn 'Arabī,* trans. Ralph Manheim. Mythos: Princeton/Bollingen Series in World Mythology. 1969. Reprint, Princeton, N.J.: Princeton University Press, 1998.

al-Damāṣī, 'Abd al-Fattāḥ al-Sayyid Muḥammad. *al-Ḥubb al-Ilāhī: Shi'r Muḥyī al-Dīn Ibn 'Arabī*. Cairo: Dār al-Thaqāfah li-l-Ṭibā'ah wa-l-Nashr, 1983.

Davis, Dick. "Sufism and Poetry: A Marriage of Convenience?" *Edebiyāt* 10 (1999): 279–92.

De Bruijn, J. T. P. *Persian Sufi Poetry*. Richmond, Surrey: Curzon Press, 1997.

———. "The *Qalandariyyāt* in Persian Mystical Poetry, from Sanā'ī Onwards." In *The Legacy of Mediaeval Persian Sufism*, edited by Leonard Lewisohn, 75–86. London: Khaniqahi Nimatullahi Publications, 1992.

De Jong, F., Hamid Algar, and C. H. Imber, "Malāmatiyya." *EI2*, vol. 6, pp. 223–228.

DeWeese, Devin A. "The *Kashf al-Hudā* of Kamāl ad-Dīn Ḥusayn Khorezmī: A fifteenth-century Sufi commentary on the *Qaṣīdat al-Burdah* in Khorezmian Turkic (Text Edition, Translation, and Historical Introduction)." Ph.D. diss., Indiana University, 1985.

Dupré, Adam. "Expression and the Inexpressible." *Sufi* 23 (Autumn 1994): 5–9.

Elmore, Gerald. "Sadr al-Din al-Qunawi's Personal Study-List of Books by Ibn al-'Arabi." *Journal of Near Eastern Studies* 56, no. 3 (1997): 161–81.

Elias, Jamal J. *The throne carrier of God: the life and thought of 'Alā' ad-dawlah as-Simnānī*. Albany: State University of New York Press, 1995.

Elmore, Gerald. "Sadr al-Din al-Qunawi's Personal Study-List of Books by Ibn al-'Arabi." *Journal of Near Eastern Studies* 56, no. 3 (1997): 161–81.

El-Rouayheb, Khaled. *Before Homosexuality in the Arab-Islamic World, 1500–1800*. Chicago and London: The University of Chicago Press, 2005.

Ernst, Carl W. "The Stages of Love in Early Persian Sufism: From Rabe'a to Ruzbehan." *Sufi* 14 (Summer 1992): 16–23.

———. *Ruzbihan Baqli: Mysticism and the Rhetoric of Sainthood in Persian Sufism*. Surrey, UK: Curzon Press, 1996.

———. *Words of Ecstasy in Sufism*. Albany: State University of New York Press, 1985.

Ghomshei, Hossein Mohyeddin Elahi. "Poetics and Aesthetics in the Persian Sufi Literary Tradition." *Sufi* 28 (Winter 1995–96): 21–27.

Giffen, Lois Anita. *Theory of Profane Love among the Arabs: The Development of the Genre*. New York: New York University Press, 1971.

Gloton, Maurice. "The Quranic Inspiration of Ibn 'Arabi's Vocabulary of Love." Translated by Cecilia Twinch. *Journal of the Muhyiddin Ibn 'Arabi Society* 27 (2000): 37–52.

Graham, Terry. "Fakhro'd-Din 'Eraqi: The Master of Lovers." *Sufi* 12 (Winter 1991–92): 27–31.

al-Ḥakīm, Su'ād. *al-Mu'jam al-Ṣūfī: al-Ḥikmah fī Ḥudūd al-Kalimah*. Beirut: Dandarah, 1981.

Hämeen-Anttila, Jaakko. "Journey through Desert, Journey towards God: The Use of Metaphors of Movement and Space in Ibn 'Arabī's *Tarjumān al-ashwāq*." *Journal of the Muhyiddin Ibn 'Arabi Society* 37 (2005): 99–125.

Ḥaydarkhānī, Ḥusayn. *Samā'-i 'Ārifīn.* Tehran: Intishārāt-i Sanā'ī, 1374 *hijrī-shamsī.*

Hillenbrand, Carole. "Mu'īn al-Dīn Sulaymān Parwāna." *EI2,* vol. 7, pp. 479–480.

Hirtenstein, Stephen. *The Unlimited Mercifier.* Oxford/Ashland: Anqa Publishing/White Cloud Press, 1999.

Homerin, Th. Emil. *From Arab Poet to Muslim Saint: Ibn al-Fāriḍ, His Verse, and His Shrine.* Columbia: University of South Carolina Press, 1994.

———. *'Umar Ibn al-Fāriḍ: Sufi Verse, Saintly Life.* Mahwah, N.J.: Paulist Press, 2001.

Hoos, Mark. "The Unknown Treasure: The Metaphysical Aesthetics of Ibn 'Arabī." *Journal of Turkish Studies* 26, no. 1 (2002), 1–14. Guest editor Jan Schimdt, Department of Near Eastern Languages and Civilizations, Harvard University.

Izutsu, Toshihiko. *Sufism and Taoism: A Comparative Study of Key Philosophical Concepts.* Berkeley and Los Angeles: University of California Press, 1983.

Kadkanī, Muḥammad-Riḍā Shafī'ī. *Qalandarīyah dar Tārīkh.* Tehran: Intishārāt-i Sukhan, 1387 *hijrī-shamsī.*

Karamustafa, Ahmet T. *God's Unruly Friends: Dervish Groups in the Islamic Later Middle Period 1200–1550.* Salt Lake City: University of Utah Press, 1994.

Kemal, Salim. *The Philosophical Poetics of Alfarabi, Avicenna and Averroës: The Aristotelian Reception.* New York: RoutledgeCurzon, 2003.

Lawrence, Bruce B. "The Early Chishti Approach to Sama'." In *Islamic Society and Culture: Essays in Honour of Professor Aziz Ahmad,* edited by M. Israel and N. K. Wagle, 69–93. Delhi: Manohar, 1983.

Leaman, Oliver. *Islamic Aesthetics: An Introduction.* Edinburgh: Edinburgh University Press, 2004.

Legenhausen, Muḥammad. *Islam and Religious Pluralism.* London: al-Hoda, 1999.

Lewis, Franklin D. *Rumi: Past and Present, East and West: The Life, Teachings and Poetry of Jalal al-Din Rumi.* Oxford/Boston: Oneworld, 2000.

Lewisohn, Leonard. "The Sacred Music of Islam: Sama' in the Persian Sufi Tradition." *British Journal of Ethnomusicology* 6 (1997): 1–33.

López-Baralt, Luce. "Saint John of the Cross and Ibn 'Arabi: The Heart or *Qalb* as the Translucid and Ever-Changing Mirror of God." *Journal of Muhyiddin Ibn 'Arabi Society* 28 (2000): 57–90.

Losensky, Paul E. "Linguistic and Rhetorical Aspects of the Signature Verse (*Takhalluṣ*) in the Persian *Ghazal.*" *Edebiyāt* 8 (1998): 239–71.

Lubis, H. M. Bukhari. "The Relationship Between Sufism and Poetry." *Sufi* 4 (Winter 1989–90): 26–29.

Lumbard, Joseph E. B. "From Ḥubb to 'Ishq: The Development of Love in Early Sufism." *Journal of Islamic Studies* 18, no. 3 (2007): 345–85.

Lutfi, Huda. "The Feminine Element in Ibn 'Arabī's Mystical Philosophy." *Alif: Journal of Comparative Poetics* 5 (Spring 1985): 7–19.

Massad, Joseph A. *Desiring Arabs.* Chicago: University of Chicago Press, 2007.

Meisami, Julie Scott. "The Body as Garden: Nature and Sexuality in Persian Poetry." *Edebiyāt* 6 (1995): 245–74.

Morris, James Winston. *The Reflective Heart: Discovering Spiritual Intelligence in Ibn 'Arabī's Meccan Illuminations.* Louisville, Ky.: Fons Vitae, 2005.

Mudarris, Muḥammad 'Alī. *Rayḥānat al-Adab.* Tehran: Chāpkhānah-i Shirkat Sihāmī, 1948.

Murata, Sachiko. *The Tao of Islam: A Sourcebook on Gender Relationships in Islamic Thought.* Albany: State University of New York Press, 1992.

Murata, Sachiko, and William C. Chittick. *The Vision of Islam.* New York: Paragon House, 1994.

Nadeem, S. H. *A Critical Appreciation of Arabic Mystical Poetry.* New Delhi: Adam Publishers and Distributors, 2003.

Najmabadi, Afsaneh. *Women with Mustaches and Men without Beards: Gender and Sexual Anxieties of Iranian Modernity.* Berkeley and Los Angeles: University of California Press, 2005.

Nasr, Seyyed Hossein. *Islamic Art and Spirituality.* Albany: State University of New York Press, 1987.

———. "Persian Sufi Literature: Its Spiritual and Cultural Significance." In *The Heritage of Sufism,* vol. 2, edited by Leonard Lewisohn, 1–10. Oxford: Oneworld, 1999.

———. *Sufi Essays.* Albany: State University of New York Press, 1991.

Nettler, Ronald L. *Sufi Metaphysics and Qur'ānic Prophets: Ibn 'Arabī's Thought and Method in the Fuṣūṣ al-ḥikam.* Cambridge: Islamic Texts Society, 2003.

Nicholson, Reynold A. *The Mystics of Islam.* Beirut: Khayats, 1966.

———. *Studies in Islamic Mysticism.* London: Cambridge University Press, 1921.

Pourjavady, Nasrollah. "Stories of Aḥmad al-Ghazālī 'Playing the Witness' in Tabrīz (Shams-i Tabrīzī's Interest in *shāhid-bāzī*)." Translated by Scott Kugle, *Reason and Inspiration in Islam: Theology, Philosophy and Mysticism in Muslim Thought, Essays in Honour of Hermann Landolt,* edited by Todd Lawson, 200–221. London: I. B. Taurus, Institute of Ismaili Studies, 2005.

———. *Sulṭān-i Ṭarīqat.* Tehran: Āgāh, 1358 *hijrī-shamsī.*

Pritchett, Frances W. "Orient Pearls Unstrung: The Quest for Unity in the Ghazal." *Edebiyāt,* n.s., 4 (1993): 119–35.

Radtke, Bernd. "A Forerunner of Ibn al-'Arabī: Ḥakīm Tirmidhī on Sainthood." *Journal of Muhyiddin Ibn 'Arabi Society* 8 (1989), 42–49 .

Ritter, Hellmut. *Das Meer der Seele.* Translated as *The Ocean of the Soul: Men, the World and God in the Stories of Farīd al-Dīn 'Aṭṭār,* trans. John O'Kane. Leiden/Boston: Brill, 2003.

———. *Das Meer der Seele: Mensch, Welt und Gott in den Geschichten des Farīduddīn 'Aṭṭār.* Leiden: Brill, 1978.

Rizvi, Sajjad H. "The Existential Breath of al-raḥmān and the Munificent Grace of al-raḥīm: The *Tafsīr Sūrat al-Fātiḥa* of Jāmī and the School of Ibn 'Arabī." *Journal of Qur'anic Studies* 8, no. 1 (2006): 58–87.

Rosenthal, Franz. "Ibn 'Arabī between 'Philosophy' and 'Mysticism:' 'Sūfism and Philosophy Are Neighbors and Visit Each Other;' *fa-inna at-taṣawwuf wa-t-tafalsuf yatajāwarāni wa-yatazāwarāni.*" *Oriens* 31 (1988): 1–35.

Rundgren, Frithiof. "Love and Knowledge according to Some Islamic Philosophers." *Journal of the Muhyiddin Ibn 'Arabi Society* 7 (1988): 17–27.

Rypka, Jan. *The History of Iranian Literature.* Edited by Karl Jahn. Dorderecht, Holland: D. Reidel, 1968.

Safi, Omid. "Did the Two Oceans Meet?" *Journal of the Muhyiddin Ibn 'Arabi Society* 26 (1999): 55–88.

———. "On the Path of Love Towards the Divine: A Journey with Muslim Mystics." *Sufi* 78 (Winter/Spring 2009/2010): 22–38. Reprinted from *Journal of Scriptural Reasoning* 3, no. 2 (2003).

———. "The Path of Ṣūfī Love in Iran and India." In *A Pearl in Wine: Essays on the Life, Music, and Sufism of Ḥazrat Inayat Khan,* edited by Pirzade Zia Inayat Khan. New Lebanon, N.Y.: Omega, 2001, pp. 221–266.

———. *The Politics of Knowledge in Premodern Islam: Negotiating Ideology and Religious Inquiry.* Chapel Hill: University of North Carolina Press, 2006.

Scattolin, Giuseppe. "The Key Concepts of al-Farghānī's Commentary on Ibn al-Fāriḍ's Sufi Poem, *al-Tā'iyyat al-Kubrā.*" *Journal of the Muhyiddin Ibn 'Arabi Society* 39 (2006): 33–83.

———. "The Mystical Experience of 'Umar ibn al-Fāriḍ of the Realization of Self (Anā, I) The Poet and his Mystery." *Muslim World* 82, no. 3–4 (1992): 274–86.

Schimmel, Annemarie. *As Through a Veil.* New York: Columbia University Press, 1982.

———. "Eros—Heavenly and Not So Heavenly—in Sufi Literature and Life." *Sufi* 29 (Spring 1996): 29–42.

———. *Mystical Dimensions of Islam.* Chapel Hill: University of North Carolina Press, 1975.

———. "Shams-i Tabrīz(ī)." *EI2,* vol. 9, p. 298.

Schuon, Frithjof. *Logic and Transcendence.* Translated by Peter N. Townsend. New York: Harper and Row, 1975.

Sells, Michael A. "'At the Way Stations, Stay' Ibn 'Arabi's Poem 18 (Qif bi l-Manāzil) from the *Translation of Desires.*" *Journal of the Muhyiddin Ibn 'Arabi Society* 18 (1995), 57–65.

———. "Ibn 'Arabī's Garden among the Flames: A Reevaluation." *History of Religions* 23, no. 4 (1984): 287–315.

———. "Ibn 'Arabī's 'Gentle Now, Doves of the Thornberry and Moringa Thicket.'" *Journal of the Muhyiddin Ibn 'Arabi Society* 10 (1991): 1–8.

———. "Longing, Belonging, and Pilgrimage in Ibn 'Arabi's Translation of Desires." In *Languages of Power in Islamic Spain,* edited by Ross Brann, 178–96. Ithaca: CDL Press, 1997.

———. "Love." In *The Literature of al-Andalus,* edited by María Rosa Menocal, Raymond P. Scheindlin, and Michael Sells, 126–58. Cambridge: Cambridge University Press, 2000.

———. *Mystical Languages of Unsaying.* Chicago: University of Chicago Press, 1994.

———. *Stations of Desire: Love Elegies from Ibn 'Arabi and New Poems.* Jerusalem: Ibis Editions, 2000.

Shaikh, Sa'diyya. "In Search of 'Al-Insān': Sufism, Islamic Law, and Gender." *Journal of the American Academy of Religion* 77, no. 4 (2009): 781–822.

Shamīsā, Sīrūs. *Sayr-i Ghazal dar Shi'r-i Fārsī.* Tehran: Rāmīn, 1376 *hijrī-shamsī.*

———. *Shāhidbāzī dar Adabīyāt-i Fārsī.* Tehran: Intishārāt-i Firdaws, 1381 *hijrī-shamsī.*

Stetkevych, Jaroslav. *The Zephyrs of Najd: The Poetics of Nostalgia in the Classical Arabic Nasīb.* Chicago: University of Chicago Press, 1993.

Suvorova, Anna. *Muslim Saints of South Asia: The Eleventh to Fifteenth Centuries.* New York: RoutledgeCurzon, 2004.

Takeshita, Masataka. "Continuity and Change in the Tradition of Shirazi Love Mysticism: A Comparison between Daylamī's *'Aṭf al-alif* and Rūzbihān Baqlī's *'Abhar al-'Āshiqīn.*" *Orient: Report of the Society for Near Eastern Studies in Japan* 23 (1987): 113–31.

Trimingham, J. Spencer. *The Sufi Orders in Islam.* 1971. Reprint, New York: Oxford University Press, 1998.

Valiuddin, Mir. "Reconciliation between Ibn 'Arabī's Wahdat-i-Wujud and the Mujaddid's Wahdat-i-Shuhud." *Islamic Culture: An English Quarterly,* Jubilee Number, pt. 1, 25 (1951): 43–51. Islamic Culture Board, Hyderabad-Deccan.

Wafer, Jim. "Vision and Passion: The Symbolism of Male Love in Islamic Mystical Literature." In *Islamic Homosexualities: Culture, History, and Literature,* edited by 107–31. Stephen O. Murray and Will Roscoe. New York: New York University Press, 1997.

Wilson, Peter Lamḅorn. *Scandal: Essays in Islamic Heresy.* Brooklyn, New York: Autonomedia, 1988.

Yarshater, Ehsan, "Hafez: (i) An Overview." *Encyclopaedia Iranica.* Vol. 11, 2003.

Yazici, Tahsin. "Qalandariyya." *EI2,* vol. 4, pp. 473–74.

Zargar, Cyrus Ali. "Aesthetic Principles of Islamic Mysticism: Beauty and the Human Form in the writings of Ibn 'Arabī and 'Irāqī." Ph.D. diss., University of California, Berkeley, 2008.

———. "Kashf o Shohūd." *Encyclopaedia Iranica.*Vol. 15, fascicle 6, 2011.

———. "The Satiric Method of Ibn Dāniyāl: Morality and Anti-Morality in *Ṭayf al-Khayāl.*" *Journal of Arabic Literature* 37, no. 1 (2006): 68–108.

Index of Qur'ānic Verses

Index of Traditions (*aḥādīth*)

General Index